T5-CCM-957

A Celebration of Poets

of Poets

EAST
GRADES 7-12
SUMMER 2009

creativeCOMMUNICATION
A CELEBRATION OF TODAY'S WRITERS

A CELEBRATION OF POETS
EAST
GRADES 7-12
SUMMER 2009

AN ANTHOLOGY COMPILED BY CREATIVE COMMUNICATION, INC.

Published by:

creativeCOMMUNICATION
A CELEBRATION OF TODAY'S WRITERS

1488 NORTH 200 WEST · LOGAN, UTAH 84341
TEL. 435-713-4411 · WWW.POETICPOWER.COM

Authors are responsible for the originality of the writing submitted.

All rights reserved. No part of this book may be reproduced or transmitted in any form or by any means, electronic or mechanical without written permission of the author and publisher.

Copyright © 2009 by Creative Communication, Inc.
Printed in the United States of America

ISBN: 978-1-60050-298-9

FOREWORD

"The times they are a changin'."

When Bob Dylan coined this phrase, his times were changing. It was 1964 and a much different world than we have today. However, to every generation the times change. The students today cope with issues that earlier generations could not even conceive. Each generation has its own unique problems. Today we have terrorism, the economy, the environment, swine flu and the list goes on.

However, the hopes of each generation is one thing that is constant. Everyone wants to make it through the stresses of school, have positive relationships, and generally succeed in life. The writings in this book give the reader an insight into each of these students. We are allowed to view, if only for a moment, what is important to each author.

It has been a joy to have published student essays and poems for over 15 years. For each contest, students send in their hopes and dreams of becoming a published writer. As most of the entries in our contests are not invited to be published, we congratulate the students that were selected to be included in this book.

We hope you enjoy reading what our authors have decided to share. As our "times change" we have hope, as our youth care about their world and want to make it a better place.

Thomas Worthen, Ph.D.
Editor
Creative Communication

WRITING CONTESTS!

Enter our next POETRY contest!
Enter our next ESSAY contest!

Why should I enter?
Win prizes and get published! Each year thousands of dollars in prizes are awarded throughout North America. The top writers in each division receive a monetary award and a free book that includes their published poem or essay. Entries of merit are also selected to be published in our anthology.

Who may enter?
There are four divisions in the poetry contest. The poetry divisions are grades K-3, 4-6, 7-9, and 10-12. There are three divisions in the essay contest. The essay divisions are grades 3-6, 7-9, and 10-12.

What is needed to enter the contest?
To enter the poetry contest send in one original poem, 21 lines or less. To enter the essay contest send in one original non-fiction essay, 250 words or less, on any topic. Please submit each poem and essay with a title, and the following information clearly printed: the writer's name, current grade, home address (optional), school name, school address, teacher's name and teacher's email address (optional). Contact information will only be used to provide information about the contest. For complete contest information go to www.poeticpower.com.

How do I enter?
Enter a poem online at:
www.poeticpower.com
or
Mail your poem to:
Poetry Contest
1488 North 200 West
Logan, UT 84341

Enter an essay online at:
www.studentessaycontest.com
or
Mail your essay to:
Essay Contest
1488 North 200 West
Logan, UT 84341

When is the deadline?
Poetry contest deadlines are April 13th, August 18th, and December 2nd. Essay contest deadlines are February 17th, July 15th, and October 19th. Students can enter one poem and one essay for each spring, summer, and fall contest deadline.

Are there benefits for my school?
Yes. We award $15,000 each year in grants to help with Language Arts programs. Schools qualify to apply for a grant by having 15 or more accepted entries.

Are there benefits for my teacher?
Yes. Teachers with five or more students published receive a free anthology that includes their students' writing.

For more information please go to our website at **www.poeticpower.com**, email us at editor@poeticpower.com or call 435-713-4411.

TABLE OF CONTENTS

States included in this edition:

Connecticut
Delaware
Maine
Maryland
Massachusetts
New Hampshire
New Jersey
New York
Pennsylvania
Rhode Island
Vermont
Virginia
Washington D.C.

Summer 2009 Poetic Achievement Honor Schools

* Teachers who had fifteen or more poets accepted to be published

The following schools are recognized as receiving a "Poetic Achievement Award." This award is given to schools who have a large number of entries of which over fifty percent are accepted for publication. With hundreds of schools entering our contest, only a small percent of these schools are honored with this award. The purpose of this award is to recognize schools with excellent Language Arts programs. This award qualifies these schools to receive a complimentary copy of this anthology. In addition, these schools are eligible to apply for a Creative Communication Language Arts Grant. Grants of two hundred and fifty dollars each are awarded to further develop writing in our schools.

Anthony Wayne Middle School
Wayne, NJ
Lauren Tuosto*

Beacon Middle School
Lewes, DE
Nicole Catanzaro
Doris Elaine Person*

Blue Mountain High School
Schuylkill Haven, PA
Verna Dresch
Edward Palamar

Blue Ridge Middle School
Purcellville, VA
Lee Martin*
Virginia Walker

Carson Middle School
Herndon, VA
Barbara Poole*
Leigh C. Toweson

Chickahominy Middle School
Mechanicsville, VA
Kathleen Martin
Cynthia Sinanian*

Christ the Divine Teacher Catholic Academy
Pittsburgh, PA
Lucille Bishop*

Christ the Teacher Catholic School
Newark, DE
Sharon Pater
Ann Voloshin

Cleveland School of Publishing and Technology
Newark, NJ
Howard H. Morton
Michele A. Williams*

Covenant Life School
Gaithersburg, MD
Denise Griney*

Depew Middle School
Depew, NY
Joseph P. Cena*

Ephrata Middle School
Ephrata, PA
Debbie Nelms*

Floral Park Memorial High School
Floral Park, NY
Emma Naughton*

Garnet Valley Middle School
Glen Mills, PA
Christina Dean*

Hammarskjold Middle School
East Brunswick, NJ
Jane Dougherty*
Michele Green*

Haverhill High School
Haverhill, MA
Katie Eisenhauer*

Manasquan Elementary School
Manasquan, NJ
Andrea Trischitta*

Maple Point Middle School
Langhorne, PA
Stacy Flaville-Boop
Diana Turek-Gever*

Massapequa High School
Massapequa, NY
Elyn Coyle*

New Jersey United Christian Academy
Cream Ridge, NJ
Sonia McCain*
Melissa Ryan

Ocean City Intermediate School
Ocean City, NJ
Martha F. Godown*
Sonja Parker*

Our Lady of Grace Elementary School
Pittsburgh, PA
Brenda Serbicki*

Pine-Richland Middle School
Gibsonia, PA
Dr. Susan Frantz*
Jennifer Latronica*
Gregg Somerhalder
Angela C. Srsic

School of International Studies at
Meadowbrook
Norfolk, VA
Katina S. Dunbar
Andrew Sytsma*

St Agatha School
Brooklyn, NY
Rosemarie Paredes*

St Stephen's School
Grand Island, NY
Daniela Schmidt*

The Bronx High School of Science
Bronx, NY
Andrew Bausili
Alessandra Casale
Dermot Hannon*
Sophia Sapozhnikov

Thorne Middle School
Port Monmouth, NJ
Joseph Puzzo*

Township of Ocean Intermediate School
Ocean, NJ
Christine Fogler
Robert Klinger
Kathleen Whille*

Trinity Middle School
Washington, PA
Lindsey Greer*
Elise Wray*

Unami Middle School
  Chalfont, PA
    Dianne M. Pizzi*

Westwood Jr/Sr High School
  Township of Washington, NJ
    Theodora Pavlou*

Language Arts Grant Recipients 2009-2010

After receiving a "Poetic Achievement Award" schools are encouraged to apply for a Creative Communication Language Arts Grant. The following is a list of schools who received a two hundred and fifty dollar grant for the 2009-2010 school year.

Arrowhead Union High School, Hartland, WI
Blessed Sacrament School, Seminole, FL
Booneville Jr High School, Booneville, AR
Buckhannon-Upshur Middle School, Buckhannon, WV
Campbell High School, Ewa Beach, HI
Chickahominy Middle School, Mechanicsville, VA
Clarkston Jr High School, Clarkston, MI
Covenant Life School, Gaithersburg, MD
CW Rice Middle School, Northumberland, PA
Eason Elementary School, Waukee, IA
East Elementary School, Kodiak, AK
Florence M Gaudineer Middle School, Springfield, NJ
Foxborough Regional Charter School, Foxborough, MA
Gideon High School, Gideon, MO
Holy Child Academy, Drexel Hill, PA
Home Choice Academy, Vancouver, WA
Jeff Davis Elementary School, Biloxi, MS
Lower Alloways Creek Elementary School, Salem, NJ
Maple Wood Elementary School, Somersworth, NH
Mary Walter Elementary School, Bealeton, VA
Mater Dei High School, Evansville, IN
Mercy High School, Farmington Hills, MI
Monroeville Elementary School, Monroeville, OH
Nautilus Middle School, Miami Beach, FL
Our Lady Star of the Sea School, Grosse Pointe Woods, MI
Overton High School, Memphis, TN
Pond Road Middle School, Robbinsville, NJ
Providence Hall Charter School, Herriman, UT
Reuben Johnson Elementary School, McKinney, TX
Rivelon Elementary School, Orangeburg, SC
Rose Hill Elementary School, Omaha, NE

Language Arts Grant Winners cont.

Runnels School, Baton Rouge, LA
Santa Fe Springs Christian School, Santa Fe Springs, CA
Serra Catholic High School, Mckeesport, PA
Shadowlawn Elementary School, Green Cove Springs, FL
Spectrum Elementary School, Gilbert, AZ
St Edmund Parish School, Oak Park, IL
St Joseph Institute for the Deaf, Chesterfield, MO
St Joseph Regional Jr High School, Manchester, NH
St Mary of Czestochowa School, Middletown, CT
St Monica Elementary School, Garfield Heights, OH
St Vincent De Paul Elementary School, Cape Girardeau, MO
Stevensville Middle School, Stevensville, MD
Tashua School, Trumbull, CT
The New York Institute for Special Education, Bronx, NY
The Selwyn School, Denton, TX
Tonganoxie Middle School, Tonganoxie, KS
Westside Academy, Prince George, BC
Willa Cather Elementary School, Omaha, NE
Willow Hill Elementary School, Traverse City, MI

Grades 10-11-12

Note: The Top Ten poems were finalized through an online voting system. Creative Communication's judges first picked out the top poems. These poems were then posted online. The final step involved thousands of students and teachers who registered as online judges and voted for the Top Ten poems. We hope you enjoy these selections.

Top Poem Grades 10-11-12

Towards Sound

An instrument stumbles over this opening note
and we watch it fall. It lingers and rolls on the stage floor
and is stomped through the planks to a majestic muteness.
How curious the notion of a spun web punctured.
From flute to trumpet, the musical wilderness topples
and the stage is silent.
The maestro becomes the lone performer,
and the audience thus, exits.

But behind these waves of muteness stripped bare,
there is indeed still that one enigmatic maestro.
How angrily he had flung inky notes on paper,
hostile allusions to sunsets and flowers plucked
meticulously into a tempest of mobile color,
and how the orchestra hadn't enough heart
to pry those hot coals of music from this man's fist.
Nor may we, the lowly audience,
driven away by a proud man defending
an uncoordinated love between child and meadow.

Each note though, does play.
The song sprints to its immaculate doom
and silently dies only for the maestro.

Tommy Chen, Grade 11
Stuyvesant High School, NY

Top Poem Grades 10-11-12

Sleep Amongst the Stars

Fathom the eternal drowning of the mind
Permit your lips to speak the broken masses of reverberation
The universe is waiting,
Estrange yourself from the dissident prating of society
Where night sleeps
Sun talks
No longer streams
To Earth — goodbye noblesse oblige
Acquiesce to the stress of the shooting star
Gliding through an endless abyss
Amiss,
Joie de vivre awaits,
Gravity escapes you
Vanity berates you
Ensconce yourself within a cosmic cloud
Blackness consumed
The ocean sands the hardened shells of man
Soft and bared unto the world
Galaxies swallow whole his fate
He yearns to float amidst the sheep
To sleep amongst the stars.

Danielle Cromartie, Grade 11
Boston Latin School, MA

Top Poem Grades 10-11-12

Quiet Queen*

Early spring light brightened the gleam
Majesty of a quiet queen
Her sleek black gown sparkled gold
A dazzling reflection burning the cold

It was in silence we expressed
Our humble honor to be her guest
With promise, command, and spirited class
Carefree, she waltzed on a floor of glass

Balanced with grace, then one misstep
Fatefully tugged at royalty's breath
Alone on a night without a sound
Destiny's kingship brought her down

Gone from the sunrises, fading through time
Ribbons of red have tied back her shine
Legend her dance, nature her throne
Her powerful voice is in how she's alone
Her jewels are the stars, her castle the sea
Majesty of a quiet queen

Pamela Curtin, Grade 12
Derry Area High School, PA
In memory of the "Titanic"

Top Poem Grades 10-11-12

I Cannot Write Poetry

I cannot write poetry, I do not have the ear
To listen to my inner voice and hence translate it here;
I do not have the patience — lack the will, the way, the word,
And all my greatest rhymes were spoken in the past and heard!
I starve myself of lyric beat without support of tone.
Ideas take arms against me, form a nation all their own!
My rhythm naps in corners, does not look me in the eye.
My meter, packs, walks up, walks out — "Good riddance, sir! Goodbye!"
They never even pay the rent for crashing in my brain —
Their jargon and their revelries will soon drive me insane!
Diction likes to drink a lot and curse me in the night;
Enjambment takes a swing at me with unrelenting might!
Simile's like torture, like an iron-coated whip
That licks its tongue across my back, a stinger for a tip.
Metaphor's a nuisance, yes, I say — a dunce, a twit!
The more he speaks, the more I smell his decomposing wit!
I cannot write poetry, I do not have the strength —
The only tools I've left to me are mockery and length!

Nicholas Anthony D'Elia, Grade 12
Osbourn High School, VA

Top Poem Grades 10-11-12

A Search for Meaning

Interrogate me and you
will find out something you never
wished to know.
You'll curse your curiosity
and call me Lucifer.
Let's go to Hades and question
the meaning of sanity.
Wait!
There is none.
Fling reason against anarchy.
Laugh at the futile attempts
of democracy.
Then crown me king.
"Look upon my works, and despair!"
But do not dare call me Ozymandias,
nor Shakespeare, for I am no wordsmith.
But perhaps…call me Apollo.
For I will strum my lyre and make you beg
for an end
to eternity.

Anthony Douglas, Grade 12
Saint James School, MD

Top Poem Grades 10-11-12

A Stranger's Nose

On my pale face lives the nose of a stranger,
Not conceived by plastic surgery, oh no,
Yes, purely genetics, and yet I am assured,
It is not my nose but a stranger's, oh yes,
A stranger, a great man I am told,
Gave me his nose, though not on purpose you see,
Though it must truly be, for I hear and I hear,
You have the nose of my father, you do,
Coursing through my veins is a stranger's blood,
Though I've had no transfusion, it's been there since birth,
But it's his all the same; I'm told it is true,
His genes he has shared, though willing or not,
A handsome face faded in time,
A nose I inherited but never set eyes,
The glint in her eyes, the smile on her lips,
She admires him so; did he know the places she'd go?
I study the faces in that old frame,
Weeping for the extraordinary gone before my time.
Would he be proud to share his nose, I shall never know.
I am proud to possess it, this I am sure.

Sydney Hetrick, Grade 11
Oley Valley Sr High School, PA

Top Poem Grades 10-11-12

New English

to express the thoughts in this head of mine
i'll rewrite English 'til it fits and it rhymes
you call it gibberish I call it right
don't tell me I can't it will be out of sight
i'll do it in secret when no one is there
rewrite it all make it whatever I care
if someone once wrote it down i'll have to revise
English is too hard i'll cut it down to size
no more such thing as a silent letter
i'll rewrite that bit i'll make it all better
i'll make it so that every word has a rhyme
so when writing poems it will save so much time
and last but not least no punctuation
so take a deep breath and begin your recitation

Kyle Knox, Grade 11
Erskine Academy, ME

Top Poem Grades 10-11-12

International Smile

Let's exchange a thousand words for that smile.
All the accents, the dialogues,
Even the different languages that set us apart,
Don't ask como estas?
Or tell me je m'excuse.
Take back your konichiwa,
The ti amo,
Especially the até logo.
Give me that smile, that international smile.
No need for words, no need for translation.
All I want to hear is silence, and
That international smile.

Cecelia In Lee, Grade 10
Westborough High School, MA

Top Poem Grades 10-11-12

Chosen

A crowd of words waits outside the gate
The pen calls some in
Shuffling through files, checking their credentials
Then slowly unlocking the gate, allowing in the elite few.

The gate is closed again leaving disappointed words behind but some still hope.
After all, it's not certain. Some words are banished and new ones are invited in.
A word used too often is pushed to the back of the line.

There are copies, extra copies of all of the little words.
They're not worried about getting chosen
They are guaranteed. Their fate is set.

The long, obscure, and difficult words have already given up
They lounge together on the sidelines exchanging stories.
When words exit the gate, some wear sad expressions
Others skip out, claiming they'll go back in a few stanzas.

Words exit one by one, words exit by the stanza, or by the line.
Adjectives are the most unpredictable, followed by verbs, then nouns.
Nouns stick to their own kind, forming groups that giggle in a huddle
before filing into the gate all together.

Words are called in, escorted through the gate in a formal manner.
Words are barked out from the chewed-up cap.
The pen bouncing and ink splotching.

Nadia Mulvihill, Grade 12
New Paltz Sr High School, NY

Top Poem Grades 10-11-12

Ode to an Artist

Thou forted goddess of pencil and paint,
Such splendor doth thy hands make.
Canvas of the heavens virgin and pure,
Seeded with thy hues of eternal wake.

Strokes from enchanted brushes birthing,
Mountains and valleys defenseless against thy will,
Shorelines and skies cease back under hands,
Of thine wander'est goddess wand still.

And in thy palms feeble forms weave,
Cowering and fragile to thy pillaging strokes.
Tips of graphite pierce the paper below,
Where thy eraser dare to provoke.

Yet in thine perfection among the arts,
Honor reflects such in another aspect of thee.
Thy heart flutters in syncopation to all,
Laughter quaking thine lovéd in boisterous glee.

Paint and pallet hath no knowledge,
Of wondrous elements birthed by thee.
The joyous moments thou hath created,
And how much they mean'eth to me.

Erin Sinnott, Grade 12
Saugerties Jr/Sr High School, NY

My Sweet Escape

I opened my eyes to a moonlit sky. Each layer of the atmosphere glistening with the rainbow colors. As I stand in the middle of an arched bridge, I hear the bending of woodwork. My feet trudging across the splintered surface, moving toward the handcrafted rails. Staring at the sparkling meadow, so calm and peaceful, I have the sudden urge to dive in. There are beautiful reeds and rosebuds surrounded by soft sand found near the bottom.

Then I imagine the feeling of submerging my feet into the sand. If only my spirit could be lifted from this abyss…

He glanced at me with a slight grin, somehow knowing my happiness. Standing beside me, in the very corner of my eye, he said, "that feeling never fades, if you simply believe in your dreams, captured by this image."

He opened the cardboard box, the picture is sealed, and my sweet escape is forevermore.

Jenna Raia, Grade 10
Kings Park High School, NY

Dear God*

Dear God,

For the past year and a half, I've been trying to figure out what life really means there's so much going on. I've lost a part of me. My life feels so incomplete there's a open gaping hole in my heart, from all the times I let myself get hurt. I start and wonder where and when I messed up and that it was all my fault. Please God help me go back in time and let me be a ghost or the voice in my head who tells me right from wrong. If You can't do that Sir, please send me another angel, because the first one I already let go, I know that I messed up, but I want another chance to fix my mess. God I ask that wherever my first angel is, you let her know that I am sorry for the harm I caused and that thanks to her I am sitting here thinking about the times I messed up, and that I should've listened because now I am paying the price, and please God also let her know she's not a zero she's my hero. Now there's nothing more to do except wait for a miracle until then I'll sit here all alone with no one to turn to except this pen…and the pages of this notebook

Ana Aguilera, Grade 11
Kennett High School, PA
*Dedicated to Briel Kobak

A Guide Forever by Thy Side

"Come to the edge He said. They said, we are afraid. Come to the edge He said.
They came. He pushed them, and they flew."
— Guillaume Apollinaire

When the storms of life brew, look through thine eyes anew.
Never doth faith linger, for He is always at thy finger.
Thou must believe He will come hither, for only He hath the power to direct whither.

He will come to prithee durst, for then thy troubles will be traversed.
For He wrought ye, and doth thus beseech thou to see,
Beyond thy grief, fulsome with belief.

When the storms thrust thee to the edge, thou must allege,
To give Him thy trust, and to adjust;
To the obstacles He directs thy way, for He hath not left thee astray.

Only then wilt connected thou be, to the holiness He hath offered thee.
For He gave thou the faith to fly, and transcend a life that hath gone awry.
Through a perspective that is renewed, and rooted in the faith that He hath imbued.

So count thy blessings and thy burdens as one, for He hath directed them to thee, as thou art His Son.
Giveth He to thee so thou can fly, because with faith thou will soar high.
Explore the worlds He hath opened to thee, for it is His intention to guarantee,
That when one hath exhibited faith that is great, His flight shall not long await.

Kristen Starkowski, Grade 11
RHAM High School, CT

I Am, I Am Not, I Believe

I am like a fish swimming in the river of knowledge
I am like an arrow with purpose and direction
I am who I was raised to be
I am unlike the others

I am not just a fish in the sea
I am not a mainstream mind
I am not simply words written on a piece of paper
I am not your average guy

I believe I can choose who I want to be
I believe that my imagination is limitless
I believe boundaries are set only by our minds
I believe in me

David Heaton, Grade 12
Frontier Sr High School, NY

The Angel with Sapphire Eyes

The sun rises
As crimson spills over pale mountains,
And pours out form within deep valleys
The flood captivates the eyes of an Angel,
An Angel hiding from the light
Blue, sapphire eyes gaze at this sight
In horror, in wonder, in fright
Quickly she floats away from this place,
This place where anxiety takes hold
The path she takes becomes a vortex
As she spirals out of control
The Angel is lost in the darkness.
Unable to find a delicate comfort,
She's forced to wander
In the fiercest wilderness of life
Here you can hear the sickening screams
Of the Angel without her light
The sun has set.

Jessica Roupp, Grade 12
Southside High School, NY

Romeo and Juliet: Act 3

Romeo kills Tybalt to take vengeance
This outburst made the Prince's anger grow
Nurse tells Romeo's deed and his sentence
Grieving for Tybalt, she blames Romeo
For his death, Juliet is struck with grief
The nurse promises to bring her lover
Romeo prefers something quick and brief
He can't bear to live without his treasure
So about Juliet, he asks the nurse
At her response he attempts suicide
And says, "Let me die! Living would be worse!"
"You should be grateful!" the friar replied
With a safe plan the three of them plotted
So the two lovers could be united

Neha Singh, Grade 11
Essex High School, VT

Untitled

He asked me.
He asked me
if I'd ever been in love.
And I took a long, hard look at him,
his brown moon of a face soaked with gold.
His eyes were like diamonds,
brilliantly shining
in the light of his smile.
He stood there, tall and lean and fiery,
with a smoking heart made of coal
just for me.
I looked in to the eyes of my one and only love,
and shook my head from left to right,
my smile weak, my tears running.
"What about me?" he asked, his voice deep,
his eyes sleepy.
I leaned in and kissed him sweetly upon the cheek,
ready to answer in his ear;

"I reckon that's been my question for you."

Selorm Quist, Grade 12
Seneca Valley High School, MD

Imaginary Sunset

Drifting through an imaginary sunset,
Making up this fantasy, to get
Up to collect flowers for a gift,
Hoping to give my spirit some lift.
Grassy meadows swallow the cliffs,
Whispering winds reveal new myths,
My hand goes down, to fetch sand off the free beach,
But the sand turns to memories, just out of reach.
A great wind, blows me to the Great Waters,
Navigation of these places were dreamt by our forefathers,
But navigation is impossible in this land, I forget,
That this place was just, my imaginary sunset.

Ray Almeida, Grade 12
Warwick Sr High School, PA

Change

Obama is here
He's now the president
Stay positive because yes we can
He the 44th man to step into the house
Get use to it because he's going to be around
Soon to be four good and happy years
He's a good role model for all the young peers
Before he came he had to beat some opponents
Like Clinton and McCain but I ain't showboating
1-20-09 I will never forget
When John Roberts said "Congrats Mr. President"
In four more years you know who to vote
BARACK OBAMA yeah you know

Garrick Beauliere, Grade 10
Roselle Catholic High School, NJ

A Hidden Memory

A hidden memory.
Gold and silver leaves.
The glazed winter forest.
The sun stinging my body.
A gentle breeze kissing my face.
Blissful laughter gorges the air.
A burning sky with vibrant rays,
Beating down on the distant hill tops.
A promise sung close to my ear,
With the melody of spring.
Dust covered images.
A mask of clouds,
A maelstrom of haze.
Clear thoughts of past memories,
A lost mist of mind.
A hidden memory.
            Ariana Woodson, Grade 10
        Appoquinimink High School, DE

Crazy?

As the rain falls, falls from the sky,
        The roads sigh
        From the weight of cars
        As they drive by.

I walk, walk onto the sidewalk,
        And talk,
        Talk to myself.
I talk to myself about this and that.
I talk to the dog and my cat.

I cannot tell you why I do these things,
        These crazy, crazy things.
        But I can tell you this:
        You do them too.
            Charlotte Taney, Grade 12
        Northwood High School, MD

After the Crash

Soft gentle drumming
rain falls gracefully
against the window

Water runs from a
drainpipe down rushing, rushing
yet going nowhere

Puddles rippling
droplets dripping from above
filling divots more

Hush, hush, says the rain
now is not the time to cry
be glad you're alive
            Melody Tomlinson, Grade 12
        Manhasset High School, NY

I Looked in the Mirror and Saw Me

I looked in the mirror
I saw me
I looked in the mirror and saw a girl that was happy
I saw me
I looked in the mirror and saw a girl that was never hurt
I saw me
I looked in the mirror and saw a girl that wasn't treated like dirt
I saw me
I looked in the mirror and saw a girl that never shed tears
I saw me
I looked in the mirror and saw a girl with no fears
I saw me
I looked in the mirror and saw a girl that had emotional control
I saw me
I looked in the mirror and saw a girl that had a beautiful soul
I saw me
I looked in the mirror and I saw a girl that really was who I wanted to be
            Tatyana Gonsahn, Grade 10
        Bishop Francis P Keough High School, RI

Sweet 16

Mom take my third candle with pride,
Because you are always there for me even when I may push you aside.
You give me inspiration with everything I do,
Although it may not always seem like it, but I truly do love you.
I wish that there was a way for me to express my gratitude,
For every time I was sick or gave you an attitude.
I appreciate every time you were standing by my side,
Mom thank you for being my role model and being my guide.
            Kathleen Westervelt, Grade 10
        St Anthony's High School, NY

Summer

With the taste of sweet summer air,
wind blowing gently against tree branches,
and the delightful smell of fresh flowers in the air,
I know it's time.
Starts with disbelief it has arrived,
waking up in soft, light sheets at noon,
lying in bed, listening to birds.
I know it's time.
Then comes soft orange sunsets with hints of magenta.
A sight to kiss your sweetheart to,
I know it's time.
If you think hard enough,
you can smell the chlorine in the pools, the salt in the ocean.
You can hear children playing in the crashing waves.
I know it's time.
When the bright sun burns over a group of conditioning athletes,
the brutal whiff of a hard workout. Then a deserving clean shower.
I know it's time.
When it all comes to an end
and I start day dreaming again,
I know shortly, it will be time.
            Leah Haas, Grade 10
        North Allegheny Intermediate High School, PA

Alone

The rain started to pound but there I stand my ground
This house is not my home my life, I'm all alone.
Smile, I am broken. Laughing, I am choking
On what I never say there is no end today
I write from what I know that you will never go.
The rain is still going, pouring down, all knowing
Mixing in with the tears, you are my greatest fear.
You take everything and leave me with nothing.
This house is not a home, I am always alone.
I will always blame you, what is there I can lose?
I write from what I learn, hatred will always burn.
Well up inside of me, you are just a memory.
So don't understand as I slap away your hand.
I never wanted, needed it. You just don't fit.
Not my friend, not my mother, you are just another
Who will never hear me say, the truth I've delayed.
This place is not my home, I want to be alone.

Nikki Betts, Grade 11
Mechanicsburg Area High School, PA

A Shooting Star

All of the sudden, you appeared in my life.
You were so magical and wonderful.

The time I spent with you was like no other.
But in the blink of an eye, you were gone.

You left with a trace or any explanation why.
You didn't care if I hurt or cry.
You just disappeared into the summer night sky.

You are my shooting star.

Alicia Escoto, Grade 11
Albert Einstein High School, MD

Time

Constricting of life
and keeper of the order you structure
you hold our universe together
but you remain unseen
the forgotten one
we base lives around you
often overlooked but always ticking away
chipping away at our lives,
as we grow old
watching faces wrinkle
and landscapes change
you remain the same
but forever changing
stationary, but always moving,
forward into life and existence,
you keep score,
in a game where you are always the winner
you are never held back
always advancing
no way to stop you.

Cory Monique, Grade 10
Advanced Math and Science Academy Charter School, MA

Who Ever Knew Life…

Who ever knew life could be so hard
Leaving you mentally, physically, and emotionally scarred

Who ever knew life could be so fun
Giving you space to laugh, play, and run

Who ever knew life could be so blind
Sneaking up on you, attacking you from behind

I knew these things about life since the day I was born
That was the first day that I sworn

That I would live life by the rules
And take life as my school

To work hard and succeed
And it gives me the need

To thank the one I love
And that is the man above

Ka'Deazha Weeks, Grade 10
Norview High School, VA

My Dark Palace

at night I stay hidden;
in my dark gloomy palace
in my palace I have no worries
no screaming, bickering, or fighting
the only screams are my own
I cry out in misery and in pain
feeling alone and abandoned in my own home
I want to runaway and get out
I have my palace deep in the crevice of my soul
no one can tell me that I'm not good enough
because its my heart, my soul, and my creation.
in my heart I am good enough
I'm stuck in my hole, no way out.
not wanting to move
my heart is damaged and torn apart
I'm this small tiny little girl that no one wants.
no one is perfect.

Amanda Kloc, Grade 11
Norwalk High School, CT

It Is Love

I'm yearning to reach out and touch your face,
To feel the spark when your soft lips touch mine.
I yearn to lie in your arms,
And to look into your beautiful eyes.
All I want is to be next to you,
To feel your love for me and to witness its strength.
To make our love shown,
Becoming closer and closer each moment of our lives.
You are my one, my true love, my everything.

Chelsea Waltman, Grade 12
Vincentian Academy/Duquesne University, PA

Relationships

Love is painful
it's like a wound
that I wish never heals
because I know it's real
so I don't want to reveal
how he makes me feel
by looking up at the moon
I hear him
as my own personal tune
knowing my chances are slim
but still hoping
our relationship will
get over this hill
moping along
waiting to hear our song
thinking of what we've done wrong
so sinking with doubt
remembering how he felt
I am just breaking down
and wanting to shout
love is difficult, it can make me frown

Melissa Kent, Grade 10
Mohawk Jr/Sr High School, PA

On Fear's Shores

The shores of twisting moors
My heart fills with sorrow
When day breaks to break
Shadows of frightful knight
From these billowing nightmares
My heart will soar
This is the darkest hour
My mind vacant with
Every intake of thy heart's soul
Let the eternal breath carry
My whims until evenings slumber

Nikki Bowers, Grade 10
Oakcrest High School, NJ

Beautiful

There's something that's beautiful,
Like a bright, red rose.
But what it is,
Nobody knows.

She's quiet and independent,
Yet, she's left lonely.
No one sees who she really is.
No one sees her inner beauty.

She's gentle and kind.
She's delicate like a red rose.
She stands independent.
She is the one that's beautiful.

Alyssa Grassadonia, Grade 10
Odyssey Academy, NY

My Questions

I am writing this because I want to
My heart tells me to
My mind's not drifting, it's staying…in place
Today must be my lucky day

I'm trying to rhyme but I can't
Rhyming takes time…too much of it
These words though are chosen with a lot of care
They're coming from in here, but where?
Are they coming from my heart or mind or do the two work together?

And what about death? When will I die and how?
Will I die tomorrow, years later, or never?
Will my soul, my spirit live on forever?
Will I never die like Dickens, Shakespeare, and Gandhi?
Perhaps I am asking too much and will never know
Or perhaps time will tell the course my life will take
And as for now, all I can do is wait
And write…
These words are my own
They come from my heart and from my soul
They just flow
I have no control

Amina Haidar, Grade 12
Academy of American Studies, NY

What Has Changed?

Some say that people change over time

As I look upon this old photograph taken in 2005 I notice many things
Austin is lying on the ground, posing like an idiot
Colin is making a facial expression that makes him look ridiculous
Chris is the smallest one in the picture, and spikes his hair
Jake has a bizarre haircut and doesn't seem to mind it
Greg is smiling
David is wearing braces
And I am very red faced because of the football game we just played

As I Look upon this photograph 4 years later I realize something
Austin still poses in every picture we take
Colin still makes facial expressions that are ridiculous
Chris is still the smallest out of all of us, and still spikes his hair
Jake still has a weird haircut, and still doesn't care
Greg can still always be found smiling
David still has his braces
And I still get very red faced after every game I play

Some say people change over time
As I look upon this photograph now
I realized that we haven't changed at all

Mac Milewski, Grade 10
Haverhill High School, MA

If God Is Here

If God is here
Then why are His footprints no longer by my side
Yet I hear that is when He carries me
If God is here
Then why are these swollen eyes holding on to tears that hold a story
Yet this story unfolds as a mystery

If God is here
Then why does my heart still shake when I hear the sound of screaming
Yet my heart still beats even when it breaks
If God is here
Why then has the light nearly gone out inside my world
Yet I have hope for the light that awaits me

If God is here
Then why is the movement of love always mocked
Yet love is always the answer
If God is here
Then why is the hallway long and lonesome
Yet they say if one door closes another one opens

If God is here
Then why is the thunder still echoing? Though the clouds have passed the sun was found
So again I will ask if God is here then where am I?

Kiersten Palmer, Grade 12
Hammond High School, MD

Freckles

I know it sounds absurd but every single word that I'm about to say is true
I know every freckle on my body where I got it. When I got it. How I got it
Ha! Don't believe me? Well then I'll prove it to you!
The very first freckle I ever found is on my right hand, second finger
It was the day we met with awkward hellos you were wearing blue and me in green
You then walked off with her at first I thought it nothing

The next is right above my left knee barely noticeable to anyone that night
The night of lights and dresses and music we didn't say much nor dance much at all
But maybe there was something there that made my mind start to swirl
The next freckles amount to a hundred or so and are in the oddest places
They dot my stomach, my back and even my ears but each one is a conversation with you
'Til the early morning sun we'd talk about life and love and us

The freckles on my cheeks are tears I've cried for you when you walked out of my life
It took me forever to come back from the pain but the tiny freckles on my nose are from looking into your eyes
When everything that had gone wrong finally became right
Hundred of freckles are on my arms and they're the kisses we've shared
The very first awkward kiss secret kisses passionate kisses the kisses you give when I need you most
And the kisses that say everything without words

My favorite freckle is hard to spot
It's small and light and not shown a lot but it's on my heart and it's easy to see
I love it because it connects you with me

Kimmy Sosonka, Grade 11
Colts Neck High School, NJ

What I'm Forced to Love About You

I know you think I hate you,
I know you hate me too,
But there's something that I want to say,
You might not think it's true.

I love the way you don't take showers,
I love the way you spit,
I love the way you smell like garbage,
I don't find it gross one bit.

I love the way you call me names,
I love the way you swear,
I love the way you steal my things,
You never learned to share.

You aren't the most lovable person,
It's hard to stay on course,
But since you are my brother,
I think I'm kind of forced.

Danielle Hrubo, Grade 10
Haverhill High School, MA

Thunder

Quickly, quickly, rapidly
It slices the air
This jagged knife of white hot fire
It tears down from the heavens
Blink it is gone
Watch again for another trickle of gold
Painting the world with a lilac mystery
Why, where, how
Who knew
But now I do
Do know
What is
Lightning

Paula McCarter, Grade 10
Charter School of Wilmington, DE

Dark River

Oh dark river, how deep are you?
I cannot see your bottom.
Your body is the darkest blue,
complementing orange autumn.
Your flow is too strong for the fish,
they cannot keep up.
You force their path even against wish,
throwing them many a hiccup.
Why do you not slow or clear?
Are you so cruel?
You inspire such fear,
with your iron rule.
I am leaving you, dark river.
I choose not to drown.

Kyle Lawrence, Grade 12
Colonia High School, NJ

Answer My Question

Why does it take longer to pick out a watermelon than someone's fate?
Why is it so hard to care but so easy to hate?
Why are you drowning in laughter when your eyes are drowned in fear?
It's easier for you to shed your skin than to shed a tear.
You see a target and you wanna throw a dart,
you think it'll ease your pain or relax your heart.
You walk every day with a fake smile on your face,
thinking that's all you need to win life's race.
Why is your pride bigger than the sky?
What makes it so big, when you can't even fly?
If your watermelon is rotten or bad you can throw it away,
but a person is different and you can't treat him that way.
If your heart's made of metal, it's nobody's fault,
you do what you feel like no matter what you are told.
However even metal can be melted or at least made warm
and you're not a robot, so your heart isn't metal, or cold,
it's been warm ever since you were born.
So what's your excuse for being so stubborn and cold?
Now maybe if you answer this question you'll deserve an award.

Liza Alksne, Grade 11
PALCS School, PA

Love

Is there anything that can compare to how amazing you are?
The way the sunlight reflects off your beautiful eyes
With the smile you get as you listen to the crash of waves afar
And it all seems to get better with the temperature rise.
With you it gets brighter and brighter each day
And it would feel great if the weather stays like this forever
But soon it starts to get colder and fade away
And we will lose are wonderful time together
I don't want to say it but we both know it's true
The sun will be covered by snow clouds and your eyes will no longer shine
It will be tough but it is something we'll both get through
And then you will no longer be mine.
But with everything I have to remember you by
The thought of you will never die.

Jessica Lynch, Grade 10
Garnet Valley High School, PA

Emotionless

Quick, like an epiphany,
Stiff — as a heart attack.
A blinding realization that dumbfounds you,
The fact that an emotion can substantially change a decision,
And a decision…
Can change a circumstantial difference in whether you are independent…
Or if you ciphen a decision from a mind that you have yet to control.
To leave a standing chance on whether you let your heart decide
Or your head besides your subconscious…
Stands between you and your emotional backfield.
A young-minded, naïve, childish brain cannot stand to make such a decision…
So for now, I stand…
Emotionless.

Olivia Williams, Grade 10
Deep Creek High School, VA

Never

You waste your time
Waiting to see
Some improvement
Some miraculous change
But he will always be the same
He could never be
The person you want him to be
He won't fill the void he left in your life
He will never be there to tuck you in at night
He will never teach you something
He couldn't learn himself
He will never care for you
He doesn't know how
Good luck dreaming impossible things
He couldn't change for me
And this is the same
He is the same
He could never change

Alexis Galagan, Grade 10
Greenwich Jr/Sr High School, NY

Gone

Don't sit there and tell me these lies
These subtle, soft, sweet lullabies
With your smiles that glitter like sun through the rain
Your kisses that drop to clear away the pain
Don't tell me everything's going to be all right
Because then you're gone and I cry through the night
Wishing that you'd still come back for me
Sickened with fear, even as I see —
You do this on purpose, to catch me off-guard
To watch as my life breaks, and pick up each shard
With your voice soft as butter you call out my name
And we go back to playing your grief-stricken game
Where you are the king and I am your pawn
And I struggle to remember just whose side you are on
So when you come home, don't expect me there
I've decided to leave; I've taken my share.

Alexandra Swanson, Grade 12
Marlborough High School, MA

The Restless Thoughts of You

Laying here restless
I feel no resentment for you loved
the moment I touched your mahogany skin
my throat quenched out
a reliable source
love flew still
my heart whispered like frozen snow in the wind
our two energies collide to make one ray of heat
my restless thoughts of you
are done
why I just lay here…
Restless

Timothy Booker, Grade 12
Penn Wood High School, PA

A Different Desire

If you desperately want to leave,
do not think twice.
Get on that ship and explore the high sea.
Travel wherever your heart desires.
Shall it be Tibet, Istanbul, or the unchartered lands
go as far as you desire,
for then, it will be worthwhile.
But if you desire something different,
something new,
something somewhat quite exquisite,
then pick up that dusty book.
To relive the past.
To live what's never been lived before.
To feel emotions never felt before.
To see things a way never seen before.
So sit obediently in that chair
as if entranced by a wicked spell, or bound by barbed wire
entangled in it — incapable of moving an inch or more
while fulfilling, that desire.

Luiza Maciejak, Grade 10
The Bronx High School of Science, NY

Shattered Glass

My heart felt broken and yet it still beat.
It was similar to shattering glass;
A multitude of pieces on the street.
Lost by all, memories free to bypass,
Frozen in the grief, unable to feel;
A personal lone cosmos of cold ice.
Putting up walls, I forgot what was real.
This empire of darkness would suffice.
I stood, my slowly beating organ fixed
On the blockade to disconnect from pain.
The numbness began to fade, feelings nixed.
There could be healing, and then I could gain
Restoration, if at the least grow strong.
And it would stay with me, my whole life long.

Elizabeth Hart, Grade 11
New Jersey United Christian Academy, NJ

what do you see?

what do you see when looking at me
do you see a black minority
or do you see someone who loves to read
do you see someone who wants to be
someone important someday
someone who will find a way
someone who doesn't quite fit in
not because of the color of my skin
but the way that i am
call me a pariah
cal me what you feel
call me what ever you like
but don't call me late for a meal
just know that when you look at me
i am what you see.

Virginia Ayers, Grade 11
DCF Middlesex Campus, NJ

The French Revolution

Years of oppression building up to this
Seems as though the way things were before for the French citizens was just a hit and miss.
Now they've resorted to violence and murder
Revolting against the government has just gone a step further.

Guillotines, riots, blood baths, and rage
The anger boiling in the peasants looked as if it would never fade.
Chopping the heads off of Marie and King Louis
Their anger caused by oppression was becoming unruly.

The National Assembly made up of French people alike
Decided to address the abuse of their natural rights.
And from this revolution of oppression and devastation
Came the Rights of Man and Citizen woven into a French Declaration.

From 1789 to the present times we live in the French were able to have the opportunity
To gain back their natural rights of life, liberty, and property.

Chelsey Pellot, Grade 10
Townsend Harris High School, NY

Life: Grief, Loss, and the Unknown Aftermath

'Tis the tale of life of struggle and strife
Of love and hate that entwine our fate
With a fall into a short abyss to rise again and restore to right all that were amiss

Ought we to cogitate on the past with bitter frustration and rue? Or look onto the morrow for a start anew?
Our painful losses and our blissful gains do so very paint the bittersweet skies with sweet and sad rains

Does inheritance of loss exist truly? Is it an insurmountable temptation that we allow ourselves to succumb so cruelly
To relinquish hope, happiness, and life? Can we call melancholy inescapably rife?
Can we call this the bitter end? To give up, to draw a path to an ultimate abyss to wend?
To suffer loss from a tender age, the realizations suffice to more than a gage
To be inundated with mixed thought, should all this grief really be for naught?
Or is this the test of survival, faith, and resolution that shall issue forth our restitution?

Saima Mir, Grade 11
The Bronx High School of Science, NY

Gratification from a Scholar

Please understand that along with my ambiguous mind,
comes an altruistic benefaction to the pleas of those that lie dearly in my heart;
know that I will at times become capricious,
but still, be apprehensive that I acquiesce when you believe in me and my morale.

You've come to acclaim without the brevity of my candid virtue.
This sudden appease has withheld the arbitrary foolishness and hostility, which I used to hold.

Thank goodness for the benevolent apathetic sensuality that I've realized from my blasphemous and biased actions;
which, in some circumstances have been expelled so banal.

And now, I speak with articulate and eloquent language:
I understand that learning is the willpower collaborated with knowledge.

You have helped me blossom my soul into many things that the world itself cannot compute.
My, my!!!! You've got aesthetic qualities, and now I'm more aloof.

Clara Brooks, Grade 11
Hempstead High School, NY

Masterpiece

Being in love is not something you become.
It's something you're made into.
Like fresh clay in the hands of an artist
you are shaped with passion and intensity.
And like the clay, in the end you become a masterpiece.
Pieces of nothing brought together by an artist

and yet…

you can't just be brought together.
There has to be fire.
Consider that every work of art
…every…masterpiece…
needs a special artist with their own special eye.
Every artist has their own look on life,
a special appreciation of the world.
An artist's art is based on how they see the world.
You are that masterpiece.
Their idea of the world.
When you become…in love…
when you become…a masterpiece…you have been molded.
So now all that's left to wonder is
…how does my artist…see the world?

Patricia Liggins, Grade 12
Oxon Hill High School, MD

The Experience

As I was racing home from school one day
I stopped to stare at a stemmed flower bed
To ponder at its blissful beauty.
All around me stood nature's young children
Blessing me with their youthful joy
And inviting me to revel in their fun.

Never asking a single question
Only living in the moment of innocence
I accepted their humble request.
Believing that life possessed endless boundaries
Each with it's own unique possibilities
Without any suffering or hardships.

Upon arriving home I was greeted
By the frosty chill of my uncle's voice
Which was a knife that struck deep within my chest.
"He didn't make it" was what I was told
As I was struggling to stand upright
And keep my composure without crying.

One second I am on top of my life
While in the next I fall ten stories
And see my innocence come crumbling down.

Raheel Awan, Grade 12
Rockville High School, MD

800

His heart raced, body tightened,
Boddom. Boddom. Boddom.
His mouth mummed,
His body sweats with fear,
Boddom. Boddom. Boddom.
"You're ready, are you scared?"
"No just pumped."
Boddom. Boddom. Boddom.
Legs wobbly, hands numb,
Boddom. Boddom. Boddom.
"On your mark…get set…Pow!!"
Ahhha, ahhha, ahhha, ahhha.
Boddom. Boddom. Boddom.
Skin sweating, nose running, heads hurting,
Hands shaking, legs sleeping, heart's growling,
Mouth's drooling, eye's tearing.
Boddom. Boddom. Boddom.
"It's ok man, you'll get 'em next time."
Boddom. Boddom. Boddom.

Nasir Francis, Grade 11
Alfred E Smith High School, NY

Season of Regret

A season of life; of joy; of hope; of beginnings.
Of the sweet scent of pink petals blooming on a cherry tree.

What about this season fills me with sadness?
This season of hope fills me with despair.
This life makes me feel of death.
A joy leaving nothing but sorrow.
Beginnings smelling only of an end.
The world gazes forward, but I look back in regret.
Dreams like cherry blossoms lay listless on fallow fields.

Nick Takaki, Grade 11
Valley Regional High School, CT

Inspirational Love

You are more beautiful than the sunset,
My love grows for you each and every day.
I could never love you enough, not yet.
I don't think it's possible to ever say.

It's so hard to find words to show I care.
Your eyes are like pure, intense love.
I will be with you when I am not there,
Watching your moves from the sky like a dove.

My heart sinks to the bottom of my soul,
If I need your help I know you'll be there,
When I need help to get out of the hole.
When I see you all I can do is stare.

You are my love forever there and true,
Despite everything I'll always have you.

Chris Morel, Grade 10
Pittsfield Middle-High School, NH

More to a Tear

A tear is not
Just a simple drop of water

There is more to a tear
Then an expression of feeling
It holds memories
And shows pain

A tear is like the claw of a tiger
Powerful
Ripping the skin
Leaving a permanent mark

You can't cover up the scar
Or hide the pain

It's like a window
Showing your life
Exposing the secrets
Inside your heart
Sarah Burgess, Grade 10
Paint Branch High School, MD

I Love You

I love you so I try not to cry
But sometimes I can't help it
I look deep into your clear blue eyes
But those eyes are not the ones I know
The ones that were as pure as snow
They are endless pits of darkness
Deep trays of despair
But I know when I stare at you
With your body frail
And skin so pail
That you are not the one lying there
You are already gone
Already free
In the place you wanted to be
And you are happy so we should be too
We are all just so happy
That we knew you
Sally Michals, Grade 10
Amesbury High School, MA

School Dances

The bass making the floor rattle
Jumping around with all your friends
Being crazy and not caring who knows
Everyone laughing, having a good time
Light flashing different colors
People never thinking that they could
Have such a good, exciting time
On school grounds
Julianna Fisher, Grade 10
Victor Sr High School, NY

How to Cope: A Poetic Essay

A writer, is a coward
Hiding behind pretty words, telling tales
Of a better place
But never going about making one
Poets have a surprising inability to string words
When direly necessary
And an essayist cannot voice an opinion
Without an hour beforehand to brainstorm
Those that ink in first person only boast arrogance
Focusing spotlights on I I I, me me me
Those that write in second person
Don't want to be found out, switching attention to readers
If only to protect themselves
And those that pen in third person
Are so content to sit and listen and fade
That they take out the factor of
You and I entirely
A writer can't wrap a pen around reality; they cower and retreat behind paper
Writing down things unequivocally too human
Hoping tomorrow will be better
Alyssa Ciampaglia, Grade 10
Cherokee North High School, NJ

Of Forgotten Times

Oh of what we lose.
Oh how they lose us.
Oh what we do, of all things.

Ode to those long lost.
For some never forget.
Some never regret,
yet some never sing.

For warm airs rise.

Some words our hearts enthrall,
and so I say to Paul, do good.
Thrive.

Days through, another breathes.
God knows
we all undo the stitches sewn
how we please.

Of the beauty we choose to follow.
Of respect that is undone.
You think you've won,
but maybe only
change is the prize.
Maria Cassidy, Grade 12
Blackstone Valley Regional Vocational Technical High School, MA

Gone

The playing and laughing demolitions in to the warmth of the Earth's core,
A true love's kiss fades away into the dark and lonely abyss,
In the end, it's all lies, never letting go of what is beautiful and pure,
Like a black hole sucking in all that is true to you, it's just all gone to me and you.

Amythist Francis, Grade 10
Lyndon Institute, VT

Noah Walker

All my life I was looked down upon or pitied, even in a passing stranger's glances.
I saw the sorrow they felt through their teeming eyes.
Summer was ending and fall was near,
Everyone around me seemed to be unexcited except me.
I was more on the apathetic side on the whole idea.
I didn't have nothing to look forward to or miss.
I have been feeling like this ever since that day.
That day my life fell apart, my mother had left us when I was 3
My father died when I was 13, after that I bounced from foster home to foster home
Until I emancipated myself at the age of 16, couldn't bear those pitiful eyes any longer
But then I saw her for the first time, she looked at me.
These eyes were different though, they had no pity, just a heartwarming look to them.
But who was she? Does she know about me?
At that point I didn't know but I wanted to meet her.
Her name was Lucy. Lucy Smith changed me. Showed me not everyone was alike.
We started dating, went steady for awhile, I was happy as can be.
But then I got that sudden feeling that something was up.
She told me about her past, and how she had been fighting cancer since the age of 13.
I was angry she didn't tell me sooner, but I soon got over it when I found out her days were numbered.
She died on August 15th, but she still lived on inside of me.
With her kind and gentle memories. I was happy the day they buried me right beside her.

Alexis Suarez, Grade 11
Bronx Theatre High School, NY

Smooth Criminal

With patient eyes, a voice like honey, and a smile like a fox,
You knock every young girl off her feet. But I'll tell you once, that you'll never get me.
Smooth Criminal, you stole my heart like a thief in the night.
Disregarding all the laws you broke, my heart.
With your hair like silk and your body resembling that of a god, I can't help but to stare.
My heart beats frantically, flutters like a trapped bird.

I've been caught.
But I play coy, denying the fact that I've been trapped.
In disbelief. Could this be true?
You've cast your spell.
I, a mere caged parakeet, yearning to be set free.
The worst is you don't even notice me. I swear, I say you look at me! Was it not your eyes that met mine in the crowd?

I'm a fly on your wall. Nothing, Invisible.
I'm the fish you want to throw back.
I, a nervous wreck, mind racing, and contemplating about that day I swear I heard you say my name.
Smooth Criminal, you stole my heart and now I'm falling apart.
But to you, I'm just another broken heart. Not letting myself love you no more.
Your trickery and your games are through, Smooth Criminal.
But, why am I still wishing I was still with you?

Ashley Arkhurst, Grade 11
Manlius-Pebble Hill School, NY

Fire

Faster than light
The fire blazes on
Ignited by his hands
The beauty amazes you
And you sit and wait
For it to rise
You say it will happen
So you wait
But as you watch
The flames fall
Fast and hard
And you look all around you
To find he is gone
And you're lost in the darkness
Blind to the rest of the world

Samantha Heilig, Grade 12
West Islip High School, NY

Out There

I look to the stars and wonder,
"Is there someone out there?"
The night remains silent though
As I continue to stare.

With so many planets
The odds are quite high
That there really are beings
From out of the sky

It'd be nice to know
That we're not alone
And that we have neighbors
Far away from our home

And I know, galaxies from here
A little green person, too, stares
At the night sky and wonders
"Is there someone out there?"

Matthew P. Elder, Grade 12
Massapequa High School, NY

Untitled

I think the
Color of hunger is red,
Bloody and injured,
Grabbing and
Shoving,

A battle cry at
The lunch line,

Snipping and biting
Like ravenous
Wolves.

Amy Morkys, Grade 11
Holy Cross High School, CT

I Wait

I wait
No matter how many hours pass or sunsets dawn
I wait
And am counting the moments when I can so softly and gently whisper in your ear
I wait to be the voice in which you find comfort
To be the voice in which you yearn to hear
When you speak to me the tones of sound that leave your lips
The highs and lows and this crisp, smooth, sweetness that is exhaled
With every gasp of air you have so slowly and tenderly inhaled
Is the most precious thing
And the most beautiful
That keeps me coming back
And keeps me waiting

Madeleine D'Almeida, Grade 12
Lehigh Valley Charter High School for the Performing Arts, PA

Tantalus

They were so close, the luscious skins reflecting the vivid rays of sunlight,
    that gleamed through the openings in the foliage.
His arms, reaching out towards the irresistible fruits, luring him closer,
    yet as he clawed at the branches, his hands remained empty.
The water, frigid and calm, enveloped him, beckoned him down
    into its depths, the bottom an endless pool of forbidden.
Head curled forward, lips barely touching the silky liquid,
    before it rushed, pulling away from him.
Left, sand slipping through his fingers, crushed against his knees,
    a barren desert, leaving him with only a longing.
Forever, he will be this way, pleading to deaf ears,
    hunger gnawing his stomach, thirst drying his throat,
    tantalized. Forever. Forever…

Dorie Schwartz, Grade 10
The Bronx High School of Science, NY

The Tree

In the dark, lonely woods of Eerie,
Lies a tree in perpetual pain
Withered by sorrow it lies weary.
While leaves dance by it becomes teary,
Hoping that some day it could dance the same.
Then he cowered his head in the midst of shame,
Veiling it's undeniable beauty from the world.
It was lonely and wanted domain
To dance in the sun,
Not the piercing rain.
He wanted its leaves to lay unfurled.
It prayed for the devoted fidelity, to uncoil its arms and dance in Alacrity
And learn the dance of life with Acuity,
To become intoxicated by the candied song of life.
A cool breeze skimmed by this lonely tree,
And kissed it with the lips of hope and affection.
And its branches extended to the diamond kissed sea.
And danced to the sweet melody.
Now he can hold his head high with
Sweet Perfection.

Katelin McDonald, Grade 12
Penn Wood High School, PA

Drifting

Salty winds that buffer rocks,
drift over the drifting blue,
hulls and sails reach heavenward,
and seagulls sing to God.

Lulls and whitecaps sink and rise,
while heaving crests and troughs tempt air,
to wane and wax in lonely space,
across the gleaming, fickle wake.

Failing lofts descend the sea,
submerged in water, ceased to be…

Patrick Gasparini, Grade 12
Midlothian High School, VA

Someone

Someone who wiped away the tears that slid down my cheek.
Someone who helps me look and seek.
Someone who has their heart all worried about me.
Someone who has the power to make me happy.
Someone who cares about what I do.
Someone who is there with me during the old and new.
Someone who gets hurt when they see me hurt.
Someone who doesn't treat me like the black, muddy dirt.
Someone who cares about my feelings, whether good or bad.
Someone who doesn't like to see me depressed and sad.
Someone who told me that my feelings are a part of me.
Someone who opened my eyes, so I can see.
This someone is a friend who is so true.
Thank you so much, because this friend is you.

Basant Tawfik, Grade 10
Bayonne High School, NJ

Dear Mom

I understand we stand in America,
Quality of life at its best,
Allegedly.
Vitality of nice doesn't rest,
Supposedly.
Then.
The world: mean, just obscene, life: extreme,
trying to swim upstream.
All those which-should-not, did.
If all the voices did not, hid.
What if Mohandas stayed quiet?
All he saw — dare he deny it?
A voice
A noise
The choice
Destroys
The tyranny.
Speak to me, mummified.
Keep mum,
Why?

Simranjit Singh, Grade 12
Townsend Harris High School, NY

Letter from a Stranger

Where is my son now, where is my gentle child.
Was he hiding behind trees in my stormy mind?
Will his springtime memory of me be ever kind?
May his windy soul grow wild.

Many seasons passed since I've glanced upon his face.
Put the blame on me son, it was I who was the clown.
For I vanished down the road and I let you down.
May he be, unlike me, seldom fallen from grace.

My war was the smooth roar of a young troubled tide.
It was the burning pain of a wound unseen.
In moonlight and dawn I remain in between.
On the wings of angels, someday, may he ride.

Fallen leaves of autumn drift farther away.
Will his rambling thoughts ever wonder of me?
Or his mother's forgiving eyes will I ever see?
If only I could come back to them someway…
If only I could return to stay.

Kevin Phoenix, Grade 12
Liverpool High School, NY

Catch and Release

In a boat on the lake I cast out my line
As the wind carries me away, I let the line go slack
Suddenly the line goes taut, a fish is caught
I pull it out then throw it back.

The fish I catch are all different types
Carp, bass, catfish, sunfish, and bluegill
Shining scales, gills, and tails
Catching them all is my thrill, my test of skill.

I look at each fish before I throw it back
Into their unblinking eyes and gaping mouths
Pondering the simple fish's life, free of pain or strife
Their wonderful simplicity makes me say, "WOW."

The rolling waves, the gentle breeze
The amber glow of the setting sun
Fulfilling my wish to go out and fish
Making the catch and release all the more fun.

William Ratledge, Grade 10
Bishop Denis J O'Connell High School, VA

love

love is true love is false
love is long love is short
love makes smiles love makes tears
love takes days love takes years
love is old love is new
love lives and love dies
love is a wish upon a star in the sky

Jeremiah Robinson, Grade 10
Nashua Christian Academy and High School, NH

To Monsieur Dumas

I beg your pardon, Monsieur Dumas, but I have a favor to ask of you.
I would like to meet this friend of yours,
Monsieur Edmond Dantès, or the Count of Monte Cristo, whichever he prefers.
From what I have heard, he is a noble and (sometimes) honest man
who is a firm believer in revenge.
You see, his story is relatively famous where I come from,
and his perseverance and resolution in the face of betrayal is astounding.
Now, I request this meeting with him because I would like to know
how he dealt with those events that affected him. A chance to compare notes, in a way.
I, unfortunately, am in a situation similar to that of the Count.
My friends were jealous of my success.
They would stop at nothing to tear down my spirits.
One told the man that I love that I had died. She wanted him. I am not dead.
I fear that there is a thicker plot here than meets the eye.
Nevertheless, I need to show them that I am not one to sit back and take attacks.
This is where the Count would be incredibly helpful, you see.
If you could relay this message to him, I would greatly appreciate it.
I will be in a cave off the coast of Sicily.
I feel that he will be able to find me if he would like.
Also, if you could keep my whereabouts between you and the Count, that would be fantastic,
as my return will be much more dramatic if people go on thinking that I am dead.

Courtney Lippa, Grade 12
Our Lady of Mercy High School, NY

Sweet Surrender

i sit patiently on the floor
the floor seems so peaceful these days unlike before
when all it represented was departing footsteps, tearful faces, and breaking hearts
not now, now it brings me home, closer to you
even though i have no idea to where you may be
it reminds me of the moments,
the moments that flow past my mind when i lay
i feel as if, at the exact minute i imagine you, you do the very same
sit and dream that i am by your side
it is an exhilarating feeling to me
the one so familiar with being left behind
a second importance to people as they selfishly worry about themselves
but never mind the past it is a tragic memory that helps bring strength
love takes more than strength it takes two people, two hearts, two souls
willing to take a chance and face fears buried inside to produce something so indescribable
so beautiful it puts the rising sun to shame
it is incredible to think we were once children without a care and we grew to care for each other
our lives will someday end for our emotions, on the other hand they will continue to thrive within us
and that is the gift that brings tears to our eyes
tears that can only be described as
the indescribable.

Victoria Laureano, Grade 11
Dracut Sr High School, MA

Heartbeat

To feel my heartbeat you have to love me. Love me like the sun loves to shine, like a flower loves to bloom. Without you I feel like I cannot lose. Out of all the options their was for me to choose, I wanted someone who I couldn't lose and that was something that you proved. It seemed so hard to open up to you but at this moment I feel comfortable around you. The only thing you said to me was I love you and ever since, that's when I loved you enough to let you feel my heartbeat.

Jasmine Sanders, Grade 10
East NY High School of Transit Technology, NY

Marie-Alix

I reach out, you seem so far away
To retreat now, you seem so far away
Come to me. Still you seem so far away!

I dream the like, closer you are today
Soul touch and flight, closer you are today
Come to me, will you seem closer today?

Swift to anger perceived was my mistake
Jabbing of saber perceived was my mistake
Flirting with danger perceived was my mistake
Choose to flee. Still I seem so far away…

Laugh of the wind, are you closer to stay?
At a kite to a sin, are you closer to stay?
Come to thee. Will you be closer to stay?

Flower to bloom, a rain dance in May
Pond under moon, a rain song in May
Time's with me. Will there be dance in May?

Marie-Alix, don't feel I'm far away
Marie-Alix, don't feel I'm far away
Gondolier to you, I am here to stay
You feel not far away.

Christopher Pasch, Grade 12
Leonardtown High School, MD

The Way the Rain Falls

I love the way the rain falls and glistens
As I splash through a puddle of diamonds
And all I hear, all I feel
Is the melody
It's different every day
And I think it's lovely
The storm finishes its song
And then the clouds move away
In beat to the whispery voice of the wind
The wind that dances up and down
Along with me as I walk by
Then the sun emerges
Like a grin in the sky
And the birds sing joyfully along
As everything perks up and grows
Receiving the song
Just like I am
It's different every day
This music, this harmony
And I think it's lovely
How every day is a surprise.

Rachel Chuang, Grade 10
Thomas Jefferson High School for Science and Technology, VA

Hope for the Future

I wish the world could just live in peace and happiness
Yet in today's world, the ground is drenched with blood
I hope for a bright future, one that is a joyful bliss
Yet in today's world, I see immense suffering

Yet in today's world, the ground is drenched with blood
I searched vigorously for a sparkle of human kindness
Yet in today's world, I see immense suffering
I wonder when we will live pain free lives

I searched vigorously for a sparkle of human kindness
Genocide occurs destroying every family
I wonder when we will live pain free lives
Meanwhile, war engulfs everyone with prickling pain

Genocide occurs destroying every family
I hope for a bright future, one that is a joyful bliss
Meanwhile, war engulfs everyone with prickling pain
I wish the world could just live in peace and happiness

Tracy Ng, Grade 10
Colonia High School, NJ

Heart Broken

As I sit across the room from you
You seem confused and lost
All I can say is that I miss you
And I'll be okay just for today.
Just answer one question, why did you lie?
I wish I could cry but my eyes
Are all dried out from all the pain.
Someone once told me
"A man that makes you cry isn't worth your tears"
But for some odd reason I can't cry…
Maybe it's because you know me too well
Maybe it's because you had me at hello
Maybe it's because you made me believe you
Maybe it's because you are unique or
Maybe it's because I love you.
I don't know anything anymore but one thing
I know for sure is that no one
Will ever help my heart find a cure.

Natasha Rodriguez, Grade 12
Linden High School, NJ

But Then I Remember Your Smile

It doesn't taste as sweet.
The color of the petals seem to fade.
All desires and wants run away.
My cares are no more.
My vision is obscured.
All because I am crying, was crying.
I can't stand it any longer.
But then I remember your smile.
Everything seems to be okay, I want to run.

Sarah Kamenetz, Grade 12
Windsor High School, CT

It Said I Love You

To see the way you look into my eyes
and chase away my fears
and hold me until I cease from crying,
the years of held back tears.

The moon filters into the room,
as you sit at the foot of my bed.
It feels so easy, so clear
but then thoughts go into my head.

I can feel my eyes get wet
the water balloon finally broke
and my tears come flowing out again
but this time I start to choke.

The feelings in my heart
can't match the feelings in my head,
so I got myself together
and slowly got up from my bed.

I walked you to the door
and I wished that I was dead,
so I wouldn't have to say goodbye
but my heart spoke before my head
and it said, "I love you."

Kaitlyn Reynolds, Grade 10
Lampeter-Strasburg High School, PA

The Book of Life

Is each person's life
just another story
with a beginning, middle and end,
weaving together and apart
when their stories cross?

Or are they interconnected,
forming one grand tale
with a little bit of everything:

Mystery
Tragedy
Romance
Comedy

And as time goes on
and the pages turn
the story unfolds:
new settings,
new plots,
new characters,
each waiting to play their role
in the grand tale known as
Life.

Jina Zablan, Grade 10
The Bronx High School of Science, NY

I Do My Best Work on Coke

I do my best work on Coke
Soda that is
But I dilute it so it doesn't hurt my stomach
Then I sit down with my feet up pondering
What another double entendre I could use,
For this poem worth writing

So I sit here scribbling
Fake words that have no meaning
Then you pop into mind but I'm tired of writing love lines

And right now I can't think of anything that has substance worth spilling
So I guess Ill talk about something like how I watched
This Coke bottle fizzing
And how it left a ringlet mark
Bubbling, foaming, and sudsing

Just like how you left a stain on my brain and a scar on my heart
You're dark like Coke Cola

With the slogan taken from Maxwell's brew
You're good to the last drop

Darren Frett, Grade 12
Plainfield High School, NJ

Ring Goes the Bell

Ring! Goes the sound of the bell at 7:45
The clock is ticking for those who trail behind.
Ring! Goes the sound of the bell at 7:50
Everyone who is late, get your tardy passes ready.
Getting ready to start the day,
Always gets interrupted by the morning announcement delay

Get in dress code now! As our school dean mentions,
But students really don't listen, unless you write them a pink slip detention
Cell phones in pockets, skirts rolled up high
Really isn't a surprise, as the school day goes by.

Hall passes are needed to walk the halls,
You even have to carry them with you in the bathroom stalls.
Half the day has gone by, now I am eating lunch, with a coke and some fries.
Now here comes period eight creeping by
Wait there it goes rushing by!
Ring! Now the day is done, because the bell has rung.

Running to your lockers, excited as can be.
Hugging your friends is always an after school priority.
Now many school buses are waiting outside, oh no!
You missed your bus, do you have another ride?

Candice Beards, Grade 11
Paramus Catholic High School, NJ

Last Night

My hands are shaking
My body is trembling
The beast came last night.
Storming in, it shook my house
My parents' faces contorted with horror
Fear filled their eyes,
My brothers hid under their beds,
Their mischievous grins were replaced with scared confusion.
I ran, afraid it would find me
And there I stood in front of the mirror
Saw a reflection of red, fierce eyes, a twisted smile
I flinch with repulsion, I finally understood:

I am the monster and the monster is me.

Pamela Leo, Grade 11
Plainview-Old Bethpage JFK High School, NY

Misery Is a Tree

How on earth can a tree be happy?
Growing up can be a dangerous journey
Only ones with deep roots can survive
Thunder, lightning, wind and rain,
Can be a traumatic experience for a little sprout.
Having children always climb you must tickle your sides;
When kites fly into your branches it must sting, yet
Squirrels and birds build tight nests that keep you warm.
But when you feel that evil orange "X" mist across your trunk,
It poisons your insides and rots your soul,
Knowing that one day soon will be your last.

Meghan McNeice, Grade 12
Tucker High School, VA

Two-Face

Your mask was a face in itself,
As it stopped me in the path,
And looked into my veins.
The gushing red told you what was coming.

You were just a great, bold lion,
Wrapped in a devil's skin.
As he lay beneath your feet,
You smiled and laughed,
Because I saw that you looked just like him.

I stood there and took you for the trenches,
But your truth told me that you were the ocean.
An ocean that held no such trenches,
A sun that looked below as he kept his vigil.
Keeping quiet, the day that he would fall from his peak,
With teeth like razor blades, protecting the place in which he'd begun.

And his eyes, were not the ocean, nor the sun.

Russell Zintel, Grade 10
Warwick Valley High School, NY

The Rear View Mirror

Yesterday was once tomorrow,
An unpredictable pursuit,
The possibilities were endless,
The potential was all but minute.
Reality was unwritten,
Fate's votes were not yet cast,
The hours oozed with promise,
Too bad the day has passed.

Ari Fish, Grade 11
Central High School, PA

My Day at the Zoo

I walk in the entrance,
To the elephants we walk,
I'm immediately bit by a mosquito,
The bug found me like a hawk.

I lead the group aimlessly,
But to the elephants we advance,
I pull out my camera,
And get in my photo taking stance.

We look at the map,
And find the house of birds,
We walk up a steep hill,
Talking with nonsense words.

We soon exit the building,
And now the great apes,
Swinging about their see-through rooms,
With behinds of various shapes.

So now we must travel,
In this giant, yellow structure,
Leaving the all animals behind,
But the memories on picture.

Stephanie Ekstrom, Grade 11
Kennard Dale High School, PA

Sister Bond

We laid together under the sun,
Waves rolled up the beach.
You whined when sand got in your eyes,
And the towel was just out of reach.

I brought you the towel
And I helped you withstand the waves.
You laughed at squirming sand crabs,
And picked seashells for us to save.

I kept all of our seashells,
And I'll never forget the day
We spent together on the beach,
When life was just a game to play.

Abbey Lichtenberg, Grade 11
Kennard Dale High School, PA

What's on Broadway

Birds are singing flowers blooming on an afternoon's bliss
Counting stars make a wish and hear twilight's gliss
A couple under mistletoe, oh will they ever kiss?
Beauty turns bad but better to have loved and lost
Wipe away those tears dear, men should not bring tears
Man has done it all, meddled in alchemy, made it snow during fall
Powers an illusion and a one man show
Should we watch Act 2 or should we overthrow
Cause one man cries when the other man roars
One king owns a river but drinks nothing but wine
While another works a week only to earn a dime
Standing over seas watching water weave and twine
Why can't we wash out Act 3 today?
So we may live together, love forever, and let children play
Or will we leave a man chanting "make peace, not war" so he could die in gore?

Hisham Madkour, Grade 12
McLean High School, VA

Genuine Young Love

Internally I cry tears
That makes a flood in my body,
It hurts me physically and emotionally,
But you don't seem to care about the hurt I feel
Because all you do is make me feel worse,
You're suppose to do the opposite,
By keeping the one who truly loves you close,
Keeping her because she will be there for you no matter what,
Keeping her because she understands you more than anybody else,
Instead you just push me away as if you don't feel the same
As if you're afraid
That I will hurt you one day as people have done in the past,
Get your thoughts together and think about what you want
Because you're hurting me by not making your own decision,
All I want to do is love you and be there for you,
But now your privilege is gone and your key can't unlock what it once could, my heart.

Chelsea Walters, Grade 11
Excelsior Preparatory High School, NY

Past in Present

Remember when he took her to visit the tall, tall trees?
They were luscious green, with their own beautiful grace.
They were the only ones there now, not one human trace.
The glass shards on the ground and the rocks that skinned their knees,
The wind whistled and scattered the glorious leaves
Moved away from the trees. And the sun on her face,
Creating patters as intricately weaved as lace.
He says this place is a secret; she nods and agrees.

They were stealing glances at each other,
Walking into the woods, the thriving core.
Silence unsettling and moss-covered rocks, what a sight.
Though it wouldn't last, for a while they were lovers,
This was a place we could see before,
But we can't reinvent the light.

Kaila Shubak, Grade 12
Colonia High School, NJ

My Mirror

What is that I see?
In the mirror; it is me.
My mirror tells me to look up
And into its eyes.
And in it lies a beautiful prize.
It's glorious and shining,
And clear all around.
No specks or marks are found.
My mirror never takes a break,
It is always awake.
My mirror shows me that
True beauty lies within,
And time and time again,
When I look into my mirror
I am still the same person.
Regardless of whether I change my clothes,
Or my hair,

The same girl is still there.

Melissa Koffie, Grade 11
Nottingham High School – North, NJ

Maybe

Maybe, just maybe I can't get you out of my head
Maybe, just maybe you're supposed to be there
Maybe, just maybe you actually do care
Maybe, just maybe I'm going insane
Maybe, just maybe this is all some kind of game
Maybe, just maybe the lie isn't what I thought it was
Maybe, just maybe I imagined it all
Maybe, just maybe this afternoon you will call
Maybe, just maybe you will tell me the truth
Maybe, just maybe my heart will heal
Maybe, just maybe, or maybe it won't

Brittney Clark, Grade 11
East Stroudsburg Sr High School – North, PA

Destiny

The end of the beginning is starting;
From the world we'll be departing.
But when?
Soon enough;
We can't wait until then.
So today, decide
To love;
The opposite of hate,
It will decide our fate.
Now is the time;
— The minute is prime —
To let your heart open wide
And let God be your guide.
So slay your pride,
And live inside…
Before it's too late.

Kaleb Kalbfleisch, Grade 10
New Jersey United Christian Academy, NJ

Threshold

Slumbering yet;
the fiery declaration of love,
of beginning.
unruly heart! and tamed too.
a threshold
but come not, await.
Heart! in what crowd lies my future?
seek him out! Beckon
to the threshold

In softness of cradling night
I dream
of him who shall step past my mountain.
Heart lose no hope! There beyond lies a doorway —
Abundance of purity! Cold, clear, tranquil waters
reflection of heaven above — within

But take heed, heart!
Cradle my purity as night cradles her stars.
Deeper than earth's core, higher than our universe
lies one love.
reach for that before you reach for me.
Call out, and I shall come.

Mary Dowell, Grade 11
James River High School, VA

Home

The most perfect place on Earth
My summer get away
My escape from it all
All day in the warm sun
I don't want to leave

Singing songs and laughing loudly
Giggling during rest hour
Shadow puppets on the tent
Talking all night long
I don't want to leave

Always freezing in the morning
Always sweating at night
Running for the good shower
Brushing our teeth at the spicket
I don't want to leave

The final days are teary-eyed
Candle light ceremony brings us all to tears
The final group hug is given
We all walk away in the saddest state possible
I don't want to go home

Kristi MacDonald, Grade 10
Haverhill High School, MA

Life

As you travel through life there are always those times when decisions just have to be made,
When the choices are hard, and solutions seem scarce, and the rain seems to soak your parade.
There are some situations where all you can do is simply let go and move on,
Gather your courage and choose a direction that carries you toward a new dawn.

So pack up your troubles and take a step forward
The process of change can be tough, but think about all the excitement ahead
There might be adventures you never imagined just waiting around the next bend,
And wishes and dreams just about to come true in ways you can't yet comprehend!

Perhaps you'll find friendships that spring from new things
As you challenge your status quo, and learn there are so many options in life,
Perhaps you'll go places you never expected and see things that you've never seen,
Or travel to fabulous, faraway worlds and wonderful spots in between!

Perhaps you'll find warmth and affection and caring and somebody special who's there
To help you stay cantered and listen with interest to stories and feelings you share.
Perhaps you'll find comfort in knowing your friends are supportive of all that you do,
And believe that whatever decisions you make, they'll be the right choices for you.

So keep putting one foot in front of the other, and taking your life day by day…
There's a brighter tomorrow that's just down the road — don't look back! You're not going that way!

Sandrene Foster, Grade 12
Bassick High School, CT

He Let Go

The world falls apart when I'm not with you because you are my eternal heart. The pain tears me apart and this is where it starts. Falling. Trying to pull you with me but you can't bear it. You push me away. Unknowingly throwing me into that abyss. Locking me away never to be heard again. Lying drenched in my sorrow. Cowering in my despair. Whispering he loves me through cold guarded eyes. How to believe in a soul when all you now know is regret for every time you stay vulnerable blatant rejection rushes back at you. Ripping your heart oh so more until it is thought that you can finally die. But every tear is mended by tears. Growing your heart back mangled and gruesome. With nothing left to beat for but lost love.

Kristina Garcia, Grade 11
Spackenkill High School, NY

Creed of Clichés

I believe in fate
In the strength to hold your head high
In the silence that says everything
In the crazy power of love
In the eye contact that shows everything
In the power of a hug,
    a hand,
    a smile.
I believe that when you are down,
The only place next is up
That good things come in all packages
That even if you try the only way to see it,
Is that the glass is half full.
I believe in the power of others,
But most importantly yourself.
I believe in hope, it will inspire you, faith will guide you, and strength will keep you afloat.
I believe that you have the power to turn the odds.
I know that hope, faith, and strength will help you survive.

Anna Winberg, Grade 12
North Allegheny Sr High School, PA

Springtime

It's that time of year
I see the flowers coming up
purple, red, and yellow.
I see the trees blooming
dark greed, light green, even yellow.
I see the sun is high in the sky
Glowing white, orange, bright yellow.

It's that time of year
I see rabbits hopping
soft and fluffy.
I see woodchucks searching
round and sleepy.
I see birds singing
graceful and bright.

It's that time of year
When I feel as though I'm just waking
been hibernating all winter.
When I remember the sounds, sights, smells of life
remember what flowers and birds are.
When I realize what time of year it is
realize that it's spring.

Suzanne Weiss, Grade 10
Advanced Math and Science Academy Charter School, MA

Tiananmen Square

Fragile flesh and brittle bone
Against a behemoth of steel
On paper you're dead
Hot lead to the head
For their nature is hardly genteel

Is it suicide?
Or a bid for new life?
Have you thought of your mom?
Friends, kids, or your wife?

What's going on
That could make you do this?
Standing alone against Deng's iron fist
The bodies of brothers lie broken behind
Eyes blind
Eyes blind

Some might call you nuts
But perhaps you've just got them
'Cause through what you've done
A new battle is won
It's a lesson in courage you've taught them

William Cuneo, Grade 10
Haverhill High School, MA

Bittersweet Lemonade on a Scorching Summer Day

As the suns rays beam down
It reminds me of the way you taste
I long for you, the sweet but sour flavor
The endless craving that you leave me with
Your forever lasting taste on my lips
All I want is another chance
For you to be my savior, not a bittersweet remainder
On a scorching summer day
It's as if your presence will remain
But faster than the summer breeze blows
You slip away
I had you for a moment
You quenched my pain
But now our past experience is all
In fade

Kerry Eccleston, Grade 12
Sachem High School East, NY

Do Not Fear

Do not fear
for even though love may fade,
It never truly disappears

Do not give in to the heartache
for it is only temporary —
Love is merely taking a break

Do not lose hope
in what you know is sincere,
Believe in your ability to cope

What you truly value
will find its way back,
And remember that you can make it through

Now throw away concerns
and trust in fate,
For true love always returns.

Brianne Beyers, Grade 11
Kellenberg Memorial High School, NY

Me

I'm short,
    I must be immature
I'm blonde,
    I must be dumb
I blush,
    I must be insecure
One look,
You've predestined who I will become.
Just look deep inside my soul
See what I have to say.
See me for who I was, who I am, and who I want to be.
Only I can judge me.

Christina Hadford, Grade 11
Georgetown Visitation School, DC

Loss

Tires screeching, "Stop! Stop! Stop!"
The loss of all control
Twisted metal, crushed glass
Acrid smoke billowing
And then silence
Only silence

Sirens wailing, lights flashing
Rushing to the scene
Tearing open the wreckage
Another young life taken
Long before it is time

Shock, Sadness, Disbelief
Grief beyond grief
Words can never express
So mementos left behind
Say, "We will not forget"

Flowers wilt, candles burn,
Pictures fade away
But never the memory
Of this young life
This beautiful life not completed.

Gaby Dawson, Grade 10
Haverhill High School, MA

The Life Long Lost

The sun has set
What have I done
Words said in anger
Dreams forgotten long ago

What have I done
I left her for the rest
Dreams forgotten long ago
My mistakes haunt me

I left her for the rest
Tears run down their faces
My mistakes haunt me
Don't rest until I am gone

Tears run down their faces
I cannot apologize for the pain I caused
Don't rest until I am gone
The end is near

I cannot apologize for the pain I caused
Words said in anger
The end is near
The sun has set

David Trompeter, Grade 12
Massapequa High School, NY

Apostrophe to the Truth: A Search for Verity

Truth, why are you so hard to find?
I thought I knew where to search for your dwelling place,
Yet it was disguised!
Now foolishness is the ill quality I bear,
Lost in the deception of those who love you not.
Now the benefit of doubt, in my cogitation will rot.

Ne'er again will I be beguiled.
Ne'er More! Ne'er More! Ne'er More!
I denounce those foes who indulge in calumny.

Some appear virtuous, and moral enough.
But under that aspect, there is nothing but distrust.
You are hidden until their actions reveal all.
For almost none can foretell the change from fair to foul.

Truth, you are but a charm so rare.
I fear I may never find you, searching for you is no longer a care.
Such deceivers beguile in mirth.
As if to have no remorse, for their self-humiliated worth!

"Truth I say to you, aspect is deceiving;
Yet actions hold all verity in a conscious being!"
The quest for you continues on,
Like the wait for a mighty Salvation.

Roddell Johnson, Grade 12
Archbishop Curley High School, MD

My Passing

Don't say you never thought of the day in which you go,
Through the gates so ever dreamed of into a world of which no one knows.
If it happened now what would become of you?
Live inside people's memories, and for eternity be clung to?

Or will you be forgotten, no memory to spare.
Certain loved ones may remember, but to others, no despair.
Who would cry, who would mourn the death of one so close?
What true, hidden feelings would this sudden tragedy expose?

Does anyone really know you? Know your thoughts, know your feelings, no they don't.
With your presence presupposed, will they miss you when you pass? No they won't.
Forever is a rarity. "Remember forever" is even worse.
How many lives have you touched, how many lives would this tragedy reverse?

Beloved son and brother, would that be all it read?
So much feeling left to rot beyond this gravestone head.
Don't say you never thought of the day in which you go.
Will you be mourned forever? or will your memory be buried...

with you down below

Justin Goldman, Grade 10
The Bronx High School of Science, NY

The Choice of a Mother

Everything is going wrong in your life
Wandering aimlessly anywhere you roam
Trying to escape from hardship and strife
Your last safe haven is your mother's home

In the comfort of the arms that will hold you
Never allowing you to fall to that bottomless pit
Never letting go till your problems are through
Encircling your inner devil and destroying it

But what happens when you're a child of two
Does this mean that there is less love for one?
The choice of a mother, if only you knew
Who would they be with when life is done?

What if they had to make a choice?
Between saving one or another from death
Is one confident or has one lost their voice?
Who will she pray for with her final breath?

Only able to help one from that dangerous fall
A mother's choice is the hardest of all
In the end she saves one but chooses to die with the other
So never take for granted, the choice of a mother

Christina Nam, Grade 10
The Bronx High School of Science, NY

I'll Miss Her

We may not be the closest of sister, but in a few months I'll surely miss her.
I know that the worst will be the pictures, seeing her every day was a pleasure.
But now that the many years have progressed,
It's up to our time together to withstand the test
Honestly, I have only one request
That her time away from me is expressed
Through letters, emails, ims or texts,
I wish I knew what would happen next.
My thoughts are endless and will never rest,
Of all sisters you are certainly the best.
I love our petty fights and arguments
Because you'd help me bother the parents!

Here, back at home I don't know what I'll do,
When I walk in the door I'll ask for you
Until I remember to find a clue.
Your absence will make me blue,
Before I believe what I hear is true.
She may only be going to college,
In order to acquire more knowledge,
But does it require all that mileage?

Christine Pavia, Grade 10
The Bronx High School of Science, NY

Never Forget

She was hoping for him,
But he wouldn't speak.
She'd cry late at night.
He didn't make a peep.
She wondered what would happen.
He still lay there asleep.

Crying didn't do her any good.
No words from him made it clear,
That he didn't love her,
And, yet, she sheds a tear.

For all the things,
That he never said.
Her pain that he made,
Lay restlessly in her head.

He dreams of her the next morning,
Preparing, for her, a love song.
But when he turns over,
She's already gone.

Papers with words were all that she left,
But a few words made him tear,
"It's you, I will never forget."
Meghan Denny, Grade 10
Odyssey Academy, NY

One Polaroid

I've seen the pictures
I've heard the stories
But I never got to meet you.
I wanted you to be a part of my life,
And I to be a part of yours.

I know I could have loved you,
But why did you have to go?
A dark cloud in my father's eyes,
Etching the lines day after day.
Why didn't you stay?

But wait...
What do I mean, "could have,"?

I know I love you with all my heart
Even though,
You are not here
To share the joys,
And share the tears.

I know I love you,
Dear Grandpa,
For now
And forever.
Lucy A. Kane, Grade 10
The Bronx High School of Science, NY

The Path

Just so tired. Cannot sleep.
No time to rest. Keep pushing forward.
Pointless goals. Golden mirages.
Where is the end? What is tomorrow when I could die today?

The road to unknowns, possibly fair, possibly horrid.
My mind too weary to pick a direction, just one foot in front of the other.
Wander on to secret oblivion, chased by haunting expectations.
Can I do it? Can I not? Can I just lie down and not get up?

I wish to veer from this dusty path, but clouding fatigue makes the feat unfeasible.
A gentle nap, a dream's caress.
My true objectives, my simple aspirations. I need no more, I need no less.
But these plain desires are trodden beneath dragging feet.

Someone, anyone?
Sing me to sleep.
Give me the pill to let forgiving slumber
Lift me from this worn road of exhausting disappointments.
Jennifer McGough, Grade 11
Madison High School, VA

La Lune

Follows me in my harrowed path of isolation
A mere delusion of comfort
But a source of comfort at that
Mystified, iridescent rays throwing faces into ghastly relief
Metamorphosing the most angelic of beings into a demonic state of mind
Until the exodus from finality to commencement comes to the close
When the creatures of the dark return to their facade of normalcy
The secret of the night remains unbroken
Shared solely between you and La Lune.
Sarah Wrigley, Grade 12
Randolph High School, NJ

A July to Remember, a July to Forget

Whenever I hear a plane take off
It is mid-July and I am in Government Camp, Oregon
I'm snowboarding in the sunny summer on shimmering slushy snow
Learning new tricks, and having tons of fun
Seeing new faces, and those from magazines
Hanging with bunkmates, who shortly become best friends
Plenty of Cobra Dogs, a handful of goggle tans
A million memories, and endless nights of laughter

But this is not my story
My story is my grandmother with a burst brain aneurysm
Squirming in a hospital bed, unaware of those around her
Undergoing hours of painstaking neurological surgery
Kicking her feeble legs oblivious of her motions
As I talk on the phone to my mom from camp
I ask, "How is everyone?! How's Bermuda?"
"Bermuda's fun! Everyone's fine! We miss you."
She replies from a cold, tiled hospital room staring at her sedated mother.
Megan O'Brien, Grade 12
Massapequa High School, NY

It Happens

You didn't know it was happening
    You never knew
You didn't understand how it came about
    You never will
You weren't even sure if you wanted it
    Too late now
You tried your best to stop it before it began
    And you failed
You fell in love
    And there's no turning back

Rebecca Finnigan, Grade 10
Haverhill High School, MA

Another Stop Another Shot

It's a pleasure to see your face again,
That sensual smile and taste again.
It's really a privilege to talk once more,
To spill out our hearts and open the door.
For a chance, again, another time
To give it a shot, cause our love is like a subway train,
Just as it gains momentum it stops again.
But the journey never ends, it runs all day
And each new stop opens to a new runway.
From there we fly, higher and higher
And hope that we don't die, or catch on fire.
Be like the Apollo and reach the skies
And hope not to fall like a failed satellite, now let's arise,
Back to reality, drop! Here's gravity
And now we're back on Earth, what a calamity
Sadly we have to say goodbye, once again,
Till next time.

Michael Fuzaylov, Grade 10
The Bronx High School of Science, NY

Calm Yourself

Calm your mind, calm your soul
You must learn to stay in control
Calm your thoughts, Calm your heart
Stop tearing yourself apart

Stop your mind from hurting you
It's you that makes this pain true
Calm your spirit, calm your mind
It's time for your soul to rewind

Go back into the past
Where your happiness was able to last
Where you were free of pain
Where you had fun in the rain

Back to when you had innocence and peace
Back to when your pain would only decrease
So calm down and breathe slow
And get back your peaceful glow

Timothy Jordan, Grade 12
St Mark's High School, DE

Reading

A man sits on the bench,
Warm, sun kissed,
Decked with shards that sparkle.
Open in his hands, is a magazine,
One, Two, Three
Minutes pass by.
Still he is, on the same page
Turn it already!
He glances from time to time
From his magazine.
Up he looks from his magazine,
And down again at the same page.
I don't know whether
It is the magazine he is reading,
Or the world.
The world seems to be winning.
For it is forever turning pages.
And never the same or on the same page.
But who can help it?
On a grand day in Washington Square Park.
Finally, he turns a page.

Chun Yun (Amy) Hsu, Grade 12
The Bronx High School of Science, NY

Said "I Love You"

First he said "I love you"
but he cheated
And I kept taking him back
Now I won't say a word to him

The he said "I love you"
but he lied
He made me cry
Day after day

Then it was him who said "I love you"
but then he "died"
He left forever
Without a single goodbye

Now you say "I love you"
but do you really mean it?
My heart can't take anymore
The real "I love you," I hope it's from you

They all said "I love you"
and I said "I love you, too"
But now with you
I say "I love you more"

Bryanna Hoffman, Grade 10
Noble High School, ME

Tell Me

The saddest song sang sweetly through,
The lips of my angel as towards the sky you flew.
You told me everlastingly you'd be by my side,
Now all that you are is my celestial guide.
How dare you leave me alone with my mind,
I told you I'd go crazy if you left me behind.
The irreality leaves me numb but I know I've got scars,
Thought you'd always be here, thought the world was ours.
I can't bear to face the day when my senses return,
Rather feel nothing at all, let my insides burn.
Memories do no justice, painted pictures in my mind,
I'll keep my eyes shut from now on, frightened of what I'll find.
If I'm worth anything any more give me a sign that you're here,
Cause I swear I can't make it on my own, don't leave me alone with my fears.
Life without you isn't life at all, but crimson regrets as tears do fall,
Tell me you didn't mean to leave me with the fire, tell me it'll be okay, I'll call you a liar.

Emily Key, Grade 10
New Hyde Park Memorial Jr/Sr High School, NY

Insomnia

I've always lied to myself about the reason why I could never get over my feelings for you, why I could never stop thinking about you, why your face always seemed to haunt my dreams, and why your beautiful smile always seemed to be the objects of my paintings. You are the reason for my Insomnia, the reason I could never look at a man. I'm trying to let you go but this, this, this hold you have over me has to stop. I have to get you out of my system. I can't let you be the bane of my existence anymore. I'm sick of memories of us together eluding my mind and regenerating new feelings for you. When did things become this bad that I actually had to fight myself in fear that I would forget you? That's the reason I've deprived myself sleep for so long. I'm afraid I'm going to forget you and then I'm going to lose myself and slowly but surely I'll fade away. I feel so sick to know that I can't get you out of my mind. It's been years and now I'm starting to question my sanity and the reason why I allowed myself to die slowly because I'm pretty sure I'm dying. Slowly of course. Why can't I be more like you impervious and fickle? Why…Why?…Why can't these feelings of us together which seemed to be in a state of disuse move on to haunt you? Your mind? Your life? When? Maybe this really isn't even Insomnia…

Shakeira Broughton, Grade 12
Acorn High School for Social Justice, NY

When You're Gone

Who knew life could be so hard, and to get ahead you have to run the extra yard,
live, laugh, love but lose it all, we all struggle all fall,
But only the strong can have the strength to succeed, the greedy will get crushed by their own greed,
so I have learned to give more than I take, and accept my mistakes,
People these days don't even see the flowers, too caught up in counting the hours,
of the ticking hands on the walls, but they will have lost count when death calls,
Enjoy each breath it may be your last, death seems to come so fast,
grandma went one day in July, and it seems all we could do was cry,
It's been a month she may be gone, but not for too long,
we will all meet up in whatever exists after this, for every human being has to give death a kiss,
Pain runs deep in me since she left sorrow stole my soul, seems every day I become less whole,
can you hear your clock ticking it's tickin' away, so enjoy each day,
I work so hard to try to succeed, I never succumb to greed,
I hope to make my father proud, but he will never praise me out loud,
Overcame the depression that stole my light, lost and alone on those dark nights,
but love touched me and healed the scars, holding his hands staring at the stars,
When everyone else left and I was alone, he was the guiding hand to lead me home,
he saved me when I was lost and led me to light, someday I'll be standing next to him wearing all white,
Until then a dreamer can only dream, living life caught in between, not quite a women but more than a teen.

Leane Rumson, Grade 12
Milford High School, NH

Life, a Moment's Glance

His brows drew closer together,
wrinkled lines rooted into his worn, weathered face
in the depths of his hazy eyes
a fierce battle raged
he ran across barbed fields into no man's land
dust clouded the air,
every step, treacherous
with hidden danger lurking beneath
at this his heart pounded
then dear Rebecca held his hand
saying everything is going to be all right
but a dark veil flew over her
and the tune to the sad hymn came back to life
a glistening tear dropped from his eye,
and his eyes stole a look at the cotton fields above
Then Hanna, just four-months-old, rocked in his arms
her tender cheeks, bubbly mouth, moonlit eyes
and fingers that grasped his hand and wouldn't let go
and his brows loosened
his eyes closed
and he slept.

Matias Tong, Grade 10
The Bronx High School of Science, NY

Lover's Bay

My vibrant visions, senses are astray.
No more possibility of mending.
Everything still, yet walls and waters sway.

His heart and mine, his veins and my own lay
apart, yet I still yearn for his tending.
My vibrant visions, senses are astray.

I cannot live or laugh or love another.
Lover's Bay holds my heart captive, lending
to my distanced, crazed thoughts, always in sway.

The bay, it fills, with my own tears each day.
I was a lover once, heart pained, bending.
My vibrant visions, senses are astray.

My heart that feels such sadness and ache may
grasp and envelop strong feelings, fending
off the man I stood beside. My thoughts sway,

soon it's temper and hate, then another day
my heart overcomes its sadness, mending.
My vibrant visions, senses are astray.
Our hearts want and wish, but still apart, they sway.

Berit Henrickson, Grade 12
Manhasset High School, NY

School

I tried my best in school
Could have sworn it was cruel
To charm our future schools
But did I have the tools?

I look at the choices before me
There are way too many things to see
I'll save my decision for next week
On a day where it's not so oblique

Once I have decided, will I get in?
Or will this be what Shakespeare calls my fin?
Or will I get in and not like the school?
And transfer and be proclaimed as a fool?

Nicholas Hill, Grade 11
Vincentian Academy/Duquesne University, PA

Season Changes

How beautiful the winter season can be,
When it is near, I would much rather be by the warm sea,
The cold can make you feel so lonely,
But gives you the chance to be warmed by your one and only.

When the white blanket of snow has covered the ground,
Everything is peaceful with almost no sound,
The sun will soon break through its cold icy shell,
The light will shine through the clouds and begin to expel.

The cold of winter will soon melt away,
And the children of summer will come out to play.

Noel Dembo, Grade 10
Kennard Dale High School, PA

The End

Falling up.
Opposite of down.
Reverse right to wrong.
In a cube that's round in shape,
Explain what has happened to the order of things.
Red is blue, inverse in state.
Purple is not the colour they join to make.
Bruises aren't real, their pain yet true.
Hurting the youth in many ways, not few.
The old are young, the small are old.
Feeling their last days grow cold.
People die, children are made.
Never exactly leaving "this place"
The cycle goes on with fear, every day
About life after death and in turn the same.
Falling down.
Opposite of up.
Sense is made.
In a problem with no meaning.
In a problem with no end.

Stephen Hedges, Grade 11
Bernards High School, NJ

Darkness and Hope

There is a sound
One not meant to be heard
It echoes from loneliness
It cries for no one

The sound is darkness
In it you hear nothing
You can sense it there
It's waiting to capture, it's hiding

Darkness is a fear
Not a happy place
Darkness is the unknown
The sadness upon a face

But where there's Darkness lies Hope…

Another sound is out there
To chase Darkness away
The sound comes for a second
But it's never here to stay

Hope is the other sound
You don't hear it for long
But it leaves you with Hope that
Hope will never be gone.

Shauna Freeman, Grade 12
Saranac High School, NY

When the World's Dressed in White

A thin white layer covers the ground,
The world is silent all around.
The trees look ever so bare,
How crisp is the surrounding air.
Animal footprints mark their path,
While snow clings to the lattice lath.
Oh what a sight,
The world is covered in white.
Kids are laughing while they play,
Some are sledding with their sleigh.
The wind blows and bites your nose,
It chills the air as well as your toes.
Hot chocolate is what you should get,
When you come in soaking wet.
Oh what a sight,
The world is dressed in white.
Each flake is unique and cold,
More beautiful and special than gold.
All around the world is white,
It is the most magical sight.

Ashley Paholski, Grade 10
Valley Regional High School, CT

What Is a Hero?

What is a hero?
A hero is someone who saves, saves a city or people.
A hero defeats evil, all types of evil.
What is a hero?
Does a hero have to run on rooftops? Have a secret identity?
Does a hero have to have special powers?
Why does the hero save? Why does a hero protect and guard?
Does a hero protect because he can?
Because he has the power to?
No, that is not a true hero.
What is a true hero?
Not someone with special powers, not someone that hides who they are.
Not someone that runs on roof tops.
What is a true hero?
A boy? A girl? Young? Old? Human? Animal?
What is a true hero?
A hero is someone who saves.
Someone who saves without knowing they do, someone who doesn't try.
Someone who does good because they are good.
Someone who is not asked to be a hero.
That is a true Hero.

Laure Herzog, Grade 12
Bishop Ireton High School, VA

Villanelle of a Lost Tune

I once knew the young winds that whistled a noble tune,
Tame in the palm of the sun's cupped hand,
Now lost, lost in the shadow of the eerie blue moon.

Thoughts of change never wandered into our safe cocoon,
Maybe I wasn't watching the not so distant sea strand,
I once knew the young winds that whistled a noble tune.

Escape is always desired from life too attune,
I thought in my embrace the winds would sway to my command,
Now lost, lost in the shadow of the eerie blue moon.

I tried to sing sweet song of sunny days and warmer afternoons,
But these winds crave the danger of the moon without operand,
I once knew the young winds that whistled a noble tune.

Upon my shoulders trouble is festooned,
As I peer through my glass at the wind's broken wasteland,
Now lost, lost in the shadow of the eerie blue moon.

I see the winds swirl and swoon,
To the wind's new taste, I must have gone bland,
I once knew the young winds that whistled a noble tune,
Now lost, lost in the shadow of the eerie blue moon.

Paige Kostanecki, Grade 10
Albemarle High School, VA

Cleanse

I leave the land where schedules and stress consume my mind.
I go to a place where I can leave all that behind.
The work, the phone, I set them all down,
and escape for awhile, to a refuge in town.
I enter a land of paradise this day,
filled with noises and flowers and beauty in disarray.
No voices, no talking, just me all alone.
At one with nature I brighten my tone.
And as the wind blows through the towering trees,
so soothing, I want to fall to my knees.
Like a kid on Christmas with a shiny, new toy,
the calming feel and the rush of joy.
The peace and harmony take their toll.
I thank God for all and clean the stress from my soul.

Tommy McEwen, Grade 11
Thomas High School, NY

Freedom

Freedom is fading away
On this dark and cold day
Tears fall down my face as I say goodbye to the life I knew
Mama looks so upset so confused and I don't know what to do
War is upon us and my home is lost
My freedom is to pay the cost
I don't know where we're going and I don't know why
I'm so scared I might die
Everyone is restless everyone is scared
I wonder if anyone ever really cared
The train is slowing on this tragic day
Freedom is fading away

Lauren Blood, Grade 11
Collier High School, NJ

I Love You

Tonight you said 3 words I'd never been told before
3 simple words that meant so much
I love you
I took them in with everything else,
But didn't think I could repeat it
I was scared and wanted to be sure I meant it
So we went home and that's when it happened
I couldn't get you out of my mind
I replayed the night again and again in my head
I wanted to see you right then
Though you had only been gone a few moments
I wanted to call you just to hear your voice again
I kept smiling, because I couldn't get your face out of my mind
I read your letter over and over again simply because it was from you
I knew I would do anything for you, even die
I couldn't imagine my life without you
I didn't know what I would do if I never saw you again
And that's when I realized,
I love you too.

Nicole Petersen, Grade 11
Roanoke Valley Christian School, VA

A Seafarer's Lure

It seeps. Seeps into the air
And you absorb it.
Absorb it and internalize it.
From the island it calls you.
Calls your name,
And his simultaneously,
Beckoning you forth
To your own demise.
But that sound!
Oh, that sound!
That beautiful, treacherous sound.
Like bait, it temps you
Until you give in.
It taunts you,
Until you are caught.
And yet it does not cease.
It resonates to all.
Like Sirens.

Eugenie Dubin, Grade 10
The Bronx High School of Science, NY

Look into My Eyes

Look into my eyes!
Babe, what do you see?
Do you see the physical me?
Or do you see my inner qualities?
Can you sense what I sense?
Can you feel what I feel?
Are you just a magician,
playing Houdini tricks on my mind?
Am I the fool?
Did your love rob me blind?
Look into my eyes!

Ashley Ramsey, Grade 12
Pleasant Valley High School, PA

Life

Throughout life
People come, people go.
But there's always that one
The one who's always there,
Never strays away.
Well that persons you
No matter what
You're there.
We have our ups
But, we also have our downs.
Still we're here,
Together
Always and forever.
I can't imagine
You not being here
Each and every day.
Thanks, for being you.

Nathan Williams, Grade 12
Saranac High School, NY

Do You Know?

There he is, in the distance, getting closer and closer.
I can hear a heartbeat now, I can almost feel his warmth.
The laughter, that smile, oh that sweet smell.
Waiting in the dark is something so new, something out of the ordinary.
Strength and courage is all I need now.
Fear of loving someone or something that you may lose.
Here it comes, that embrace you've been waiting for,
the acceptance of another being, the feeling of being important.
This feeling is so addicting, the feeling of having someone always.
The feeling that you can't let go of.
This feeling, this word, this meaning is so strong,
you must understand its true dynamics before attempting its beauty.
This word, that feeling and that strength is only known as one thing,
almost one thing only
Love.

Taylor Stevens, Grade 10
Wall High School, NJ

I Am

I am intelligent, and I am strong.
I wonder constantly about my purpose here.
I hear no comforting voices helping me through this time.
I see a path laid out for me.
I want closure.
I am intelligent, and I am strong.

I pretend I do not fear my future.
I feel like my composure could be ripped out from underneath my feet.
I touch upon each and every one of my inner thoughts.
I worry that one day all I will have is instability.
I am intelligent, and I am strong.

I understand error is acceptable.
I say I don't have a care in the world.
I dream of my worry free childhood.
I try constantly to remain in the present.
I hope that one day I will rid of these petty worries.
But for now,
I am still intelligent, and I am still strong.

Marissa Villafane, Grade 10
Haverhill High School, MA

Words That Leaked

Days and nights perceive to be identically repetitive,
differentiate between motives and the difficulty to respirate.
singularity of vocabulary which I have learned to appreciate.
perspectives are various, but what we know is vague,
because what we retain in common is almost same.
Do focus on the rain or the untouched space that lays.
wrinkles occur to age, try to relate time with words, is it questionably sane?
Practice is gratitude, learning is of a higher magnitude.
scales and models put us on the same wave length.
But it's universal we can all agree,
we breeds and species have unusually different words to speak.

James Reinhart, Grade 12
North Andover High School, MA

Soldiers

As soldiers march off to war
We all sit back safe and secure
They are willing to sacrifice for you and me
To make sure our country remains free

They die each day
Their families will never be the same
As they suffer through loses
We feel no pain

Those who return, do so proud
As they walk onto land they expect a crowd
But no one is there, they begin to feel despair
As we all just sit back like no one cares

Mentally wounded, they cannot survive
They go through life just managing to get by
We should provide for their every need
But most of the time we pay them no heed

Thomas Gavin, Grade 10
Manhasset Sr High School, NY

An Ode to Life

Life is full of struggles
We never see them coming.
How do we ever redeem ourselves?
Is it even possible? Every day you're blamed,
It seems the easiest way. You feel like you've let
The whole world down. But you know it isn't true.
You know you're not the person they all say you are —
Only you know you're true self. Don't let anyone tell you
Who you are or what you should do. It's your life and
You're in control. As you grow older,
You realize that you're accounted for more and more.
Every action has a reaction —
And every mistake, a consequence.
As you grow older, my little one,
Just remember that at the end of the day,
It all comes down to you. You are the writer of your destiny;
The spark of your inspirations.
So just live your life,
And hopefully your life will live for you.

Zohra Roy, Grade 10
The Bronx High School of Science, NY

Underwater

Above there is noise and commotion around
It only becomes peaceful once I've submerged down
Underwater life stands still and calm
I daresay I wouldn't hear a bomb
If my air supply would only last
I would stay underwater until an eternity past
When life is stressful and hardships are seen
I think of being underwater and suddenly life is serene

Jacob Kramer, Grade 12
Harborfields High School, NY

here for you, forever*

i'll be the chuckie to your tommy pickles,
always ready for a play date.
the robin to your batman,
let's go fight some crime.
i always got your back,
here for you, forever.

i'll be the kfed to your britney,
no matter how crazy you get.
the patrick to your spongebob,
we can go jelly fishing in bikini bottom.
i always got your back,
here for you forever.

i'll be donkey to your shrek,
even if you're a smelly ogre.
the pedro to your napoleon,
you can always borrow my chap stick.
I always got your back,
here for you forever.

no matter where we go,
i'll always be there for you
just like you are for me.

Lauren Shea, Grade 10
Victor Sr High School, NY
*Inspired by "Sideman" by Paul Muldoon

Mother Earth

She has caramel colored skin,
The texture of soil and everything green.
She laughs with such power it shakes the trees bare in fall.
Her smile clears the skies, awakening the sun from its nap.
Her graceful strut sends the storms in retreat.
She is my Mother Earth!
Her steady hands bear the fruit we eat.
Her green thumb is what brings springs back every year.
Her heart is where we make our nest, our homes.
She's always been there for us,
She is my Mother Earth!
When she cries our oceans flood,
When she screams yellow streaks of lightning break the sky,
When she trembles our buildings collapse.
We mustn't upset Mother Earth.
So there, there, wipe those tears away,
Walk to school another day.
Pick up the trash we've left behind.
Un-melt those glaciers, un-pollute those rivers,
She is my Mother Earth and I love her!

Betty Diop, Grade 12
Bronx High School for Medical Science, NY

American Dream

America what is America
America is a fat man with a Big Mac in one hand and a welfare check in the other.
Dream what is a dream
A dream is an honest lie wrapped like a present secretly a time bomb synchronized with my alarm clock.
Hope what is hope
Hope is just a dream with a very long timer set on the bomb.
Truth what is truth
Truth is a 9 year old boy breaking through a white picket fence after riding on a pink slip-n-slide
Lie what is a lie
A lie is the same boy 7 years later when the fence has turned a slight shade of yellow and the slip-n-slide has had a few more riders.
Friend what is a friend
A friend is a reflection in the mirror that listens to all your hopes and dreams, truths and lies.
Goal what is a goal
A goal is a perfect blend of hopes and dreams slowed down by lies sped up by truths and made easier with friends
An American dream what is an American dream
An American dream is you cutting the blue wire on your time bomb, simultaneously setting off an explosion of happiness and when it's all over it's a smile.
Smile what is a smile
A smile is the white picket fence guarding your hopes and dreams and goals and broken down by a 9 and 16 year old boy after flying off of a pink slip-n-slide.

Tyler H. Martin, Grade 10
North Allegheny Intermediate High School, PA

The Real Me

I am genuine and amiable.
I wonder how language is formed.
I hear the world screaming for help.
I see that in every evil wrong doing, there is an actual intention of good.
I want to be extremely successful as a person and help others.
I am genuine and amiable.

I pretend I am a chef on a cooking show when I cook.
I feel immense pride in my country for its strength.
I touch the hearts of those I help.
I worry about life after death.
I cry when I think I may not have as much time as I think with those who I love.
I am genuine and amiable.

I understand that life is as quick as the speed of light.
I say each person should live each day as if it was their last.
I dream of one day providing for my own family and giving my children one prodigious life.
I try to please, and make everyone as joyful as can be.
I hope I will live a long, prosperous life.
I am genuine and amiable.

Stephanie Psehoyas, Grade 10
Haverhill High School, MA

Love Out of Reach

Words of the wise and scholarly become the words of a simple fool.
Yet like a thief I wish to steal you from your place and hold you close to me. Should I even wish on the bright star? Oh how they envy you and your shining light.
Every word you speak is the song of the nightingale and a smile is brought to my face as snow pale cheeks become shadowed in pink. Speak to me again is all I ask; so let me again hear your song. Leave me not in silence, leave me not alone and cold but grant the warmth of the sun that is your smile.

Maria Calia, Grade 11
Abington Heights High School, PA

Too Late?

I am bursting with goose bumps and butterflies,
When I see your smile.
That full faced, crooked grin.
It makes your eyes squint,
That's all the better.
It's refreshing to see your smile again.

I made a mistake,
Will you forgive me?
I chose wrong,
Will you still take me?
I waited too long,
Is it too late?

Just say "no,"
I'll surrender.
Move on like you have,
While I waste away.
She can have you, I'll back off,
Only if you say you don't want me.

I will try my hardest to turn away,
But before I do it, I need to see your smile,
One, last, time.

Dara Wissinger, Grade 10
Campus Community High School, DE

Fantasy Ride

Like the souls of the dead
My mind wonders
In such forms that is not understood
Mesmerized by your touch
Hypnotized by your smile

Like the heart of an unborn child
You keep me alive during times of thunders
You give me hope in my livelihood
You don't provide much
But the little that you give is what makes me shine

Sunflowers grow with the comfort
You provide, the love you give
But you're nonexisting
You're an image of the imagination

Your time will reign when rivers stop
Flowing and lives no longer live
You'll be mine when men see the ocean's ending
But I'll be here, waiting for the physical confrontation

Merttchyne Fenelon, Grade 11
Edward R Murrow High School, NY

The Calm of Night

When the night is calm and the breeze is light
by far your greatest creation is the stillness of night
some feel alone some feel scared
others in wonder and me…aware

I stand in awe I look in wonder
I feel transfixed by being under
something so vast something so strange
I feel at home in your range

It gives me joy it gives me proof
to know you're there to know the truth
while people search for a home I know where mine is
the stars tell me that it's far greater than this

A land paved in gold and full of love
somewhere more perfect than the skies up above
I stand in wait to see my dreams come true
to feel at peace and worship you

Keith Crawford, Grade 12
Winslow Township High School, NJ

Guardian Angel

Raining, pouring, crying, weeping,
Black dresses on this mournful day.
Lying in the casket looking like she was sleeping,
The baby was in heaven far, far away.

Wishing, wondering, having a dream
That somehow I could have my sister back.
Though impossible it did seem,
Somehow I had to get my life back on track.

I had to put this behind me,
And leave Blake to God up above.
Something special she will always be,
My guardian angel whom I dearly love.

Jenna Rodrigues, Grade 12
Westfield Sr High School, NJ

Untitled

Why does my heart love
Such a man
That I pushed away
And let shatter my heart
Now undeserving of him
For disappointing him so
I still long for him
He let me have his friendship
But if it makes him happy
I'll stay away
Not knowing when it will end
My broken heart aches yet
Still flutters at the sight of him

Kathy Munroe, Grade 10
Northeastern Clinton Sr High School, NY

Time

There is something there
Something unexplainable
Doubt if anyone could understand it

It's there showing itself slightly
It never will fully reveal itself
Yet never will it truly be hidden

I don't know what it is
It is there no matter what is done
Watching though shining, silted eyes

Is it good or is it bad;
Is it happy or is it sad;
Or maybe it just is, just there.

It is time
Time itself to be revealed
Time just simply time

It is a great asset but also
A most feared enemy
But it still marches on.

Haley Hayden, Grade 11
Nokomis Regional High School, ME

Ode to an Old Piano

You're more of a decoration, aren't you?
The ornament, the *And did you know it's so antique, it has ivory keys?*
the extra piece of furniture.
I gave up,
my mother gave up,
my grandmother gave up;
you were merely a phase
for all three generations.

The damper pedal is still missing
from my 8-year-old-mother's outburst,
most of the keys above treble C are flat,
and some corners are missing
from being moved in and out of houses
to the Bronx, Bayside, and back.

Inside the unsteady bench lie my theory books and scales and sheet music, scattered.
The metronome doesn't keep time anymore.

So maybe I'll break the old cycle.
I'll sit down on the old bench, switch on the old light, carefully lift the old cover
and begin to clumsily pick my way back through "Minuet in G."
I'm not as good anymore.
You are, though.

Lauren Javaly, Grade 10
The Bronx High School of Science, NY

Keep Me Safe

Lay me down,
Upon this ground,
Let me sleep,
And let me weep.

Let me say,
This month of May,
How your love,
Thus from you above.

Made me say,
I wish I may,
Dream sweet dreams,
That make it seem.

As if I,
Can never say bye,
For I love,
Just like a dove.

Kiss me sweet,
And let me sleep,
In your arms,
Keep me from harm.

Simon Mohr, Grade 10
Holy Spirit High School, NJ

The Wicked End

Man's becoming more corrupt now. Godless, wicked and cruel.
The soulless man stood silenced, his word rang so true. To chastise all.
Words were worse than the flood, worse than disease. Words are wicked.
We swim in this life of misery, face cruelties of life each day.
Voice your prophecy, shed us some light, feel sorrow, feel pain.
Can mankind survive this?
We swim in the tears of others' pain, others' sorrow, others' fear.
Only to learn, nothing.
A stab to the back, it wounds our will and soul.
Will we be here tomorrow, we wonder?
We grow in numbers, we look to others, we look for eternity.
We look to the sky for knowledge, when the stars align.
The eclipse will come, heaven will fall, what will we have done.
I have seen heaven and hell, fears and sorrows, life and death.
People see the light in others, they ignore it.
They look to darkness, when will it come?
The crowds will gather, our time is precious, will we see it?
Will we change? Humans just don't understand, they try, but fail.
Will we ever see the light and the goodness around us all.
Ask yourself. Look to the heavens, answers are there.
If we listen.

Samantha Gavin, Grade 10
Winslow Township High School, NJ

Skiing

The chill of the breeze hits the face
It travels through the body with quite a pace
A feeling that not everyone may know
Of when your skis first hit the snow

The sky seems bluer from up here
The place where all the world's mountains seem near
The power one feels when moving so fast
Forgetting all that has just past

There is no limit to the speed
A little snow is all I need
This is the place where I feel at home
The place where one cannot feel alone

No matter what the conditions are
A smile is not hard to spot, even from afar
The ski school children always seem so proud
Sometimes they are a little too loud

But there is no place I would rather be
Than sitting on a chair lift ready to ski
There is nothing in the world that can quite compare
To the feeling of being one with the air

Alison Kimball, Grade 10
Haverhill High School, MA

So Young

He risks his life. He looks out for others.
He puts everything on the line. He never thinks twice!
The Young American Soldier.
So young, he has his whole life ahead of him.
Risking his life, so others can be free!
The things he's willing to do. To keep the country protected.
To keep others from harm. To keep everyone safe!
A hero…to all who are threatened.
To all who are scared. To me!
I am thankful for what he does. I am glad he's willing to fight.
I am amazed by his bravery. I am so happy for the Young American Soldier.
I am proud to know he's out there. I am proud to know he's strong.
I am proud to know he's fighting for freedom. I am proud to know he's my friend!
I think about him…when I see a war story on the news.
When I hear a patriotic song. When I read a patriotic poem.
The Young American Soldier!
I pray that he's ok. I pray that he remains safe.
I pray he makes it home!
Thanks for all that you do, thanks for all that you mean to me.
Please stay safe. Please come home!
Young American Soldier!

Kayleigh Schreyer, Grade 11
Richland Sr High School, PA

Eraser

Love is like a
eraser first it is
brand new and has
never been used but
give it time it soon
slowly fades away
until there is nothing
left but a tiny piece
that can't be held
anymore.

Ron Lord, Grade 10
Sharon Middle/High School, PA

Life Is Like the Clouds

Life is like the clouds
They seem so slow
Yet move by so fast
You stare at them
Without a thought
And don't see that
You see them angry
As lighting crackles
You see them sad
As rain falls down
You see them happy
As the sun shines
Just like in life
You see people angry
As fists tighten
You see people sad
As tears are shed
You see people happy
As smiles appear
Next time you look up
Remember that life is like the clouds

Christina Dunnington, Grade 11
Osbourn High School, VA

Strange Noises

bumps in the night
whine of the dying light
scuttling just out of sight
drips in the kitchen sink
dishes on the counter clink
sinister mutterings on the stairs
hiss of the cat caught unawares
creaking of a twisted door
muffled footsteps on the floor

screams
then
. . .

silence.

Katherine Spreadborough, Grade 10
Haverhill High School, MA

Complications

Can it be, that you're the one? That I'm the Earth, and you're the Sun.
Revolving around you in my constant spin, it's not fair, baby you've done me in.
Not close enough to feel your touch, far enough to miss you much.
Cast away this hopeless dream? Things are not what they may seem.

Two souls destined to be not apart, yet I can't feel your beating heart.
Words and wonder, the building grief, I'm calling out for some relief.
The burning passion, steaming out, too far away to hear me shout.
Shackled in this barren land, please take hold of my helpless hand.

Can I wait for time to fly? Must I be forced to say goodbye?
To admit my weakness would complicate, further destroy my weakened state.
The hours pass, but you remain, this relentless nightmare must be slain.
But do I want it to go away? Can I live, if you stay?

Can't live with you by my side, still I can't run and hide.
Rescue me, you must take hold, revive me from this grasping cold.
The thoughts don't stop, I'll go insane. Speak my words, I must refrain.
Don't ask me questions, for I will not lie, but my answer, may cause me to die.

Richard Douglass, Grade 12
Patchogue-Medford High School, NY

Most Poems Rhyme
(Ode to the Judge)

Roses are red violets are blue
This one's for points so it does, too.

At least, it rhymes.
Syllables may be off at times
Prob'ly a bear to read, but hey you likely at least get minimum pay.
If not you may want to find a different way
to spend the time that is your day.

If you are expecting something deeper then stop.
And do something productive.
Unless you like this.

Like it says on my fourth-favorite shirt (placed so because of the hue):
Do what you like, like what you do.
You could hike, like the man on it, too.

Or you could judge poetry. Not law.
Law requires schooling.

Jim Conlin, Grade 11
Wyomissing Area High School, PA

Wisdom

He sits there in his worn rocking chair scratching his pure white beard,
watching as the children walk by, oblivious to him.
He wishes they would just listen to him,
some of the things he had to say, but they don't.
He knows he could help.
But the children never listen
so he just stays, observing the world from his rocking chair.

Justin Walker, Grade 11
Moravian Academy Upper School, PA

Truths Realized

The wind hits my face,
As I think about a name.
The world drifts away.
As I still stay the same,
I blame others for my decisions,
And never ponder why I did them.
I wish it gave me more meaning.
The wind starts to scream at me,
And I don't listen.
I am shifty like the trees,
Or as gentle as the leaves.
I will never be pleased.
Unless the needs grow dim.
I am like a hanging limb.
So come to my rescue…

Brandon Zegarski, Grade 10
New Jersey United Christian Academy, NJ

Innocent

I've never been shot
But I've been killed
I guess the shock gives it a great thrill
So they stabbed me with hate and I bled love
And out of my heart fly 2 doves
What a beautiful demise
People say as they walk by
Looking at me from a distance
Mom and Dad so close yet so distant
This is sane,
I die as the innocent
While the rest run free
Please in peace leave me
But walk by and drop a rose

Amari Soria, Grade 11
Cedar Crest High School, PA

Diwali

Festival of lights,
Fun fruitful nights,
Houses decorated bright.
Families coming together
Celebrating even if they are
Under the weather,
Colors vibrant
Red, Yellow, Green, Orange, and Blue
Flowers fragrant
Roses, carnations, lilies, and sunflowers too.
Plates full of sweets galore
Make my mouth water for more,
Baskets full of gifts
Make spirits lift.
Diwali never falls on the
Same day each year,
Yet makes my heart jump
Each time it draws near,
Diwali sparkling, radiant Diwali.

Miraaj Bagia, Grade 10
Manhasset High School, NY

Illumination

The land, so barren and empty.
Stillness encompasses everything.
She becomes nervous, and begins to run.
She sees no faces, in the quietness of the terrain.
The tree branches begin to interlace like fingers
As she looks up, the sky is disappearing,
The light is gone.
Darkness terrifies her —
She calls out for help.
Nothing responds.
In a panic, she is about to give up.
She sees a spark, glowing in the shadows.
Gladly, she sprints to the glow.
Her fearful worries disappear,
And there is the boy,
Holding a lantern to guide her to him —
They embrace.
He knew he would find her again.
The boy puts his arm around her
And guides her back to where they belong.
Together.

Skyla Budd, Grade 12
Plainview-Old Bethpage JFK High School, NY

Sometimes All I Need Is You

There are days I feel I've hit the point of no return
And days I feel like my mind is suffocating
Days I feel I'll never learn
Sometimes all I need is you

There are days I wish I could see your face
And days like this your eyes would sparkle
Days I feel that I'm in a race
Sometimes all I need is you

There are days I hate what I have said
And days I cry "I'm sorry"
Days I ask God why you're dead
Sometimes all I need is you

There are days I whisper into the dark
And days it whispers back
Days I remember all those marks
Sometimes all I need is you

These are the nights I sit alone and cry
And nights spent wondering what happened
Nights that I remember how hard I tried
All I need is you

Natalia Kaya, Grade 12
Cranston High School West, RI

Divine

You are beautiful, you are Divine, you are one of a kind
Beauty cometh not with struggle but with the same ease of which you'd breathe
Elegant and eloquent none in comparison
Gifted with wisdom, taste impeccable, surely the heavens lament for the loss of their angel
A jewel in the eye of the beholder yet more precious than any diamond or garnet
Adorned with grace and a character most noble
Superwoman I shall call you, powers unimaginable
Able to bring out the best in anyone
Never faltering or misguiding
Heavenly, delightful, blissful, marvelous all of which sublime leading me to this last loving line
Divine, Divine, Divine truly you are one of a kind most precious beyond belief

Chidi Agbaeruneke, Grade 10
Benjamin Banneker Academic High School, DC

What You Have Done to Me

Anger swells deep within my veins as it suffocates my blood vessels
Thickening steam pours out of my ears, enveloping every inch of me
My pupils are overwhelmed by the roaring blaze shimmying around them
I count backwards in my head hoping to calm down
Yet my entire bone structure becomes fragile making it shake profusely
The soles of my feet burn against this evil bondage you hold tightly over me
My mouth has forgotten saliva letting my sandpaper tongue rip wildly against my brittle teeth
The color has flung from my skin leaving me with a ghastly complexion
My muscles have evaporated into thin air contributing to my weakening mind
For someone so weak you have total control over my once sturdy being
You have become a sponge absorbing everything in your path
I grip for peace struggling to peel away from your absolute negativity

Eva Bleyer, Grade 11
Smithfield High School, RI

The Darkest Cloud

His nose pointed up towards outer space
There was never anything too tough for him to face.
With his head resting happily on a puffy white cloud,
This boy smiled proud and his heart beat was as loud as his chest would allow.

This boy met this girl; they took the subway and vanished into the city.
Nervous at the sight of her; she's so pretty he thought.
Talking eye to eye, time flew by — he forgot all the negative things about love he was once taught.
Look how happy this boy was that cold December night,
Their conversations kept them warm while circling around the same block, neither of them cared for a clock.
This boy with his new pretty sharing the view of a lit up city skyline —
They were lost in time, until the clock suddenly struck nine.
Hand in hand they sat beside each other and conversed awkwardly on the subway.
He collected enough courage and finally asked her if she would like to stay.

Ready to drive her home, he realized that was something he could not do.
The boy may have forgot all the things he was once taught about love,
Just as he lost track of time circling the block and gazing into her eyes —
The boy had lost sight of his keys!
They looked around; keys were nowhere to be found, they must be forty-five minutes back inbound.
But he didn't care; he shrugged with a laugh —
He lost his keys but his love was found. They made it home safe and sound.
That crisp December night left his heart pounding faster than it ever used to pound.

Sarah Hobart, Grade 12
Framingham High School, MA

Emily Margaret Stevenson

I am what you are scared of.
I am going to be the one to succeed.
I may not realize it now.
But I will get through my insecurities.

I am stronger then you can imagine.
I am an ox on a cold winter's day.
I have gotten through it all with my head held high,
if all that I had was myself.

I am who I am, and that will be a success.
I am from amazing people, a great family.
As admired as a leader amongst their people.
I will be all I can be, an amazing person,
even if I don't see it yet.

I am an individual, different from the rest.
I am fighting life battles like you are,
a warrior in the toughest of wars.
The unkind words are sticking with me.
The strength of my soul has shown the way.

I am going to be a dream come true.
Do you want to come with me?
I WILL SHINE.

Emily Margaret Stevenson, Grade 11
Newfield Sr High School, NY

My Prince

My prince has eyes that shine like sapphires blue.
My prince has locks that glisten like gold spun anew.

He has a melody in his voice that envies all birdsong,
And his words could serenade me all night long.

He rides a horse with hair pearl white,
And dons chain mail armor that refracts the light.

He rescued me from the tallest tower,
And ne'er leaves me, even for an hour.

He slays mighty dragons and is honored by kings,
But tells me I'm worth more than any of those things.

Off to his castle, me he will whisk,
And never depart without leaving a kiss.

Though wonderful is the prince in my head,
I would so much rather to have you instead.

Cheryl Hicks, Grade 12
Nottingham High School – North, NJ

17?

He was planted in the ground,
A fruit that was forbidden.
The garden was far enough from her —
The trudge alone…exhausting.
She heaves the distance to the tree —
Its leaves would be her life
Entwined with its branches, she would be one, new.
For but when she reaches it, she stops —
The fruit is gone —
He has grown too fast;
She cannot compensate for what she lacks,
His fruit has grown beyond her own.
She contemplates planting herself, as he —
For then she would be permitted.
She ponders her own growth — then stops,
Then remembers —
She is young.
She will not give into the forbidden.

Erica Tasch, Grade 12
Massapequa High School, NY

President of America

Startling, surprising, fabulous.
Sometimes, some days, even some moments
come somehow.
I can remember yesterday
as an instance,
a brand-new story for America.
I would love to say it is
more than history,
or not history at all?
It is some version of truth,
a true story.
Obama did it.
We proved that we are not
segregating, separating, differentiating
human beings
at least…
by their race.

Tanzin Fatima, Grade 12
University City High School, PA

Her Eyes

When I look at her, when I look into her eyes I see love
Love she gives to no one else but me
Her eyes are strong
Her eyes give me solace in my troubles
Her eyes make me long not to leave her side
I see love
When no one else gave me a chance
Her eyes at one time gave me a second chance
When you look at her you won't see it
But look at her while she looks at me
You will see the love that I see
And that special love that I see is just for me
I see love, and I pray, one day so will you.

JC Colliluori, Grade 12
Osbourn High School, VA

Tears of the Past

Tears that fell so long ago,
From broken hearts forgotten,
Echo in a song.
Memories are surfacing.
Lover's fond farewells forlorn,
Whisked away by wind.
Treacherous secrets whispered soft,
Consumed within Time's shadow,
Lurk lost messages.
What haunts the walls of strongholds?
Their ancient stones eye witness,
To all that was there.
Emotions, strongly rushed then.
Ambitions, fated nations,
Passions, fiercely burned.
So much is forever gone,
Misplaced by spell and weather,
Never to be found.
Time is unrelentingly
Pursuing all of our steps,
Engulfing in mists.

Rachael Forgét, Grade 10
Webster Christian School, NY

All Alone

A dark winter night
The woods all around
He sits in a hole
Covered in dirt
He lays as beauty hits the stars
Lively staring
He realizes she is gone
Perhaps a good thing
Maybe not
Wondering what had happened
Thinking to himself
My love for you is great
My lust for you is grand
Where have you gone my love?
Will you miss me?
I guess this is the end.

Alexandra Papadakis, Grade 12
Massapequa High School, NY

Erratic River

Your love was like a river
Winding, turning, never-ending
But as you spiraled across the land
You were perpetually bending
Into a shape, a form
I could not comprehend

Lela Ross, Grade 12
Liberty High School, VA

Same Place

I step on the treadmill on the wooden stage, in the auditorium,
youthful and ripe.
And I push the button. "On."

I run and run, and I grow a beard,
and I see the same lights, and I see the same curtain,
and in front of me is the boy that looks awfully familiar.
The boy is me.

And the boy pulls a hand-drawn set,
a 20 foot tall roll: scenery on a spool, my drawings.
The drawings of my dreams.
My future family, my unconditional love for my passions.
I continue to run. My legs hurt, I wince.

The boy comes to the end of the roll of drawings,
The drawings I look back at while I run.

My knees buckle, and a cry echoes,
and I collapse in front of the scuff marks,
the scuff marks made by my shoes
as I first mounted the treadmill.

And just before I close my eyes,
I see the same lights, and the same curtain. And it closes.

Joshua Jacobs, Grade 10
Andover High School, MA

Don't Let Go

My heart stops every time you call me
When I hear you say "Hello Katie"
"What have you been up to lately?"
I get weak every time you speak I never knew how much it means to me
Oh I can see it just as I dreamed it
With your arms around me so
And I am begging you please don't let go
Oh no Oh no please don't let go
Every time I see that face
That face is so hard to erase I leave it there for just in case
In my mind I know you are mine from the beginning to the end of time
Oh I can see it just as I dreamed it with your arms around me so
And I am begging you please don't let go
Oh no oh no please don't let go
You stop by every once in a while
Just so I can see your wonderful smile
For one I would drive a thousand miles
Oh I know it's been too long since the day that you been gone
Oh I see it just as I dreamed it with your arms around me so
And I am begging you please don't let go
Oh no oh on please don't let go

Kathrine Alt, Grade 12
Bishop McCort High School, PA

Ode to Pens

The pen lying there in its infinite glory.
Master of words and ideas,
It truly knows all
Throughout the ages its importance has never changed
The pen as it slides along the paper reveals all for all
As the blue black red or green ink sink into the surface
More and more is revealed
And without the pen none would be possible
The pen therefore should be honored and praised
For with its wisdom we have been raised.

Stephen Greenberg, Grade 10
The Bronx High School of Science, NY

Ode to Cherry Chapstick

Among the store shelves you sit proud.
Your cherry red color shining through the clear plastic.
You make my lips glisten with sparkles.
As you brush my lips,
The smell of sweet cherry floats up.
As I lick my lips
The faint taste of red cherries rests on my tongue.
When my lips flake with dryness
You come to the rescue,
With your healing powers.
You make my lips smooth and soft.
You must have been created by golden arms.

Meenu Rajendraprasad, Grade 10
Advanced Math and Science Academy Charter School, MA

If Everyone Was Purple

If everyone was purple would we finally be equal
To our brothers and our sisters standing 'round us far and near
Or would our strange, abnormal world find something else to judge?
The wealth of one, perhaps,
If all mankind was purple, would be judged upon instead of the color of one's skin.
If all society were purple and had the same amount to spend
What would be judged upon then?
The size, perchance, would decide if one was ridiculed or loved.
If all humans were purple with all the same cash flow and all the same size
What then would be founded wrong or right?
The residence, presumptively, would decide whether one is weak or strong.
If all persons of this world were purple
All with the same income and all the same proportion
All residing in equal abodes what next would the world criticize?
I, myself, am sure that some one person in this world
Must be cleverly dense enough to dream up something to determine
Who is right and who is wrong
Even if everyone in the world
Was of the color purple

Breze Lee, Grade 10
Cosby High School, VA

Death

Death is the moment
That we hope to
Never encounter.
It is the moment
Where we feel guilt,
Regretting what we
Never got to say
To those
Closest towards us.
Death is the moment
When a lover
Sacrifices himself to
Protect his love, not
Realizing the
Inflicted pain.
Death is the moment
When a young girl
Feels hollow inside,
Not understanding
What just happened.

Sonal Agarwal, Grade 10
The Bronx High School of Science, NY

Knowledge

Library
Silent, eloquent
Learning, imagining, growing
Periodicals, novels, records, treatises
Destroying, burning, consuming
Oppressive, destructive
Fire

Tyler Maley, Grade 10
Blue Mountain High School, PA

Questions

What is life?
What is death?
Why are we here?
Why do we leave?
Why is there love?
Why is there loss?
Who are we really?
Who is our real creator?
When did it start?
When will it end?
Why do we ask?
Why do we answer?
Who is our soul mate?
Who will they be?
What is our purpose?
What do we think is our reason?
Who? What? Where? When? Why?
Where will we be in later years?
Where will you?

Daniel Byrne, Grade 11
Osbourn High School, VA

The Original Love Song

What ever happened to the true love story?
You keep hearing songs that somehow express
How love is this tingly, sensational, phenomenal feeling in which we live our lives
No one actually tells about what love does to your body
Or how love can affect your mind
And if love ever departs, you suffer from withdrawal
I'll tell you what a true love song sounds like

It's like saying: ever since I met you, I feel like I could fly
If you ever left, I'd feel blue; if you ever left, I think I would die

It's like proposing: just steal away with me — no one would ever know
I love you; I think you love me — I'll be the Juliet to your Romeo

It's like praying: don't ever leave me, please don't say you will
I thought that you'd complete me but now time has stood still

It's like composing: a love song that fits you, it describes you so well
I don't like feeling blue; being with you makes my heart swell

Love can make us fools
It can make us do things we've never thought we could do
If love had not been there with us the entire time through

Kaitlyn Beausoleil, Grade 10
Dracut Sr High School, MA

Sunset Escape

The orange hue decorates itself slowly in the sky,
As the blazing sun cools, making its way into the sea.
Your kisses become distant then, as you stare at the horizons;
And I look at you, your beauty, your perfection.

Comparable to a sun, bright and warm;
But you fade as night takes over your day.
And I sit on the beach, the same way you left me,
Waiting for the sunrise, waiting for your presence.

Hoping the sun rises and never sets again,
And you stay with me forever.
But I know why you cannot and I enjoy anticipating your return,
The return you make after your sunset escape.

And when you arrive,
My heart beats faster,
My words are jumbled,
And I know that we're in love.

No matter how long you drift from me,
You come back, brighter than before with more stories to tell.
And I smile, listening to this beautiful entity tell me its journey,
And when you've finished, right before your escape.

I kiss your blazing yet gentle lips, and you warm my spirit.

Alexandria Ashley, Grade 11
Aquinas High School, NY

Time

Time flies by,
When no one seems to know.
One second you say hello,
Then when you feel like you just said hello,
You have to go.
Hours can turn seconds,
Like love can turn to lust.
Time is confusing,
Yet it controls all.
You can go out for an hour,
And the hour feels like a minute.
Why is it that some people,
Are so fascinated by time?
Time is controlling,
But can be loving as well.
When no one seems to know,
But when everyone seems to care…
…Time flies on by.

Shelby Berner, Grade 10
Brick Township High School, NJ

Facade

Sunshine buried beneath gray sky
Absence of light as the weeks go by
How do we know that what's done is done?
How do we know that this race can't be won?
Walking through life with no worries or cares
As if everything's perfect and nobody dares
To upset the balance of life without fear
You hold on to emotions and bury them near
Only to find that they've not gone away
But rather are fighting to break through the gray
The mask you put on to hide what you feel
All along waiting for someone to peel
Through all the layers of life that you hide
You try to forget all the nights that you've cried
For something you know has been lost with the sun
And you find that there's no other places to run
You go back to the place where your journey began
And discover the infinite fallacy of man

Melanie Colson, Grade 12
Christian Central Academy, NY

Fear

Fear is a snake
Green, slithering
Hiding in the corners and holes in the earth
Springing at unsuspecting moments
Thrashing the flesh
The venom spreads
Fills the veins,
Stops our hearts
Our minds
We slip into shadows
And rise
Only as the serpents we once venerated

Michael Guardiola, Grade 12
Massapequa High School, NY

Black Hole

The house moaned and creaked
Its wooden bones screaming violently
Into the cold December night
And I, listening upon its agony
Lay in tormented anxiety
My pupils digging black holes into the ceiling.

Within my head, I dreamt of falling down the
Gravitational pull of the inescapable vortex of nature
My physical body being stretched and pulled
To the limits of my creation
And as I free fall into the nothingness pit lifeless,
I have but a quiet and serene warmth covering my aging face.

Down — down I spiral into the unknown
My desperate heart silenced for I do not fear this unknown
But long for it welcome it
Rush head first into its seductive allure
Rejecting the mundane of past realities
Soon I will be swallowed whole.

But do not fret nothing shall hurt me
It is I the unknown fears
I who took the courage to leap vulnerable and unafraid.

Sarah Frazier, Grade 11
The Prout School, RI

The Dance of Youth

Silently, she dances,
wisps of hair flying behind her,
the wind softly blowing her pure white skirt.
Her bare feet lightly tread the grass,
as she bounces across the field.
Just a girl, of merely five years.
If you look closely,
her wings from heaven still peek out.
Before her, a butterfly flutters,
and the girl giggles,
as it flies around her face,
finally landing on her outstretched hand.
As she leans in, to take in the animal's beauty,
she notices something.
A slight, barely noticeable, tilt of the head,
as the creature seems to stare at her,
directly into her eyes.
Then suddenly, without warning, it takes off.
Toward the dark forest it flies,
and without a second thought, she runs after it,
into the dark unknown.

Erin Chapman, Grade 11
North Point High School, MD

The Accident

Speeding, the wind surrounds you but you cannot breathe.
Confusion sets in as you hear the sound of the thunder so heavy it shakes you, your warmth is seized
You know it will come.
The trees and homes all start to fly,
Everything you once knew passing by
In a frightening blur all else is gone
Slamming into the air, time is stretched so long
Then a sudden burst of heat and pain
No matter how hard you open your eyes you know you will never see the same again
The pain drips from inside you
Your skin and heart torn, you find you cannot move
In the heat you are frozen
You breathe. Broken peace. A sigh of relief.
So empty you cannot speak.
It's all over now, this is how it must be.
You will remember it because it will suffocate you, leave its mark
But your heart will skip over those moments
That are too hard to bear

And even though he is a world away
You will always hear his breathing
But he will never hear your screaming

Kelly Walsh, Grade 12
Suffield High School, CT

Bitter Sweet Remorse

Something is ready to burst forth.
The tighter I will hold it
Needing to shout to find no voice to cry,
Regretting everything to have done nothing immoral.
The more I take of this cool crisp air, the harder it becomes to breathe,
Being numb, the pain is still felt to be a playful tickle.
While joyfully laughing through choked back tears,
Kissing the wounds that have done me harm,
My chest seems impossible to bear, and yet it is the happiest I have ever felt.
Could this feeling possibly be a righteous kill, by doing me good while doing me wrong?
Why must something so beautifully simple be so complexingly confusing?
The more I take from it, the more I want it, and the more I hate it.
My heart is racing,
All I can hear is its pounding echo in my head, trying to tell me something.
Logic can't reason with it, arguing inside of me fighting with myself
I am spinning out of control, with the ground remaining perfectly stable.
Could love be any harder to understand?

Alaina Breed, Grade 10
Marblehead High School, MA

Thunderstorm

A sudden boom, rumble, and crash echo throughout the ashen sky.
Quick and slender bolts of lightning emit from the heavy, rotund, pearl-gray cotton balls above.
A streak of light illuminates the dark and ominous sky, if only for a short moment.
I breathe in the balmy, yet refreshing, air which engulfs me.
The rain becomes a light drizzle and the radiant rays peak through the now hollow, happy, and hoary clouds.
As the sun gently touches my skin, I feel cleansed, serene.
Peace has come at last.

Morgan Mihelic, Grade 11
North Allegheny Sr High School, PA

I Let Go of You

You see right through me and not in a good way
When you don't know I exist — is a typical day
But to keep me hoping and dreaming for you,
You sometimes talk to me like you always knew
Who I was; you make me so confused

So let go of whatever you think the problem is
And pretend that you don't know what's wrong with me
Cause I know — deep inside of you; you must like me too

I hear you talking, talking about me
But I just keep on walking, hoping you don't see
And sometimes when you call my name,
My heart stops beating, my cheeks go aflame
I start hoping you meant somebody else
Then you look at me; I smile —
I bet you're pleased with yourself

After a long long time, I started thinking of you
And what you did to me what felt like centuries ago
I wanted to call you, and you know what I would've said?
I would've gone, "It's been so long; now I don't care a shred
After all those nights and imaginary tears that I shed,
My heart's no longer yours — my love for you is dead."

Leighton Suen, Grade 11
Staten Island Technical High School, NY

Atlas

ATLAS
I got this world on my shoulders but it's light.
Heavy burdens I carry 'em
Shhhh. Quiet I bury 'em.
Put it in da dirt 'n neva look.
Back turned to dis justice
I go hard. Hard as in balla
Keep movin' 'til my feet are no longer cemented.
Bound to this world my hands are strapped.
UNMOVABLE.
My fingernails clawed I will never drop it.
My bones break, my back gives out.
I stumble with this endurance
The stars shall never revolve.
With one knee down
My head is well built.
With my arms weakening
My heart is,
DYNAMIC
'Til the end comes
ATLAS.

Oliver Brown, Grade 12
Rockville High School, CT

The Beauty of Failure

It comes crashing down like a wave
With all your dreams whisked away by the ocean
You know deep inside you need to be brave
But at the same time you have no emotion
It is time for you to swim ashore
For you to get back onto land
Put it all aside because it doesn't matter anymore
You're almost there, almost reaching the sand
You look back to see the sun rising along the line
The beautiful view is something to adore
It's time to see the beauty of failure shine
Because you are now better than before

Camila de Souza, Grade 10
Henry P Becton Regional High School, NJ

Dad

Someone asked me today how you were doing,
but I couldn't answer.
I can't believe no one there knows I'm gone.
I wish I knew how you were.
I have only seen you once in the past seven months,
and it was only because we passed each other while driving.
You didn't even wave, but then again neither did I.
I wish it didn't have to be like this,
you chose her over your own kids.
What is it that you see in her,
that no one else can see?
She's like a nightmare,
except when I wake up she's still there.
I know the way it happened was my fault,
because I finally had enough and walked away.
You will always be my dad,
we just don't talk anymore.
That part is not just my fault;
it takes two to communicate.

Jessica Kenneally, Grade 12
Pittsfield Middle-High School, NH

Oblivious

you look but do not see
you hear but do not listen
you touch but do not feel
you are oblivious to the beauty that surrounds you

you don't know a good thing when you've got it
you never stop to smell the flowers
or to feel the rain come down on your face

you don't hold on to the things you treasure
you just watch them go
without a single thought about them
she floated away from you
like a dandelion seed in the breeze
and it never occurred to you to go after her

Elizabeth Travers, Grade 11
ESM High School, NY

Things That I Find Infuriating

I hate that gum hearing
Am disgusted by nose clearing
Am annoyed by water leaking
Am vexed at chair squeaking
I sigh at self confident lacking
Darken at continuous clacking
Anger at assumed knowing
And stiffen at the voice affections flowing
I am exasperated by distracting voices
And maddened by unintelligent choices

Nicole Evancha, Grade 10
Haverhill High School, MA

When

When you get mad,
When you get scared,
Think of me;
When life is bringing you down,
Always remember me;
Life is tough,
But if you remember
That someone loves you.

Hanna Plummer, Grade 10
Grace Christian High School, VA

She Waits

She grows,
She goes to school,
She goes to work.
She waits.

One comes,
One courts,
One cheats.
She waits.

Life continues,
Life alters,
Life tells her to move on.
She waits.

He comes; she thinks it's a joke.
He courts; she looks the other way.
He leaves.
She waits.

She dies.
Waiting and alone.
Why wait
When we are blind
For that which we seek?

Lizzy Kribbs, Grade 11
Haverford High School, PA

Us Vets

Praise us, Honor us, Respect us

We have both served and given
To a woman we all adorn.
Her beauty is breathtaking from sea to shining sea.
Majestic mountains and prosperous plains
To the potent people with prestigious personalities.

We've had hope, we've lost hope.
From the wet monsoons to the scorching deserts.
We've never lost sight of your red, white, and blue.

Now it's time for our honor.
For our praise, for our salute.
Monuments, holidays, recognition.
This is how we want to be remembered.

Our valiance be praised, our courage too.
May we never forget those who died and never made it back.
Their lives lost but their spirits true.
Never will they be forgotten.

So, may those who've lost
A brother, a son, a mother, a father.
Always remember them and we will honor them too.

Nicholas Eng, Grade 11
Bunnell High School, CT

And It Was Sapphire

There I was standing at the gateway,
towering bastilles of stone above me, rustic marble below me,
venturing on into a viable road, with hope for a meaningful end.
And I was emerged, this nostalgic presence,
pathways crossing pathways, under gray skies,
but showing the potential of a summer's day,
with a refined sense of triumph on the air,
and a warming comfort for all the fears I could ever have.
Up and down, following the lights and returning,
a spirited hue running through edifice upon all,
as if God had doused his bristles in an elegant blush,
to show what was truly waiting in any days to come,
to spend my days within such humble ambiance.
Had I known to be welcome, from the start to the end?
To walk through closed doors, and see what is veiled,
to be apart from the norm, impulsive and colorful,
apart from the accepted approach, independent and fearless.
And everywhere was sapphire, and emerald, and pallid,
in each direction I turned, where St. Thomas of Villanueva would sleep,
two hallowed towers watching with bated breath,
quite a salvation for me, as it was.

Thomas Przybylowski, Grade 12
Brick Township Memorial High School, NJ

Forever You and Me

It feels like only yesterday
You promised you'd always stay
Guiding me through each new day
You weren't supposed to pass away

What do I do, now that you're gone?
I don't know how to carry on
When you died, my whole life changed
The world I knew was rearranged

I'm too young to be without you
I miss your love, so gentle and true
When it is quiet, I still hear your voice
I know that this was not your choice

My love for you remains deep and wide
Along with you, my childhood died
In my mind, your face I see
I hope that this will always be

Your beautiful heart was so loving and kind
You filled my youth with peace of mind
When my life is over, and we're together again
My broken heart will finally mend

Maureen Busund, Grade 12
Williamstown High School, NJ

Nothing Remains

My mind has been taken with anger
Fear controls my body
During nights I scream for help
It feels like eternity trying to find a glimpse of hope
I can't imagine a time when I woke up with a smile
But as I lie on the ground
I realize it's too late
I have been sentenced to eternity in this awful place
Where I'm my own companion
I can't smell the flowers in full bloom
To touch the warmth within me
The coldness moves through my heart, soul and mind
The way I often feel is the reflection of loneliness
My tears are cold and wet as they fall on my face
My soul bleeds little by little
Nothing remains
If I could get up and move I would move without a backward glance
Building my courage and becoming strong
And heal myself one step at a time
But nothing remains in this empty place
Just a nameless and hopeless girl

Stephanie Millien, Grade 12
International High School, NY

Life

Music songs concert noise
Bark animal play toys
Fun rest beach swim
Child run fall skim
Stand legs feet toes
Sneakers shirt pj's doze
Sleep bed pillows head
Hair brown black red
Hot vacation hotel lobby
Wait time dedication hobby
Ballet dance rhythm poise
Music songs concert noise

Tara DeNucci, Grade 10
Brick Township High School, NJ

Dreams

Every night I lie away,
Thinking of the day.
Wishing things can be
Relieved and forgotten.
I drift off, dreaming of nothing.
Wishing I could live a life,
Of adventure and suspense.
My dreams take flight,
Life taking hold.
These little thoughts that
Never seem to be alone.
They dance through my conscience,
Taking a definite form
I fly away with them,
And play till dawn.

Charlotte Hoar, Grade 10
Sacred Heart High School, NY

The Awakening

The awakening is coming
I feel it in the air
By the lift in the trees
And the yawn of the bear

The buds of the flowers
Bloom more with each passing day
Robins, finches, and hummingbirds
Come from every which way

The sun shines down
Upon all for long
Each animal awakes
To sing a new song

"The spring has now come!"
O anthem to the skies
The earth is reborn
It wears no disguise

Susanna Floyd, Grade 11
Koinonia Academy, NJ

Oh, Man!

Oh, Man
Where has all the time gone?
It seems just like yesterday
We were out, playing in the lawn
It was me, who begged you to stay

It's been three years, since last May
The red lights is where it all began
What an unforgettable day
OH, MAN!

They said she would be fine
They promised to take good care of her
They were medicine men I thought it was a good sign
A few years later it happened again, so now I'm not so sure

They said her heart was broken
It still is to this day
It hurts so much, so now your name is unspoken
You could change it all, if you didn't leave that May

Sometimes I just think at how different things would be
If mom hadn't gotten sick
You could come home to us, you could be free
We could go back to normal, 8 years and you'll have the right to pick

Stefani Vadeboncoeur, Grade 10
Haverhill High School, MA

Life

A collective noun for all the experiences I wish to collect: Life.
Is it wrong, even in the slightest, to want to live purely,
Unadulterated,
Unhindered.
Certain things,
Certain moments,
Fill me up, make me whole.
Like the crab that feels momentarily winded,
Amazed on the shore, but complete, belonging to the ocean floor.
What is a metaphor but a fitting example,
An illustrated advocacy for what I'm trying to say.
I wish I could take all those beautiful, fleeting seconds
And turn them into a lifetime, the sunlight, the moonshine.
I'm not broken, I'm slightly fractured.
I'm not hopeless, I'm slightly failing to dream.
I know for fact, for fiction,
That this Earth, this world, has so much to offer.
But chance isn't blatant. With time or with effort?
It cannot be both.
Present yourself,
Life.

Reem Abdou, Grade 12
Fort Lee High School, NJ

Life for Me

Why can't you accept the fact that I'm intelligent
Snickerin' and swearin' at me is irrelevant
Hatin' on me is really not needed
Cuz I'm not cocky PSH I'm conceited
Conceited for the fact that have so many reasons
Cuz even when I'm not asleep I'm still dreamin'
Education is my drug and yeah I'm fiendin'
To get my 40 acres and buy back my freedom
Though they slay me yet will I trust 'em
And though they play me yet will I crush them
No other option I'm goin' to the top
Success won't wait and I'm never gonna stop
I'm gonna be the best and I'm not gonna flop
I'd rather you HATE me for who I am
Than LOVE me for who I'm not

Anthony Hyland, Grade 12
Thomas Fitzsimons High School, PA

The Sources of My Smiles

A friend's helpful words.
Chirps of the morning birds.
An unexpected note.
A sweet root beer float.
Reminiscing on lost years.
The fall of refreshing tears.
Smelling newly baked treats.
Dancing to the wild beats.
Knowing someone truly cares.
New shoes, all the pairs.
Confidence, enough to show your true self.
The cheer face of a Christmas elf.
Feeling a sense of being worthwhile.
Being able to make someone else smile.

Sammi Donovan, Grade 10
Haverhill High School, MA

Mother Used to Sing

My mother used to sing to me
before the moon came up above
the trees every night.
She used to lay me down to sleep
with my dolls next to me
in my twin-sized bed.
She used to comb my hair until
I fell asleep.
One day, when I was older,
I asked my father if he liked
my mother's voice.
His answer was, with a smile,
"I love her, but her voice can break glass."
I turned to him and giggled,
then turned to the window.
All I could remember as I looked
at the moon above the trees
was how beautiful her voice was
when mother used to sing.

Katrina Carbone, Grade 11
Coe-Brown Northwood Academy, NH

Sisters

Their DNA is linked,
They are relatives by blood.
Closer than even they think,
Bonded by more than love.

Since birth they were together,
Friends by pure default.
Their futures are intertwined forever,
Until their breaths shall halt.

Connected in an embrace,
As just young girls, like angels, on the sand.
Two very similar by face,
Standing there hand in hand.

As they grow so does their bond,
And another photo on the beach.
Both are taller, their hair less blonde,
Yet their love you cannot teach.

So even though they will part ways,
As they grow and come into their own,
They will never forget those younger days,
When they were never, ever alone.

Julie Solimine, Grade 10
Haverhill High School, MA

These Final Days

Sighing, watching the clock from date to date.
How many more days left? Maybe twenty or thirty-eight.
Looking out the window to see the sun shine.
Who knows what we're learning in English class this time!
Maybe about Cyrano and his great nose?
Or if not poetry, then probably prose.
All that I know is that the squirrel out there,
Is preening his coat of fur with great care.
And the robin on the branch has found a big worm.
Ugh, look at it move. Watch it writhe and squirm.
Then with one gulp the worm is all gone!
The bird flies away, it's time to move on.
Upward he flies, he's airborne, he's free.
And inside I wish, that could be me.
Then, CRACK! like lightning, I jump from my seat!
To see the whole class snickering at me,
The teacher's ruler in two pieces lying on my desk,
I see all of a sudden, this was school, not a fun fest.
Ringggg! The bell! I rise and put books away.
Alas! We still have classes, assignments, and plays,
But my mind shall be elsewhere, these final days.

Sara Andryuk, Grade 10
Mountainside Christian Academy, NY

Current Annoyances

When there is no fruit in the refrigerator but every flavor of Doritos resides in the pantry
When nothing is on TV…Dad why can't we just pay the 5 extra dollars a month for OnDemand?!?
The spiky yellow haired boy with glasses who sits behind me in English Class
People who tend to be a little over dramatic…you should think about acting
People chomping on their gum so people in China can hear them
A little brother nagging me for a falsely promised 5 dollar bill
People who think they are better than everyone else
Children who scream and cry in the store…all I want to do is shop!
Rude waiters and waitresses…Hello I'M paying YOU!
Rain, rain, rain

Amy Tashjian, Grade 10
Haverhill High School, MA

Ode_to_Wikipedia

As a button is clicked and a word is typed, a world is opened one filled with information
Knowledge, facts, opinions, truths, disparities, discrepancies
Yet it's all there, all that one could ever need
Compilations, letters to words, words to sentences,
Sentences to paragraphs, paragraphs to sections, sections to full pages
All that one could ever need, on every subject, big or small
Significant or not, useless or vital, it can be found with such simplicity
Almost impossible to miss, to overlook, to leave unsatisfied, unenlightened, still clueless
It's not an option, it is not possible, all that one could ever need
Vast numbers of pages in vast numbers of languages
Knowledge for all, and knowledge, after all, is power.
Disambiguating the disambiguities with disambiguations
All that one could ever need. Yet when the search is done,
When the knowledge to be had is had what more is there?
A new word is typed or a new window is opened.
Yet at the same time the greatest window that of knowledge is shut
Out with the old and in with the new
As the user moves on satisfied, enlightened with the key, the answer to their inquiries solved
The source of knowledge vanished from memory, only the knowledge still remains
Yet what would we do without you, Wikipedia?
All that one could ever need.

Ethan Widawsky, Grade 10
The Bronx High School of Science, NY

Frozen Forever

On that flawless summer day so many, many years ago
With it's splendor of warmth and sapphire blue water reflecting upward
The spongy sand at the waters edge like quicksand for the eager children to build their "kingdoms" in
Parents watch with pleasure at the amusement and awe of the young
Silently wishing they could shrink and join in the wonderment even for just a moment
The surf crashes the children splash the mothers watch with beating hearts
Ice cold drinks turn warmer by the minute; the sun bakes the beach with unyielding rays
The water is ice the air an oven, no compromises today
The day with it's immaculate light, blinding the playing children who squeal and laugh with pleasure
A game of tag, a game of ball, a game of twirling 'til they fall, a game that's new, a game that's not, a game for every boy or girl
Sand relentlessly sticking to every known surface, enveloping everyone in a cocoon of itch
One day of joy that erased all of pain, one that breaks the ordinary into the extraordinary
But just for now, just for today
Tomorrow it will be just the past, just one perfect day in the mix of all the others
One solitary time of shear bliss, frozen forever in time

Molly Gibbs, Grade 10
Haverhill High School, MA

Smothered Ash

All alone and forgotten, who am I?
Doesn't matter no one cares, who am I?
Don't ask, I'm a nightmare unraveling

The shadows are my home
Living there all alone,
Heart and soul wasting away
Shutting the doors, no more sway,
Hiding my soul, forever

A cold wind smothers my fire, my love
The cold wind has a name
Hate, and he's winning, stealing
My fire, my warmth,
He hardens my soul and feels no remorse

I fear it is too late
To rekindle a fire almost spent,
I wonder where my love went
Did I lock it behind closed doors?
Doesn't matter, the key was destroyed
To save myself the trouble,
Of enduring all the pain and suffering

Trey Griffith, Grade 12
Massena Central High School, NY

Full of Heart

I was walking home last night
so late only the streetlights were bright
when I was kidnapped by a witch.
At least that's what I think she was,
because no mortal could have removed my heart
and made such an easy switch.

I wondered why she wanted mine.
Getting cold and bored?
I know I now itch for immortal spaces —
my heart longs for untouched-by-people places.

My body has no wings to fly
and my new heart knows not when or why.
It cares for neither work nor pain,
nor mortal things like loss or gain.
If I could ever find that witch again, I'd switch
and give her back her timeless heart,
but tear off some to keep for myself
as repayment for this thankless lark,
a mortal life spent with old longings
that come straight from the heart.

Madeline Monk, Grade 10
Woodbridge Sr High School, VA

Childhood

What resides in this house?
A house so small, so quaint, so dear
What could possibly be in an abode
With no windows, drapes, or fears?
What could live with these people
Of hard looks, robotic motions, and lips sealed
When the house is finally opened
And the giants soon appear?
Imagination is a welcoming breeze
dancing all throughout this tiny house
It places windows where they're suppose to be
And gives the fellow residents their mouths
Innocent imagination is what keeps a doll house alive
It keeps the stories, hopes, and dreams intact
But when the mind finally is tainted with reality
Where do the fellow residents reside?

Becca Fairchild, Grade 11
Kennard Dale High School, PA

You Only Live Once

One night.
Is all it takes
To make one mistake,
That would change your life forever.
We all wish we could take some things back,
But we're already stuck with the facts
That it happened and it can't be changed.
Only if choices could be changed.
Only if one thing didn't always lead to another.
Parties and bonfires, drinking and smoking with friends,
Sometimes you wish you could take back what you've said.
But the past is past,
And now we're in the present.
And unfortunately, unexpected things happen,
When you least expect it.
It's terrible to just die alone
Now it's over and time to just go home.
We hold hands and try to fight the tears,
But we just get past all the years,
That this routine has led our life,
And now we have to say goodbye to another one's life.

Brooke Boyce, Grade 11
North Attleboro High School, MA

Friendship

Something that seems so great,
So indestructible in your eyes.
Something ideal,
Close to perfection in your mind.
Something that has been through so much,
But still pulled through strong.
It all can change,
And become the complete opposite
Of what you thought would never happen.
It can crumble and break
In the blink of an eye.

Laura Nonemaker, Grade 11
Kennard Dale High School, PA

All Unknown

There's a rush, flowing silent.
A simple hush, somehow violent.
A calm feeling, emotions vent.
Hearts stealing, thoughts bent.

Three words I carry.
Two eyes I seek.
One heart I have.
Yours to keep.

Two for chance, one to fall.
A quiet glance, after all.
There's a secret, shyly hidden.
None forget, none forgiven.

Three words I carry.
Two eyes I seek.
One heart I have.
Yours to keep.

Nothing left, minds clear.
A devious bet, not sincere.
A frequent escape, lost alone.
Challenges that shape, all unknown.
Savannah Moon, Grade 12
Montour High School, PA

The Fire

The flames flicker in
The night sending shooting stars
Into the heavens
Steven Sloan, Grade 11
Grafton High School, VA

Frozen Soul

Tiptoeing past my heart
Fleeting through my soul
who am I to stop you
I'm not dauntless
valiant
nor bold
trails of secrecy
defeat and betrayal
leaves only you
you
whom forsaken my intellect
my comeliness
but who am I to stop you
I'm not dauntless
valiant
nor bold
Mariah Scott, Grade 12
Overbrook High School, PA

Have You Ever

Have you ever danced in the rain
Got so drenched you caught a cold?
Have you ever ridden a plane?
With weights in your stomach as heavy as gold?

Have you ever laughed so hard
That tears streamed down your shaking face?
Have you ever run through a yard
In the midst of a fast and furious chase?

Have you ever vowed to be
The best thing the world has ever seen?
Have you ever held the key
To stop society from being so mean?

Have you ever asked yourself what you can give
Rather than what you can get?
Have you ever chosen to live
Life free from the pressures of a bet?

I have done all these things. So
If you listen you will learn
It's not necessary to search high or low
Or take so much time to seek what you yearn.
The secret lies in two words: carpe diem — seize the day.

Sophia Deng, Grade 12
Montgomery Blair High School, MD

Conflict Among Words

A continuous conflict between words
The complicated meanings of simple sayings
Inspiration found in helpful understandings
Making reasons behind the combination of letters
To speak without knowledge of what to pronounce
To speak at moments with knowledge contained
Words flowing together in rhythmic form
A thought spoken out to mean not what it means; but to be heard as it's meant
Knowing the confusion in which words can be caught
A meaning to one, is different to another
The thoughts behind those words continually unknown
That thought contains a reason
That reason involves the meaning; the meaning, consists of a word
Discovering the letters to connect for significance
A message sent can be perceived in misinterpretation
The clarity of a word can be mistaken
Taken in perspectives of different translation
The confusion of conflict among words
To continue with the simple sayings
The complicated meanings that are never exposed
Making reasons behind what is said
Morgan Archer, Grade 11
Schoharie Central Jr/Sr High School, NY

Just a Twist

I can't get you off my mind
I couldn't be more blind
I should of noticed once you started to shine
In the corner of my eye
All the time in my mind
When you were just so kind
I tried to blame mankind
When me and you just started to UNTWINE

Stephen Gori, Grade 10
Brick Township High School, NJ

It's All There Is!

If I could
I'd call your name
If you could would you explain
If I could I'd understand
Why it's so good to have you around.
My mind is broken from the lies, the hidden feeling and tears I've cried
These are the thoughts of broken down these are the thoughts that are around
It's all I have
Now that you've gone
But if I could, I'd hold your hand
If you could, would you understand
That I need you around

When you're far from my sight everything is almost right
But when you come, come around, there is a risk
I may drowned.

Krista Dixon, Grade 12
Saugerties Jr/Sr High School, NY

The Song of the Lyre

Sing so sweet, Orpheus King of the Lyre
Come fly the nightingales perched upon his shoulder.
The women flocked yearning to be loyal to this song
But only would his song please
Dear Eurydice. Oh that maiden who
Faired so well with the song of his lyre.
But how it could not tame the vipers'
Fangs that took away the new resonance
And gone she was. But o' Orpheus King of the Lyre,
Sadness overcame thee. But courage too came in a new melody
Away he went with a new harmony
And He freed dear Eurydice.
And away she trailed behind his flute
O' and so suddenly a song of foolishness
Crept upon thee and around he turned
And the lyre that had been young lost its voice and grew old of pain.
No longer would it tame nor soothe
O poor Orpheus now just a mortal torn, broken, lost his passion
And now upon his tomb rests the song of silence.
O' singing so sweet, Orpheus
Come fly the nightingales perched upon his grave.

Mei Xin Luo, Grade 10
The Bronx High School of Science, NY

Back Stabbed

Betrayed and unwilled
Pesky barbarian talk
Words that hold no truth
Fists clench, body tightens up
Slowly ease off with great pride

Tereza Olson, Grade 10
Woodlynde School, PA

Merry Go-es Round

Merry go-es round
around sounds
cranked from
disused organs

toy horses
in motion:
a perpetual chase
in a dead heat race
for (First place)

up down
   down up
strapped and stuck
in her own shoes
too fast to lead —

down up
   up down
up never lasts

So long.

Eithinzar Lwin, Grade 12
Stuyvesant High School, NY

Putrid Savior of Mine

The hand by which I am delivered
Lays cold beneath the sea
Like shells within the morning sand
The hand delivers me

And when the tempest's storm
Passes slow with age
The hand controls the sails mad
As sunlight burns the sage

Thus comes the sickened winter
The fury wrought with cold
Riddled with the snowy banks
Ill with tales told

The hand by which I am delivered
Rests leagues beneath the earth
Quiet like the wind of night
Dead upon my birth

Emily Baer, Grade 11
Woodbridge Sr High School, VA

If You Are by My Side…

I'm ready to fight the world for you, just stand by my side
I'll be ready, no matter how high the tide

Just give me that support and stay by me
And promise me that this will be what will make you happy

Struggle and strife to me, will not mean a thing
Because for you, the effort is worth persevering

If I can have your trust, I will promise to make that try
And will keep making an effort, so nothing will go awry

Don't fight and divide yourselves, because it hurts and divides me
Staying together and united is the magical strength beneath this beauty

If you say that this will make you content and smile
Then that is all the assurance I need and it will make the effort worthwhile

But the effort may also be worth nothing, if you don't stay united
It is like forgetting structure and form when endeavoring to create a ballad

If you are by my side, I can accomplish any task
And any golden destination or treasure…I can unmask

Himani Gupta, Grade 10
St Dominic Academy, NJ

Following Steps

Cautiously, timidly, I tried to impress my prints
In your strong firm steps.
Yet, mine was not like yours,
And yours was not like mine, it came to be twice of my size.
The whisk wind can easily sweep
The outlined powder of my steps so I tried again.
Over the fence, the empty unmarked seesaw
And stiff swings made no shriek.
There was no usual honkings of cars or the yells of old men at the chess table
So I tried your steps again, only a few.
The snow had saved your path for me, I believe
Watching your stride, I wanted to follow you.

Only now it's no longer the same.

The wind beats against my back
And thrusts me forward.
But now, there are no steps I can follow.
All I see is the indefinite path in front of me
Yet, I have already come thus far without any sorrow.
I have left my own steps in back of me, as they lie there freely,
The wind sweeps it away just like any other debris.
But I continue my tread steadily.

Julie Chen, Grade 10
The Bronx High School of Science, NY

The Cry of the Soldiers

Long ago a shadow fell over the battlefields of Gettysburg.
North against South, brother against brother,
It was the shadow of death.

As I walked on those same fields,
The tears came to my eyes
I can feel their pain
I can hear their cries.

So many wounded, missing or gone
Stones in lines with numbers, names unknown
Where the Blue and Gray find common ground.

How many thousands died on the ground where I stand?
This land before me is holy
These fields remain untouched since 1863 to honor these men.

As the cold wind blows against my back
I see the shadow again
And in the sunset I cry.

Shivonne Hancock, Grade 11
Wayne Hills High School, NJ

Broken and Put Down

I smile
In another part of the world a child cries
Why can't anyone hear her?
One world broken at the seams
Our laughter outweighs their cries
We drown them out; we put them down
Not our problem; not our fault
Ignorance can save us
But can it save the child with no food?
Open our eyes; let us see
Today we will dry their eyes
And tomorrow there will be one less cry
Let's put together the pieces of this broken world
And so we smile

Kara Eichelmann, Grade 12
Central Bucks High School-East, PA

A Note for a Friend

I remember that you were once a friend
I remember the time that we used to spend

I look forward to the day where together we walk
I look forward to the day where together we talk

I know at times we could fight
I know there's still hope, still a light

I acknowledge we can't hang out in school
I acknowledge the status and I'm not cool

I hope you know that I won't wait, thus if we never speak
Just remember that you were the one on popularity peak

Ryan Grippi, Grade 11
Patchogue-Medford High School, NY

Asteraceae*

I waited for him, burning passion, burning
Incessantly
His soldier suit, dark and browning
Myself only, gossamer, Smooth, like a face flooded with tears
His cap, his sensual aura, and then, his silk,
Beautiful shirts, the Great Gatsby

I was held, closely to him
He embraced, raced, and cased my Heart,
Told me he loved me quite shyly, coyly.
Pennilessly in Louisville. The feeble Gatsby. Jay Gatsby,
James Gatz, whoever you are — of my — Life.

He deserted me, left me to wait for him
Time ticking, the hymn, the opera,
The Maestro ending, his orchestra
Of passion, desire, that carnal hunger, for his face
Gone, yet still, that lingering Phase

The horses' heads, racing, gloomy, overcast skies adjacent
Life set in a cornice, innocuous daughter, unfaithful husband
What choice — if Any — does she have?
Tom's verdant nature, muscular, manly, a Yalee
But a Romeo he is Not — Jay, it's been five years too long.

Junyoung Choi, Grade 11
Bergen County Academies, NJ
*Inspired by "The Great Gatsby"

Lost

A silent move, toward a goal unknown.
With a forest of people to appease.
Silent, the stream of thoughts.
Deadly as can be.

Hush. Hush. It whispers in my ear.
To hear it not, I choose.
Succumb to the rules that come my way.
Yield, as a tornado of torn leaves approaches me.

My compass is broken. I'm not on a path.
Fear me not, I bring no gust of my own.
I choose to do, what I do not.
I hope you do not notice my only power is your own.

I push aside a thorn, with good intentions.
Those intentions, are not my own, but it's.
It warns me, cries for me.
Tells me, to go onto open road.

And right as it may be,
Regret my fresh wounds, I do not.

Elizabeth Shvidky, Grade 10
Stuyvesant High School, NY

Just Push Pause

Believe in something with an uncontrollable faith,
That will inevitably inspire the young youth of this age in time.
Stop for one precious moment in the never ending fast pace life
We are all living and just breathe in and out.
Look to the horizon to witness an amazing sunrise or sunset that glistens over the
Ocean's waves and sandy beaches that are too perfect and too beautiful to exist in this world.
Listen to the wind as it guides the autumn leaves to fall
And fly and land on the ground so graciously.
Think about the future and ask all the questions possible, and wonder if it'll all work out in the end.
Wish things were simple and everything was meant to be, but never regret a loss or mistake made.
Feel the warmth of a loved one lying snugly next to you on a cold winter night,
As the snow softly covers the streets with a pure white blanket of innocence.
Smell the freshness of rain as it pours down with madness,
But then breaks away to reveal a remarkable rainbow.
Teach and learn every lesson meant to be known by sharing and laughing with your neighbors.
Love and be loved for those are the greatest feelings one can have, so do not let love go.
Treasure and remember every moment lived.
Live your life to the fullest because you only get one chance to make it the best.
Realize you are strong only because you are weak.
Just push pause and capture all the beauty of your life.

Bridgette Patton, Grade 12
Math Science & Technology Community Charter School, PA

My Horse

As I fly through the meadow on my horse I see that we are meant to be.
We could ride all day and still not be tired.
We could ride at night if mom wouldn't tell us we have to retire.
As I lay in my bed I think of her.
When I think of her I think of a cheetah, a fast beautiful graceful animal.
As I sit doing school I think of us
The minute I'm done I go jump on and ride 'til the sky is so dark you can't walk nor ride.

Madison Carpenter, Grade 10
Commonwealth Connections Academy, PA

Searching for a Clean Slate

How did the world become this way in which the price that all men pay
Is death and the loss of security due to the absence of purity
When did people forget humanity to test every fiber of moral sanity
Committing atrocities without a soul falling into evil's dark, bottomless hole

Is it possible that the problem lies within that causes us to alienate from everyone, even our kin
Does this looming shadow bring out the beast which society likes the least
What difference can a person make in order to retake
That which has been lost like a flower in the wintry frost

Does the world simply need a hero with the heart of a Leo
Can the public give this person the power to shut off the villainous shower
But this ideal desired by many believers of hope is not real
Where are these supposed vigilantes for good to stop crime before it can brood

Maybe we can subvert hate in small strides driving away those inclined along a tide
Splashing opportunities to create a path that escapes a chaotic and disharmonious wrath
Whether it be community service or charity, anyone can invoke change having infinitely-spanning range
Granting the helpless with the chance to overcome personal strife allowing a new lease on life

Peter Hess, Grade 10
The Bronx High School of Science, NY

Wish Upon Rain

The rain falls down,
From the silver clouds in the sky.
We ask ourselves about life,
And wonder why.

Why does the rain fall?
Why does the sun shine bright?
Why does the wind blow?
Why do the stars twinkle at night?

If you look out,
On the wet window pane,
Drops are scattered like the stars in the sky,
So can we wish upon rain?

To wish upon rain, I don't know.
Can we?
Should we?
They fall from the sky.

The sky has stars we wish upon,
So why not rain?
Their silver glint in sunlight is like stars.
Will our wishes come true?

Emily Chambers, Grade 10
Odyssey Academy, NY

After Death

Bury me next to the famous and brilliant
Bury me next to the poets deaf

For I feel as if real recognition comes to you only after death

Since no one cares what you are in life
Just so long as you have merit once you've left

Bury me next to Miranda and Ferdinand
Bury me next to them, for reveries

My life has been full of ardor
My life has always had amity

No matter what I do now
I hope people will come to visit me

Bury me next to the thinkers and winners
Bury me next to you

For I know, love, you are brilliant too

Stephanie Provenzale, Grade 12
Seneca Valley High School, PA

Now Here and Now Gone

Now that you're here forever with doubt
And now that you're gone I'm forever without
With love in my heart
And hate in my soul
Shaking and screaming without a control
All around me I'm so full of fear
But what can I do without you here
'Cause I'm wishing
And hoping
And praying to God that He'll never ever spread us apart
I love you so much it just hurts to say
So I hope you feel the same exact way
I just want to tell you you're my everything
So please don't leave me forever
Come back to me

Kristina Segarra, Grade 12
Chicopee High School, MA

The Way of the Heart

To the mind it seems a difficult choice
To logic it seems a pointless battle
To the body it seems a random act
To the senses it seems a confusing struggle
But to the heart the choice is simple and clear
The battle is easy to conquer and win
If you listen, it will become neat and organized, and you
Will finally understand what is truly worth fighting for.
The heart decides what is meant to be;
Who you love, who you hate,
What you want, and what you truly think
You can trick the mind, you can fool any logic
You can cover your body, and you can mask the senses.
But deep down inside you know in your soul
That you love who you love, and that will never change.

Marina Van den Broeke, Grade 10
Penn Foster High School, PA

Look Around

Look Around
As the petals reach the water
There's a breeze up in the air
The seasons change as the years go by
People laugh
People cry
People living long
People who died strong
Fear is driven far
Bravery is just a word
Surreal is our bible
And fake is just another routine
Lies become our dictionary
While truth is just garbage
Money is no longer important
Unaffordable becomes the new trend
Look Around
This is the life we live

Adalene Lam, Grade 11
Plainview-Old Bethpage JFK High School, NY

Ode to the Cherry Blossom

Newly clothed branches
Capped with light pink snow.
Never melting,
Yet with a life all too short,
Basking in the light
Of a newly awakened sun.
Cherry blossom —
Your name does you no justice
Delicate white-pink rimmed
With alluring red-pink
More beautiful
Than any cherry.
Petal-arms spread wide,
Inviting the world
To stop and stare.
What other blossom
Could compare?
Almost-white fleshy stars
Floating slowly downward
On the gentle breeze.
A warm springtime flurry.

Sanaa Virani, Grade 10
The Bronx High School of Science, NY

The Panther

Spots are undetected by the first glance.
A mysterious animal that stays to himself.
Calm as the sea breeze,
But rough as a crashing tide.
Every day is a new adventure.
He struggles to become the best.

Brendon Patrick, Grade 12
Gar-Field High School, VA

Remnants

She used to whisper
In twirls of color
Inside my waiting ear.

But somehow,
The colors drained
And the contrast faded,
The photograph of melody
Crinkling about the edges.

My ear still waited,
Listening to her blank silence.
Listening even as that silence
Ebbed into the darkness,
Remnants of its once-ago colors
Still dancing on my closed eyelids.

Devon Bacso, Grade 12
Peddie School, NJ

Beauty in Simplicity*

The background painted, a lemon yellow.
Blue irises placed in an orange vase.
Beauty can be found in something mellow.

The contrast of the colors makes it glow,
The warmth through his brush strokes creates such grace.
The background painted, a lemon yellow.

Although Van Gogh was such a sad fellow,
He often painted portraits of his face.
Beauty can be found in something mellow.

And yet, some amongst us still yearn to know,
Why flowers wilt, from blue to brown, to waste.
The background painted, a lemon yellow.

Often found in old men's loud, rough bellow,
Or maybe found in young lovers' sweet chase;
Beauty can be found in something mellow.

Does beauty in simplicity still flow?
Things as simple as flowers in a vase?
The background painted, a lemon yellow,
Beauty can be found in something mellow.

Katrina Mendoza, Grade 10
Townsend Harris High School, NY
Based on Vincent Van Gogh's "Vase with Irises Against a Yellow Background"

Remember

Remember you mother's advice she gave to you
It doesn't matter if you listened or not
Remember the special times you spent with your father
Sometimes it's all that you got.
Remember the sidewalks you skipped down when you were a kid
With every bump, turn, pebble and crack
Remember whose hand was there to hold
Treasure these moments 'cause you'll never get them back

I'll remember all the faces I have seen in the hall
All my friends, old and new
I'll remember the peaceful street I was raised on
All the secret hiding places I once knew

All these memories I will keep with me
Until the day I die
I will never forget the ones I love
Even if I'd said goodbye
I will appreciate them to the fullest extent and beyond
'Cause you never really know what you got, until it's gone.

Christina Lounsbury, Grade 10
Campus Community High School, DE

The Tide of Basketball
The ebb and flow of the tides of basketball
Sway from one hoop to the other.
The force of the slam-dunk crashes hard on
The sandy shores of the court.
Oh, how sweet the three-point breeze
In the sweaty heat.
And yet as the tide turns, its rhythm is only dictated
By the stars.

Max Kiss, Grade 10
The Bronx High School of Science, NY

To Be Loved
I want to be told how beautiful I am
And that I am the funniest person in your world
And that my intelligence makes you flustered more than anyone else
But most of all, I just want to be loved.

I want to be held by you when I am sad
And cared for when I am sick
And to come home to your warm smile and embrace
But most of all, I just want to be loved.

I want to be looked at with such desire that I get goosebumps
And be touched with such gentleness that I melt to the floor
And have my cheeks hurt from laughing at your jokes all day
But most of all, I just want to be loved.

I want to be your everything and for you to be mine
And for you to reach into my soul and shake the darkness away
And for you to squeeze me when times are tough so that all I can feel is you
But most of all, I just want to be loved.

Kirjah Huff, Grade 10
Paul V Moore High School, NY

No Poem
I'm never going to write a poem ever again.
Because not writing a poem is the most expressive thing you could ever do.
I used to write beautifully and articulately,
My emotions flowing like energy and motion through a magnificent being.
I also used to feel.
I felt universes explode within me.
I felt deathly downpours drown me in dark waters.
I felt the instantaneous bloom of one thousand cherry blossoms.
I have also felt those same cherry blossoms wither and die.
But now, I can't describe how I feel.
I don't even know what I feel.
I couldn't describe this infinity.
It's so great, that it has changed life within me,
And caused my feelings to reincarnate into something beyond poetry.
No expression.
The ultimate feeling.
I shall now write my final poem.

Jacob Klein, Grade 11
The Sound School, CT

Wake

When you awake
You finger and toes curl as your body test itself to see if all still works
As the ligaments and muscles grows taunt under your skin, you twitch
A low soft grunt vibrates in your throat as you give your body new air
Your eye opens slightly as the gooey seal on your eyelids is pulled apart.
The fog left from the night's stagnant tears slowly fades
Gradually does the mind begins to process that which is laid out before you
Complex things aggravate your sleepy mind, as you body fights your slow awakening
Visions of last night's dreams swirl freshly in your mind, as you wonder what is real
You long for more sleep so you roll to your other side and shift on your pillow
Searching for the coolness of the air on your sheets hoping that might help you drift back to sleep
You replay your dreams, close you eyes, and relax your muscles,
But it is too late your mind has already begun to spin you can't escape it
You have already become much too conscious of the strip of sun that lights the room
Your thoughts and body have already awakened, no longer can you find sleep
Reluctantly you push yourself from the warm bed, casting aside the soft quilt
You take those first aching steps, marching towards the new day.
All the while, consoling yourself with thought that later when the sun has fallen you'll nestle back into your bed
And let your consciousness ebb away.

Kelly Groglio, Grade 11
Greenwich Academy, CT

Heaven's Mercy

As the sons and daughters of God cry out for peace,
Genocide and war never seem to cease,
Mothers, fathers, sisters, and brothers,
Friends, close ones, those intimate lovers,
Groan for all creation to realize,
The glory and weight of their promised demise,
If not the hearts of mankind fall to their knees,
Asking the Heavens to rend in response to their needs,
The necessity of God's mercy and grace,
To let the light of His countenance shine upon man's face,
To give courage and strength for those hurting souls,
To wipe creation's tears for establishing the paradigm of nurturing in full,
To bestow hope in the minds and hearts of all,
To love unconditionally on every tribe, tongue, nation and people regardless when they fall.

Timothea Vo, Grade 12
Brien McMahon High School, CT

Typical Tin Foil

Typical teenager.
Wears her heart on her sleeve. Praying for that one boy, that won't ever leave.
Dreaming of the prefect kiss. Lost in an ignorant bliss.
Wishing on a wishing star. She wonders who, and where you are.
A prince to sweep her off her feet, lead her up a stairwell. You she'd like to meet.
One boy to slay her dragon, and calm her empty fears. She only needs one guy to stop the flowing of her tears. A pretender in distress, to try and find the one. Knowing that it's just a test.

Typical teenager.
Lonely to the bone. She knows she wants to talk, but she won't pick up the phone.
Wears her heart on her sleeve. She knows what she wants, and she would never let him leave. Was he really unloyal?
Could she deal with him not being a knight and shinning armor, but a stupid boy in tin foil?

Samantha Mariotti, Grade 11
Scio Central School, NY

Breezes No Longer Blow Here

Screams and yowls
Trembling as children rumble through
Back from school
Off to hole up in regulated capsules
Passing a little twig surrounded by wooden poles
And white twine
In the middle of a lawn
This tree has no challenger
Or neighbor
Just the grass
Closely trimmed to a regulated 1 and 1/2 inches
Who also wishes to wave and tremble
Breezes no longer blow here

Catherine Cummings, Grade 11
Kingsway Regional High School, NJ

Escape

I am a depressed isolated soul.
I anxiously search for something
to escape the burdens which
I am unable to control.

My eyes begin to close.
I come in contact with a counterpart
that I, but no one else knows.
I am extravagantly amazed
as I gaze into its enchanted glow.

I gently prop myself on a cloud of serenity.
I perform a breathtaking harmonizing melody.
I have reached my anticipated destination.
A journey beyond any imagination.

Elaina Vaughan, Grade 12
West Allegheny High School, PA

A Scoop of Life

"one small scoop, plain vanilla"
the weary old man says.
sits down, takes one bite
and looks at the reflection in his metal spoon.
what stares back at him
not an 80-year-old prune, but instead a wide-eyed child
skin smooth as velvet
gobbling a jumbo ice-cream sundae.
cherries. hot fudge. sprinkles. whip.
savoring every bite. pure bliss. no regrets.
the world at his fingertips.
spooning each scoop while it's still there.

the old man puts a smile on his face.
looks back at the counter.
think. think.
struggles to get up one shaky leg at a time.
goes back up to the counter and asks for two more scoops.
cherries. hot fudge. sprinkles.
and whip.
extra whip.

Samantha Markowitz, Grade 10
The Chapin School Ltd, NY

Silence

Understand my world.
Between sight and sound,
colors emerge victorious
noises dragged out and caged.

I once knew
lockers slamming, crowds cheering, horns blasting.
I once knew the sound of my own name,
wind rustling dried cornstalks,
birds' free spirited songs.

Nothing distracts me from my sleep now.

Thunder no longer wakes me,
sirens do not warn,
doorbells do not ring in my friends.
Alarms do not wake me on these dark winter mornings.

Laughter and crying can only be seen
my name spelled out across familiar lips
I do not remember how it sounds.

My world is silent.
Soundless waves caress my feet

Madeline Benz, Grade 11
Villa Walsh Academy, NJ

Love?

Something you grip
Something you hold
Something that turns your heart cold
You keep it until you grow old
When your own heart starts to fold
Love should be there till the end
Like a lifelong dream or a childhood friend
Love should help you be what you want to be
Do what you want to do
At no point should love hurt you
Many times you have your doubts
He assures you it's the right way out
He will never leave
He will never go
And there is no one else
He'd rather spend the rest of his life with
Its no myth
From the moment you met
To the minute you die
He will always be at your side
Because in your heart you know he's the guy

Megan McLaughlin, Grade 10
Blue Mountain High School, PA

Blue

Blue
Makes me think of serenity
Like a howling coyote
In a frostbitten tundra
Justin Knowles, Grade 10
Haverhill High School, MA

I Miss You Pt. II

It's been so long,
but only a year.
There's so much to tell you,
I just hope you will hear.
You are now my inspiration,
for everything I do,
The reason I write,
its all because of you.
When I got the news you were gone,
it stabbed me like a knife.
It officially became,
the worst night of my life.
Just thinking of you,
brings tears to my eyes.
Knowing that you'll never come back,
makes me want to die.
I'll live my life for you,
with you close inside my heart.
Always thinking of the good times,
this is my restart.
Will Ercolano, Grade 10
Atlee High School, VA

Alienated

As I sit translating
Latin so foreign in tongue to me
but so close in soul to me

the epics of heroes, order, and reason
sing to me their stories
planting scenes of courageous deeds
straightforward evils
and triumphant good, always

as I sit translating
overhearing a conversation
so close in tongue to me
but so alien in soul to me
I fail to notice any reason
any rationality, sense
the queer actions
of my contemporaries
force me to question
how tangible is my sanity
perhaps I belong in another age
an epoch that understands me?
Andrew Alves, Grade 10
Haverhill High School, MA

Decay

Looking at a blank world slowly losing itself: a little bit more goes away every day.
All the colors are pastel grey, delicate, fading, a loss of former glory
As each day passes with no sign of change.

The blue paint on the walls sees a new chip, a new crack, every day. Not this again.
Each day it's a little less blue, more washed away.
Music is muffled, softer now. The deep glory is merely
A faint breath of the wind, fighting an unfelt heat.

Laughter is fading. Friends look around, pondering
What laughter was ever for, where it went, why it's gone.
Hearts beat with less insistency — not so keen to work anymore.
What's worth beating for anyway?

Everyone looks around for some saving truth
Some comfort to show that it's not all yet lost
They search, so frantically, but the hope is gone.
And it's so hard to search when the colors are fading
When the world is so quiet, when the laughter is running away.

And the heart says "but why, but why, why bother, why try?"
And it slows more and more and begs for a rest.
Says, "I've been beating too long, do we have to go on?"
And each thump comes slower, softer,
It's okay, just sit, relax, just be relieved it's almost over.
Alexandra Demers, Grade 10
The Bronx High School of Science, NY

My Inner Belligerence

Shivering on a gentle summer night,
Not of chills, of fear,
Tears crawling down tanned cheeks,
Lips part, drinking my despair,
Toil has led to dreadful nothing,
May I climb my ladder alone?
Vines cover the steps, I can see nothing.
Release it!
I demand recovery.
I scream silently, teeth clenched,
Hands freeze, eyes squint.
Enough is enough.
I shall clean out the vines.
The dishes are washed,
Sweetly, with lime detergent.
My floors are swept smooth.
My sheets smell fresh, like summer.
I showered.
And I cooked.
And I carried myself away. But climbing that ladder, I tried and failed.
And I still cried.
Allison Chen, Grade 11
Princeton High School, NJ

Drumming Heartbeat

He was a strong man,
This I know.
But it is so hard,
Just to let him go.

Yet, he lies there,
Coughing and aching.
Laying there still,
Withering away to nothing.

God takes us,
At the end of our lives.
He takes us to wherever we go.
At the time we die.

I sit here next to him,
Tears in my eyes,
Then all there is, is silence,
As the sound of a drumming heartbeat dies.

Jessica Post, Grade 10
Odyssey Academy, NY

Comes to Dying

People live, people love,
watched over in guidance
from others above.
And while some will hate
and others will care,
when comes time to dying,
they both will be there.
No matter how many say they hate
in their own eyes,
when life comes to death,
they will sympathize.
Little prayers join hands
in this time to console,
people see their hate,
place it with 'nother role.
When comes time to dying
while everyone's crying,
paths of roses and tears be lain,
in the grave which he'll be lying.

Noelle Blanchard, Grade 11
Greater Lowell Technical High School, MA

It's the Memories

Down by the railroad tracks
I saw your sweet smile
We were mature and sincere
You taught me more than anyone
We are the Romeo and Juliet of today
And the feelings that we grew together
It was something no one else would understand
Only we could sit by the railroad tracks
Without a care except for each other
We proved the statement
— It's the memories —

Kathryn Angers, Grade 10
Norton High School, MA

Power to What?

Power to the People?
Power to what People?
The people that fight, kill and steal?
People that shoot and deal...
Drugs that uncareful thugs
Find as love, for the people
Then I start to think, I should.
I should? Help the community that was up to no good?
For our minds, bodies, or souls
Yes! We can reach our goals!
Then we power to our People
The people that is black and proud!
The people that is bold and loud!
The people that is not afraid to speak,
And beat
The violence that we're running from.

Tiffany Eason-Robinson, Grade 11
Law Enforcement and Public Safety High School, NY

I Let You In

It's crazy to think that I let you in,
Let you get in,
Deep underneath my skin.
I watched you drive away,
With a smile on my face.
I didn't know it would be goodbye.
I didn't know what would happen that night.
I thought that everything was going to be all right.
You told me you'd never be the one to make me cry.
You told me you'd be there to wipe the tears from my eyes.
Everything you told me was a lie.
You left me here,
Trying to forget,
Trying to erase,
But every time I close my eyes.
All I can see is your face.

Blake Zeiger, Grade 11
Home School, RI

Another Life

Do not mock me
Do not hurt me
But please throw your money at me
Because I am a bum
I have spent my life
Underneath a cardboard box
Living life off of change
Pennies, nickels, and dimes
My sole meal of the day
Consists of bread and water
I spend my day wandering through the streets
Rummaging through garbage
In hope of finding something useful
A chair, a tarp, scraps of food
The street life
Is the only life I know

Kyle Morose, Grade 10
Haverhill High School, MA

The Hockey Goon

When the puck drops his opponents will fall
after the whistle he'll go after them all
with hip checks and cross checks and sticks that are high
there'll be bruises and cuts and even black eyes
some play for the money and some for the fame
but he simply plays for the love of the game
putting the puck in the net makes heroes for the fan
but putting guys in the hospital makes him the main man

Nick Tyler, Grade 10
Brick Township High School, NJ

The Dark Clouds

The clouds are dark in the sky above
And here we all are
Cloaked in our deepest shades
All is silent
Not a soul wishes to evoke the unmentionable, intolerable knowledge
None dare to disturb this evening as the sun begins to fade into oblivion
But there is one drop
A solitary noise to break the silence
And then another
The cool water surrounds us
Floods our thoughts
And there you are
Staring into my spirit
I see your eyes
They mimic the clouds as all of ours do
With the dark clouds above
On this evening

Tyler Bonham, Grade 11
Kennard Dale High School, PA

Too Young

You say I am too young, but how old is too young.
10, 15, 14 or 6 months
Girls getting raped at 10, pregnant at 15
But one close to me was gunned down at 18.
So many hopes, so many dreams
Shattered by the offensive age of 17
So how old is too young 7, 13,12
Boys in childish acts at 7 in gangs at 13
And off to college at 18.
So how old is too young 2, 6, 12
Taken away by the depths of night at 2
Moved from home to home 'Til 6. Then to be sexually abused at 12.
Or is it 16 or 17
Then to be faced with life's addictions at 16
And being faced with the reality of my sexuality at the age of 17.
But wait didn't you say I was too young.
I may be young, but not too young to understand life.
So tell me how young is too young.
To be only 18 I have been through some of life's toughest challenges.

Feleisha Thompson, Grade 12
Springfield High School of Science & Technology, MA

I Am

I am the howling wind of the night
Whose wrath goes unspoken,
I am the feeling of sandpaper
Smooth on one side but completely different on the other,
I am a turtle
Meek and shy except to those of my kind,
I am the daughter of justice
Striving to do that which is right,
But the cousin of infidelity
Who falls and slips in a sea of lies,
I am a birthday,
Full of surprises both good and unpleasant.
I am simply,
Myself.

Siqing (Lucy) Liu, Grade 12
Montgomery Blair High School, MD

As We Say Goodnight

God bless the weak, who cannot stand alone.
God bless the strong, who tears have outgrown.
God bless the freaks, who suffer the world's scorn.
God bless the druggies, wishing to be reborn.
God bless the drunks, drinking away their pain.
God bless the heartbroken, standing in the rain.
God bless the homeless, begging on a corner.
God bless the infants, who never make it older.
God bless the wounded, as they try to walk again.
God bless the sick, who pray for the end.
God bless the war and the people that are dying.
God bless the hopeless, who've given up trying.
God bless the lonely, in Your arms, hold them tight.
God bless the pregnant girl, who has nowhere to sleep at night.
God bless the nation, God bless the people,
God bless our friends, and God bless the evil.
God bless the soldiers, God bless the world,
God bless the animals, and the little boys and girls.
God bless the wrong, God bless the right,
God bless us all, as we say goodnight.

Claire Werkiser, Grade 10
Unionville High School, PA

I Have Lost You

My darling, my friend
I have lost you again
Where, in this test of life, have you failed?
This world is cold; your soul, jailed
These are the chains you just couldn't see;
These ones that now cannot let you free
My darling, my friend
You've fallen for it again
And now with every letter I send,
I seek no reply, only an end
My love; for you, my heart weeps
For in your falsities you sleep
Unaware, my darling, my friend;
That you have lost me once again.

Elisabeth Lambert, Grade 12
Garnet Valley High School, PA

Life

It's from the time it starts to the time it ends
Starts out you being pure to creating sins
What's crazy is worse once you become of age
It quickly skips chapters then page by page
Seeing emptiness and unfamiliar faces
Its twists and turns, its constant disgraces
The painful yet happiest feelings that come from the heart
Just another way of saying "A Work of Art"
The pieces to the puzzle seem to be everywhere
Even when there is a picture the concept is still unclear
You sit around and think trying to figure out that feeling
Not realizing moving on is a start to your healing
Your days are young, happy, sad, and old
And what keeps you going are the memories you hold
It seems so tiring because it takes so long
You have to stay focused and try to stay strong
You may not know whether things are wrong or right
Just know that it's this little thing called LIFE

Karen Velasquez, Grade 12
Harlem Renaissance High School, NY

A Tourist in Chinatown

The funniest thing I've seen in all of my days
Is laughing at tourists and all their ways

As they pick up their chopsticks with both of their hands
And refuse to drink tea and rather, soft drinks in cans

I do this on Sundays or on days without work
Where I sit in the corner with rice and roast pork

Where the insides hurt deep through the laughter and fun
While their "I Love New York" hats and shirts bathe in the sun

They cannot order in Chinese, as their speech grows very still
And watching them articulate is what I find a thrill

The busy sounds of restaurant work conceal me in my pit
As tea and pleasure join me, while I hide in dark and sit

And as I turn to pour another warm, moist cup of tea
I see only another man, who sits and laughs at me

Jonathan Tam, Grade 11
Manhasset High School, NY

Remember

Your first kiss
Your first car
Where you went to high school
Your first real date
First night on your twenty-first birthday
The picture of your grandmother from the last time you saw her
Your wedding day
Your first child
Your last child
Your last dinner with your wife
Loneliness…emptiness

Nicholas Aveni, Grade 10
Haverhill High School, MA

City

Walking along, looking around
The buildings stand tall like giants,
But are minute against the sky
Trees frame the path,
A splotch of green,
Against a canvas of white,
The city is full of life,
As if it is alive itself,
And feels the warmth of the sun,
And the coolness of the breeze,
White marble, grey steel, infused with green
Civilization and nature are one
Looking up to the sky,
Looking down on the world,
It is all enormous, overwhelming
Powerful, beautiful.

Greg Mercer, Grade 12
Tucker High School, VA

Wait

The words they don't come
Then they do. All suddenly.
Forming fragments or
Sentences.
You want the poem or story or thought.
Just to be good.
Now that the words do come
What do they mean?
Nothing at all?
Then what is the point
Just for a minute you realize
It doesn't matter.
Then again it does matter all the more
Or at least now it does.
Since those words had to be said
Really they did need to be said
In that order, no.
But said, yes.
Wait. For what?
For the words to be any good?
It doesn't matter if they are. I have poetic license.

Jamie Pitter, Grade 10
The Bronx High School of Science, NY

Things I Could Be Doing Instead of Poetry

Listening to music by Michael Jackson.
Drawing a fancy picture.
Watching MTV.
Saving the world from crime.
Writing a tell all book about my life.
Googling my name.
Building a house.
Trying to read a book.
Cooking a feast for my family.
Trying to learn Chinese.

Henry Benitez, Grade 10
Haverhill High School, MA

The Rose

Another soothing sun arose
Beside it a crescent moon shivers cold
Mist and haze astray
Comprises a luminous ray

Daisies upon the fields of Casablanca
As white as Agadir's snowy tops
Amidst all a reddish Rose
Reaches to the heavens above

I am the Rose,
With thorns like needles
A color so peaceful
A deep red as dreamy as the starry Moroccan sky

In every petal a memory
In every shade happiness
Looming upon the cascading whiteness
The perennial plant; The Rose.

Chaimaa Makoudi, Grade 12
Douglas MacArthur High School, NY

71%

Why am I so unknown, when everyone knows me?
While a blanket of life for many
Yet a chilling fear for some
I hold many in my accepting arms
Yet no one has held me
The laughter of children never dies
But in these arms some have
The things I see never cease to amaze
Yet you mistreat me, misuse me
And misunderstand what a wonder I am
Without me, there is no life
Yet I will always be treated this way
But when I'm upset, it's a national emergency
You are all effected, and lost by my endlessness
Whether survival, recreation, sports or an escape
You couldn't function without me
But at the end of the day I have my Father
And his words comfort me
And God called the gathering together
Of waters he called the seas; and God saw
That it was good

Brianna Gipe, Grade 10
Shippensburg Area Sr High School, PA

Grades 7-8-9

Note: The Top Ten poems were finalized through an online voting system. Creative Communication's judges first picked out the top poems. These poems were then posted online. The final step involved thousands of students and teachers who registered as online judges and voted for the Top Ten poems. We hope you enjoy these selections.

Top Poem Grades 7-8-9

Standing Strong

Sitting at lunch with people that don't understand you
Thinking to yourself, I don't need this
Hold your head high
Be the better person and be kind to others even when they are unkind to you
Take a deep breath and let it go in one ear and out the other
Gain confidence
Look them in the eye and delete your fears
Don't worry about what they may think of you
Mind your own business
Tell yourself you can do this and never give up
Remember you are just as important and special as them
Keep going
Even if you fail the first time, try again and again until you reach your goals
Face your intimidations and conquer them
Plant your feet firmly into the ground
No one can move you without your permission
Don't give them your permission; you are in charge of yourself
The better person wins in the end
Love yourself and don't let anyone get you down
Only you can change your future
Stay strong.

Callie Andro, Grade 9
Pine-Richland High School, PA

Top Poem Grades 7-8-9

Ode to Twilight

Dear Twilight that I extol proudly,
That is my heart and sky
You are a compelling magnet that pulls and attracts me to you
Why is this so?
I do not understand because you are a page turner that can capture anyone like a buzzing bee to a pure and beautiful flower

Your stories, from the onset to the end, are extinguished with passion and grace
Any who reads you will melt in your addicting flames
You are like a home run in a baseball game
The sun in the day and the moon at night when the sun sets
You are like a dazzling, yet popular, Golden Retriever in a huge group of puny, identical Chihuahuas

You, a clever book, are as romantic as a rose on Valentine's Day
When people read and turn your soft, sensible pages, they are awestruck and crave for more like an extremist yearn for challenges
Your call is as sweet and silk-like as a tune that no one knows
Being both stunning and fascinating, you are similar to El Toro because you thrill us all to a pallid and rhapsody state
Unlike the other and apathetic books out there in the open, you are an angel that has fallen from the sky to touch and kiss our very souls.

Ida Chen, Grade 8
Thomas Edison Intermediate School, NJ

Top Poem Grades 7-8-9

Ich Liebe Sie Jude

You probably knew how I felt
a little school girl
wide eyed loving you.
And you too feeling the same.
But we were hopeful and they took your brown eyes away.
No more lips to comfort me.
No more boy to shelter me.
My blonde hair saved
me from Birkenau, Dachau,
Belson, Treblinka.
You died in that little
red house forever mine.
Another Jew forgotten in
the ashes of time.
Why wouldn't you
see why couldn't
you see how
he was
equal to
me?

Julia Clark, Grade 8
Charles S Pierce Middle School, MA

Top Poem Grades 7-8-9

Not Our Last Goodbye

I lay in bed and wonder why God took you away
I wanted you forever. Why didn't He let you stay?
The aching in my heart, I yearn for you so much.
I miss your warm big hugs, and your soft, gentle touch.
I stare off into space and I think about you still.
The loneliness in my heart, I guess I will forever feel.

So I lift my head up and tell myself once more
You're in no painful suffering, the cancer is out the door.
I know that it's a blessing, the disease from you is away,
But I still shed those tears, when I know that you're not here today.

I know that you're in Heaven, as happy as can be,
But I still hope that you're proud of me.
I've been through a lot, matured and grown
But there are still times when I feel alone.

Even in a crowd of people, it's scary to feel like this,
But just thinking of you, puts me in a state of bliss.
I'm fighting very hard and moving along.
Heartbreak and your passing have only made me strong.

So I'll look outside my window, and I look into the sky
"This isn't the end, Grandma. This is not our last goodbye."

Erin Connor, Grade 8
Monsignor Haddad Middle School, MA

Top Poem Grades 7-8-9

Oceanic Lullaby

Soft and pink ivory shells
The sound of the ocean ringing like bells
Lapping and shaping the sand on the shore,
Like an uncontent potter who re-forms and shapes even more
Gulls dance and drift in cloudless skies
As each new wave crashes and dies
Rising and cowering
Finding and scouring

A gentle voice humming a sweet melody
Singing the mysteries of the sea
Haunting, wondrous lullaby
Rising and falling tones so shy
Sparkling diamonds on the land
Seemingly placed there by God's own hand
Cresting and falling,
Laughing and calling

Ocean.

Shay Hostetler, Grade 8
Selinsgrove Area Middle School, PA

Top Poem Grades 7-8-9

The Truth Is in the Eyes

The truth is in the eyes.
Every smile and every giggle does not work.
Unless of course,
The eyes play a part in the joyful emotion.
What you say is not always what you mean,
And the eyes will reveal just that.
The heart can hide and slowly wither,
But your eyes can tell the tale.

If there were no eyes,
We couldn't grab hold of another's jealousy
Before it creeps up
And taps them on the shoulder.
We couldn't listen or be listened to as intensely as we show
We couldn't cry for help
We couldn't cry at all

Without our eyes,
No one would understand
When we are stressed, grieved, or mournful.
No one would feel passion through their love's deep eyes.
No one would know,

Because the truth is in the eyes.

Rebecca Malaret, Grade 7
Carson Middle School, VA

Top Poem Grades 7-8-9

Under the Cherry Blossom Tree

Under the cherry blossom tree,
The blue sea above
Is dappled with pink clouds,
As the wind wraps around my waist,
Tugging at my bronze hair,
Under the cherry blossom tree.

The afternoon sun is blinding,
Casting short shadows of
Minnows darting along the jade grass.
The blushing blossoms dance above me
As I sit
Under the cherry blossom tree.

Now night falls
And I must depart,
But I'll never let myself forget
Those swirling rosy petals hovering
Just above my head,
While I was dozing
Under the cherry blossom tree.

Hannah Matangos, Grade 8
Ephrata Middle School, PA

Top Poem Grades 7-8-9

Tickling Ivory

Fingers flitter in black and white,
Every beat is struck just right

Notes are bludgeoned, notes are kissed,
But all float into wondrous mist

Blending, mixing, mellow tones,
One's work of art indeed one's own

Hear what dots and lines become,
All in all the music comes

Escape the world, and blinding light,
Enter cool and fanciful night

Pedals or petals, which more soft,
More is learned than ever taught

Discover swirling fantasies,
Dreams that flow through ivory keys.

Mary Mount, Grade 9
Unami Middle School, PA

Top Poem Grades 7-8-9

A Walk in the Woods

its bright and blissful wind dances with the trees,
a delicate tango simple and at ease,
it dances to sunshine glistening and ringing,
but then i soon realize the earth is singing,
fish dance down a babbling brook,
to serenading sounds everywhere you look,
from the playful branches swinging their leaves,
to the soaring birds exploring each breeze,
they defy gravity with the flap of their wings,
every tree in the forest stands tall and sings,
it's an ancient song of ancient voices,
golden sounds and beautiful noises,
from blazing sunsets to flowers blooming,
the echo of song is always looming,
it's sung by trees, flowers and deer,
if you listen closely you might hear,
an enchanting natural melody,
the whole world in perfect harmony.

Madeline Robert, Grade 9
Granby Jr/Sr High School, MA

Top Poem Grades 7-8-9

With Her Hands

With her knobby, twisted hands,
she has felt the silt of soil on the jungle gym,
she has touched the grit of the sandbox next to her playmates.

With her knotted, pockmarked hands,
she has dabbed on the vibrant lipstick of adolescence,
she has brushed her salty tears away following her first relationship.

With her yellowed, blue-veined hands,
she has received her golden marriage ring,
she has reverently swaddled the softness of her first child.

With her shaky, mottled hands,
she has scrubbed the last layer of hardened oatmeal off the bottom of the cracked bowl,
she has pressed the button on the camera to take the photograph of her only son in his graduation gown.

With her discolored, uneven hands,
she has placed the multicolored pills carefully into the days of the week medicine holder for her husband,
and then caressed the engravement "a father to all" on his tombstone.

With her arthritic, weakened hands,
she has eaten her cream of wheat, alone, at a table set for three.
She has reached in the morning to embrace the family she can no longer hold.

With her wizened, loving hands,
she has held the world, she has moved a mountain, she has molded a life.

Danielle Rose, Grade 9
High School North, NJ

newfangled

words that aren't really words
buzzing and whirling
how much more, really
revolving doors
always bring us back to renaissance
throwing away tracks left before us
tossing out lessons worn down

Rachel Lin, Grade 9
Thomas S Wootton High School, MD

Julius Erving

Dribbling down the court
Boy he must love this sport
He is in the zone
The other coach letting out a groan
Oh he's going to swing
He is the king, the king of the court
He never comes short
He invented the Dunk
Boy this is bunk
How does he transport
To the other side of the court
What a nice call!
Now he's shooting the ball
What a nice shot
He's got the slot
MVP, not for me
Dr. J is here to stay
Steals the show 2nd free throw
Swoosh it's in
He wears a big grin because it's a win

Kiera Klaum, Grade 7
Floral Park Memorial High School, NY

The One

At the dance I saw him.
The music played and I waited.
Waited for him to ask me to dance.
Watching, waiting, anticipating.

He crossed the room and came to me.
Asked me to dance.
The music was slow and smooth
Rocking, swinging, swaying.

For those two minutes,
I was on top of a cloud.
The room felt silent.
Quiet, hushed, calm.

The dance ended.
We went our separate ways.
I will never forget that night.
Romance, everlasting, memories.

Janine Curran, Grade 9
Unami Middle School, PA

My Haven

Climbing up mud, bending under vines,
With the comfortable sound of crunching leaves
Towards my haven, my home
To escape to a paradise engulfed by trees,
With the dried out waterfall and many trails to explore
Towards my haven, my home
Above all is the flat stone looking over the homes hidden in weeds
Oh to be there, to take a breath and be calm
Finally I'm at my haven, my home.

Sarah Shaw, Grade 7
Trinity Middle School, PA

Smile to the Music

Smiles sound like your favorite music when listening to it.
You are in an amazing mood.
Dancing to your music
With friends or not.
A smile is like your favorite song.
When someone smiles it's contagious, just like if someone shows you a new song,
And you get addicted to it.
Smiles are repeated choruses in a song.
People smile repeatedly,
Like lyrics in music.
Just like music, people won't be able to live without smiles.
Without smiles,
Personality and everything else will become boring.
Smiles are you favorite part of your song.
When you see parts of people's personality.
When you listen to everyone's types of music,
You can see their personalities also!
That's the life of music and smiles.
That's what a smile sounds like to me.
What a wonderful sound.

Krystal Kim, Grade 8
Seneca Valley Middle School, PA

Snow

A frozen ocean lies before me, awaiting the arrival of my feet,
The crunch, crunch, run and stomp, and the thump of my heartbeat.

The cold, blustery wind stings my face.
I see in the sky a snowflake that looks like hand-woven lace.

In the frosty chill of the air,
I hear the whoosh of the wind everywhere.

I see rolling drifts that sparkle like droplets of fairy dust.
I lay down, swinging my arms and legs to make an angel, that's a must!

I want to close my eyes and sleep,
Not make another sound or hear another peep.

But the cold creeps up my spine like the chill from a bad dream.
I drifted away, but floated back on a sea of frozen cream.

Alyssa Blundo, Grade 7
Westwood Jr/Sr High School, NJ

Shopping

Designer shoes, size seven,
Oh. My. Gosh. These look like they were made in heaven.
Three new tank tops…one red, one blue, and Oh!
I think I might like pink.
A gorgeous new t shirt,
And maybe a matching mini skirt.
New jean shorts, with a few rips.
These fit perfectly on my hips.
Capris that come to the knee,
And sunglasses so big I can hardly see!
An oversized coach bag,
Ew! Not that one, it makes me want to gag!
Silver necklace, bracelet, and maybe a ring,
I'll look like a superstar with all this "Bling-Bling."
Colorful flip-flops for by the pool,
I think I'll buy these ones, they look so cool!
Lastly, I need a bathing suit.
This pink bikini is so cute!
There's so much to buy at the mall today.
I hope I have enough money to pay!

Keri Wieczerzak, Grade 7
Anthony Wayne Middle School, NJ

Suzy Q

With a canter like a rocking horse,
we leap over the jumps.
Suzy, like a white canvas splattered
with chestnut brown paint.
Just like a lamb, so sweet and gentle,
and lively as a foal.
She first carried me, then my sisters.
To her, I was not just a rider, but a student.
Suzy was never impatient,
and a great listener too.
She retired so suddenly,
and was in so much pain for months.
Trapped, in a dark wooden box stall,
listless, lifeless, with sad eyes.
I can still see those eyes,
those eyes like melted brown sugar.
And I didn't get to say goodbye.
There will be no other one like her.

Hailey Mowrey, Grade 7
Trinity Middle School, PA

Blue

Blue is the color that spreads through the sky
As the day passes by, the river flows by me
And I let my feet sink into the cold water
Looking at the blue calming sky
While watching the blue jays fly high and low
Seeing the dark clouds roaming in
The smell of the fresh new rain
Quenching the thirst of the blue violets

Nick Chong, Grade 7
Sanford School, DE

Three Trees

Three small trees,
their slender trunks aligned.
Though at the top,
their lengthy branches intertwined.
Their leaves create a canopy,
as heavy rain falls from the sky.
Although the surrounding trees get soaked,
the sheltered ones remain dry.
The three trees act as a symbol,
of how the nation should be.
At the bottom we live our separate lives,
but at the top always united for our country.

Breana Tate, Grade 7
Carson Middle School, VA

Injury Daze

There is a large issue these days with me,
not the popular video game craze,
a problem that creates an ill at ease.
Sports injuries leave quite an angry daze.

Every year since the days of fifth grade,
me getting injured comes up end on end,
and not a full season has been played.
The couch has sadly become my best friend.

Mind over matter does not pertain here.
I must strive to overcome and conquer this,
to the point where I play with fun, not fear.
Will I leave this frustrating abyss?

Hard work and determination are key.
Then I will be able to play stress free.

Will Sasser, Grade 9
Unami Middle School, PA

Not Real Love

He is just using you
And you need to get a clue.
You need to accept he doesn't love you,
Just because he gave you a kiss or two.
He's found someone new,
And when you find out your face is going to be blue.
You gave him your heart,
But he's just ripping it apart.
You're offering him everything,
Just because your relationship has a little thing.
It's not really glowing,
And his love is not flowing.
You give him your all,
But he's just letting your relationship fall.
He cares about the other girl more.
To her his love is pure.

Tanajah Baldwin, Grade 7
Link Community School, NJ

Rid the World of Darkness

Hate is a wildfire
That tears through the world
And burns up everything in its path
Swift as the wind
It feeds on anger and despair,
Spreading darkness across the globe
Until there is no safe place left.
All hope is lost,
Families are torn apart
In hate's reign of terror.
Sometimes it may seem
That hate will rule forever,
But that is not always the case.
When people learn to love,
To treat each other with kindness
And bring joy to those in need,
That love will build up and grow.
Against hate, love is stronger
With help, it will last longer
To ride the world of darkness
Once and for all.

Nicole Becker, Grade 7
Depew Middle School, NY

One Window

One window is all I need,
To let myself go free,
To see the world,
To be more than a face in the crowd,
To have the sun shining on me.
All I need is a chance.
All I need is a moment.
To think. To breathe. To take it all in.
Then I'll take a step, make a move.
And then I'll reach to that window,
And break it open.

Arthi Nithi, Grade 7
Anthony Wayne Middle School, NJ

Foxy

I once saw a fox.
It was smaller than an ox.

It was slick as can be.
As it can trick a hunter with its speed.

It can see a bunny from afar.
Soon after it will charge.

It seems like a saint.
But it is so taint.

For he could pull a trick.
For he is so slick.

Stephanie Grozio, Grade 7
Hammarskjold Middle School, NJ

Set of Keys

My family is a set of keys
My father is the master key
That you can't duplicate
My mother is the key holder
That holds the family together
My sister is a key chain
That brings fun to the family
My brothers are the house keys
That connects us together
I am the mail key
That brings in the good news

Jaime Santana, Grade 7
Simon Baruch Jr High School 104, NY

Waterfalls

Water drops trickle
And fall down a rocky ledge
In a careless way.

Dropping faster now,
The droplets frolic and laugh —
Misting up the air.

They splash at the end,
Back in the river to play
And giggle some more.

Victoria Loughborough, Grade 7
McDonogh School, MD

Summer

The blue sky
The green leaves
The bright grass
The tall trees

Sparkling waters
Creatures everywhere
Smells of barbecues
A warm, soft air

Neighbors walking dogs
Playing children are in sight
The best sunset of the year
Crickets humming late at night

School is let out
Fall is far from near
Relaxing all day long
Summer's finally here!

The universe is balanced
There's nothing else to say
From black and white to color
I hope summer's here to stay

Stephanie Neville, Grade 8
St Stephen's School, NY

Tornado Ballet

Beep! Beep!
A siren sounds.
Warning! Warning!
Here I come!
Spinning, twirling
A tornado's dance.
Gracefully I spin,
Daring you to get in my way.
Hail applauds me
As I dance across the earth.
Destruction behind me as I leave
Returning to the sky
Where I will wait
To dance again.

Rebecca Gonzon, Grade 7
Christ the Teacher Catholic School, DE

There's a Mountain on My Face

There's a bump on my forehead.
The hugest zit around.
I felt it when I awoke,
And then was mirror-bound.

My trip down the narrow hall,
Was overflowing with thick, dark, fright,
With anxiety and dread,
Of the thing I developed last night.

It's not a bump, but a hill.
No, not a hill, but a mountain,
A huge mountain on my face.
What a slumber that must have been.

But my reflection said otherwise,
When I viewed the face I'd seen a lot.

When I scanned my whole forehead,
I saw only the tiniest of tiny dots.

Sophia Barakat, Grade 7
Carson Middle School, VA

Last Day of School

Day dreaming in school
As school is about to end soon
No homework
And bossy teachers
No more getting up early
Sleeping as late as we want
Having fun all day
And partying all night
No more silly fights
Like goofing off and running around
As I hear a cling
The bell rang

Amy Tran, Grade 7
Hammarskjold Middle School, NJ

I See

Sometimes I'm sad and alone up here
I see little things like a smile or tear
    I see people running to go to recess
I see people working doing their best
    Sometimes I see kids passing a note
And I hear the teacher quote for quote
    I see a new kid look up at me
She is kind she is shy and her name is Shale
    I see kids walk away down the hall
Some running, jogging, or bouncing a ball
    When everyone's gone I feel very sad
Because they all leave me so very glad
    They leave me way up high on my stool
Because I'm the only clock in the school

Hannah Neidermyer, Grade 7
Grandview Heights Christian Academy, PA

Sudden Loss

At such a happy time you left us all with
countless memories many I recall
Before they told me I already knew
that you were gone here was nothing I could do
I never would have imagined your days would be rationed
I was wrong to say you'd be there the next day
Ever since the crash there's been a missing part
but I can only find you in my heart
Sometimes I wonder how God could let this be
maybe it was meant to
but how could this happen to me
I hope you hear me when I say
I love you very much and I miss you every day
Life without you is like a puzzle's missing piece
lost and forever gone
now that you're deceased
There is not a day I don't remember
there is not a way I could forget
our love is a never-ending song
if only I could hear you sing along

Katherine Cheney, Grade 8
Our Lady of Mount Carmel School, VA

Montana

Montana doesn't have a beach in sight,
but it does have a sun that is brighter than bright
and a quiet peaceful sound
even with rivers and streams flowing around.
As I look at the large mountains topped with snow
back to Delaware, I dream of never having to go,
I sigh, then breathe, and sigh again;
Montana is such a beautiful serene place to be,
with so much wide-open space to feel free
as I finish my horseback ride to the lake
nothing here comes close to being fake.

Brienna Pavlik, Grade 8
Beacon Middle School, DE

Behind Those Eyes

Behind those eyes I see the true you.
You talk to yourself when you're filled with the blues
You dream randomly about what could be
To only find out it could not be.

Deep inside your heart starts to break.
You can't hold the gates from letting it escape.
You start to feel trapped and so unsure.
To realize it's present tense not the past anymore.

When I look through your eyes I see the good and the bad.
But when the mirror reflects it only shows the sad.
The tears roll down your face even though you hold them back.
To not be seen by anybody else but the truth lets it out.
When I look into your eyes I see the lies.
But when you say it outloud I start to breakdown.
From believing you when I was turned around.

Krista DiMeglio, Grade 8
Floral Park Memorial High School, NY

nature

the grass dances to the wind
they clap their hands and stomp their feet
they all boogie to the wind beat
they dance with the trees
as they swat fleas
and the ants grow a pact
to get food and get back
the sun is looming over the trees
as they all went to sleep

Jadon Jenkins, Grade 7
Ghent Elementary School, VA

Running

First comes stretching,
The most important part
Then I'm off
I start with a nice, steady pace
I spot the first mile marker
And am feeling great
I look around me
And enjoy the scenery
Next comes mile number two,
I am doing well
When I reach three miles, my legs start to tire
Keep on going, I tell myself
Mile four is pretty far
My whole body is screaming to stop
But I have the will to go on
At last I reach the fifth and final mile
I drop to my knees on the cold, damp ground
And raise my hands
In victory but suddenly I feel the grass on my face
Then the blue sky turns black

Christopher Suh, Grade 7
Carson Middle School, VA

The Ship

At sea on a beautiful day
The ship sails out of the bay
Enjoying the fresh sea air
Enjoying a day so fair

A lighthouse is on the shore
Warning sailors from so far
Enjoying the cool sea spray
Enjoying the warm summer day

Watching a white sea gull
The day never growing dull
Enjoying the fresh sea air
Enjoying a day so fair

Julia Moore, Grade 7
Whitin Middle School, MA

Out of Fear

You sometimes act out of fear
And often forget what is real
Do you not know that this is true?
That sometimes you're not even you
Out of fear of what they think
Afraid to sometimes even blink
To me this all seems fake
But you just sit and learn to take
All that has been thrown at you
Do you not know that this is true?
Often you even frighten me
That someday this is what I might be

Angela Cutler, Grade 9
Giles High School, VA

State of Play

Answer your
questions!
Watch the
heart monitor
help
the cause
with color.
Sale!
Bat now.

Robert Mainardi, Grade 9
Unami Middle School, PA

Sun/Moon

Sun
Yellow, bright
Blinding, gleaming, blazing
Inferno, illumination, crater, eclipse
Waning, waxing, orbiting
White, lunar
Moon

Mitchell Clemons, Grade 7
Christ the Teacher Catholic School, DE

What's Love

Love means a deep compassionate feeling for one,
Love helps relationships grow stronger with every step taken.
Love the one that means the most to you.
Even when you're down he should pick you up always.
Make you feel at home when you're millions of miles away.
Love is when you give it up just for a single soul.
Love surrounds us every day,
From the people you see to the living things all around us.
Love is when you tell them how much you care about them, and what you feel.
Love is unique, an emotion of passion while you do the impossible,
Forget the negative, enjoy the positive things.
Love is like an ocean of water floating all around.
Love fills me with the best glee.
When I'm hugging the one I love I hope he will be the only one for me.
I understand the concept of losing all I have for you.
The most wonderful person there,
The one that will hold me when I'm scared.
Lift my spirit when I'm feeling down, his love surrounding me all around.
He is my knight in shining armor in my soul.
He is the only one in the world for me.
Love is a compassionate feeling, be ready to face the real world, scary but fun.

MyKayla D. Podish, Grade 7
Trinity Middle School, PA

Someday

Someday I will find myself and really see who I am.
Someday I will help less fortunate people so that the world can be a better place.
Someday I will face hardships that will knock me down, but I will get back up.
Someday pollution will disappear, and the Earth will not die.
Someday world peace will come so that people and nations don't fight.
Someday I will be a better person and try to make all these things happen.
Someday…

Jong Hoon Kim, Grade 7
Anthony Wayne Middle School, NJ

Just a Thought

The world today, take my hand,
I will show you what has become of our land.
Instead of bringing hope we bring wars,
Instead of spreading love we call upon the corps.

The world has changed in a very cruel way,
When 6.5 million people die each year that is surely something to say.
I envision a new nation where we will wake up and behold,
That If we stand together a better world will unfold.

Open your eyes, look around,
To the polluted smoky skies.
Take a moment and tell me what you see,
Is it the way you imagined it would be?

Just a thought, if we added a little extra dedication
Couldn't we make a better world for the future generation?

Neha Khurana, Grade 7
Carson Middle School, VA

The Rose

Many different colors,
Filled with different meanings.
Each has a mind of its own,
And speaks for itself.

A thorn that kills,
And the blood red that stains.
Eleven roses in a bouquet, and a dozen just for you.
Leaving an impression forever in the lover's heart.

Yellow is for friendship,
The friendship that is priceless.
Something that is irreplaceable
As long as it is true, they'll forever be by your side.

The rarest of all is black,
Deadly yet scarce.
You'll be lucky if you find one,
But probably doomed for all eternity.

There are many more colors,
From blue to purple to pink.
All mysterious and hold such beauty.
Sweet smelling fragrance enchanting us all.

Annie Kong, Grade 7
Simon Baruch Jr High School 104, NY

Laura Ling and Euna Lee

Laura Ling and Euna Lee
Two American journalists who should be set free
The North Korean government is calling them spies
But they are women of integrity who tell no lies
They now have been sentenced to hard labor for twelve years
That was one of their family's greatest fears
With pleas from Hillary Clinton and Al Gore
Our nation is looking for their freedom and more…
North Korea's nuclear device
Is the reason these women are paying such a steep price?
We hold this vigil tonight to pray
They're in God's hand, let Him show us the way.

Matthew DeNapoli Champagne, Grade 8
Monsignor Haddad Middle School, MA

Happiness on a Stick

Lollipops are a piece of heaven entering your mouth,
they are so delicious.
Lollipops are a bonanza for your taste buds,
it makes them go wild.
Lollipops are a big ball of sugary goodness,
it shrinks right in your mouth.
Lollipops are a small present,
you can't wait to get it unwrapped.
Lollipops are happiness on a stick,
it can bring joy to people!

Kaitlin Lorditch, Grade 8
Ephrata Middle School, PA

The Road of Life

The Road of life is long and different for each who travel it.
Some will drive sports cars, zooming off at lightning speed.
Some will drive vans, bringing along those close.

Some will take the nearest shortcut.
Some will creep along.
Some will drive past others.
Some will stay and wait.

Some will zip right through its treasures of views
From point A along to B.
Some pause to wait and see
What the road has to offer.

In the end, it's your choice
To drive fast or drive slow.
And the way you choose to go is up to you to know.

Patrick Carr, Grade 7
Ocean City Intermediate School, NJ

Mi Amor

O mi amor,
For this love there is no cure.
When you walk by my heart skips a beat,
And I turn my head as you walk down the street.
You never spare a passing glance,
But still you put me in a trance.
Your beauty is beyond compare,
You're only mine and I won't share.
Your divine aura is too much for me,
I'm truly in love as you can see.
You will only receive the best,
I hope that I will pass your test.
I love you with a burning passion,
You've always had a lot of fashion.
Your eyes sparkle like two pools of blue,
Please accept my love for I need you.
I can't live a day without your smile,
For you I would run a mile.
O mi amor,
For this love this is no cure.

Timmy Flynn, Grade 7
Hammarskjold Middle School, NJ

I Miss You

I miss you
I miss your hugs
The way you would hold me in your arms
I miss the way you told me you loved me
But now you're watching over me
Hard times come and hard times go
But I guess this comes to show you
We don't know what tomorrow holds

Dana Martinez, Grade 7
Thorne Middle School, NJ

Elements

The sun, a bright ball of exhilaration
the ocean, a living wasteland of water
the wind, a tour guide of the seasons.

Without these elements,
there would be no life.
Imagine a vast land of no water,
no movement, no colors;
just frozen ice creating
an empty world of nothing,
Devastation!

Luke Kelly, Grade 7
Ocean City Intermediate School, NJ

As the Clouds Go By

As I laid there on the ground
I saw the clouds moving past me,
thinking of how time goes by.
Lying there wondering if anything
will ever change.
And when the clouds disappear
I saw one thing.
In life things will pass
and change
as your times goes by.

Sam Lisa, Grade 7
Thorne Middle School, NJ

Why Not?

Why not party to shake
things up a bit!
Treat yourself more
and put your best foot forward.
Have your moment
in the sun
with room to relax.
Take care
for you are flippin' adorable.

Elise Baranak, Grade 9
Unami Middle School, PA

Concussion

I do not remember you or me
I do not know what's the sky or the sea
I do not know hate or love
I cannot tell what's down or above
I wish I knew what was what
Then I would be out of this rut
However, everything is a blur
And my words start to slur
My head fills with a painful ache
Like I'm scratching it with a rake
I wish I could remember that day
But all I remember is black and gray

Sarah Gosnell, Grade 9
Unami Middle School, PA

Feelings About You

Through every broken dream and every hopeless day
I wish to find someone that isn't you
Someone that can fix the pieces to the heart you broke
Anyone out there that could give me back
What you have taken from me
Someone that can hold me close and kiss me in the pouring rain
Someone that will hold me close and protect me from my greatest fears
Someone who would risk their life just to save mine
A person that will run away with me
Wherever I want to go, and not ask why
A person that would wipe away every tear I shed
And know exactly what the reason is I'm crying and why I'm so upset
Someone that will hold my hand each and every day
Someone who will scream I LOVE YOU
To the sky and not care who hears or what they say
Someone that calls me beautiful instead of ruining my day
Someone that brings sunshine to my day
Someone that will love me for who I am
And not make me change my ways

Caroline Habib, Grade 7
Hammarskjold Middle School, NJ

Beauty

Beauty: The first thing that comes to your mind,
Is the look of someone on the outside right?
Well, I have learned that beauty,
Is so much more than that,

Beauty is strong
Beauty is the way you feel,
And the way you act,
Don't be fooled,
Looks can be deceiving,

Just because someone is beautiful on the outside,
Doesn't mean they're beautiful within,
And don't think that just because someone isn't as beautiful on the outside,
Doesn't mean they're not raging with beauty on the inside,

It is hard to find,
But I believe once you find it,
You should hold onto it forever,
And never let it slip through your fingers.

Chelsea Moriarty, Grade 7
Westwood Jr/Sr High School, NJ

I Miss You

I'm growing up and I miss the old things we did together.
You were by my side for everything.
You would wrap your arms around me and I knew you would never let go.
You were there for hard times and always good times.
I love you so much and I promise that will never change.
Even though you may not be living with me in my home;
I am still your little girl and I always will be.

Paige Butkiewicz, Grade 7
Thorne Middle School, NJ

Dreams

Hold onto your dreams
As long as you can
Let them take off
But only when you are ready
Some people might put you down
But don't let them stop you
Even when it hurts
You know yourself better than anyone you know
You know exactly what you want
And the way you want it done
Live your life the way you want to
Not the way others might want you to
Take a chance
Dream your dream

Victoria Petherick, Grade 7
Depew Middle School, NY

Fill the Gaps

We were in love, it was great, it was awesome.
I enjoyed watching our love blossom.
Watching our love spiral down,
Completely oblivious to everyone around.
You let me go, our love to die.
It was so hard to say goodbye.
Now our love, completely dead,
Me still hanging on what you said.
Here I am, all alone.
I just want you to come back home.

Kiersten Ferguson, Grade 8
Ephrata Middle School, PA

Doomsday

Vibrant, cheerful, happy day
The sun's bright, everything's okay
Happiness, joyful, kids at play
Just another wonderful day
After coming home to a sensational sway
Turn on the basketball game, watch the replay
Suddenly, breaking news, everything is gray
Didn't want the reporter to say
An asteroid coming to hit the Earth today
Your happiness is broken like a liquid crystal display
Everybody is in panic, everyone scurries away.
This beast is called Apophis, and it is here to stay
Let's all stop, hope, put our hands together and pray
The flaming ball of fury is in our air, shining a bright ray
The news reported it shedding radioactive decay
Life is flashing before our eyes nothing left to say
Suddenly a bright light leaves us paralyzed, makes us stay
The explosion near the ocean, creates a spray
All of us frightened away
You're up in your bed; it was a dream, HURRAY!
Maybe you shouldn't have watched horror movies all yesterday

Justin Mazzola, Grade 8
Floral Park Memorial High School, NY

Broken

You all are the same
So why am I so different?
I had a heart
A big one, too
A heart that you destroyed
All I wanted was to be your friend
But you rejected me
Now my heart, once so very big
Is now so miserably small
You taunt and mock me in the hall
So when someone reached out to me, I pushed them all away
And now I'm all alone; when someone tried to comfort me,
I tried to make them leave
But they stuck by me and plucked me from the darkness
That had once engulfed my heart
And my world, which was falling down, rebuilt itself again
My heart is still small
My mind is still closed
But now they are being treated
All because someone tried
And finally succeeded

Caia McGee, Grade 7
Pine-Richland Middle School, PA

A Journey

Climbing, climbing
Around each corner
Leaping, leaping
Across each stone
The bubbly water shimmers like jewels
It trickles down the side
Slipping off the edges and forming pools
Cooling daring climbers who had slipped inside
Finally it's time to go
Down to the safe ground below
Most likely the most astonishing place I've been
The magnificent rocks of Catoctin

Danielle Combs, Grade 8
Covenant Life School, MD

A Whole Other World

Everybody dreams
About a life that's unreal
People dream about everything
Some dreams come true, others don't
Everybody wishes that dreams were a reality
But dreams are out of this world
Dreaming is like a whole other life
A life that you can make your own
That's what I call a dream
A place where choices are endless
And where fantasies become reality
A dream
An endless place

Sierra Clinton, Grade 7
Depew Middle School, NY

The End

If the world was ending what would you think about?
Would you spend those last seconds thinking about your family?
Would you spend those last seconds thinking about your faults?
Would you spend those last seconds with your life flashing before your eyes like in all those cheesy movies?
Would you spend those last seconds thinking about what you never did?
Would you spend those last seconds thinking about who you never forgave?
Would you spend those last seconds thinking about the friends you lost that you wish you did not?
A mournful, morbid end
The end is like a new beginning
Good or bad it's still new

Katie Cagle, Grade 7
Westwood Jr/Sr High School, NJ

The Meeting of Good and Evil

The Being told me "I am glad you came."
   I shuddered with fright.
The Being asked me, "Why did you betray me?"
   I trembled and panicked with deep rotting fear.
The Being commanded me, "Go help the needy, those poor in spirit."
   I denied, scolded, and begrudged with ignorance and malevolence.
The Being commanded me, "Redeem yourself by caring for others and the soul of goodness more than yourself."
   I raged, grieved, despised, and disdained with animosity and aversion.
The Being commanded me "Become pure of heart, let your soul shine and illuminate with rapture and justice
rather than darkening and descending into malice and fiendishness."
   I renounced, dreaded, scorned, abhorred, and loathed with insolence, hostility, Satanism, and repugnance.
The Being told me, "Deep down you can be considerate and loving, you can change the evil and nightmares that haunt the good
and peaceful. Transform yourself into an example of hope and sanctity."
   I detested, execrated, infuriated, spurned, quivered, and dismayed with wickedness.
The Being told me, "Instead of power from death, deceit, and darkness you can gain even greater strength from corroborating
with those in need and reigning tranquility and serenity. Do this is my name. Reunite with me in my Kingdom of Heaven, that
is the kingdom of harmony and fondness."
   I contradicted with timidity, iniquity, and disturbance.

Stephen Troiano, Grade 7
Our Lady of Fatima School, NY

Chills and Butterflies

you give me chills. and butterflies too. just by me thinking of you.
the sound of your voice is so sweet. i get lost in your eyes every time they meet.
i feel my nerves taking control of me.
and all i want is for you to hold me.
i know we don't talk as much as i'd like.
but you always seem to be on my mind. maybe i am just blind.
by the fire burning in your eyes.
calling me softly and ever so sweet. the voice that makes my heart skip a beat.
i want to see if this feeling is real. and know truly just how you feel.
is it more than friends. are you here till the end?
or am i alone, waiting for this to end.
you don't know how bad i feel. all of my pain is so real.
my life was blank. until you came along. and decided to change what could've been wrong.
all of my life i waited for this. waited for something worth the risk.
i know you don't see it. but i surely do.
i like you so much. do you feel it too?
all the chills and the butterflies too.
you're giving me whiplash but it's nothing new.

Julie Abraczinskas, Grade 8
Central Columbia Middle School, PA

Broken Stars

She ignites the sky with fire, burning it in the far west
Shining it like a last sign of life for the sun,
Its final battle with the sky as the moon is born.

She cradles the world in her hands.
Her tears carry storms and her smiles bring warmth
As she watches her children grow

She participates in the constant struggle of life
Battling with love and hatred
And the thin thread rests in between.

Whispering sweet words of solitude
She disappears into her shroud of shadows
Fading away into the night sky of broken stars.

Jessica Dunlap, Grade 9
Unami Middle School, PA

Hunting

Hunting is one of the things that I love
It brings peace to me, like a flying dove.
I go whenever I can
Even if it is months away, I always have a plan.

Although I don't get something every time
I keep my mouth shut, I'm a mime.
I like going out for a duck
It's hard to hit one though, you need good luck.

I also like to go for turkey
You can't move though; they're quick to flee.
Sometimes I go out for deer
But they also have a lot of fear.

Hunting season comes and goes
Each with a set of highs and lows.
It seems as nature talks to us
We must listen, it's a must.

If we don't we won't get
We would let
The catch of a century go away.
Now I must go, it's time to play.

Robert Wisniewski, Grade 8
Floral Park Memorial High School, NY

The Homework Machine

Her laptop was on her lap.
She heard a ticking sound then a bell.
She walked up to the huge homework machine.
Her homework was done,
And she was free to hang out with her friends.
"Are you done with your homework?" her mother asked.
"Of course," she said with a huge smile on her face.

Allie DiRocco, Grade 9
Fairfax Collegiate School, VA

Let It Go. Hope Is Here.

In our lives we are faced by critical moments.
Clueless, we are completely lost
Like little children in a city with no guiding angel
Afraid and scared it will leave you,
We sometimes take the wrong path,
The path that leads to failure
We feel small; we hide,
Putting everything behind.
Then we shout, scream for answers.
Through the sunshine, we hope, we dream.
Living in a cycle of life,
Hard moments leave. Hopes bloom to embrace us
We smile, forgetting about the past,
And look forward to tomorrow as painful memories ease.
Fresh start, New Life, Hope, Dream
Our true lives begin starting now.

Jin Kang, Grade 9
Middlesex School, MA

Transition

Green grass
Fallen leaves
Yellow sun.
Fall days

Apple trees
Winter squash
Sunshine lost.

Stagnant water
Frozen ice
Winter here
Summer gone.

Hannah M. Clark, Grade 9
Morgan Math and Science Academy, MD

Mystery…

I know a secret which can hurt many souls
A secret not ordinary,
For you to devour.
Nor can I tell, nor can I stop
It's all waiting there for me to drop,
Time to make some hard-core choices.
Hearts will be broken, tears will be shed,
Next thing I know I'll be the one to regret.
Some will benefit, some will be harmed
I just don't want to get burned.
Who knows what lies ahead,
What a dark secret it is
Engraved in my heart.
Can't stop thinking about it 'til the day I turn to dust
Whatever it is
It's called life.

Irin Begum, Grade 9
Newtown High School, NY

An Easy Two Points

Past the defense
Among a crowd
Toward the goal
Above the rim
Over a defender
Through the hoop
I slam the ball
Back I go
To play defense
And get the ball again.

Avery N. King, Grade 7
Trinity Middle School, PA

Hockey

I skate down the ice
with my stick in my hands
I pass the puck with my team
as we skate end to end

We all cheer, pass,
check, and skate
we shoot the puck
to score a goal maybe eight

We do our best
giving it our all
we skate very fast
trying not to fall

We practice our hardest
from day until night
we all have good sportsmanship
nobody gets into a fight

Hockey is fun
hockey is the best
I love hockey
way better than the rest

Shane Mullin, Grade 7
Trinity Middle School, PA

Stormrise

Electric calm fills the air,
my body, my soul
while the earth awaits its touch
bringing life and love,
death and hate.
A distant power, unpredictable
turning, spinning, roaring.
The Storm:
a wonder, a mystery
a thunderous roll,
a rapid strike of light,
a blackened sheet of rain.

Shannon Farrell, Grade 7
Ocean City Intermediate School, NJ

Secrets

Although sometimes small, a very big emotion is responsible for making them.
That feeling deep inside that something is chosen to be hidden.
Whispers, hands covering mouths, passing glances.
Jealousy, anger, betrayal, love, friendship.
It may stay with someone for a short amount of time or
It may last for years to come.
Those are the most dangerous
Because that small thought, emotion, or fact,
Is deliberately being hidden from another.
Finally, when all is revealed: anger, fear, happiness
Or confusion is the result.
These powerful emotions are always known by someone
They are like a cave's entrance; sometimes hidden or
Sometimes open for all:
Secrets.

Angela Prendergast, Grade 8
Unami Middle School, PA

Poets

I wish I was a poet, with a mind as wide as the sky
With a wit as quick as a cheetah, all the pure truth, none of the lies
Poets seem to know everything about the world around
They can have their head in the clouds, while keeping their feet firmly on the ground.
They are dramatic, spastic, oddballs, containing imaginations that run wild.
Poets are serious, ironic jokers, yet have the heart of a child.
Poets reach beyond expectations, flying beyond all doubt.
You never know why or how, or what they're all about.
Poets are confusing chickens, their minds as great as the sea.
Although their criticism makes sense, you don't see them helping me.
Poets often start out poor and feeble, owning just the clothes on their back,
But once they hit it rich with their poems, their rhymes are something they lack.
But once their fame is over, because their poetry begins to fail,
Their egos are quickly resized, and the poets start again with their wail.
Poets wail for a new beginning. Poets wail for a better end.
They try to fix the world with words. Those words they twist and bend.
I wish I was a poet, with words so extraordinary,
But for now I'll just stay as I am and dream as necessary.

Kathleen Moran, Grade 8
Monsignor Haddad Middle School, MA

Losing a Friend

The things that happened, the memories we shared,
For a quick second I actually believed that you cared.
Obviously not if this is your conclusion,
All I ask is why you left me in so much confusion?
I guess nothing really mattered; it was all just a lie,
Now you've left my heart out to slowly sit and die.
I thought we could make it; it was all so easy to believe,
But it is true now, looks can really deceive.
My heart was all yours, all yours to keep
You were my new beginning, the start I soon would seek.
I guess everything I thought was real came to its final end.
I just didn't know that it would involve losing my very best friend.

Sade Swift, Grade 8
Upper Room Christian School, NY

Always There

Green coats the earthly floors of the world.
She streaks across the top of a white Corvette.
Her beauty stops at the end of a burnt forest,
that was destroyed by red.
Her lovely parents yellow and blue are proud.

She kisses yellow and steps on blue at the middle of ark of love.
Her enemy, red feuds and fights as he burns her.
Green envies her step sister purple for her royal elegance.
After all of her hardships she loves and cares,
and she will always be there.

Ryan Saul, Grade 8
Martin Meylin Middle School, PA

My Good Friend

You sit up there watching me
Silent above the clouds
But never shy my good friend
Always talking to me

Always telling me when you're sad
Sending tears that fall from above
And numerous roars
When you are mad

But let's not forget the joyous days
Which you and I love the most
When you shine that ray of light
On the world I have come to know

But one day I will know a new world
Never quiet above the clouds,
Because I will be talking to my good friend
And whispering secretly down below

David Camero, Grade 7
Garnet Valley Middle School, PA

Summer

Summer is so much fun.
I love to play in the sun.
I go to the beach,
And hopefully I don't get a leech.
Sometimes I will get burned,
I now wear sunscreen, I learned.
Summer is a blast.
It goes very fast.
Summer is hot.
That is why I want a yacht.
Ding ding ding,
The children fling.
Everyone runs to the ice cream truck.
Be careful not to run through muck.
Summer is so much fun.

Grant Hettinger, Grade 8
Christ the Divine Teacher Catholic Academy, PA

Life

One window is all I need to wonder
About the past, about the present, about the future
That's all I need
To succeed, to prevail, to live

One window is all I need to believe
About my calling, about my gifts, about my reason
That's all I need
To understand, to know, to live.

Michael Elia, Grade 7
Anthony Wayne Middle School, NJ

A Day of Snow

The snow, crispy as a burnt marshmallow
Hard underneath
Hard as a horse's hoof,
Hard as a frozen ice cube
Hard, hard as hard can softly be.
The animals wander,
Leaving their every movement
Cemented into the snow.
Crunch! Stomp!
Your foot plops in the snow.
The flying music players
Alert the animals of your presence,
Making them scurry in every direction.
As the sun plays hide-n-seek,
It shows glimpses of the blinding whiteness
Lying on the ground
Slowly melting the wonderland away.

Erika Addison, Grade 7
Christ the Teacher Catholic School, DE

The Game

When I step onto the hardwood
The crowd, the noise, the emotions
They disappear into thin air
When the ball hits my hands
I see nothing but the net
I make one move
Past the first defender here comes the help
And there they go I'm unstoppable
I sore through the air
Like a fish jumping out of water
The rim is closer, closer
Then I feel as if for this one moment
I'm Michael Jordan trying to win the game
As the clock winds down
I reach for the rim
And as I slam it down I awaken
But this dream will stay with me
Until the next time I step onto
The hardwood and play
The game

Derrick Sekuterski, Grade 7
Depew Middle School, NY

The Game

The plate is covered with dirt
The boxes undefined
Cleat marks in the paths
Where the players trudged for nine

The grass is all torn up
The bench is covered with seeds
A single, ball alone
Sitting in the weeds

Not a single person left
The fields are all alone
Not a soul in sight
They've disappeared and gone home

This will be repeated
In a week or two
Another gamed played
One team will win and one will lose
Megan Waleff, Grade 8
Central Dauphin Middle School, PA

Without You

I feel so alone,
My world has no air.
It's because you left me,
And the pain is hard to bear.
It is hard to live without you,
Will I live to see another dawn?
I don't think I can stand it,
Without you it's hard to go on.
Please come back to me,
I need you.
I don't know what I did to deserve this,
To lose you.
I need to have you back,
To keep me going.
It feels like I'm drowning
And everything is going black.
Please come and save me,
Bring my heart back.
Alison Lindsay, Grade 8
Dutchess Day School, NY

iPod

Old school black or white
anything but
stuck in the past —
think of it as
future perfect
and
the winner is
a certain ubiquitous
device
Katelyn Davidson, Grade 9
Mainland Regional High School, NJ

Falling

Sometimes I find myself falling
Even when I'm asleep
And sometimes when I'm dreaming
I know that what I'm seeing
Isn't what's really there
Even when I'm falling.

Falling seems like fun
When you're not the one
Falling from the sky
Falling from up high
Falling from your needs
And all you are is falling.

Falling…
Falling from up high
And all your dreams can fly.
When you fall…
Falling from up high.
Anthony Perugini, Grade 9
Unami Middle School, PA

Loved One

Sitting
    Waiting
        What to do
Shaking
    Tapping
        No new news
My heart races
    And skips a few beats
Sitting
    And wondering
        How he will be

The suspense is so hard
    It goes on and on
Oh please
    Oh please
        Just let him go on
The doctor walks in
    You can tell by the look in his eye

That this is the end
Time to say good-bye…
Deanna Garofalo, Grade 9
Jackson Liberty High School, NJ

Build Life

Life ignites war.
Build life as an all-star,
Untamed speech faces violent content.
Live dreams together.
Memories rely on living.
Bliss Brannon, Grade 9
Unami Middle School, PA

Tornado

I am a tornado
    I twist and turn
Watch me
    Run across the road
        Like an animal
    Running from fear
I cut through your house
    Like a knife through butter
I stomp on the earth
    Harder than a wrecking ball
But when the moon turns
    I run away
Like a roaring freight train
    To a faraway land
Brandon Anderson, Grade 7
Christ the Teacher Catholic School, DE

Dream Freedom

Quiero mañana
When the sun will shine
Where freedom will be mine
Quiero mañana
Where earth hugs my feet
Where the sky cries on my skin
Quiero mañana
Where the sun awakens me
Where the moon kisses me good night
Quiero mañana
O how I dream for tomorrow
Magalie Kalukula, Grade 8
Visitation BVM School, PA

My Life Behind the Surface

My life behind the surface
Is extremely hard to see
My brother chasing after the bees
Right behind the trees
My mother making dinner
And my brother becoming a winner
They are all amazing to me

My life behind the surface
Can be strange, too
With my father down in the dark
Not playing a game
And my brother hiding in his room
With no one knowing what he is doing

My life behind the surface
Can be strange and fun
But hard to see
You might want to make some changes
But if it was up to me,
I wouldn't change a thing.
Jessica Kernan, Grade 7
Trinity Middle School, PA

Feeling Blue

An emotion so excruciating
Not fitting in
Hearing snooty remarks
Seeing people roll their eyes
Straight at your face
People looking at you
As if you "pulled a Charlie Gordon!"
The taste of your tears on your tongue
Running instantly to the bathroom
To pour your heart out
Only to be heard by the eavesdropping sink
Being ignored at lunch
It hurts inside
I feel so mad
I feel so sad
I just want to prove
That I am an amazing and astonishing person
And they deserve to have me as a friend
They deserve to feel blue
To feel the agony of being an outsider
Ouch.

Sneha Iyer, Grade 9
Pine-Richland Middle School, PA

My Cello

I start to play
Beautiful music fills my ears
Music coming from my cello
Every inch of the strings vibrating
Like a thousand little speakers
Projecting sound across the room
Sound, coming from the deep reddish brown body
Sound, coming from the smooth hairs of my bow
My fingers fly across the strings
Unhindered by anything, just flying
Soaring
And then, abruptly, the song ends
I sit there for a moment, pondering
Then I play it again
Joyously
For I can't help but be happy
When playing my cello

Aaron Reckless, Grade 7
Carson Middle School, PA

Mysteries of Life

Life can be full of happiness, joy, misery, pain, or sorrow —
with questions concerning what will happen tomorrow.

I try to fill my days with thoughts of hope and love.
I trust in God's guidance which he gives me from above.

Make the most of life — love, laugh, live, and smile.
Our moments on Earth only last a while.

Jelisa Smith, Grade 8
Mary Mother of Peace Area Catholic School, PA

Chasing

I have never been to the end of a rainbow, have you?
I hear it is impossible, yet I try and try and try
When it is raining and the sun comes out, I wonder
How come they say there is a pot of gold?
I know it is a myth, yet I find it so hard not to believe.
So again I sit there, wondering
I run and run but never catch it
It disappears just as I creep close
It taunts me with its majestic beauty and color
Rainbows are untouchable. Unable to capture
They do not have a beginning or an ending,
Just an arch of color in the sun
I do not wish to find a rainbow's end
Yet somehow I still believe.

Angelina Marie Tiano, Grade 7
Trinity Middle School, PA

The Rhythm of the Water

The rhythm of the water falling from the sky,
Like a drummer in a band,
Patting gently, with little effort, little worries, little care.

And as the water gets louder and heavier,
The drummer taps harder,
But still remains peaceful.

Soon the water starts blaring,
And the drum begins to boom,
And the entire world is filled with sound.

Next the lighting and thunder appear,
And the tireless drummer strikes the drum with great force,
Like a fierce animal strikes its prey.

But then the water calms,
And the drummer returns to his quiet, steady beat,
And the rhythm of the water changes once again.

Sarah Golon, Grade 8
Floral Park Memorial High School, NY

Just Because I'm Skinny!

Just because I'm skinny
I'm not weak
I'm not breakable
Just because I'm skinny
I'm not a loser
I'm not a track runner
I'm not small
Just because I'm skinny
I know I'm not overweight
I can't always be who you want me to be
I'm not a twig
Just because I'm skinny — let me be that way!

Aleksander Koroman, Grade 7
Anthony Wayne Middle School, NJ

A Tree

The roots reach through the soil,
Deep into the ground.
The trunk stands strong and tall,
Making not a sound.
The branches stretch to the sky,
Swaying in the breeze.
The leaves wave all around,
Saying hi to other trees.

Rachel DePalma, Grade 7
Christ the King School, VA

I…

Some say God is light
I say God is darkness
Some say God will save us
I say God never came
God gave us darkness
I created light
God gave us disease
I created Medicine
I created bravery
I created justice
I created faith
I created words
I created love
But

God created I…

Sungwoo Park, Grade 9
Poolesville High School, MD

Lies

Lies
Spreading like wildfire
Burning their victims
Sparing no lives
Lies are a curse
A dream crashing down
A future destroyed
Without common ground

Nothing has changed
Not one single bit.
You're still the same girl
I met in comp. lit.
The one who toyed with fire
Ending up burnt
A scar left by evil
They're for eternity

The past is unchangeable.
The future is unreasonable.
And yet, the present's unbearable.
Lies

Elena Weikel, Grade 7
Garnet Valley Middle School, PA

Hollow Path

Many feet trod heavily down a straight
hollow path toward an ending point unseen.
Until suddenly a fork appears,
causing fear, in judgment to be made.
Some people trudge on left dismayed
while others traipse on right into the haze.
But as for me, paths I see are three,
another cut and dry, between the two,
a mystery beckoning me to find out where it lies.
This path is different from the hollow line
where flowers bloom and sun shines through an overcasting sky.
Others look, if only brief, before they walk on by,
not seeing what I believe, a path hidden from their eyes.
So without them I give a grin, this new path all my own.
On I press, without distress even though I walk alone
for only I may travel by this third path,
a new road, called life without strife.
I call this path my home.

Cole Carlin, Grade 7
Ocean City Intermediate School, NJ

Unnoticed Reality

We all see the petals on the daffodils
Each of them looking as if they were little pills
They're like capsules of life as they brighten each lot
And think, they brighten the world, but are only a little dot

You never know when they will die
Petals just fall off time after time
Yet no one seems to notice until they're totally gone
Still it makes no impact because there will always be another dawn

What if the daffodils were people living lives
Every day more than a few die
Does that even make an impact?
Too bad it's somewhat like a fact

By number it's a statistic
Somebody needs to fix it
Let's open our eyes not just hide in disguise

Bianca Grimshaw, Grade 9
Northeastern Clinton Sr High School, NY

The Prehistoric Giants

As I run away from the stage of fake grass, I see them,
The Prehistoric Giants.
Some were sea dwellers and some soared the skies of blue.
Some ate meat and some ate plants but it made no difference to me.
Their sharp, pointy teeth and spiky tails had me convinced they were real,
But later I learned that the ferocious beasts were merely the work of a genius.
The beast I feared were giant machines covered with fake muscle and rubber,
Programmed to move and roar like real prehistoric giants.
Even thought the prehistoric beasts were proven to be fake,
I never returned for the beasts had struck fear into my soul.

Clayton Moriarty, Grade 7
Trinity Middle School, PA

A Walk in the Park

Walking through the park on a beautiful winter day
Seeing all the kids laugh and play
Everything covered in snow and ice
Makes it look like a pretty sight
Looking at all of the couples talk
As they take their daily walk
Walking through the park on a beautiful winter day

Brandon Mandile, Grade 8
Floral Park Memorial High School, NY

nightingale

the nightingale's sweet call
past the high upon the wall
over the willowing trees
hidden under leaves
enchanting that loving moon
never caring about morning's noon
oh the larks cry comes
and so the nightingale hums
the story of night
left only in starlight
awakening from a dream
lost to the gleam
for a nightingale's song
only to wish to dance along
to be abruptly awakened by the lark's call
to wake and stand tall
and to stare upon the wall
waiting to listen under night's shawl
the nightingale's sweet call.

Nicole Melillo, Grade 9
Monroe Township High School, NJ

Sam

You were only fourteen when they took you away
You said you would never forget that day.
Millions of innocent Jews were killed at any cost
No one can bring back the precious lives that were lost.
You entered a world of hate and sorrow
Praying you would see the light of tomorrow.
You carried a heavy burden upon your back
You worked very hard; you didn't slack.
Your extreme hunger grew more and more each day
As those murderous villains continued their foul play.
They killed your people; that terrible deed can't be undone.
Out of three thousand people in your village,
Only 10 were left; you were one.
Nobody helped you — not because they didn't care
But because they were afraid of the cruel Nazis there.
You are definitely braver than most, but your kind is now few
You touched my soul deeply; your words stuck like glue.
Be proud of the things you have done.
You beat the odds, a million to one.

Maggie Rhamy, Grade 7
Medford Township Memorial Middle School, NJ

Terrorism

Terrorism is like a pen;
You never know when it is going to run out or go away.
Annoying as a wasp,
People are unknown,
Life threatening and hidden,
Evil, and can be so powerful behind our backs,
Bombing, attacking, don't know what.
Osama bin Laden and Al-Qaeda,
So cowardly and they will not show their faces,
We are tired of asking them to stop.
This is the moment of truth. Here we go; we got them!
Finally, we're done with the bombing and attacking.
No more bad stuff and having to worry just walking in the street.
The war is over! Yes!

Jeremy Fowkes, Grade 7
Pine-Richland Middle School, PA

Our Furry Friends in Need

Living in alleyways; nothing to eat but trash
Wishing for a loving family to help
Living in chains that hold firm
Wishing for their rightful freedom
Kicked: wishing they were kissed
Beaten: wishing they were loved
They are treated like dirt
And wish for you to know their pain
Open up your heart to a furry friend
Open up your home to your life's new companion
They are waiting for you to hear their plea
They are the dogs abused every day

Jennifer Lott, Grade 7
Pine-Richland Middle School, PA

The Beauty of Spring

Rain sprayed on the sea of freshly cut grass.
Raindrops fell freely like crystals from a broken glass.

As the moisture seeps rapidly through the coarse dry earth,
Sleeping buds of flowers open up declaring a new birth

The tulips of spring time were awakened by the sound,
While squirrels stayed hidden with the nuts they just found.

Thunder erupted, hidden by covers of clouds in the sky.
It startled the little robins as they prepared themselves to fly.

As the raindrops dissipated slowly from the day,
They left clouds of hazy mist lingering to stay.

The leaves swayed lightly as raindrops coated their backs.
Now, the creatures emerge leaving mud on their tracks.

The beauty of spring isn't hard to miss.
Witnessing it will reward you with a pure, unadulterated bliss

Frecelyn Dela Peña, Grade 8
Floral Park Memorial High School, NY

Eulogy to a Pal

You have been a pal for many years,
You gave me hope,
You filled my soul

You have kept me company through
Michigan,
Florida,
Ohio,
And even Virginia

We picked flowers,
We drew shapes,
We built a leaning tower

You helped when I was lonely,
You helped find new friendships

In your final days you sputtered,
Just give me one last squeeze,
I am lonely without you,
My dear Squeeze Cheese.

Meghan Kaminski, Grade 9
Unami Middle School, PA

Stars

Why do the stars twinkle?
So that if you're lost
You find your way back
Bright little dots high above
Letting your mind find itself
Showing the light back to reality.

Jaclyn Bonlarron, Grade 8
Hauppauge Middle School, NY

June

The days are hot,
The weeks fly by.
School lets out,
And vacations begin.

Thunderstorms roll in
While sweat beads rolls off
Hard working athletes,
And their focused coaches.

The taste of chlorine
Is always in the air,
Beside the wafting smells
Of hamburgers and hot dogs.

Summer just began,
And stress just ended.
No more tests or quizzes,
Just beaches and boardwalks.

John Gote', Grade 8
Martin Meylin Middle School, PA

Thank You

Oh Mom,
Without you in my life would go down like a slope.
But when I look at you I think of hope,
I know I don't tell you how I feel,
But she is the only mom that had the power to heal a broken heart.

When I think of you I think of love.
That is why you are as sweet as a morning dove.
Without you I will fall apart and feel blue,
When all I need is to say the words "I love you."

You are always there for me
If they are good or bad,
You are truly the greatest mother that I ever had.
No one can replace you,
You're smart,
You're talented,
You're kind,
You're sweet.
All the things needed for a nice loving mother.

I also know I may sometimes be a pest,
With all your beauty it's no contest.
That is why I say to you I love you.

Ryan Osborne, Grade 7
Westhampton Beach Middle School, NY

Time Is Limited

Life is like a mountain,
Once you reach the top,
There is nothing left,
The end has arrived.

That is why we shouldn't waste,
The life we have.
Soon it will be gone, and nothing will be left.

Would we want to look back and say,
"My life was great and enjoyable,"
Or with much regret saying, "It was completely horrible?"

There is no one in the world,
Who would waste God's greatest gift,
No one who would think about, wanting to throw it away.

Life can always come back to haunt you
When your time is almost out,
And you will feel like your life was misused, wanting a second chance.

Many people think life is like an endless road,
And that all the time in the world is yours,
But it isn't, and you need to make the best of it.

Matt Montanari, Grade 7
Pine-Richland Middle School, PA

Taliban

Terrorists that show no mercy,
They cannot tell right from wrong or good from bad.
They are hungry lions, who will never stop eating,
Showing no respect for rules,
Or any other beliefs.
Only one way is right — their way.
They cause religious wars, which we know will never end,
Like a fighter who can't throw in the towel.
Everyone else has moved on.
Why can't you give it up?

Zach Skirpan, Grade 7
Pine-Richland Middle School, PA

Ocean

Where the waves crash down, over the rocks
And the boats are still, sitting in their docks,
Where the sky is darkening, yet still a pretty blue,
And land is safety, but in the distance too,
Where the water is colorful, as blue as a dream,
And the ocean is rocking, though still it can seem.
Where the sea is vast, and the shoreline is far,
And the fish are swimming, even the gar.
Where the wind is blowing, stirring the sky,
And the waves are smashing, from very high.
The wind is blowing west, there is a storm approaching near,
And though it's a beautiful place, I am leaving here.

Nicole Sherlock, Grade 7
Whitin Middle School, MA

Alone in the Crowd

Alone in the crowd
Walking through a hallway
Lockers on both sides
People who used to be my friends
Now turn their heads away
Refusing to meet my eye

People who I don't know
Chuckling as I walk by
Laughter in the air
Everywhere I go, every corner I turn
I hear lies, whispers
Deceived by so-called friends

Clusters in ever classroom
Hands cupped around their mouths and ears
Spreading a constant stream of endless gossip
Hurtful words fly at me
Piercing me with their cruelty
And the minute hand moves slower and slower

How can I go back to the way I was?
How can I act the same around these "friends?"
Did I do something wrong?

Deebas Dhar, Grade 7
Carson Middle School, VA

The Momentum

Do you ever get that funny feeling,
The one where everything's passing you by?
Or that you know that your fate is sealing,
But you can't figure out the reason why?
Sometimes the Earth spins a little too fast
And everywhere, it's so quick and stealthy.
I blink and today's already the past,
Leaving so little time to stay healthy.
I know it's silly, maybe even dumb,
But I wish the world could take a breather,
Or pause, block everything out and go numb,
So you and I can watch but feel neither.
We must embrace every moment we live
For we don't know how much it has to give.

Samantha Usman, Grade 9
Fox Chapel Area Sr High School, PA

Time Machine

As I stood before it, wondering if it was a sin.
Choosing which to stay or go, finally I got in.
Not knowing what to expect, I saw images all around.
People, battles, nonsense, but I couldn't hear a sound.
Clank! It stopped, the doors did open wide.
I couldn't see at all, then I got outside.
As I stepped out of the darkness, I was embraced in light.
My eyes soon adjusted, but was it day or night?
The first thing I saw, sent trembling through my knees.
It was a creature ten feet high, let it be friendly, please.
The creature did not harm me, it simply walked away.
Even though it scared me, longer I would stay.
I saw many other things, that did amaze me so.
After I'd had my share, it was time to go.
I did see an amazing sight, there was so much to see.
Yet best of all, no one knew but me.
The doors shut behind me, my trip was so sublime.
I wonder what will happen next, when I go back in time.

Nathan Koehler, Grade 7
Perkiomen Valley Middle School East, PA

Rays of the Sun

The heat of fire grows stronger
until rays extend upon
the cool Earth, creating life.
Plants thrive, animals prosper;
an abundance of life lives
through provided nurturing hands
which nourish, support,
and cherish nature's splendor.
Sinking down into the mountains,
she pulls the blazing waves off the ground,
knowing that her work is done,
only until the next day
when she starts her cycle, again.

Erica Watson, Grade 7
Ocean City Intermediate School, NJ

Makeshift Family

My makeshift siblings.
They are closer than my blood ones.
Maybe because my makeshift family is better loving,
In ways my own blood is not.

They protect me when I'm being teased.
They encourage me in something I slowly understand.
They think I'm the best and can help conquer my worst.
Making me happy when I'm in the dumps and happy go cheery when it's time to Glomp!

They don't mind my normal self.
Like my psychopathic and childish ways.
Because I love them all and
I always want to stay with them all.
No matter what happens I love them because we went through them all.
As my loving makeshift family, who's always there for me
That understands me.

Realitie Vittoria Butler, Grade 7
School of International Studies at Meadowbrook, VA

My Dear Grandfather

My dear grandfather, you are so near and dear. When I was just a few years
I would look up to you, with awe, as if you were a shining star.

My dear grandfather, you are so comforting, warm and safe. Remember when I was just a babe?
I would hold your finger tightly, in my little tiny hand as if it were mine.

My dear grandfather, you are so sweet and kind.
You would hold me when I cried, and kiss away my sadness, always staying by my side until you saw me smile.

My dear grandfather, I'm so thankful you're still alive.
You are the twinkle, the moon, the sun, and even the stars in my brown eyes, so full of wonder, so much like your own.

My dear grandfather, when you walk into the room,
You always "have me at hello," to borrow a line or two from our favorite show. "You complete me," don't you know?

My dear grandfather, I never want to let you go but I know that one day you will have to.
I want you to know that before you do, I will say these words for you: "If you shall die before you wake, I pray the Lord your soul to take."

My dear grandfather, so caring and understanding, you have walked me through my life, and have guided our whole family.
There is still much more to come for me. But when your time comes and your life is done, that's a moment I cannot think about,
When my dear grandfather has finally gone.

Gabrielle Irving, Grade 7
Garnet Valley Middle School, PA

Unlikely Art

A spider works busily all night,
twisting and turning, only working by the moonlight.
The night grows longer and dew forms on the spider's art,
making a finishing touch and an impression that will last forever.
The sun slowly rises, spreading light to all parts of the world and illuminating each tiny strand.
Flowers bloom, time passes and the spider finishes.
A work of art in something so simple.

Zoë Paris, Grade 7
Gananda Middle School, NY

Summer Seas

Rough ocean waves and the calm cool breeze
Giant sand castles and sailing the seas
The beach is the best place to eat a peach
The hot scorching sun is fun when you're young
Bring a beach ball and you will see this is the best season of all
You can run, jump, and slide in the sand
And even watch a band
Don't forget to use sun block
For the suns rays are very hot
The beach is the place I would want to be
Because it is fun for you and me!

Jocelyn Penteck, Grade 8
Floral Park Memorial High School, NY

For You

I fall even deeper in love when I speak with You
I dance for joy when You look at me
My heart moves beneath my chest when You touch me
I need to be with You every waking moment
You are first on my mind in the morning
And last in my thoughts at night
Still yet I dream of Your passion
I sing praises to You
And worship Your most high name
I know You don't expect perfection
Or require this of me
And for that I am grateful
For I would only let You down
I wait for the day when I see You
Long for the hour I meet You
I grow impatient for the second I spread my wings
Am lifted up by heavenly winds
And fly towards the Son.

Lilia Tkach, Grade 8
Maple Point Middle School, PA

The Place That Keeps Me Cool

Emotionless, blown away from the pack,
running away to the place that is safe,
from all the outside world.
This place is peaceful,
computer games to my right,
and a comfy bed to my left.
Trying to forget about the past,
trying to move onward,
to the future.
The false feelings leave,
relaxing my nerves,
the feeling of relaxation engulfs my self-being.
No more anger,
and no more pain.
The train of emotions stops,
and is slowly cooling down.

Brandon Golden, Grade 8
Pine-Richland Middle School, PA

Changing

When I think of changing
I only think about me growing up
and reaching my dreams
which is to play in the NFL.

All dreams can come true if you believe in yourself
When your dreams come true you'll be happy.
Reach for the stars to find your dreams.
When I think of changing I only dream.

I know I can make it I just need to try
I need to work hard and one day
I'll be running out of those dark tunnels onto the field
to do what I love best — that is to play football.

Isaac D. Glendenning, Grade 7
Trinity Middle School, PA

Weekends

After a long week's wait
Thank goodness it never comes late
The weekends
A beginning of a whole new slate.
But first we have a little time to celebrate,
The high things
The low things and sometimes no thing at all.
You see I work at a factory
They say I fit the category
Come in early
Stay too late
But the pay rate is nothing to celebrate
I guess that's why I celebrate the weekends oh so much.
So as I pull the clutch
With one touch the garage door opens
My daily commute is over.
Time to slumber and to contemplate as I stargaze length ways
And width ways as my as day replays over and over again.

Alston Clark, Grade 8
Morgan Math and Science Academy, MD

Soar

Happy moment's happy days
Come to me in cheerful praise.
Love that loves and love that's true.
Do to me as I do to you.

Sunny morning and moonlit nights.
Hold on to this so very tight.
Kindness without a second glance
No more upright figures and backward stances.

Unfold your wings tired from misuse.
Stretch those wings with inner youth.
Fly into the sky the heavens is your limit.
Soar boastfully and gracefully never loose or timid.

Michael Frazier, Grade 8
School Without Walls, NY

Summer Fever

I'm in the classroom
Sitting so sad.
Looking out the window
At the beautiful day.

I see a family of deer
Walking so calmly.
All I can think about
Is being free.

The bell rings
It's finally here.
We all scream
SUMMER.

Trevor Stammel, Grade 8
Central Dauphin Middle School, PA

My Parents

My parents are very responsible.
They are very honorable.
They give me good advice.
They make me tasty rice.
They take good care of me.
Like an apple in a tree.
They tell me to save my money.
And don't spend it on some honey.
They tell me to eat my veggies.
So I won't get a wedgie.
They wanted caring cats.
But I wanted roaming rats.
My parents are very special to me.
They let me be what I want to be.

Basmeh Mohamed, Grade 7
Depew Middle School, NY

Rain

Wishing,
Wanting,
Waiting,
For the rain to freefall from the sky.
Trickling down your beautiful face,
Watching your life fly by.
Tasting,
Feeling,
Seeing,
Your sorrows and regrets lift away.
Into the wells that bring us hope,
Bringing life to a new day.
Crying,
Cheering,
Mourning,
As your memories stop to say,
"That you and yourself and the rain,
Are one! Which you must obey."

Deanna Terrazzini, Grade 7
Ocean City Intermediate School, NJ

Who Am I?

Who am I?
That's always the question you ask yourself.
You always try to figure it out.
Sometimes it doesn't come to you right away.
It happens over a certain period of time.
You would always ask yourself this until you figure it out.
This question may seem simple, but it's very tough once you think about it.
Some people will know it right when they hear it.
Others will look like they know the answer then they don't when they try to answer.
I still don't know the answer to this question.
I hope I will one day.
But, for now I don't know.

Victoria Ost, Grade 7
Floral Park Memorial High School, NY

Trailer

Life is like a 50's movie
There's the black, there's the white, and the gray spots in between
There are things that you know and things you're unsure of
But unlike the movies, happiness is not always in the final scene
If only we were sure of the ending
Life might be a much simpler dream

Like the movies, there are smiles all around
But you never know who to truly trust
The unscripted lives of those unfamiliar smiles
Questioning life is something you must
Hold youth close and let your mind wander
Don't let the faces fool you or your curiosity rust

See in color when you can
Don't think of what you know but what you want to learn
Don't let your life be outlined in the black and white
Rather take those gray spots in your film, don't let the solids return
Take the medium and run with it
Who knows how your life will turn out, that's not my concern

Christine Gamache, Grade 9
Unami Middle School, PA

One Weird Summer Afternoon

One sunny afternoon I was walking down the street,
Listening to music and dancing to the beat,
I saw this little boy singing along,
"Oh hi there," he said, "What a beautiful song."
"How do you know what song I'm listening to?" I asked surprise?
"Well, I could hear it in my heart and I could see it in your eyes,"
"Wow," I jumped, "That's just weird,"
But later things got weirder as came a long a man with a beard,
Then I asked him, "Who's that man that looks real sad?"
"Oh that's my dad and his day has been bad,"
"Come on son we have to go or else we'll miss the bus,"
"Okay dad," the boy said with a fuss,
When I got home my dad said, "Hey how was your day?"
"Oh it was actually kind of fun," I answered, "but in a weird way?"

Sreeja Bapatla, Grade 7
Benjamin Franklin Classical Charter Public School, MA

Yet Again

The sun creeps away on silent feet.
Its color changes from a lemon to an apple.
Blending like a watercolor painting.

Better than a magic show.
Better than Broadway.
Better than a brand new car.
Less and less remains.

A day at the beach is the gold medal of fun,
But watching the day end is better than how it begun.
Silent as sleep, the sunset shines.
The ocean is a mirror reflecting the sun's beauty.

This magical moment happens every day.
Too bad it only lasts for a few seconds,
Which seem like years as the sun falls down the horizon,
But then it ends so fast, so suddenly.

Night arrives as if it's at a party.
The day has gone, the day has passed.
Yet again.

Emilie, Grade 7
Westwood Jr/Sr High School, NJ

The Fears of a Child

A little girl lies there, with no movement, cold in bed.
Monsters creeping around in the house she fears in her head.
The floorboards go CREAK!
Drip, drip…the faucet starts to run.
She yells to her older brother,
"Stop it! This isn't fun!"
The little girl can't call her mom, for she has gone to work.
Now the monsters have more time to lurk.
They hide in your closet and under your bed…
This is the nightmare that all young children dread!

Samantha Malnick, Grade 7
Westwood Jr/Sr High School, NJ

A Look at Love in the Right Eyes

I see the wide eyes of love before me
And inside them I stare at the sorrow
A pain that I shall never wish on thee
Your words once said were hopes for tomorrow
But those hopes are all but a memory
And now my heart is empty and hollow
Thoughts from our past will haunt and torment me
When you said those three small words in a row
You lied unconditionally I decree
At first you deny it but now you know
The real truth inside your black heart for me
I must move on to sunny and yellow
Out of the dark cage and finally free
The eyes I see are bright, and now they show.

Megan McDevitt, Grade 9
Unami Middle School, PA

Spring Time

Birds coming back form the south
The smell of spring fills the air
Children playing outside with their friends
School is almost over for the year
The snow from winter melts from the warm sun
Tulips start to sprout out of the ground
Garden work is starting to be done
People begin to camp in the outdoors
Rain and wind gusts happen
Summer is very close
Mosquitoes arrive out for a long time
Don't think about the bad things
So enjoy spring while it lasts

John Sosnowski, Grade 8
St Stephen's School, NY

Love Is a Myth

I used to think that love was just a myth
Impossible to find
No more than just a kiss
Then the day I saw you
Is when the sky faded to blue
Then I knew, it must be true

Because now I know that love is real
Not a fantasy nor surreal
If you just pay attention and look in my direction
Then you'll see
That love's for you and me

Jayda Hill, Grade 7
School of International Studies at Meadowbrook, VA

I Am Me

I am me, just me, and nothing can change that
I am said to wear my heart on my sleeve
I am a perfectionist, always wanting things to be right
Bright is something that isn't always me,
I am not stupid, I just have my off days.
I tend to get paranoid easily, but that is just me.
I hate seeing people sad or mad,
I would much rather them be glad!

I constantly wonder about the "unknown"
Always curious about everything, but that is just me.
I am a believer but I'm not easily fooled,
I think of myself as a caring person, neither mean or cruel,
I may seem a little quiet to you,
but I promise when you get to know me I will probably be
one of the most outspoken people you will ever meet.

You don't have to like me,
but this one thing I will say to you
I am me, and no one can change that, not even you!

Baylie Ann Swart, Grade 7
Trinity Middle School, PA

The Lamborghini

The Lamborghini was great;
it used to be first rate.
But the gears had a glitch,
I drove in a ditch,
and now it is something I hate.

Max Stauffer, Grade 8
Ephrata Middle School, PA

Love

a giant elephant
that is rough
to the touch
changes your life
right in front of you

a sour piece of candy
goes from
sour to sweet
sticks to your teeth

a light switch
turn it ON
happy, bright
turn it OFF
dark, sad

yellow
like a lemon
bright, exciting
shines like the sun
so everyone
can see it

Bridget Smith, Grade 7
Jamesville-Dewitt Middle School, NY

Beach Babe

Chillin' at the pool.
In my sunglasses,
Lookin' so cool.
Swimming with my family.
Eating snacks,
And having laughs.
Getting thrown in the pool,
Flying through the air,
I look like I don't even care.
Splash!
Water fights with my sister,
Wishin' I didn't kick 'er.
Getting sunburn was a bummer,
But I got to swim in the summer.
Leaving was a drag,
But I'm not gonna brag
'Cause my summer
Wasn't that big of a bummer.

Brooke VanDenBogart, Grade 7
New Egypt Middle School, NJ

Into the Night*

I creep out of bed for tonight
Past the window of fading light
Past the kitchen in the dark
It is there I begin my flight

Out the door and into the cold
I sit and watch the sun grow old
As all light in the house is out
I watch night and let it unfold

My teddy bear must think it queer
To have not one fluffy bed near.
His glassy eyes hold a protest
But he does not show sings of fear

The stars are bright and comforting,
But I choose to go on my wing,
For I must fly before I sing,
For I must fly before I sing.

Freddy Levenson, Grade 7
Rippowam Cisqua School, NY
*Inspired by "Stopping by Woods on a
Snowy Evening" by Robert Frost

March

March blows though the door
Snow starts to melt
As flowers start to grow
Celebrations of birthday
And the luck of the Irish start to flow
March leaves blowing out 42 candles

Rachel Lynch, Grade 7
Garnet Valley Middle School, PA

The Shadow of Light

The dark is unknown
Impossible to see
Inescapable, deathly shadows
Horrors that rest inside of me

Stars go out,
But the darkness lasts
When the lights fall away
Shadow remains

The light is protection
A shield against evil
Indisguisable, bright clarity
Hopes that rest inside of all

Stars go out,
But they never die
A candle lights
Even the darkest shadows

Austin Hong, Grade 7
Anthony Wayne Middle School, NJ

Love

Love is a cloud floating by
It can be plentiful
It can be dry
It's beauty is great
It's power is strong
It keeps you distracted
All day long
Only some feel it
A feeling so grand
The feeling you feel
Seems like warm, soft sand
Love, love can save
Love can heal
Love can make your heart start to peel
Thump, thump goes your heart
When the love begins to start

Christina Robinson, Grade 7
St Hilary of Poitiers School, PA

My Loving Dog

Dear Gordo, you have been a good dog.
Well, to me you're a human,
but to people you're a dog.
You have been like my brother,
my son;
but you're my dog.

Rafael Mendez, Grade 7
Life Academy, PA

Tree

You gather my thoughts,
Like the leaves on your branches.
You lift my soul,
Like the water in your roots.

You emerge with your silent colors,
And display life's diversity.
You stand tall after a storm,
And demonstrate your strength.

You are a shelter,
For tiny, feeble orphans
You are a window,
To one's past and future.

You taste of silence,
And you smell of magnificence.
You feel of grace,
And you look of tranquility.

You observe everything,
But do nothing.
You affirm life's magic,
But without a word.

Abhishek Chaturvedi, Grade 8
Thomas W Pyle Middle School, MD

Ice Skating

Whipping, slipping, and spinning.
The moves are precise and stunning.
And my competitors tough and surprising.

The ice is white, cold, and frozen.
I hit the cold ground hard,
Only to get back up again.

Singles, doubles, triples.
I land my spins and twists.
And show off my moves to the judges.

From all the sacrifices, hard work, and pain.
They only leave me in suspense.
And leave me curious.

After all this waiting.
After all I've gone through.
I make it into second place.

Dorothy Hurtle, Grade 7
Selden Middle School, NY

Farewell

Rain cascades onto my eye,
Down to my perfectly curled lash,
Masquerading my every tear,
Intensely, but gradually deepening
As I swam into the depths of my thoughts.

If you must know my excruciating pain,
But I simply detest to say it again.
My delicate heart turned desolate in the blink of my eye,
That's all I have to say but I let out a discontent sigh.

Goodbye my lover, my only true friend,
Hope we get to see each other prior the solitary end.

That's all I will tell,
All you will know,
There's one last thing to say,
Farewell.

Denee Oliver, Grade 7
Westwood Jr/Sr High School, NJ

The Summer

Endless blue skies
hot blazing sun.

Warm humid nights
summer's just begun.

People swim in the sun
they have so much fun.

Luke DeCello, Grade 7
Our Lady of Grace Elementary School, PA

Beauty

To most people,
Beauty is perfectly toned muscles,
Or flowing waves of hair.

To most people,
Beauty is like a radiant face,
Or as a songbird sings.

To most people,
Beauty is an "ooh," an "ahh,"
Or a quick "uhh!" of breath.

Beauty really is,
The crash of waves on a sandy beach,
The light of a full moon on a cloudless night.
The first bright, shining light of dawn.
Beauty is love at first sight.

Paul Antonick, Grade 7
Westwood Jr/Sr High School, NJ

Painful to Realize

Sleeping like an angel
With his innocent eyes
Going back to childhood memories
When life was good

He knows the situation he is in
And he tries to help
But people mistake his actions
And turn the table around

Even though he tries so hard
They succeed at bringing him down
Like a picture on the wall
But as he dreams he goes back in life

As he pushed his sisters on the swings
Laughed and hugged his mom
Tears streamed down his cheek
As he wakes and realizes

It was just a dream

Danielle Rodgers, Grade 7
School of International Studies at Meadowbrook, VA

Football

F eet scrambling to get away from defenders.
O ffense driving the ball down the field.
O ffensive line knocking the defense off their feet.
T remendous catch on 4th down saves the drive.
B all whizzing through the air.
A ll eleven players working together as one.
L ed by the quarterback, the
L ubricious offense scores a touchdown.

Michael Kaplan, Grade 7
Unami Middle School, PA

Despair

Love is unfair
Something that the mind cannot bear
And the heart always left in despair
I gave my all to you
And all my dreams did not come true
Just like Eris and Dysomnia
Our hearts are broken in two
I loved you
My eyes could not come off of you
This is my disease
My infection
My loss
The person I left in you

Gaston Touafek, Grade 8
Monsignor Haddad Middle School, MA

My Dogs

Bailey
Cute, furry
Amusing, exciting, caring
Always wants to cuddle
My dog

Maxine
Bashful, timid
Caring, charming, appealing
Barks way too much
My other dog

Zach Manuszewski, Grade 8
St Stephen's School, NY

Sun and Moon

Sun into moon
Dark into light
The day is moving swiftly
From morning to night.

Kaylee Kilkenny, Grade 7
St Hilary of Poitiers School, PA

Stranger

There's a stranger looking back at me.
Who is this girl?
And why does she look so much like me?
She copy's my every movement
I wave she waves
I dance she dances the same way.
She's extremely familiar
But I can't put my hand on it.
I think about it for a second
Oh no!
This stranger is me!
What have I become?
This isn't me
Is it?

Kiana Mitchell, Grade 9
Woodbridge Sr High School, VA

The Feather Falling War

I saw a feather fall — when I bashed the pillow over her head —
The Egyptian cotton covering the pillow — had a nice feeling —
"BANG!" she got me right in the face —
Then I saw a feather fall —

I knocked him over with my pillow —
Then smacked him with the pillow until I saw a feather fall —
The feather fell like a maple samara seed falling from a tree —
Trying to catch it would be impossible — it goes its own ways —

If you look around — all you see is feathers —
Feathers — feathers — feathers — feathers everywhere —
Sit down and you'll feel like you're on a cloud —
Floating away to an amazing place where rain is falling feathers —

Sophie Anthony, Grade 8
Hoboken Charter School, NJ

I Don't Understand

I don't understand why the world is the way it is,
So many questions fill my head every time.
Few answered, many not figured out yet.
I mean what is everyone fussing about?
I don't understand why bad things can happen to good people.
But, great things can happen to the bad people.
I guess that's the way things are…plain and simple.
I don't understand why kids can be the ones who get
The after affects of their parents' stupidity.
It's all such a pity.
I don't understand why there are wars.
Why can't we all make love and peace?
If there are two roads to choose from, why does everyone take the same?
Why can't someone stand up once, and make a change?
I guess I don't understand a lot of things about the way the world is today.
So maybe I will never figure it all out or someday I will.
Either way, everything happens for a reason; good or bad.
I'll have to wait to find out.

Jamie Nichole Satryan, Grade 7
Trinity Middle School, PA

Writer's Block

Sitting at my desk, scratching my head with my thumb,
Not knowing what to write, my brain seems to be numb,
Tapping my pencil wildly, this is harder than I thought,
I could write about anything, I could write about a lot,
Maybe about friendship, love, or problems I face,
Or about animals, beauties of nature, or maybe even space,
But, those all seem normal, I want something out of the box,
What about going green, the weather, or types of rocks,
Good poems don't just come out of thin air,
It takes constant thinking, and then your ideas will just be there,
It just dawned on me, I know what I am going to write,
I'll write about my writer's block, though I thought with all my might.

Rebecca Grube, Grade 9
Cocalico Sr High School, PA

Back Flip

The heat from the sun on my cherry face
The big mountainous object sits on the ground.
There is no more turning back at this pace,
Sneaking on quietly without a sound.

Now soaring steep and high in the blue sky.
The familiar sound of the whining springs.
The laws of physics I hope to defy.
Off in the distance a bluebird sings.

Building up courage for an awesome feat
Quitting now would be such a giant fail.
Landing a back flip would be such a treat.
I go for the trick but do not prevail.

Practice makes perfect, so I will still try
To be jumping so high free in the sky.

Zach Schug, Grade 9
Unami Middle School, PA

The Wind Blows

The wind is whistling
Wind is like a person blowing air
It blows branches and leaves
Like a tornado blows away houses and cars
The wind flies kites
Wind can make a hot day feel good
And that is how the wind blows

Joshua Halsey, Grade 7
Norview Middle School, VA

I Am Perfect, Just Not to You

Perfection seems so important,
It's something that you can't let go.
Look at me through my eyes,
I want to show you what I know.

When I first met you,
It didn't matter to me.
You kept insisting I looked great,
But things became worse, and I started losing faith.

You tried to make me perfect.
But you missed something big,
Look through your notes,
Go ahead and dig.

I'm already perfect, just the way I am!
The little things make me perfect, because I'm me,
And I'm not someone you want me to be!
I may not look perfect to you…sometimes not even to me…

But at least when I look in the mirror,
I can see myself perfectly.

Ashley Danseglio, Grade 8
Hicksville Middle School, NY

Summer

Children playing games.
Hear lawn mowers on the grass.
Summer is so great.

Jacob Kusajtys, Grade 7
Our Lady of Grace Elementary School, PA

Ode to the Hare

You can see it bouncing from afar,
It can be dark as the night or light as a star.
It can be so soft, you'll want to touch,
The care that it needs is very much.
It can grow to be very short or long,
Loving it is never wrong.
There can be many different types,
Some rare ones even have some stripes.
It can be as pretty as can be,
Or aggravating, I guarantee.
It's pretty popular overall,
Except for the few it doesn't enthrall.

Maybe you thought I was talking about a bunny,
That strikes me as very funny,
Because that is not the story I was telling,
Maybe next time I should check my spelling.
You may not have been aware,
But I was actually writing about human hair.

Megan Cohen, Grade 7
Rachel Carson Middle School, VA

Deck

My big brother Ryan is building a deck
Don't know if its stable, or if it's a wreck

Table saw, power drill, he loves these big toys
Ryan and Justin make plenty of noise

They assemble the railing and trim work galore
What's the point of a railing if you fall through the floor?

Old deck boards are shaking, with stairs not quite true,
The family is quaking as they tip toe right through

Their project is slowing, more screws tame the wood
In hopes that the decking turns out to be good

For graduation parties and summer fun,
The date is approaching, Ryan's under the gun

They complete the new deck with hours to spare,
The guests are arriving with potluck to share

Ryan and Justin breathe a sigh of relief,
The deck is complete without too much grief.

Garrett Schweiker, Grade 7
Rachel Carson Middle School, VA

Terrorism

Terrorism is a big problem,
Especially to those it has affected most,
Like September 11 for example.
Terrorists are like assassins in the night,
Sneaky and hard to track.
I don't know how they do it,
Or from where,
But I do know they do it for no reason.
That much is certain.
I hope that Osama is alive,
So that we can capture and bring him to justice.
This isn't a war;
It is like a hunt.

Nick Trombola, Grade 7
Pine-Richland Middle School, PA

Slavery

Slavery, Slavery fighting to stay alive
Slavery, Slavery I've been working ever since I was 9
Slavery, Slavery I'm tired and scared
Slavery, Slavery my owner use to care
Slavery, Slavery my church was burned down
Slavery, Slavery I don't feel any better now
Slavery, Slavery I need to run away
Slavery, Slavery All I can do is pray
Slavery, Slavery Harriet lead me on the right path
Slavery, Slavery how long will this last
Slavery, Slavery

It's just because I'm black
Slavery, Slavery

No!!!!! No!!!!!! I want my freedom back

Niaya Greene, Grade 7
Samuel Ogle Middle School, MD

Museum

How amusing
To be
A painting
New faces every day
Gazing at you with awe
With strained understanding
Maybe, though, it would become frustrating
Not moving
Not speaking
Not breathing
Not explaining
Maybe it is better still
To be able to move at will…
How amusing
To be
A viewer.

Natasha Voake, Grade 7
Lycée Français de New York, NY

Animal Abuse

Animal abuse is a terrible thing to do
It makes animals less likely to trust humans
Animals are living creatures,
And deserve to live on this planet, too
For most people animals are a life changing thing,
While for some people they are just like another wasted space.
Animals' feelings count, too,
Though they are smaller than us,
Doesn't give us the right to hurt them,
Animals are hurt,
But if one of us takes one in,
Care for it and love,
It will become your best friend.

Ashley Augustine, Grade 7
Pine-Richland Middle School, PA

Peace

Peace is what makes the doves fly in the air.
Peace is when people sleep without being scared.
Peace is the war coming to an end.
Peace is no matter what country their from,
You call them friend.
Peace is coming together as one.
Peace is why God calls you to come.
Peace is the calling of the Lord
Peace is what comes from the core.
Peace is the word that is #1
Peace is the word that says we can have fun.
We all come together when peace comes around,
And we are all grateful for it.
We all love peace and that's a fact
Even in the bad times we all love peace.
Peace is a wonderful thing; that's for sure
Everyone loves each other because of peace.

Paul Altenbaugh, Grade 7
Christ the Divine Teacher Catholic Academy, PA

Video Games

Some are fun,
Some boring, and some make me angry.
I love playing online.
It helps me make new friends.
Talk to ones I already know.
And I know who is the best player.
I am better than my brothers,
Only in some games.
It helps me be better,
To have better reactions,
And my finger strength.
That's what I say,
But my mom says it's bad for me.
It actually can make me intelligent.
Some boy took an airplane up in the air for ten minutes.
Then he landed on the ground all from playing a video game.

Thadeus Pawlikowski, Grade 7
Christ the Divine Teacher Catholic Academy, PA

Count Down

6 hours a day, 180 days a year
Finally, 180th day is here

TICK TOCK TICK TOCK

We count down the hours
Because, when that bell rings, we have the POWER!

TICK TOCK TICK TOCK

Another minute passed,
Why can't that clock move super fast?

TICK TOCK TICK TOCK

The bell had rung,
We all jump while our papers are flung

The school year is done,
And now it's time for summer fun!

Tess Rivera, Grade 7
Hammarskjold Middle School, NJ

Just Because

Just because I'm shy
Doesn't mean I have nothing to say
Doesn't mean I don't have any friends.

Just because I'm shy
Doesn't mean I hide in the corner
Doesn't mean I'm always alone.

Just because I'm shy
Doesn't mean I blend in with the wallpaper
Doesn't mean I can't stand out.

Just because I'm shy
Please don't ignore me.
Mackenzie Faber, Grade 7
Anthony Wayne Middle School, NJ

That Child in the Devil's Mouth

I can't bear to see my people go.
I can't live without them because I am not complete.
What will happen to me?
My God said be strong but I don't see His work to help us.
I wonder why I am here standing with all these tears.
What have I done to be in the Devil's mouth?
But my people still stand strong.
In this vague place of killing.
Will this be the end of my people and me?
Is this number representing me J038153?
NOOOO because I am still here no matter what they do to me.
Phillip Mack, Grade 7
School of International Studies at Meadowbrook, VA

A Hero in Many Ways

My Uncle Graham is as old as the Earth.
Golf is his sport, but I think he
considers teasing me a sport.
A veteran of firefighting and Vietnam,
Uncle Graham probably thinks the
U.S. military should give him a
Medal of Honor for putting up with me.
He is always there when I want
to talk to him
Unless the Pittsburgh penguins are playing.
Then it is "This better be important!"
I will never forget him saying "ey bud" to me;
it's as famous as "I had a dream."
He's a hero of fire and Vietnam
But most of all,
he is my hero.

James Leasure, Grade 7
Trinity Middle School, PA

Please Don't Let Me Die

I'm sorry for all the times
I've disappointed you and for all the times
I've made mistakes and didn't come through for you
I know as the world is turning you want to keep learning.
I know I can't go back and fix this, but when you read this
I hope you'll remember the good times just like Christmas.
I know you might hate me now but that's just because,
I don't know how to tell you what I'm feeling now.
I hope you can read this and forget the past
Because if you don't love me my life won't last.
Alyssa Mannery, Grade 7
Galloway Township Middle School, NJ

One Voice Can Make a Difference

One voice can make a difference
Drastic or small
Complex or dull
One voice can make a difference.
One word could slay a being
One word could make them cry
One word could aid their seeing
One word could make them wonder why.
One voice can make a difference
Drastic or small
Complex or dull
One voice can make a difference.
One word could make one snicker
One word could make them grin
One word could help them not to bicker
One word could help them not to sin.
One voice can make a difference
Drastic or small
Complex or dull
One voice can make a difference.

Alex Shockley, Grade 7
Snow Hill Middle School, MD

the rain falls

across the sky
between the trees
over your head
under the clouds
throughout the air
against your body
outside your house
below the thunder
beyond the mountains
underneath your feet
onto the leaves
past your heart
to your arms
upon your breath and
within the dirt of the ground,
the rain
falls.

Christina Hender, Grade 7
Medway Middle School, MA

Wind

The wind howls on the earth.
It makes a good breeze.
It's very strong.
It blows the leaves off the trees.

Sydney Diaz, Grade 7
St Agatha School, NY

Two Summers Ago

I met a girl.
She was awesome.
She was beautiful like a blossom.
I asked her to dance.
She didn't reject me.
We danced until the party was over.
I'm sad because the night is over.

George Perruzzi, Grade 8
Monsignor Haddad Middle School, MA

The Ocean

Giant waves from the deepest oceans
Wouldn't keep us apart

For we'd cling to each other
And never let go

Our hearts would become one
With harmony and peace

Forever to rest
In the blue ocean's deep

Where nothing is wrong
And emotions could breathe

Ashley Eng, Grade 8
Schaghticoke Middle School, CT

What If My Name Were 'Rose'?

such a sweet thing, a Rose —
its perfume lingers
intriguing and so familiar
its soft petals
appealing and delicate.

you can look
but you can't touch:
the ethereal beauty that stands
defiant to your needs
and yet beckoning to you:
its sickly sweet scent —
alluring and tormenting.

petals begging to be touched,
dewdrops adorn its crown,
the wafting fragrance draws you in…
and the thorns shall pierce your skin!
and the point will drink your blood!
pretty on the outside,
devious by nature.
such a sweet thing, a Rose —
my name.

Annie Qiu, Grade 9
The Bronx High School of Science, NY

summertime

running and playing
splashing at the pool with friends
the smell of summer air

Nick Earhart, Grade 8
Ephrata Middle School, PA

Caterpillar

The very hungry caterpillar
Grew and grew and grew
He was green all over
With a big red face too
With fur all around him
And these six legs to move
His two purple ears
Kept him alert for his food
But when it came to eating
His appetite grew
With the longest body
To full and full and full
So when it came to night time
It would be very dark
His two very green eyes
Could keep him seeing very bright
And when it was bed time
His stomach all set
For this very hungry caterpillar
To feast the next day

Katie MacDonnell, Grade 7
Whitin Middle School, MA

Never Forget

Never forget the things that,
Truly mean the most.
Because even the littlest of things,
Have the most significant meaning,
From a laugh to a smile,
Flowers blooming in the spring,
The beat of a butterfly's wing,
The stream of light,
That comes in through your window,
When you first wake up in the morning.
Never forget,
What truly means the most,
Because the littlest of things,
Are often forgotten.

Brooke Schonbachler, Grade 8
Pine-Richland Middle School, PA

Fun!

There's a party
That's fun
And I'm going to run
Because I'm number one

People are dancing
And they're having fun
So fun, so fun
Really having fun

It does not matter what shape or size
Just that you're having fun
Dancing in the sun
While having fun

Katie Cota, Grade 7
Whitin Middle School, MA

Cancer

Cancer.
Not everyone has it,
Nobody wants it,
But we all have to deal with it.
Though karma it might be,
It still is a trouble to your family.
The young and the old,
The dads and the moms,
With their horrified children.
Even innocent children,
With their horrified parents.
As they watch their hair depleting,
The state of being sick,
Evolves to the state of being dead.
And once you think it's all over,
From the survivors and the dead,
The next thing you know,
It starts all over again.

Jenna Colasante, Grade 8
Floral Park Memorial High School, NY

What the World Could Be

I want to hear the whole world singing
just forget about who might fall,
and all the flings and scattered things
that don't mean a thing at all.

I want to see the nations dance,
overlook all the fear and blame,
and look to the sky as they frolic and fly
the world would never be the same.

I want to hear the kingdoms play
songs of happiness and joy,
cooperate as they find their fate
sounds never do annoy.

But I'll probably never meet this dream
halfway, or for that matter, at all,
for we're much to caught up in our own little worlds
to look around and hear nature's call.

Michelle Kuhn, Grade 7
Cedar Lee Middle School, VA

Nature

The sun says hello in the summer
The breeze brushes up against me
Bugs beg me for food
Clouds hang over to protect me
Trees hum when the wind blows
Grass has different moods, that's why it changes color
Bushes are lazy, that's why they don't move
Ants go marching one by one

Shi`Anne Parsons, Grade 7
School of International Studies at Meadowbrook, VA

Being Me

Sometimes I want to be someone that I'm not
Like James Bond or Michael Phelps
But I'm not Bond or Phelps
James Bond drives cool cars and travels the world
While I stay home wondering
What's my place in the world
Bond does what he wants, but
I have to follow my parents' rules
Michael Phelps gets millions and millions of dollars a day
While I clean the house and mow the lawn for nothing
Phelps has fun and parties with no worries
I play my box at home with some worries
No, I'm not Bond, James Bond or Michael Phelps
I sure don't have cool cars or millions of dollars
I'm just plain ole me
Nothing cool
Nothing special, and
I am just fine
With being me.

Ben Soyka, Grade 8
Beacon Middle School, DE

Gold

Gold is like the crisp leaves,
Swaying and singing with the breeze.

Gold is like the sun, hanging in the sky,
So bright and luminous, yet up so high.

"Gold is something that cannot stay,"
Is what Robert Frost wrote down one day.

Gold is like a shining ring,
Catching light on everything.

Gold is like a shooting star,
Seems in such a hurry, just like a speeding car.

Gold is like a summer's night,
So warm and blinding, even though it's night.

Delaney Leonard, Grade 7
Sanford School, DE

The Flower That Died

I saw the petals fall —
While I lay in my opened casket —
Everyone's clothing is as black as the petals —
There were more petals than how many years I lived —

Everyone around me sniffles and cries —
Like I did when my mom died —
The room is filled with sadness and tears —
But at least I lived a good life

My life has ended and so has the flower's —
If I could change my life I wouldn't —
Life had been but now it is time for me to go —
Maybe I will see the flower in Heaven.

Lisette Melendez, Grade 8
Hoboken Charter School, NJ

Gray Area

Are we that gray area?
The ones that fall in between,
The ones that always can't be seen.

Are we the ones who straddle a line
And obey almost all the time?
That don't really get a say,
But only told to study and play.

Are we the middle ground,
The ones who love to horse around?

So is our generation denied our choice?
So let's stand together and raise our voice.

Alina Munoz, Grade 7
St Joseph Hill Academy, NY

I Am a Memory

I am the Rainforest;
I wonder if I will still be able to hear the calls of the birds years from now.
I hear my canopy swaying to the sounds of the wind.
I want to go back to a time when you could listen,
relax without hearing the blaring horns and seeing the lit-up buildings of civilization.
I see the new generations after generations living in my branches as their ancestors did before them.
I am the Rainforest.
I pretend that I am surrounded by, enveloped by, a sense of calm, not calamity.
I say goodbye to my lost limbs as they are cut away, taken away to serve man and "progress."
I worry about my future, your future.
I was the Rainforest, a lost concept, a vague memory.

Emily Reiling, Grade 7
Pine-Richland Middle School, PA

Music

It is what makes you move, the rhythms and beats that shape a line, or a piece
The mood or tone that vibrates a single string
To create chords and then a phrase

It is a language, written all over your head and inside your mind. The words in this language,
Float in the air and wrap around you expanding in all directions.
Each sentence conveys a question, and then the next answers the call.

Your ears grab the sound into your head when it plays.
It could be as simple as just two notes, or as complex as a whole symphony of sounds.
Music is a way of life, part of a culture
Music is art.

Cynthia Guo, Grade 7
Carson Middle School, VA

America's Dream

I dream of a world
Where there is no war on Earth,
Where the deaths of soldiers will stop,
And where arguments will end.
Why don't we talk it out?

Why is it we treat others different for no rhyme or reason?
It doesn't matter what shade you are,
We all have hearts pumping,
That all need some lovin'.
Let's get to know one another.

Why don't we all spare a dime?
To help the unwealthy.
Some starve, some freeze, some can't catch a breeze,
They aren't strong or healthy.
Let's give them some strength and make sure they're not filthy.

America dreams for no lonely souls,
Nobody who is feeling down with a frown or mad and feeling sad,
Everybody needs a buddy to be funny,
So pick one to share your love and laughter.
We are the American Dream; let's stand up for what's right and never be staggered with fright.

Eddie Keenan, Grade 7
Ocean City Intermediate School, NJ

Where's My Aglet

I look to my shoelace, the end is frayed,
I wonder, where is my plastic aide?
Without it, my shoe is incomplete.
Quite a nuisance whilst I'm walking on the street,
A trouble when tying my shoelace,
And difficulty in a race.
Without it my shoelace would surely rip.
But what is the NAME of the plastic tip?

The end of the shoelace must be widely unknown,
But very vital as now it is shown,
Oh, what could it be, that little piece there,
Leaving my shoelace like tangled hair?
It keeps my knot together, at the bus stop,
And saves me the trouble, of holding the lace top.
But now the end is free to get dirty, free to get wet,
Ah I knew SOMEONE told me the name…aglet!

Eric Lim, Grade 7
Carson Middle School, VA

Land of the Free

When you see an American flag sway,
Most people shout, "Hurrah, Hooray!"

For the American flag is a sign of freedom,
Something that we have won.

In a great battle many years ago,
Where we had dealt the British a mighty blow.

And so some may not believe,
What this country can achieve.

Well, we can prove to them,
That we're proud to be American.

Zach Benson, Grade 7
Hammarskjold Middle School, NJ

The Beach

I love chilling at the beach
Then I get hungry and eat a peach
The sun beats down on my face
These are memories I cannot erase
This is a part of summer that I would love to save
The sounds and feeling of hitting a wave
Boats and jet-skis fly right by
The seagulls always try to be sly
The hot sand covers my toes
I really hope I don't burn my nose
Big sunglasses and a cold drink
Chilling on the beach can really help me think
I do not want to return to school
The summer at the beach was really cool

Catherine Fayer, Grade 9
Unami Middle School, PA

Michaella

We've seen the years pass by
And I know you have always been by my side
Between our laughter and our tears
You helped me face my biggest fears.

We've gotten so much older
Yet I still remember all the memories we've had together
As I look back to where we first met
I think about our very first bet
And I hear our tiny voices trying to be tough.

We became best friends
And I know our story will never
Come to an end.

Sandy Restrepo, Grade 7
Westwood Jr/Sr High School, NJ

In the Spotlight

Silence, except for that whispered purring
The lights come on, humming and whirring
I'm blind as a bat, but my eyes adjust
It's time to shine or bite the dust
I open my mouth to find it's dry
So suddenly, I'm very shy
But then I remember, this I love
The lights glare down from up above
They shine brighter than before
Capturing this moment I adore
I start singing, speaking, acting
And the audience starts clapping
And oh my gosh, how good it feels
I can't believe that this is real
I am in the spotlight
It'll happen again, maybe tonight

Hanna Alvesteffer, Grade 8
Our Lady of Mount Carmel School, VA

Real or Fake?

Friends. Pick them, choose them.
The question is: are they real?
Are they fake?
Would they blame you for their mistakes? (No!)
Go and find them out.
Go and see what they're about!
Do they do good things?
Do they do bad? Are they real?
Or are they fake? Go!
Find them out. Pick them, choose them,
See what they're about.
When you do, will you keep them?
Will you end with them?
Before you act, ask yourself:
Are they real or fake?
It's your choice you have to make.

Lanesa Cumberbatch, Grade 7
Life Academy, PA

Unseen Fish

Swimming casually
Through the water looking for food
Among the seaweed
Into a school of minnows
Between great boulders
Beside a fisherman's lure
Around the hook
Back into the depths
The fish swam
Unseen

Zachary E. Harris, Grade 7
Trinity Middle School, PA

Rocks

So silent and still,
Not moving, not speaking,
But seeing, with eyes unseen.
Watching history unfold.
Watching, people and places and things,
Grow and prosper, grieve and die.
All these thing it has seen,
Since the beginning of time,
And all these thing it will see again,
Until the end of time.

Maura Fisher, Grade 8
Indian Valley Middle School, PA

Luna

I watched the light
sift through the
darkness.

I wanted to touch it,
feel its precision.

I covered the light
with my finger.
The sky was completely
dark.

I suddenly longed for
the light,
its contrast with
the night sky
was all I needed.

I coaxed my finger from
its spot,
now settling next to my thumb.

There it was;
there I was,
basking in its
glow.

Flavia Martinez, Grade 7
Ocean City Intermediate School, NJ

Blinded

Tick   Tick
Life's seconds slowly depart; never to be seen again
Tick   Tick
I sit; mounted on this wall
I watch days, months, years whiz by like dry leaves, blown in the crisp autumn wind
Moments come and go; such is the way of life
Students sit below me I watch their lives progress
They come they test they worry they laugh they read they write they go
I know; for I watch it all unfold from my place above the door
I count the moments as they fly by
Tick   Tick
How I wish I could speak! To tell all below me how very precious time is
By my hands you see it pass and yet you still don't see: time is never reclaimed
You continue to worry; cliques, designer names, popularity
You never seem to notice each priceless instant as it deserts the world
You let the superficial blanket truth
Spend your time wisely, chase dreams, love, adventures
I would if I could; but I am bolted here, fastened securely to this wall
So I stay to forever remind those beneath me to enjoy life while it lasts
I would loudly shout out these lessons if I could; but I cannot so
Tick   Tick   Tick

Abby Moore, Grade 7
Olson Middle School, NJ

Mother Nature's Gifts

The rain pounds down
On the growing flowers
They stretch up
Their leaves reaching toward the sky
Sweat beading on their petals
Some creamy white flowers are like lacy puffs pinned together
Other lavender flowers hide an orange treasure inside
Lemon yellow daffodils trumpet brightness through the bleak sky
Outside of this small courtyard
Cars zip by on the slick road
Salty water splashes beneath the wheels
The usually crystal blue sky
Is gray-white
The sun is playing hide-and-seek behind the clouds
The weather makes everyone gloomy and restless
The only inspiration, the only pieces of joy
Are the perfect flowers blooming in the courtyard.

Lindsey Thompson, Grade 7
Indian Valley Middle School, PA

Sally

I have a friend name Sally.
She likes to go visit the valley.
She goes home to always be alone.
She is smart she is talented but she never wants to use her magic.
She could be black she could be white but it doesn't matter we all have rights.
She doesn't smoke she doesn't drink she obviously loves to play by the sink.
She washes she cleans she loves to eat.
She sleeps she eats the only thing she doesn't do is follow her dreams.

Junior Calloo, Grade 7
Link Community School, NJ

Confused Hope

A case of mistaken identity
Before me paths unfold but which to take
To choose the right path the first time is key
Wish to have my own path that I could make

His footsteps are visible through the sand
Should I follow them or I'll choose again
So many expectations in my hand
Pushing me to move on, don't think I can

Just be yourself take one step at a time
Wait for the course to unfold before you
Try to enjoy the journey and the climb
Who to be is the question, don't know who

To know everything, but I know nothing
Wish I could know what the future will bring

Emily Monsalud, Grade 9
Unami Middle School, PA

Puppetry Sunshine

Puppetry sunlight moves in through the clouds,
The overcast gray sky is obsolete.
Shadows cover the ground in blackened shrouds,
I watch each movement of my feet.

The thunder of doubt shirks away,
The confidence of beauty has begun:
Affection and feelings left in disarray,
Now sit in the brilliant sun.

The dark and sinister clouds of deceit,
Are no longer seen in the lit-up sky.
The familiar taste of the stinging rain retreats,
Leaving the worries left to dry.

The puppetry sun stands high in the blue oasis:
The intense light extends its loving burn.
What had been a black abyss,
Is now a wonderland of brilliance:
Filled with an adoring concern.

Alanna McAuliffe, Grade 8
Genesis @ Xaverian School, NY

Poetry

This is beat! Poetry is boring!
I wish I wasn't doing this; I could be soaring.
But I'm in the library. BORING!
I could be out with friends, chillin', having fun
But I'm sitting here…it's pretty dumb.
Nothing against poets, I just don't like it.
I'm not Shakespeare; I can't write a hit.
I'm here bored, writing this verse
But if I don't do it, Mrs. Seigel will give me a curse.

Steve Servis, Grade 9
Unami Middle School, PA

Game Winner

The count is full in the eighth inning,
A simple base hit will have the Yankees winning.
The ball leaves the pitcher's hand and you see it twiddle,
CRACK! The ball travels up the middle.
Diving for the ball is the shortstop,
It hits the dirt and goes flying by his flop.
As the runner is rounding third and heading for the plate,
The ball arrives just a second too late.
The runner scores and his team takes the lead,
The crowd cheers for the batter's good deed.
Now it's Boston's chance to tie the game,
The Red Sox can't score, and they lose in shame.
The Yankees leave with a win under their belt,
They deserved it after the performance they dealt.

Donny Killian, Grade 8
St Stephen's School, NY

I Am From

I am from dog walks with shi.
I am from chores that make me tired.
I am from dominos with my family on my yard.
I am from the piragua stand down the block.
I am from plane ride to Puerto Rico.

I am from the basketball court in San Juan.
I am from the forest looking for quenepas.
I am from the salsa we make for a party.
I am from sazone we use to make the rice.
I am from the cocorico we drink.

I am from the Arroz con Gandules.
I am from the flan we eat for dessert.
I am from the barking of my dog when she sees a cat.
I am from looking at the bats fly.
I am from Puerto Rico.

Chris Martinez, Grade 9
Hoboken Charter School, NJ

To a Friend

You're my friend
Oh you're the best, you've always helped me
You're funny, you're happy, you're sad and mad
I've helped you through rough times and you've helped me

How you have helped me
What a wonderful job you have done
Now you seem happier because I've made you feel good
We've gotten past our problems

Now we can move on
You're my friend
No one can prevent that
I know you won't bend.

Shane Schmelick, Grade 8
Township of Ocean Intermediate School, NJ

Sand of Life

Fine grains of sand.
In the mixture trash.
Shells.
Rocks.

Our own life imprinted in the
Sand.
Trash.
Shells.
Rocks.

The up, rise.
Sand.

Lies.
Trash.

Rough patches.
Shells.
The almost sand.

Anger, frustration.
Rocks.

Sand. Trash. Shells. Rocks.
Repeat.
When tide comes, sand is still left.
Kristal Sotomayor, Grade 8
Knoch Middle School, PA

Friday

My favorite day
is Friday because it's the
last day of the week.
Phillip Guzevich, Grade 8
Life Academy, PA

Sun Kissed

The sun hits the lake
so bright.
Makes you shut your eyes
so tight.
The wind
so powerful
so cool
wisps by with the breeze
that just kisses your cheek.
The chills
that roll
down your back
give you the goosebumps
so tingly
that just stands the hair
on your neck.
Sarah Baily, Grade 9
Home School, PA

Unknown Universe

Stars are gleaming diamonds
Where unknown secrets and curiosity
Hide behind their beauty

Where depression is a face
Drained of life
Eyes watery rubies
Bulging with sorrow

Where a face of joy
Is a pure flower
A smile of a thousand suns
Shimmering with happiness.
Brooke Martin, Grade 8
Galloway Township Middle School, NJ

What Would It Take?

What would it take
for things to be quiet
quiet like the snow.
What would it take
for us to live together
for stars to be brighter
for hearts to be warmer.
What would it take
for you to let me cry
on your shoulder
and you not care
that your clothes get soaked.
What will it take
for you to promise me
that you will be there
forever.
Hannah Morley, Grade 8
Beacon Middle School, DE

South Main Street

As I ride in my green jeep
traveling
down South Main Street,
there are many curves
in the road,
many tall, leafy trees.
Traveling
down South Main Street
I can see the goat farm
and the rustic log cabin.
Traveling
down South Main Street
I'm looking forward
to seeing my black dog
and my favorite cat...
once I get home on
South Main Street.
Melissa Altieri, Grade 7
Trinity Middle School, PA

Worries

A giant cloud is looming,
Dark and ominous in the sky.
A cloud of endless worries,
Slowly drifting by.

And as that cloud moves over,
At a dreadfully slow pace.
It starts to slowly form,
Into an image of my face.

My face is looking panicked,
Worrying about something new.
And as you watch me worry,
Raindrops start to fall on you.

One billion little worries,
Falling quickly to the ground.
As my face in the cloud,
Starts to fearfully frown.

But as you start to smile,
And reassuringly speak.
A ray of sunshine pierces the cloud,
One beautiful golden streak.
Zachary Fox, Grade 7
Ocean City Intermediate School, NJ

Going

I gotta get out of here
I'd rather be dead than stay here
I can't take it anymore
the SCREAMING
ringing in my ears
the CRYING
I can't take these tears
the FIGHTING
over all these years

I gotta walk. NO. run
out the door
I'm sorry I'm not sorry to say
that I'm going...

going...

GONE
Kayla Belliveau, Grade 9
Westlake High School, NY

Summer

Summer is hot,
the best season we got.
Summer is cool,
because you can jump in a pool.
Jay Peña, Grade 7
St Agatha School, NY

Just Because

Just because I'm scared
Don't talk behind my back
Don't go without me
Because I wanna go with you

Just because I'm scared
It doesn't mean I'm stupid
It doesn't mean I'm not cool
It doesn't stop me from having a good time

Just because I'm scared
You should still abide in me
Still love me
Just because I'm scared — don't leave me

Nichole Raffle, Grade 9
Unami Middle School, PA

He Is Risen

Jesus came down from Heaven above,
Pure and sinless like a dove.
He came to die on Calvary's tree.
He came to die for you and me.
Tortured, broken, and buried alone,
Then entombed by a giant stone,
Later his disciples Peter and John came,
To grieve for the One who cured the lame.
"He is not here, He is Risen," the angel said.
They were amazed to see Jesus was not dead.
They ran back to the others to say,
That Jesus had risen on that day!

Emily Melvin-Michael, Grade 7
Tri-State Christian Academy, PA

Paradise

Hear the drums play boom boom boom,
Listen to the maracas shake shake shake,
And the bongos bong ba da da da da.
Then you know where you are…Paradise.

Go sun tanning, water surfing, fun in the sun.
Feels like your summer has just begun,
Relax, take a load off, it's time to play.
Make this summer just your way.

Hear the bands rock out
The crowds getting loud
And all you want to do is shout shout shout!
Then you know where you are…Paradise.

Go sun tanning, water surfing, fun in the sun.
Feels like your summer has just begun,
Relax, take a load off, it's time to play.
Make this summer just your way.

Kelly Marie Korpus, Grade 7
Trinity Middle School, PA

Winter

When everything stands frozen
When time stops turning
When pale white flakes dance and swing
You know winter is here
Pale, cold, and solemn
Violent enough to make you afraid
One minute a blizzard could blow you away
Yet peaceful
A white blanket covering and protecting
So new sprouts could survive to the spring
Yet so quickly it has come and gone
Come back next year!

Sarah Cheng, Grade 7
Highland Park Middle/High School, NJ

Baseball

Baseball is my favorite sport.
Smack!
I hit the ball.
Crunch, crunch.
I run all the way to first.
Swoosh!
I slide at home.
I'm safe!
Hooray!!
I hear the crowd cheer for me.
Pat pat pat…
I feel my teammates pat me on the back and helmet.
We won the game.

Nicholas Panepinto, Grade 7
St Stephen's School, NY

The Battle

Looking over the hill, they're not here yet,
the cannons are loaded, we're all set.
A few minutes later, we know what's in store,
as they come marching, 'bout 7 core.
Soon after this began Picketts Charge,
I know we can defeat them,
because we're quite large.
Everyone's screaming and yelling about,
everything's running through our heads, but doubt.
The screams and gunshots carry on,
if only it was tomorrow's dawn.
As I look to my left, the tension is high,
as I look to my right, there's nothing but sky.
The battle kept on going for 3 days strong,
some men thought it was short, some thought it was long.
After all that fighting, we had won,
now ending the revolution that had begun.
Though some dead, we fought a great fight,
I'll sleep with victory in my head tonight.
Now everyone's happy, the revolution is done,
but most importantly, we had won.

Stephanie Kovacs, Grade 8
St Thomas More School, PA

A New Beginning

The past is written,
in stone.
But my future isn't.
I have a road of choices to make.
Some are clear and others
are NOT.

My life is crazy but
I can make the best of
my dreams.

I wanna be successful.
BUT,
it all starts with ME
and a DREAM.

Kayla Hernandez, Grade 9
Green Dot Academy, NY

Sisters

Three sisters are we
As different as can be
I love each of you
And they love me
Sometimes were together
Sometimes were apart
We may be separate
But not in our hearts
We are like a puzzle
When one is missing
We are not whole
When we're together
We are a team
When we fight
It's only for a night
We must never forget
Three sisters are we

Sara Hamlin, Grade 8
Caribou Middle School, ME

A Singer on the Stage

I believe that I'm a butterfly;
a singer on the stage
with a crowd of people
staring at every move I make,
every step I take.

When I sing my song.
with nature as the stage
a loving spirit inside
releases words from my inner soul
creating a radiant performance,
voices cheer for ears to listen
hands clap for the world to hear
my melody set free to flutter away.

Hadly Patterson, Grade 7
Ocean City Intermediate School, NJ

This World

What's wrong with the world today, when even the kids murder and slay?
Is it the parents' fault when they carry out the deadly schemes they've sought?
What made them so obsessed with bloodshed?
Whose fault is it that innocent people are dead?
Someone tell me who's to blame, when children play a sickening game?
Is it the music or TV shows, tell me why no one knows.
Is it the influence of people like Hitler, tell me why no one is sure.
Is it the doing of Satanism or is it the teasing and criticism?
Is it the breaking up with boyfriends or girlfriends?
Won't someone tell me, will this ever end?
The fighting, the killing, the bombings, and guns.
Why are parents making funeral plans for their young daughters and sons?
How could people we love so much, have such a deadly touch?
Was it because they were drunk or high, someone please tell me why?
They're not just trying to give a scare, they're taking lives and they don't care.
Who could be so vicious and cruel, as to put people through hell, even in school?
What drives them to this deadly sin, no one knows where to begin.
Why does this world seem so crazy, and all the answers seem so hazy?
Tell me the truth and please don't lie.
Tell me the truth and tell me, why?

Samantha Smith, Grade 9
Warsaw Jr/Sr High School, NY

A Family

My family is a car
My parents are the steering wheel
They lead me which road to take
My dad is the GPS technology
He always know the easiest road to take and
Where there is traffic and all the shortcuts
My sister is the radio
Always loud and sometimes unpleasant
My mom of course is the wheels
The main part of the car which is also the main part of my family
She is always there when she is needed
I'm the driver the one that makes everything work

Lucas Huang, Grade 7
Simon Baruch Jr High School 104, NY

Graduation

Graduation is a time, when we say goodbye.
It's a time that makes us cry.
It's too hard to let go of all our memories, they'll just fade.
It's hard to let go of all the friends we've made.
People think it's just a joke,
but when you say goodbye, you might just choke.
I'll miss you guys so, even though
we'll keep in touch, I know.
And though graduation means "the end" of our time here,
Throughout these years, we have overcame our middle school fear.
As much as we have laughed, now we'll cry
but just remember, "Let the good times roll by."

Jessica Hom, Grade 8
William R Satz Middle School, NJ

The Big Game

Today was the day of the big game
Everyone had to play a role
It was not for fortune or fame
But simply for reaching our goal

We knew there was nothing left to say
Except it was time to play
We were playing to win for the team
And also to live our dream

We scored first
Just like we'd rehearsed
And never did our opponent score
So when time was up, our fans roared a very big roar

We had won
We were number one
And we celebrated far past sunset
That day was the best, and of that I'll never forget

Cage Galupi, Grade 7
Carson Middle School, PA

Thunderstorm

I know a thunderstorm.
The smashing of a window,
the howl of the wind.
I know a thunderstorm.
The hail whipping past at breakneck speeds,
roofs and doors flying all around you.
The snapping of trees,
the falling of power lines.
Then all of a sudden the lights go out.
And the fear of the unknown takes over.
I know a thunderstorm.

Brett Nolt, Grade 8
Ephrata Middle School, PA

In the Future

In the future
Many things will be different
And will be more advanced
In the future
Some people think there will be flying cars
In the future
Some people think we will live underwater
In the future
Many people will want to be able to fly
In the future
People will be different and so will the world
No matter what happens
In the future
The future will be fun
And it will be great to be around and watch all this happen
In the future

Corianne Banks, Grade 8
Floral Park Memorial High School, NY

Swine Flu Rap

Yo, yo, yo, I think I got swine flu!
Stop sayin' that, y'all, it's more like you got whine flu!
The chicken goes "cluck," the cow goes "moo,"
But as far as I know, pigs don't go "flu!"
One man named Tom tries to stop this, it's true,
That's one guy you should build a shrine to!
Even if you've got, the flu of swine,
SUCK IT UP! You'll be fine!

Tom Evans, Grade 7
Galloway Township Middle School, NJ

Traveling Through the Woods

On an exploration through the forest,
I saw through the trees,
Some lilacs, blowing in the breeze.
Some rabbits nestling in the leaves.
What a sound!
Birds chirping a cheerful song,
While the ants are marching along.
I smelled,
The enticing aroma of berries,
All shapes, sizes, colors, tastes.
Laying my hand on the tree,
I felt it's rough, rigid skin against my palm.
I tasted the warm cool air of the summer breeze,
Oh! How beautiful life can be,
Just take the time to look and see.

Alexis Peterman, Grade 7
Pine-Richland Middle School, PA

Nothing and Everything

Nothing,
at times can feel like everything,
or simply just nonexistent.

Everything,
it is what you have and want.
That everything is consuming you have nothing.

Everything is possible.
That is what most people want to believe.

Others,
think that nothing is possible.

At times we have everything,
to make nothing.

Nothing,
it is all you have and care about.

Do you have nothing or everything?
Can you even tell the difference?

Madison Ehrenreich, Grade 7
Trinity School, MD

Like Sister Like Brother

One day my little brother Bobby, seemed like he had a hobby
For eating food; every time I saw him something was being chewed.
He was drinking like it was going out of style and he was thinner than a nail file.
I was getting deja vu and then I knew,

My mom knew it too and the only thing to do
Was to go to the hospital that day, I knew everything would be o.k.
When they put the infamous I.V. in his arm, he was shocked with alarm;
He looked like he was being chased with a knife and he was going to lose his life.

I was out all day, but when I came home, I saw my brother, he was staying at home!
I ran inside and gave him a hug, he then continued to play on the rug.
I explained to him what he was going through, he then knew
He was getting the same thing as me, with this disease, there is no reason to say Yippee!

I am very fond that our bond
Is getting stronger and hopefully we don't have to wait much longer.
Right now this cure means the world to me, one day it will mean the same to Bobby.
One day my dream will hopefully come true, and I won't have the chance of being hospitalized, every time I have the flu.

Joanna Napolitano, Grade 7
Oakdale-Bohemia Middle School, NY

Never Forget the Unforgettable

Never forget world war two, how would you feel if it happened to you?
People suffered days by days, people died in different ways.
Families getting separated, people feeling isolated.
People getting ordered in groups, Jews getting killed by troops,
Every day they would cry, most hoping to die.
Think how you'd feel if your family disappeared, that's mostly what everyone feared.
People wanted to escape, they wanted to run, if they got caught their lives would be done.
Think of all the people who escaped and died, all because they tried.
They'd hang people as a warning, people woke up and cried every morning.
Never forget this, never let it die, listen to the story and cry.
Always remember what happened back then, so we can prevent it from happening again.

Jasmine Shirazi, Grade 7
Tilden Middle School, MD

Surrounded

Surrounded,
Surrounded by nature by trees and dirt and open sky.
Surrounded by friends at your side all day and discovering new and blistering worlds within a world.
Day and night, good and bad, wrong and right.
Finding things anew not only around us but inside ourselves that truly and absolutely matters.
That matters for when we branch out and create our beginnings.

Our place in this world.
Our very own surrounding.

Alissa Feigo, Grade 7
West Frederick Middle School, MD

Wish

I wish I had someone special right here by my side. A true and wonderful friend in my world so big and wide. Someone who's caring that I can count on. In between my mysteries and my troubles someone that I can really depend upon. I wish I had a true friend who is always here with me, right until my very last breath. Until the end of all eternity.

Lhorrana Silva, Grade 8
Ann Street Elementary School, NJ

Cry

We all cry, no one knows why
Perhaps it's because we're weak
And couldn't conquer a fly
And we can't conquer our fears
And we can't hide from our tears
It seems like everything's our kryptonite

But amongst this ever flowing river,
Of our tears and fears
Rushing through our minds more violent than a hurricane
We can usually find a large rock to cling to

And no, our Superman's not scared
Of the villains within the shadows of our internal hurricanes
But even he can't take the wrath of our kryptonite
He tries so hard to fight the forces, but could never succeed.

So what do we do when our forever-strong Superman
Succumbs to this kryptonite
And leaves us feeling that not even he can't stay strong

Leaving no one safe, especially us without shoes
Where the grass tickles
And the rocks cut deep
Deeper than the kryptonite ever could.

Randi Crews, Grade 8
Charles S Pierce Middle School, MA

Green

Green as dark as the black at night,
Green for hunting military and more,
Military blossoming like flowers in spring,
Leaves come giving trees life,
Bees pollinate blossoming apple trees in the spring sun,
Come back to the hive to make dark green honey.

Dalton King, Grade 7
Alexander Middle/High School, NY

The Garbage

At the end of the day, when dawn turns to dusk
Taking out the garbage is a must
It smells so bad,
It makes my nose sad
Taking out the recycles as well
When I don't take it out my parents will sure yell
The many items in the bag weigh a ton
Even washing the dishes is way more fun
Flies buzz and buzz all around,
The garbage truck it would sure to be bound
The many rotten food and items in this bag,
Bringing them outside can be such a drag
Doing anything except the garbage is much more fun
But like the many other chores, it has to be done.

James Mendoza, Grade 7
Hammarskjold Middle School, NJ

Life Goes On

I wish I could do something
Yet I knew that I could not
I sat at her bedside as she was drifting away
I wish she would pull out of this
She did it once before
She was tired and hurt
She never showed it
We loved her every bit
We knew her body was weak as a string
But her heart was as tough as a bull

As I held her hand she said softly I love you
Then she became loosened and weak
She passed away just like that
The horrible monster cancer is
Has taken my beautiful, loved grandmother

Billy Ray Mitchell, Grade 7
Westwood Jr/Sr High School, NJ

Push Play

Push Play you're my favorite band!
You always will be.
Even though you are moving across the country,
You will forever be the best.

I can't wait to see you online,
Hopefully on TV one day.
Stars shoot around my head when I see you,
It never goes away.

Your songs are always stuck in my mind.
They rock my socks off.
You can never let anyone down,
Even when you announced your big move!
They will always get over it.

So go to California,
And have the time of your life.
I will always miss you.
Just Push Play and listen!

Lindsay Hubschman, Grade 8
Floral Park Memorial High School, NY

Tired

Long, long day
This day never ends.
People pass, people go
But little do they show
Any signs of being awake,
Yawn, sigh, and hope not to cry.
Because of all the exhaust
Need a nap, need a bed
Need a place to rest my head,
And finally…sleep…

Emma Buckle, Grade 8
Monsignor Haddad Middle School, MA

Untitled

I see
  A monster
Full of
  Gossip,
    Hatred,
      Betrayal,
        And love;
Just like a horror movie
That scares
  Us all;
In a time
  Where everything changes,
Be careful
  What you say,
    And do
Because
  High school
    Will
      Haunt
        You.

Amy Sharn, Grade 8
Northstar Christian Academy, NY

The Blank Road Ahead

I walk,
  each step, forsaking a footprint.
Each filled with memories, now left behind, lost.
      Freedom is   ahead.
The road, blank, anticipating to be filled.
    Fresh air is   S
          P
              I
          R
               A
          L
              I
          N
            G
    through my hair.
Shocking to the touch it is freedom,
  whisking through me.
I can see freedom in me.
I can see freedom in my path.
I can see freedom in the world passing by.

Kasey Ennis, Grade 7
William Penn Middle School, PA

The Future

The future, the future,
Oh, how it will be
I hope I will be able to see it to be
I hope it is bright,
I hope it is near
I just wonder what will be here
Will there be peace
Will there be war
I only want to know more and more
If the future is good,
I am going to be glad
But if it is going to be bad,
I am just going to be very sad, sad, sad
Will we be rich
Will we be poor
I wish I can know more,
But I just don't know anymore
The time will wait
For the future will soon be awake

Jameson Moy, Grade 8
Floral Park Memorial High School, NY

Credo

I believe in freedom through the lands
The past is over
The future is a mystery, which will unravel by tomorrow
The fact that no man shall fight alone
The existence of happiness
Forgiveness, faith, and culture

But when one man stands alone it's outrageous

I believe in working together as a team
I believe that success follows hard work
I believe that challenges teach you lessons, street smarts, and wisdom

And I believe day by day you experience the world in a different way

Ryan Valoroso, Grade 8
Hauppauge Middle School, NY

Speed of Biking

Slowly
Ready, anxious
Gaining, hurrying, jumping
Pacing, pumping, lifting, speed
Air, blowing, height
Jump, adrenaline
Fast

Brett Landis, Grade 8
Ephrata Middle School, PA

Lonely

Being lonely is like being like in a black hole
Sucking in other people
Never having light
There will be no happiness
There will be no hope
Like a black hole emotions are as deep as can be
No one to comfort you
You sit there floating in your mind thinking and wishing for happiness
No love to warm your heart
Every turn is nothing but black
Your thoughts are lost
Until someone is there for you or you find love you are trapped being lonely

Jarred Burke, Grade 7
Hammarskjold Middle School, NJ

The Game

The hearts pounding
The excitement of the crowd
The skates hitting the ice
Getting ready to take the face-off
The sweat coming off your face
The intensity of the game
A brutal hit everywhere you go
Racing for the puck, you then get on your stick
Getting ready to shoot
Hitting the goalie in the pads
Going for the rebound
Shooting the puck into the back of the net
The roar of the crowd

Nick Stapleton, Grade 7
Depew Middle School, NY

The Volleyball Dream

Happiness means volleyball in the fall
Changing dreams means changing time
The floor will never get a chance to touch the ball.
My hands will meet, and I will beat the ball over the net,
The rush fills me with happiness
My team runs over and yells, AWESOME HIT!!!
The buzzer rings, 1st period, we have the lead

Hearing my name means I'm being fame
I really hope famous volleyball players feel the same
Hopefully this is not just a dream
But if it's a dream I would do
It would be nothing but a dream
I'd wake up knowing it was not a thing

Volleyball can come and go
I just gotta know when it's my time to shine
Live and learn 'til the trophy is mine

Alyson J. Gregg, Grade 7
Trinity Middle School, PA

Colors

Colors exist for a purpose.
They change our emotions,
They help us understand things,
And they help us find the right direction.
But, what if colors didn't exist?
Everything would be like an old TV show.
Black, gray, and white would only be seen.
Everyone would be dull.
Our planet would be dull.
Our galaxy would be dull.
The entire universe would be dull.
That would be very bad,
But every single day,
We see colors,
And are happy that we do.

Clayton Gentilcore, Grade 7
Christ the Divine Teacher Catholic Academy, PA

The Pride in Parenthood*

Parenthood comes in many ways,
Here, the little dogs lay.
Their mama stands here so proud,
To protect them is what she had secretly vowed.

The boy sits and watches them eat,
Slurping up milk, they are so very sweet.
They whimper and wait,
For the boy to refill the plate.

Their bellies are now satisfied and full,
And the boy wraps them in a blanket made of wool.

Julia Turgeon, Grade 7
Whitin Middle School, MA
*Inspired by Norman Rockwell's work.

The Revolution

The war had started, it was a revolution,
and the people said it was their only solution.
America declared its independence,
and got away from England's ascendance.
It was a very long war,
yet the respect for America suddenly soared.
Benjamin Franklin brought out majestic France,
The English brought the Hessian's to join the dance.
The battle of Yorktown proved it would be,
a proud American victory.
And the nation that came from a war,
evolved much and become much more.
It became a world power, in technology,
education, wealth and military.
The country won many other wars,
and helped open up many doors.
All that came from a gigantic war,
on the American eastern shore.

John Zhang, Grade 7
William Annin Middle School, NJ

Hockey

It's fun to watch their bodies crash
  Sometimes right into the beach
But the best is when they go through the glass
  And they soar right into the crowd

It's amazing how the crowd goes so wild
  When someone scores a goal
Especially when it's the Stanley Cup
  You can feel the whole place shake

I hope that can be me one day
  Holding the cup nice and high
So for now I'll have to keep on working
  And hopefully fulfill my dream

Christian Whitcomb, Grade 7
Depew Middle School, NY

The Moon

Moon! Moon! Glowing bright
Guide my way through the night,
Burn thy light into my soul
With thy strength I'll find my home.
DeAnna Zecchin, Grade 9
Unami Middle School, PA

Enlightenment

These questions cease.
Life completes.

These ifs, ands, or buts fade.
Content shows them the way.

Life's questions erase.
Wisdom takes its place.

Complications are over.
Serenity starts to hover.

My vision is blurred by
The beauty of the herd.

Pulling me closer:
EVERYTHING.
NOTHING.
Alba Summers, Grade 7
Ocean City Intermediate School, NJ

The End of Eternity

My mind
Is a black hole of thoughts.
My face
Is a river with its
Tears endlessly flowing.

My ears
Hear the eternal cry of pain
Coming from the one I love.
My body
Is a pillow in which I use to stroke her
When the fire of eternity dies out
In her soul.

My heart
Then breaks to pieces.
My eyes
Can see her pain.
Myself I
Feel the fear inside
My aching heart.

When the fire of eternity dies out
In her soul, and in my heart.
Christina Long, Grade 8
Orono Middle School, ME

R.I.P.

Death is so unrealistic, it's so unpredictable
Yesterday he was alive, but now lying there still
Face white, pale and cold, emptiness in his eyes
Life ceased to exist in him, it just doesn't seem real to me
Last time I saw him,
He looked as strong as a brick wall that could never be crushed.

It was the night of October 31st, 2000, when I heard the word "died,"
Chills went up from my toes to the very tip of my hair
My head was spinning, pain throbbing in my chest
Tears formed in my eyes
Drip, drip, drip
I tried my best to resist, but my eyes kept dripping more tears

I wish I could have said a better goodbye
If time would just give me one more chance
Just one more
I would hug him the whole day
Giving him all the love I could possibly give
You will always be more than a tangential thought in my heart

Bye-bye
My dear uncle,
Farewell.

Jamie Yang, Grade 8
Fairfax Collegiate School, VA

Perception of a Year

Can you tell if you have shattered, or did your mirror break?
Can you tell if you are lying, or is it just a big mistake?
Can you tell if you are crying, or is it just the rain?
If you are only joking, then why am I in pain?

Can you tell if you are moving, if Earth spins the other way?
Remember when you're on the moon, a year is just another day.
Can you tell if that's the answer, or just a step along the way?
Are you sure it's not a circle? You put it off for one more day.

Can you tell if this is history, or a version of a lie?
Can you tell if it was tyranny, or the changing of the times?
Can you tell if dreams are fiction, if they're happening to you?
And is sci-fi just a fantasy from future's point of view?

Can you tell if you are running, when you're back where you began?
Can it really be a masterpiece if you don't share it when you can?
Are you really a musician, if you don't write your song?
Did they help you learn to draw the world? Were you able all along?

Can you tell if I don't love you when I say that you're my friend?
Can you tell if you have learned a thing once this poem ends?
Can you tell from a distance the true meaning of my tears?
Is it the ending of your part-time home, or just the ending of a year?

Rachael Aikens, Grade 9
Valley Regional High School, CT

nature

nature, nature everywhere
nature is so very calming and also very relaxing

go outside and close your eyes
breathe in the scent of our beautiful nature

Zehra Jaffar, Grade 7
School Lane Charter School, PA

A Story

As faces frown, upside down,
While cheerful flowers bloom in the spring,
You can fade away to see your world, in a different way;
Little girls laughing, playing hopscotch,
"Go Tracy Go!" they cheer;
A mother, "No, that was my only child,"
Crying, the night away;
The uplifting voice of the worship,
Fulfilling the lives that need; opposed from
The sad yearning souls in need
Of food and sleep!

As a young boy runs over to
His friends to see what's new;
The six grader, on the other side of
The field, cries, because of
Devastating news; you can't always control
The balance of life, it's up to what the
Forces of nature's council, decides for you.

Abigail Cox, Grade 7
School of International Studies at Meadowbrook, VA

Dancer in the Wind

Wind is racing through the trees,
It stirs the grass and rustles the leaves,
Of the elegant old Holly tree.
One leaf falls,
Twisting and turning.
Its movements are graceful,
A dancer in the wind.

The wind swoops down,
Taken by the dancer,
And lifts the leaf up to the heavens,
So the dance will never end.

The dancer's performance is magic in the making,
And with it comes a sense,
Of peace and healing,
And the taste of liquid beauty.

And still the dance goes on today,
The leaf the dancer,
The wind the conductor.

Chloe Vassot, Grade 8
Manor Middle School, PA

Dream

Every night I escape into a world,
Not too far, not too close,
An 8th wonder of the world,
Abstract yet so real,
A colorless, colorful place,
Where even black and white mingle happily,
Where limits are extinct,
Where the heart, not head,
Shapes this world,
Imagination is the hero,
Creativity is the king,
And fear is the servant,
A time when time is still,
Then the villain reappears,
A piercing sound,
Reality strikes,
This dream is shattered,
All eyes are open.

Aseem Jain, Grade 7
Carson Middle School, VA

Chores

I shouted and screamed, ran and roared
Anything not to do my only chore.
I couldn't, I wouldn't, I didn't want to.
Anything not to clean my room.
I whined and pouted, my mother so mad,
She even almost called my dad!
I told my mother not me not I,
I wouldn't clean my room I wouldn't even try.
She told me no friends don't even dare,
And don't you think about going to that fair.
I shouted and yelled, please Mom no!
I'll clean my room if you'll let me go!

Nikki Weissman, Grade 7
Hammarskjold Middle School, NJ

My Life

Girl: My life is horrible
Boy: Your life is fine
Girl: My life is terrible
Boy: Then so is mine
Girl: How is that possible?
Boy: I'm telling you it's true
Girl: But you're so special!
Boy: And so are you
Girl: I'm so different
Boy: Aren't I?
Girl: No! You fit in with everyone!
Boy: That's just because we tie
Girl: I don't tie with anyone
Boy: Not even me?
Girl: Of course not! You're the one I love! (Gasp)
Boy: Then I am all you need

Alyssa Belardo, Grade 8
Newtown Middle School, PA

Dare to Live

We only live life once,
Or so we do believe.
But other people think,
He grants us more reprieves.

What's on the Other Side?
We will never know.
That's why we don't live as much,
'Cause we're afraid to go.

If there's another life waiting,
Don't wait 'til you find out.
Go crazy, go wild,
Laugh, and scream and shout.

Live like there's no tomorrow,
'Cause there might not be.
Laugh and love and cry and die,
Only then can you be free.

Eric Tam, Grade 9
Parsippany High School, NJ

Blackberry

Sweet, sweet blackberry,
Standing alone on the bush,
Your turn will be soon.

Karlee Patton, Grade 8
Mattei Middle School, PA

Love Is Like a Song

Love is like a song
It is never wrong
You make it your own
It has a completely new tone
You make it line by line
It starts out very fine
At first, it is unclear
Then it becomes very dear

Love is like a song
It can last very long
Love is very deep
When some people find love, they weep
Love can be sung
Or spoken in a foreign tongue
Love comes only from the soul
Love is a life goal

Love is like a song
It is very strong
Love creates a special bond
You learn to become fond
Love will make you wise
It is the greatest prize

Victor Shen, Grade 7
Carson Middle School, VA

Dandelion Angel

I sit, waiting for my time
when the wind will come
and take me away,
away to the vast sky
where I can be free
to perform my delicate dance
twirling to my own rhythm.
I float by so quickly
that I can't be stopped,
but soon my flight will end.
I will meet the Earth once more,
and wait for my next journey to the sky.

Courtney Thern, Grade 7
Ocean City Intermediate School, NJ

Into Life

The Crystal Rose
glistens with beauty.
It sits
as if waiting
for what?
As the sun
sparkles through
the transparent wall
but, what is encased?
Is unseen
its beauty mystical
it sees
it sits
as it waits
its masters arrival
it's here
from the touch
The Crystal Rose
rises
and walks away.

Tyler Raske, Grade 8
Belhaven Avenue Middle School, NJ

School Has Done Its Final Share

Pencils and pens
All come to an end
Essays and test
Less and less
Yearbooks and parties
All just starting
No more snow no more rain
Walking to the bus was always a pain
Going to bed late and waking up early
Will there be no more
Because school is out
School is out
Scream and shout
School is out

Aniciah Jones, Grade 8
Churchill Jr High School, NJ

School

Ever evolving
To the rough problems of life
But it is with strife

Ian Montgomery, Grade 8
Cinnaminson Middle School, NJ

Wandering Child

He never knows where he goes anymore
Now that you have gone
And he shall forever wander on
Though his soles are sore

But one place alone he seeks
Though its distance lies in weeks
And though it may have grown tart
The only place is your heart

You need not build a home for him
With sheltering wood you find
The only place he longs to be in
Is forever on your mind

So cast aside your vanities
Of superficial guess
And all of your uncertainties
Remember that unless

You keep an open mind as well
As an open heart
This child shall wander on until
You have learned love's sort

Mitchell Chan, Grade 9
Holmdel High School, NJ

Joyous Light Prevails!

Darkness ruled his life
Her beauty hath been revealed
Joyous light prevails!

O tempting maiden
With the air of a goddess
I dearly crave thee!

As I touch thy skin
Warmth races through my body
How splendid it feels!

With faithful guidance
I know you won't forsake me
Be my heart's keeper!

Darkness ruled his life
Her beauty hath been revealed
Joyous light prevails!

Michael Pietrzykowski, Grade 9
Holyoke High School, MA

Common Sense

People may be different and diverse;

By their religion,
By their race,
By their culture
By their color.
But they all have common hopes and desires.
They all have common dreams.
A better future for their dear ones.
A better future for their nation.

Syed Ahmad, Grade 7
Floral Park Memorial High School, NY

Summer Love

That summer I will never forget.
It lasted merely three months,
But all good things have to come to an end.
The long talks —
Oh, such childish things we spoke.
The endless walks —
Oh, the stares we got.
Over the hill and back again, around the bend.
The way you made me feel — like I was in a dream,
The kind that I never wanted to wake up from.
The butterflies danced in my insides.
Then you kissed me goodnight on the cheek
Because daddy was looking through the window.
The sand in our toes,
And the stars in your eyes,
Little blue stars in a very big sky that would be hard to
    to live without,
But that I learned to live without over time —
My own slip from grace to clumsiness.

Anne Page, Grade 8
Cornerstone Christian Preparatory Academy, PA

0

I have no start.

A full void.
Neither empty nor full.

Friends are selected,
Outsiders rejected.

There aren't any Obstacles,
Still you can't Overcome feeling lost and insecure.

Obsolete.
The missing birth,
The missing midway.
The missing Obituary.

I have no end.

Elizabeth Suizzo, Grade 8
Southern Regional Middle School, NJ

The Longest School Week

Come and listen to my story bout my long school week;
I get up Monday morning and I feel like a freak
My mom says brush your teeth,
Then she heads out to make food;
The smell of pancakes puts me in a better mood.

School, school I can't wait till it's summer;
School, school, it sure is a bummer.

Tuesday morning still a drag; as I pack my old school bag
Then I ride off to school, with my bike that is so cool.
Wednesday is the halfway mark;
My dog wakes me with a "Bark"
Six periods to go; gosh this day is awful slow.

Thursday I'm preparing for a test in poetry;
Somehow I forgot about the studying, ya see
I hope that Mrs. Nelms will pity little me;
I need a good grade or angry my mom will be.

Friday saves the week out here
The sun is really out and the sky is blue and clear
My brother is singing one long Guitar Hero song
I'll join him on the weekend which won't last for long.

Ryan Fritz, Grade 8
Ephrata Middle School, PA

Love

Love is a 4 letter word with more than a 4 letter meaning
What is love?
Love is compassion…
Love is tears…
Love is the feeling between two people…
Love will break your heart…
Love can tear you apart…
But love can also be a remarkable experience…
It can change your life forever…
Love is one of the most powerful feelings in the world

Mirranda Leigh Metcalfe, Grade 8
Margaret Brent Middle School, MD

Summer Night

Summer night
with lightning bugs glowing, dragonflies swirling,
the moon showing, and stars shining
with rivers glistening, fish swimming
flowers closing, birds sleeping
with dewdrops forming, bees waiting for morning
winds blowing, tree leaves dancing
with bright eyes opening, dreams colliding
sunrise coming, people awakening
until next time summer night

Shyenne Deseray Durbin, Grade 7
Trinity Middle School, PA

Summer

Summer's about May flowers
turning into June showers.
Playing in the swimming pool
makes me feel all nice and cool.
No homework, just housework,
but I can't stay inside all day;
I have to go outside to play.
Walking underneath a tree
I see a happy buzzing bee;
in the shade
or on my roller blades;
on a hike
or on my bike;
drinking iced tea;
looking at the sea.

Waiting for summer to go,
just can't wait to see the snow.

Then winter's here…
Where did summer disappear?
Adrianna Linan, Grade 7
Elizabeth Seton Elementary School, PA

My Dream Land

There's a place
Out of this world
Where no drama can survive
I escape there when I sleep
I escape there when I'm awake
Vivid colors are so peaceful to me
It's a fun place
And quiet all around
Weird, wonderful creatures
And fantasies are formed
I love this world
This fantasy
This amazing creation
All mine for me to roam
I love my world
People call it my butterfly land
My reality dissolves into my dream land
Cheyenne Herington, Grade 7
Depew Middle School, NY

Flashback

It's a flashback of me,
laying down,
a track
so much time for me to
give back
You never would
have guessed
that I'd be this good.
Alex Ehling, Grade 9
Unami Middle School, PA

My Pencil

My pencil, once so shiny and long
Sharp-tipped, its rubbery pink eraser half gone
Long story short, I treasured that pencil
More than my books and my folders, and even more than my stencils
Until one day in music, I seemed to have misplaced it,
Though I searched and I searched, it appeared the earth had erased it
But the very next day, I saw it under the door,
Broken in half, it was quite an eyesore
It killed me inside, to know it had been so mistreated,
Then I saw the kid with the other half of it, silently seated
He chewed on it happily; its pink eraser was gone
I stared at him angrily, but he just sat there as if nothing was wrong
Later we made brownies in Home Ec., and I was the stirrer
But I saw him chewing the pencil again, and yelled "MURDERER!!!"
The class simply stared, and I stared back at them
Then I looked at the floor, and realized how foolish I'd been
I sat down at my desk, and acted as things were before,
Writing with only half a pencil,
I had lost that war

Lauren Binnert, Grade 8
Hammondsport Jr/Sr High School, NY

Life

The hurdles are blocking me from finishing in ease
The running and thinking and mind games are hurting my knees
There are people guarding all the bridges
And shortcuts don't get you far
So I stay on the lonely road going farther than the bar

No one can help me find my way
So I walk alone day by day
The scenery is nice
However I know it's just for show
Pine trees and pretty purple flowers
Along the side of the street they flow

Everyone else is taking side streets
But I decide to go straight
Through all the ups and downs I go
I stop only if I have to and wait
I know I won't go far if I don't try
So I'll do the best until I die
But every day I'm breathing I will not take easy street
That's just life

Kailee Oakes, Grade 7
Westwood Jr/Sr High School, NJ

11:11

This night I shall dream of your bedazzling eyes
Wrapped in echoes of your mellifluous voice
The depths of all the oceans of the universe shall never separate our love
Brilliant as a shining star, the seas greet us from afar
In the twilight we feast on our tender hearts of love
You will always be my Konstantine, the apple of my eye

Tahjé Isaacs, Grade 9
Heritage Jr High School, NY

The Girl I Used to Know

We were best friends forever
before I moved away.
Coming back felt so foreign.
Visiting her with my mom again,
for the first time in years.
Here was the big open space under her apartment,
where we used to run and chase each other,
hair flying wildly and laughing.
I held my breath as the doorbell rang,
announcing our arrival.
The door swung open.
Greeted with warm welcomes,
I was not prepared for how time made such a difference.
Hair longer, she was taller than I expected.
Yet some things never change.
She had the same exact smile when she was excited,
same personality.
As soon as she hugged me in the long awaited reunion,
I knew that we would and always be friends.
No matter what.

Myra Xiong, Grade 8
Russell Sage Jr High School 190, NY

Between Mental States

I wake up, still feeling half asleep.
Tossing and turning in the bed that has kept my shape all night.
The birds are screaming at me to get up and get ready.
I slowly get up and open my tired eyes
to see the sun violently piercing through the curtain,
filling my room with unneeded light.
It finally hits me that this is something I haven't quite noticed.
As I reluctantly take my first step out of bed, I wonder.
Has the Earth rotated faster?
Or did the birds find an excess amount of worms?
If the birds are ready to start their day, so am I.

Kaitlin M. McAlister, Grade 7
Trinity Middle School, PA

I Must Let You Go

Oh no, it's bad
As I watch the life leave your eyes
As your last breath lingers in the air
Tears rapidly flowing down my cheeks
I fall to my knees and the room fades to a blur
I ask myself why me, why now
You left me in my time of need
Months and seasons restlessly pass on
My heart is still sore and I wish for you even more
As I lay awake I yearn for your face
I visit your grave and I know I must let you go

"ILY Mommom"

Danielle Przybyl, Grade 7
Depew Middle School, NY

Life Is Good

Life is good
Sports are the teachers of life
Friends are the ones that get you to where you're going
Family guides you to the light at the end of the tunnel
Girls bring out the best and friendly side of you
Money may get you places but won't buy you happiness
Video games give you a grasp of what's real and fake
Cars get you places, but won't get you anywhere in life
Vacations give you a break from the real world
Life is good

Troy Everly, Grade 7
Garnet Valley Middle School, PA

Together

We've been together through everything,
Every little smile and puddle of tears;
Our love overpowers anything,
And so it will for the rest of our years.

We've shared this portion of our lives together,
And have the rest of it ahead;
Your love is a part of my life forever,
One I think about every night before bed.

Our love reminds me of the perfect fairy tale,
I'll be the pretty girl and you're the handsome prince;
Send my heart to heaven with every email,
My heart hasn't been the same since.

I guess through all this I'm trying to say,
I loved you then now and to the very last day.

Kerri Pennell, Grade 9
Enosburg Falls High School, VT

Oops!

In a world full of do's and don't's
Why can't I mess up once in a while?
What's wrong with an oop's?
What's wrong with a mistake?
Nothing.
Nothing's wrong with a mistake;
So why is it such a big deal?
So what?
I forgot to do my homework.
Oops!
I forgot to walk the dog.
Oops!
I forgot to study for the big test.
Oops!
I think
If
There were more "It's ok's" in the world,
Maybe
There wouldn't be as many oop'ses.

Chelsea McQuillen, Grade 7
Olson Middle School, NJ

Patricio

That annoying, single minded, (GARGH!) hypercritical, creature
That lives down the hall. And tattles like a preacher
He wears the same clothes, three weeks in a row, forgetting the creation of the mall.
He neglects the fact he needs to brush his teeth and wash his face.
He forgets to use soap much too often
And he has volcanoes (sickening!) all over that place he calls his face.
And shampooing his head usually (always!) goes forgotten.
Despite his greasy state, his room is always clean
But I am banned from his kingdom of neatness,
I take one step in, and he's an explosion of mean,
I always have to bow out from Sir Freakiness.
Kind he is to my sis and bros
I'm the lucky one, the one he loves to thrash.
Dead legs and bruises, Charlie-horses too: and I know you don't want to listen to my brotherly woes
But I dearly wish I had the strength to punch and bash.
Eighteen months apart, we are terribly close.
But we've probably been fighting since the day he was born.
Even though we fight I probably couldn't have chosen
A better brother to have, and if he wasn't born, I would have been torn —
To never have a brother like thee.

Alesia Passaro, Grade 7
Westwood Jr/Sr High School, NJ

Taking Advantage of Great Opportunities

The sky is watching over us, holding the clouds to cover up the sun. Mother Nature is furious; because we earthlings take advantage of her. The ozone layer is slowly drifting away, by us littering, and manufacturing businesses blowing out photochemical smog. Then nature has it's revenge by fighting us with acid rain, hurricanes, tornadoes, and tsunamis, we strike back fiercely and give her pollution. I have an epiphany, YES! I have the solution, if we destroy Earth we have no where to live then we all die, NO! Don't sit home and cry. We clean up Earth, and make nature happy. No more war because in the end we'll want to know what we were really fighting for? The outcome wouldn't be pretty Mother Nature and earthlings are dead. The species is gone, now we don't have anyone to carry on.

Tiyana Peters, Grade 7
Rosemont Middle School, VA

When You're Gone

When you're gone
When you're in Heaven
What will I do?
Will I think about you every day?
How many tears will I shed?
How bad will my heart ache?
Will I be devastated?
Will I be able to get through the rest of my life well without you there?
What will I do during the hard times when I need you the most?
Will you still be there in my heart every second of every minute of every hour of every day in my life?
What will I do when I need some comforting?
What will I do when I need someone to cry with?
What if I am not strong enough to get through it?
What will I do when I need love, support, and courage?
What will it be like without you here?
How much will my life change?
What will I do without you here?
What will I do
When you're gone?

Annie Gallo, Grade 8
Bailey Bridge Middle School, VA

Ode to Lady Spring

Dear Lady Spring, I am glad you arrived
with time of equal day and equal night.
It is a time for cleaning house and soul.
A time to renew and refresh as life begins to grow.
You chase the germs and cold out of our bodies and minds.
You are welcomed as fresh air and sunshine.
April showers and dew are the jobs you complete,
with fresh grass and new flowers right at my feet.
Dear Lady Spring, thank you for coming by,
bringing flowers and the beautiful spring sky.

Bridget Fay, Grade 7
Nativity of Our Lord School, PA

A Face's Tale

I walk through the flood of students
Watching what seems like hundreds
Of faces as they pass my own.
Even though we all seem to move
Like uncoordinated cattle
Through the crowded hallways,
Each face is different,
Each set of eyes
Shielding thoughts from outsiders.
Each face holds a story
It's pages are expounded on each day.
perhaps I am somewhere in that print.
I only know as much
As they let on
Or what is sent through
The Rumor Mill.
Just as the previews are never as good as the movie,
The movie never as good as the book,
I wonder what goes on behind those faces.
But, as my own story,
Maybe that is as it was meant to be.

Olivia Migliori, Grade 8
Nazareth Area Middle School, PA

Why?

The time is ticking towards the hour
   The hour no one wants to face
      Is the last
         I hope it is not
For I barely know you and already you are leaving
   Please don't go
      Stay strong for me
         I want to get to know you
            Please Please
              I beg you
                Don't go
This has to be a mistake
   Why should this happen
      Of all people
         Why me

Joelle Kozierowski, Grade 7
Depew Middle School, NY

Milkshakes

Milkshakes come from machines,
You can buy them from McDonald's or Burger King.
First vanilla, then chocolate and strawberry,
These are the flavors of the world's favorite drink.

They're cold and refreshing and sugary,
Also one of the best inventions in the world.
Extreme sugar gives people the strength,
As well as the energy to get through the day.

The machine is just as wonderful as the drink.
If I had one it would be a prized possession,
Because of the tasty and sugary drink,
The milkshake.

Jawhar Ali, Grade 7
Carson Middle School, VA

Summer Is Finally Here!

I don't understand why we go to school,
It's just not cool.
But when summer comes,
You can be a beach bum.
Or you can go outside and play,
And do it all day.
You can roll in the mud,
Or even catch a bug.
You can throw a ball,
Or climb a tree and fall.
You could call your honey,
Or even make some money.
You could hunt a bear,
Or just scream into the air.
You can buy a fish,
Or break a dish.
You could go for a splash,
Or go and spend your cash.
But when it ends,
You will miss school and all your friends.

Cassidy Kovacicek, Grade 7
Trinity Middle School, PA

Time Traveler

Stop!
Nobody move
Freeze this moment
What will you do?
10 years from now you'll look back and say
Man I should have done it this way
Everything's over in the blink of an eye
Before you know it all this time has gone by
In 10 years you'll be sitting on a swing
Thinking man I should have done it this way

Mariah Fisher, Grade 7
Depew Middle School, NY

Lacrosse

From smashing and bashing
to running and jumping
The competitions and games
along with the practices
Hard work, anticipated
blood, sweat, and anger
the sport of men only
yelling, screaming, running
on the field and off
this sport will push you
to your limits
That depends on how far
your limits go

Jake J. Swanson, Grade 7
Trinity Middle School, PA

Reawakening

The Earth is a blank canvas
on which Mother Nature
creates warm glistening rays
from the sun to shine down
upon a newly awakened flower.
Its yellow petals blossom
through shining blades of grass
announcing spring's reawakening
to birds filled with excitement
flying, leaping, and chirping
in celebration of a
perfect spring day.

Megan Kohler, Grade 7
Ocean City Intermediate School, NJ

"Good" Morning!

Today's a slightly busy day,
Push the blankets far away.
Check the time, it's 6 o clock,
Tick tick tock, tick tock tick tock.
Drag my feet across the ground,
My head too tired to not look down.
Stare in the mirror, eyes open wide,
Put my glasses to the side.
Brushed my teeth and washed my face,
Gotta have contacts here someplace,
Found 'em, popped them in real quick,
Fell back on the bed real slick.
Woke up with a startled shout,
Mind frantic, thoughts about.
Put on my shoes, grab my keys,
Run outside and feel the breeze.
But something in the air was wrong,
Something's been weird all along.
My neighbor comes and gives a wave,
"You're going to work? It's Saturday!"

Josephine Chiao, Grade 7
Carson Middle School, VA

The Haircut

I had to cut my hair,
but the price was not fair!
I had to dig in my wallet
and crawl under my bed
until I had no money to spare.

Matthew Sun, Grade 7
Hammarskjold Middle School, NJ

Broken Raindrops

Raindrops fall down my window pane
Dropping from my eyes
Pouring into the flowing river
As I lay down and cry

The clouds are thickening slowly
I can't hold back my tears
And down the raindrops fall
Exploding in my fears

My heart has torn in two
I'm building up with rain
Puddles are filling quickly
I'm drowning in my pain

A flash of light strikes the earth
Then darkness sweeps the air
I can't believe you broke my heart
I guess you didn't care

Dawn breaks the peaceful sky
While birds fly up above
I wake up with a loneliness
For I have no more love

Meghan Grubb, Grade 9
Unami Middle School, PA

Roller Coaster Ride

Waiting in line for the ride
Scared, nervous, excited
People were talking
Loud, happy, jittery
Getting scared now
Closer, closer, closer
Sitting in the seat
Anxious, butterflies, shaking
Moving slowly uphill
Apprehensive, worried, oh no!
Down we go
Screaming, frightened, adrenaline
Twists and turns
Laughing, ecstatic, hold on!
The end of the ride
Relieved, giggling, let's go again!

Jordan Onisk, Grade 7
Depew Middle School, NY

Perfect

Perfect.
That's not me.
A China doll wannabe.
Model child.
LIES.

Emotionless.
That's not me.
Too composed to shed a tear at the
prospect of your dead
grandmother.
Left alone at the casket. Not shaken,
but crumbling away inside.
Others are comforted as I stand in
silence.

Perfection.
That's not me.

Anastasia Nicholl, Grade 7
Ocean City Intermediate School, NJ

Changing Seasons

Summer, winter, spring, fall
Summer, summer fun for all
Winter, winter bitter cold
Fall, fall red and gold
Spring, spring greenish fun
It all starts again just wait for the sun
Summer, winter, spring, fall
I just wish we could have them all.

Serena A. Moncion, Grade 7
Trinity Middle School, PA

Da Vinci's Lullaby

Paint stirred tornado-like
Grasping brushes red
And in this marathon race
I am far ahead.

Texture washing sideways
Practically one-to-none
But never in a decade
Will these colors run.

Shadows lurking in pictures
Pouring pain and hearts
Catch me if you can
My picture's sweet yet tart.

Am I an artist now?
As I'm tightening ties
Hanging masterpieces
This is Da Vinci's Lullaby.

Kayla Novak, Grade 8
Logan Middle School, PA

One Window

One window is all I need…
To examine the never-ending limit of my thoughts,
To observe my guilt and my innocence,
To allow my emotions to frolic,
To watch myself grow as a person,
One window is all I need.

Vincent Rigoglioso, Grade 7
Anthony Wayne Middle School, NJ

Thoughts of Adolescence

I am…a young girl with a full heart,
hidden somewhere in an empty room…
with eyes not quite of autumn's gold,
and yet neither all of summer's green;
I see…a girl, insecure, but uncompromising,
transparent as air — less, even, than the tears
that fall in anguish about her weary feet,
salt poison united with the withered ground…
I touch…the downy wings of hope, in wonder,
in reverence, in need, in hunger;
sadly it burns my fingers as a flame
I hear…a measure of serenity, a certain silence,
the echo of alone which heals me of dreaming,
the nothing that stills the wanting,
the numb, the cold that laughs at pain;
I dream…of bluest waters, reaching
with twisted hands toward the faded sky,
of dolphins that wander in seas without limits,
carrying me past corals and clouds…
I am a young girl, only.

Erica Eckel, Grade 8
Emily C Reynolds Middle School, NJ

The Star

I want to be a rock star
but all I seem to be is a silly little girl
whose dream is too big.
Every time I tell someone my dream
I get the usual
"good luck with that" or "yeah right."
No one can see my talent unless they hear me.
They just see me standing there
with my bass in my hands
and music in my soul.
They don't see how their words hurt me.
They don't understand how their words bring me down
and how they discourage me instead of encourage me.
Just wait though
one day when I AM a star
they will see how they were wrong
and I was right.
I am a star and I will travel far.

Kelsey Buckingham, Grade 8
Beacon Middle School, DE

Chocolate Delights

Chocolate Delights
divine and so sweet
so many varieties
so many to choose
let's just name a few
first there's milk chocolate
milky and creamy, ooh lala
heaven melting in your mouth, what a treat!
next there's dark chocolate
pieces of goodness
talk about a wonderful dream, delightful
last but not least white chocolate
a very nice choice for a very special day
so unique, white chocolate
I can taste the delectable now
Wow!
although I named a few,
there's so many more
cake, sundaes, strawberries, yum
You can never get enough of
Chocolate Delights

Kelli Humphrey, Grade 7
Carson Middle School, VA

Markers

Yesterday, my mom got me new markers.
They were all watery, wonderful colors.
The markers were supposed to be used for school.
But I accidentally lost them in brambles at the pool.

I entered the edifice where my mom lives,
Afraid to tell her where the marker set is.
I told my mom of the bad news.
She got so mad I think that she blew.

She grounded me big, sending me to my room,
I felt like a prisoner in the kingdom of doom.

Now my mom won't get me more markers,
I'll miss all those watery, wonderful colors.

Grace Liu, Grade 7
Fairfax Collegiate School, VA

War

Has a toll on every one
War is the thing that ruins people's lives
War can rip states apart
War makes one place never the same
War changes people's minds and thoughts
War is the fear that haunts everyone
War is the permanent mark left on people that fought
War is the never ending pain that we all feel
War can change a well united country into a wasteland
War is the devil's game

Isaiah Johnston, Grade 7
Pine-Richland Middle School, PA

In Touch

It's been so long,
Since I've seen my friends,
I sing some songs,
But the pain never ends.
I miss them dearly,
And I wish they were near me.
But we're growing now,
And I just don't see how.

I've been told many times
That we won't keep in touch,
Well, the joke's on them,
'Cause I love them very much.

I think of them so often,
Our times won't be forgotten.
I love them like my family,
I'd do anything for them,
You'll eventually see…

Jennifer Nelson, Grade 9
Shenendehowa High School, NY

Pop-pop

Pop-pop,
You'll always be in my heart.
You'll always be in my prayers.
You'll always be a part of me.
You're not on this earth,
But you'll forever be in my world.
Arm wrestling,
Catching crabs,
Swimming in the bay,
Driving the tractor,
Going out for breakfast,
When I do these things,
I will think of you.
I've never wondered where you are,
Because I've known all along.

Aine Boyle, Grade 7
Ocean City Intermediate School, NJ

Confidence

Hold on to your confidence
Like if it was your air
No matter what anyone says
Don't even bother to care
Violence is not the answer
Nor will it ever be
Look up high
And count how many goals you can see
This is where your focus is
This is where your mind shall be set
This where you should be looking
Until the day you rest.

Walline Alphonse, Grade 8
Orange Middle School, NJ

One Window Is All I Need

One window is all I need to visualize the plan that will help me succeed.
To spread my wings and learn how to fly,
To do what it takes to reach the sky.
To realize that the world isn't such a horrible place.
To conquer my fears and realize my dreams.
To live, to laugh, to love,
And to do all the above!

Mona Hassanein, Grade 7
Anthony Wayne Middle School, NJ

Homework

The homework teachers give us is really just too much,
It takes up most of my time, I even work through lunch!

Does it help you or fail you, this answer I have no clue.
The amount of books in my backpack weighs a ton, that's true!

I have no room in there for my pencils or my pens.
The books take up so much space, I can't possibly fit in ten.

Is homework really necessary, or do teachers torture us,
And if it is incomplete, a failing grade — no fuss.

So, as I write this poem, thinking how it will rhyme,
It really is my homework taking up my time.

So, now it is done and typed for the teacher to see,
I am trying not to think of the next assignment bestowed upon me.

Michael Jeras, Grade 7
Depew Middle School, NY

Where I'm From

I am from Rambling Hills drawing with chalk on sidewalks
I am from poetry and Thanksgiving meals
I am from the tire swing glistening under my flower budded tree
I am from watching my dad get around with his IV
Who learned what I have to be grateful for

I am from soccer and making my first goal
And landing my round-off backhand spring
I am from my coaches who encouraged me and never let me give up
I am from clean your room! And make your bed!
I am from my three cousins one month, two years, and three
From memories of watching how they grow

I am from Dolores and Joe
Back flips and paintings
From the glass butterfly at home in the curio cabinet
I am from the Catholic Church making my 1st holy communion
Looking at pictures to remind me of my past
New places, old faces but still memories to me

Gina Geletei, Grade 7
Hammarskjold Middle School, NJ

Orange

As I go to the store to buy some fruit
My mom needs some more because we're out of
Strawberries, oranges too.
As we get near
The oranges bend
I smell a sweet citrus blend.
Then I pick it up and
It's smooth as can be
I say mom that's the orange
I want to take home with me.

Latesia Bailey, Grade 7
Ruffner Middle School, VA

The Truth of Friendship

Friendship is many things
Silly smiles for the camera
Laugh attacks that bring us tears
Up-all-night sleepovers
And all those fun memories over the years.

Hour-long phone calls
Parents constantly yelling, "That's enough."
Talking about boys and fashion,
Music, teachers, and the random stuff.

Gossip in the crowded hallways
Text after text on our cells
Hanging out by our lockers,
Just before we hear the bells.

Keeping secrets, sharing dreams
Listening, supporting, and caring too
This is what friendship is,
For the best of friends, me and you.

Wendy Nelson, Grade 7
Depew Middle School, NY

Playing on the Diamond

Playing on the baseball diamond is the best game
Baseball can make you wallow in shame
Or it can take you to fame

Baseball is a sport of the mind
Make you think before the sign
It is a physical fight
Running during the game all day and night

Once reach the 9th
With it tied up
It's a 3-2 count
The pitcher staring you down
You dodge a bullet the pitch is in the ground
The game is over now
You can take your bow

Kevin Jakinovich, Grade 8
Floral Park Memorial High School, NY

Xanadu Zoo

A **B** lue Bird **C** omically **D** ives for food
E agles
F ly above the clouds
G ibbons
H ang from leafless limbs
I guanas
J ump from stone to stone
K angaroos
L urk, ready to jump
M onkeys
N est awaiting their young
O striches **P** ace **Q** uietly back and forth
R attlesnakes
S lither and hiss
T urtles
U nder water swim round and round
V ultures'
W ings flap preparing to prey
X anadu
Y ear-round
Z oo life

Aria DiMeo, Grade 9
Mount St Charles Academy, RI

When You Sleep

When minutes turn to hours
and the sun asks the moon to bring the dawn
when geese graze and pigs fly over yonder moon
when clocks turn into lamps
when picture and frame turn to book
when a cloud becomes ones bed
and when flowers turn to stars in the sky
when quarters turn to candy and veggies to dust
one is asleep,
one is happy,
one is free to wish,
one is asleep.

Faye Aarons, Grade 7
Carson Middle School, VA

Miracles Do Happen

The mom was getting ready for bed,
There she sat on the edge of the bed
Thinking about the baby,
When her water broke.
It was three months early.
The baby was born.
There it laid, so small.
Doctors say
There was a small chance the baby will survive.
Little did the mom know
That miracles do happen.

Jessie Pang, Grade 7
Hammarskjold Middle School, NJ

Make Love, Not War

We live in a world filled with terror and hate.
There's so much going on
that we tend to lose our faith,
in this crazy world
that we can't escape.

Sometimes we loose sight of what matters the most,
and our fate, we must choose it.
We don't know
what we have
until we lose it.

There's only one way for our bond to tighten.
Instead of fighting,
and hating each other,
we should come together
and love one another.

We should put all of our differences aside,
and become
close friends
because no one knows how it all will end

We might fall in a hole; we might even die,
but if we MAKE LOVE NOT WAR, we just might survive!

Cierra Granger, Grade 8
Ocean City Intermediate School, NJ

My Life

During the course of history, lives change
in good ways, yet change in bad
through death, births, and experiences.
"People we love create and share tears."

Lives are never the same, ever.
In gaining new friendships,
life builds brick walls of memories
that forever become cemented into minds.

When progressing in life,
thousands of lives change every day
not even knowing it.
People sign into the guest book of life
which never becomes filled.

Time goes by and new people pass
through giving direction to new paths of life.
And no matter what is done,
life moves on in order to reach
accomplishments bringing great pride.
Times change.
Lives change.

Toni Pindale, Grade 7
Ocean City Intermediate School, NJ

(A)

he found out her story
he said he would help
tell her what book of the bible to read
she actually feels like he knows
like he had been through the same
like he actually cares
she had people pretending before
but she feels god in him
feels like he will help
feels like it will be ok to stop
she doesn't really know him
she can just sense it
just finds he cares
that he wants to reach out
but she doesn't know if she wants that
if that will be ok
so she waits now
but feels like she is important to someone
for the first time in her life.

Abigail Jones, Grade 7
Talley Middle School, DE

A Story

Dragons, princesses, wizards galore,
Animals, teachers, monsters, and more.
Prince Charming in a faraway land,
Saving a princess without command.

A final second shot goes in with a Swoosh!
Wind blows across a cold mountain, Whoosh!
A story's a place for a mind to wander,
With plenty of things for it to ponder.

With death and disaster,
A car going faster and faster,
Sunny days and rainy nights,
Summertime for flying kites,

A story can be anything you want it to be,
All you need is to grab a book and you'll see!

Erin Ring, Grade 7
Chickahominy Middle School, VA

The Jewels

I believe in hard work
The blood
The sweat
The tears
The pain and soreness
But I don't believe in giving up
I believe in myself
I believe in my team
And I believe that no matter how hard I fall
There will always be someone there to catch me

Shannon Danis, Grade 7
Carson Middle School, PA

It Can't Rain Forever

It is hear now,
A thing that I know well,
I can hear the loud booms and see the bright flashes,
And I don't think they will ever leave my life.
But then I remember these great words,
And repeat them to myself over and over:
A storm may be in you're life now,
But it can't rain forever.

Rachael Chen, Grade 7
Monsignor Haddad Middle School, MA

The Juggler

Mental and bod'ly weakness take control,
Sports hand over no peace on a school night.
Worn out limbs don't have the power to write;
Activities leave no time for the soul.
If time could be found, it would make me whole.
Teachers and coaches do not have clear sight;
Understand us students when things are tight,
Workloads are making me pay a huge toll.

Angry with myself, my eyes are bleary.
Managing time is a great life lesson.
Stick out this crisis, don't be so teary.
I'm almost there with my frank confessin',
Organizing life itself is weary
Coping. The skills I've employed; a blessin'.

Brynn Dietzel, Grade 9
Unami Middle School, PA

Untitled

Sitting in the car,
waiting for a star
A star to wish on to make things better,
but there is none in this weather
It's dark outside,
there's nowhere to hide
I wish it was brighter,
so the dark side can be lighter
Many secrets are in the streets,
while people are still in their sheets
What's there to do when the evil tempts you?
or when you're stuck between two?

The grass is greener on the other side,
over there there's no reason to hide
The roller coaster ride is no longer working,
and the evil will not be lurking
So put on your smile,
something you haven't had for a while
And be yourself,
you can't be no one else

Edienna Perez, Grade 7
Dr E Alma Flagg Elementary School, NJ

Bliss

Custer State Park, sitting on an immense rock face
Smooth and gray in its loneliness on the lake
I, a minuscule person next to the rock,
found bliss.
Staring at the crystal blue lake with the shimmering fish
swimming through the gently breaking waves.
A gentle breeze ran through my hair.
At that moment,
The world stood still.
Quiet, peaceful, beautiful.
As if life took a breath,
watching my moment, one single moment.
Not a cloud moved,
not a tree swayed.
The turning of twilight reflected the beautiful sunset off the lake.
My moment that the world watched
with me in silence,
peace from life.

Caylee Sams, Grade 7
Trinity Middle School, PA

Terrorism

Terrorism is something that affects me as an American.
Americans are affected by terrorism in many ways.
Terrorists are all around us, blending in with the crowd,
Attacking us when we are not ready,
Killing little children, women, and men.
They cannot be stopped, hiding in secrecy.
Their leaders are powerful and wealthy.
They are as silent as the wind.
All they want is destruction and to end peace.
They are the monsters of our world.

Daniel Cornish, Grade 7
Pine-Richland Middle School, PA

The Feeling

The feeling of hitting a grand slam to win the game
Thrilling
Swishing a three-pointer at the buzzer
Mind boggling
Sipping ice cold lemonade on a hot day
Thirst-quenching
Jumping into a sparkling pool
Rejuvenating
Acing a chapter test
Fulfilling
Winning a school spelling bee
Astounding
Biting into a saucy rib
Savory
A thick milkshake as frosty as snow sliding down my throat
Delectable
The feeling of being with my family
Priceless

Denis Vanini, Grade 7
Depew Middle School, NY

Soul Mate

When you find your soul mate
it's just like a play date
the journey is long
but love is strong.
It's like a song
so sing along
it does not last forever
but never say never.

Kim Brown, Grade 9
Unami Middle School, PA

Flying Through Water

A fish is a bird,
Flying through water,
Without any word,
To find food for its daughter.

It's spotted the prey,
It's diving down deep,
Soaring through the day,
To make the prey sleep.

The chase has begun,
Prey trying to flee,
Underneath the sun,
Prey thinking, "Why me?"

The prey has been caught,
Hunter returning home,
As always he's brought,
Food back to the dome.

A fish is a bird,
Flying through water,
Without any word,
To find food for its daughter.

Alden Foelsche, Grade 7
Dorothy L Beckwith Middle School, MA

Everyone Is…

Everyone is an artist.
Everyone is a director.
Everyone is a writer.
A book.
You paint the painting.
A book.
You direct the movie.
A book.
You are the writer.

A book is where you benefit from
another person's work.
A book is where you are in control,
make it your own.

Andrea DiCristoforo, Grade 8
Hampstead Middle School, NH

Always Fighting!

We fight and scream.
You punch walls.
I slam doors.
You call me annoying.
I tell you to get lost.
We barely ever get along.
We are total opposites.

We can't even be in the same room without arguing about something.
We both have started fights but sometimes never ended them.

The truth is I hate to fight.
If you ever left, I would miss you.
So what I say isn't always true,
But no matter what we say or do,
I will always love you.

Alexandra Sokolofsky, Grade 7
Depew Middle School, NY

Veterans

I would like to thank U.S. Veterans for serving our country.
I very much appreciate all the time they put into the armed services.
I hope the war ends soon, so everyone can return home safely.
I know they do not have an easy job.

I cannot say thank you enough.
We have our freedom because they risk their lives.
I appreciate the sacrifices that the Veterans have made.
I hope everyone realizes how lucky they are to be safe in their own homes.

American Veterans are my heroes.
I wish I could thank each and every single one of them.
I truly appreciate everything they do.
I hope these two words get them through at least one more day,

Thank You.

Julia Snyder, Grade 9
Dallastown Area Sr High School, PA

The Person I Love

The person I love
The person that's like a shining star above
The person who is always there for me
The person who is warm like a hot cup of tea
The person who is like my breathing air
The person who always cares
This person is a close relative
The person who is responsible for the way I live
This person has creamy, caramel skin
This person is neither thick nor thin
A person who is like a blossoming flower
A person who is like a light bulb, with so much energy and power
The person who in the beginning took care of me, then my brother
The person I love, the one who is and whom I call, my mother

La'India Santos-Phillips, Grade 7
Monongahela Middle School, NJ

Gift from the Heavens

Everything goes black and I hear,
"Your light must shine before others,
so that they may see your good deeds
and glorify your heavenly Father."
Although I don't fully understand its whole meaning,
I feel different somehow, more pure,
Like something great has just happened to me.
I can't quite put a finger on it.
It's one of those things no one understands,
Like when the wind talks to you.
Then it hit me!
I let the light of God reach me.
I've been shading myself,
But now I can no longer resist.
For the power of God has reached me.
I have now accepted and embraced it.
God has purified me,
God has simplified my life,
God has improved me.
I feel happiness.

Brendan Bagnato, Grade 9
Pine-Richland Middle School, PA

The Watchers

Ah, Bliss
lift a battered mug, sipping gentle milk and honey
two feet dangle off the stool
breathing across a woven-forest of yarns and threads
Finally slipping
onto a wooden bar slung across the chair legs

My gaze falls beyond the countertop, the grape ivy, the door,
it too rests
upon the peeling bark of two towering shagbark hickories
that seem to be two giant vultures with thin molting feathers.
They perch tall and straight in a grassy field, their
wings shading over the windows, watching;
Sentinels for what is now
home.

Melissa Liu, Grade 9
Pomperaug Regional High School, CT

Tornado

I am a tornado.
I sway and whip through the skies
with anger and power.
I travel across the land
like a bulldozer,
destroying everything in sight.
I pick up and throw objects
with no effort at all.
When the sun pokes through the skies,
I disappear
like a magician performing his final trick.

Emma Nelson, Grade 7
Christ the Teacher Catholic School, DE

Love

Love takes root and holds fast to your desires.
It's taking on a beautiful pure shape
Becoming an unconditional fire.
And your love becomes your life; it's your fate.

Love fading, wilts when you need it the most.
It's leaving, now a broken, hollow mold.
Love is a sickness and you are its host.
Love's giving, taking, leaving you so cold.

It hurts but heals. It makes but breaks, and you
No more than a child in its eyes, are lost.
It's needed, wanted but is hated too.
It's such a great prize at such a high cost.

Love is a hunger, dire to satiate.
Love is a danger and unknown 'til late.

Teva Mayer, Grade 7
Mars Area Middle School, PA

Beauty

What really is beauty?
Is it my hair or my clothes?
Maybe it's my character or my bubbly personality?
To me, I feel beauty is who a person is,
How they feel and what they like.
Not how they look.
It's not bad to have outer beauty,
But without inner beauty it is useless.

Wow, she's really pretty,
But inside lies the heart as hard as a rock.
Though another girl as smart as a tick
With the character of a precious jewel remains unnoticed
Her bulky glasses and mouth full of braces block her beauty.
No one bothers to look within, to see the person she is
Beautiful is what she is
Just look inside.

Gabriella Khalil, Grade 7
Westwood Jr/Sr High School, NJ

Advice

When writing a poem
Stay true to yourself
Understand who you want to be
Come into your own
Know what you want to tell
Let your personality shine through
Don't forget…
Find your inspiration
Whether it be nature or the people around you
Write about something you know and believe in

Courtney Greene, Grade 7
School of International Studies at Meadowbrook, VA

New Best Friend

I give the girls my meanest glare, but they don't look, don't see me stare.
They're practicing handstands in the pool. Having fun in water cool,
My sister and her new friend. I can feel my stomach bend.
My throat tightens as around I turn, and watch the pale blue water churn,
And lap at the walls. "Hey Becca," my sis calls.
I cross my arms and pretend not to hear, but she knows better and draws near.
"Come on Bec, please play?" But I'm still mad and turn away.
She finally decides to leave me alone. For sadness and anger is all I have shown.
Under the water I pull my knees to my ears, and let loose a string of sobs and tears.
I'm sad, angry, jealous, with a clenched heart, why couldn't they have been nice from the start?
And when I surface for a breath of fresh air, I give the two girls my meanest glare.

Rebecca Torchia, Grade 9
Pine-Richland Middle School, PA

No More Loyal "Tea"

The sky is darkening as we paint ourselves with the war paints of liberation
As we slip on the clothes and wigs of justice
As we review our plan for freedom and as we talk of our desire for independence.
We walk toward the HMS Dartmouth waiting in the harbor
As we think about the prize
Liberty
And the consequences we will gladly face to get it.

We board the ship and open the cartons of tea
Opening a way to our independence and freedom.
As we heave the tea into the Boston Harbor
We are dumping our loyalty to Britain and all British rule.
The waters and shores of Boston Harbor turn brown
Reminding us of how nothing will ever be the same.
Tea will be washing up on these shores for weeks
In protest of the taxes and in hopes for freedom and independence.

We have finished our job here and must return home.
As we wash off the war paints of liberation as we remove the clothes and wigs of justice
As we remember what we have done for freedom
And as we think of our momentary satisfaction in our desire of independence
We know that we are one step closer to claiming the prize of liberty and justice
And that one day we will have succeeded in shedding our British loyal "tea."

Kim Riordan, Grade 7
Commack Middle School, NY

Tomorrow

Like a lamp on a desk that is turned off,
We wait, for tomorrow.

Maybe it's broken, maybe the bulb burned out, maybe it's not plugged in. Nope it's fine, just off. So we wait, for tomorrow.

Wait, it's flickering. Slowly, the flickers speed up until it's consistent,
Then it goes out.

Wait for it, wait for it. There,
It's on and soon it will be brighter, because on the table where the light shines it reads: Hope.

Tomorrow has come.

Sam Burk Schwarzwalder, Grade 8
Oyster-Adams Bilingual School, DC

Branded

Every thought involving him is stalked by
A wave of heat that kisses my cheeks, words
Leave my mouth in mad attempts to deny
The way every time he looks at me he stirs
Feelings I did not know I had until
His eyes as crisp and clear as arctic ice
Poured crystal blue water until so full
Was my soul I could not bear it, suffice
It to say that the curves of his lips are
A temptation of the highest degree
His smile could send me to the farthest star
How he has so much power over me
Is something I will never understand
I just know I am forever branded.

Kellie Hollingsworth, Grade 9
Unami Middle School, PA

My Tree

Summer is lingering near
as I sit under my tree
with little drops of rain water drop on drop
sitting in green beds from the previous night.
Penetrating rays stain its leaves
creating movement,
a performance, a summer dance
drop on drop slithering
down the fingers of my tree.

Carly Roeck, Grade 7
Ocean City Intermediate School, NJ

The Storm

The clouds hurtle across the angry sky,
Spewing out rain in a fury of water
Fiery lightning falls down, hits the earth,
And springs back up into the clouds,
Only to strike again.
Thunder explodes through the ashy sky,
Ripping in and out of the violent atmosphere
Only to strike again.
Trees thrash in agony and pain
As the elements wound their wooded hearts
The relentless wind stings the frozen ground,
Turning it into nothing less than ice.
The Storm batters and beats the earth,
Frays it at the edges, makes it imperfect.
Gradually, finally, the clouds dissolve
The darkness lifts, the mist ascends,
And the Sun rears its shining head
Sheds buttery warmth, its lovely light
Healing it, resurrecting it…
And the forgotten Storm hides itself away
Only to strike again.

Priyanka Padidam, Grade 7
Unami Middle School, PA

Pitbulls

The kind of dog that is mistreated and misunderstood,
The little puppies are whipped by their owner's words,
Scared to leave their so called jail cell.
Pit bulls are nice, friendly dogs,
Unless their owners treat them bad,
They love to be seen,
And love to be loved back.
Unless you have no heart,
You could give the best home a dog could ever ask for,
But if you don't have a good heart, please don't judge,
This is a very gentle dog that loves to protect its family.
Unless you're very rude, this dog won't attack,
Not even dogs because they love company.

Mallory Nixon, Grade 8
Ephrata Middle School, PA

Broadway Baby

I grew up with rhinestones and glitter
I was raised with the comforting smell of flowers and wet paint
with tight ballet shoes and the light jingle of tap shoes
with rubber bands and hairspray
I grew up with singing and dancing
and never being afraid of a crowd
I was raised with make-up and spotlights
with smiles and applause
I was raised with stage crews and props
I was raised doing what I do best — performing
I was raised with Broadway and pianos
I was raised as a singer, dancer, and actress
I was raised doing what I want to do forever — be on stage

Sidney Nicole Popielarcheck, Grade 7
Trinity Middle School, PA

The Shadows of Nature

The music of my heart doesn't stop beating,
It thumps to the beat of the Earth.
The wind in the trees,
The mist, tingling down the waterfall,
The thump and splash of the ocean on sand,
The growths on the forest floor…
All of them tell my heart to beat,
Without them my heart would not beat.
A building, a skyscraper, a ruin,
Garbage, death, habitation,
Humans…
The enemies that try nature,
And harm its lovely existence,
The only thing standing in nature's way,
The blockade between me and nature.
The only shadows of nature that
Harm it, choke it, seize it.
My life in the hands of nature.
Nature in the hands of
Mankind.

Tommy Wright, Grade 8
Emily C Reynolds Middle School, NJ

Soaring

The eagle looks upon the land
Its land, fruitful and strong.
He feels the winds of change.
Warm under his wings,
And he rides with it.

What a ride!

He sees his land
And knows it's good.
Some things are wrong,
But it will be better.
It's stormy now,
But it can't rain forever.

The eagle will be brave.
He will protect and defend his land.
He promises peace and prosperity.
He knows, our land will be great.

His spirit soars higher than his flight,
And he will fight, for our rights,
Every day, and every night.
The eagle flies new colors of hope,
Over his land, fruitful and strong.
Mary McDonald, Grade 8
Monsignor Haddad Middle School, MA

Stars

Stars show up in the night sky.
It makes me just want to fly.
I need to make one mine,
And show it off by letting it shine.
Sandra Mae Fuentes, Grade 7
St Agatha School, NY

Home

Silence,
Your
Free gift
Is
a
New
House
Bigger
and
Better
Than
Your
Old
Home
Now
Flashback to
Your old life.
Mike Johnson, Grade 9
Unami Middle School, PA

The Fall of Icarus

A boy with a pride too big, and wings too frail
Fell from the sky with his father stunned and pail
Icarus flew way to high, when his father said no
With a cocky smile up to the sun he'd go

As the glue started to melt, and his smile the same
His wings were coming off down to the ground he came
With a great plop in the pond, and a weep from his dad
Others barely looked and no one looked any sad

Nature took its course and it wouldn't stop to save
The dying young boy, who too much had raved,
About his bright new wings and his talent to match
As he fished for fame death is all that he'd catch

But no one would know, of his tragic death
They were to busy with their work they wouldn't even waste a breath
They went along with their work like nothing had happened
They kept on with their jobs Icarus' destiny securely fastened:

He would die that very day, with a lesson I am sure:
If you choose to fly high, make sure your wings are very secure!
Caitlin Harrah, Grade 7
School of International Studies at Meadowbrook, VA

Far-Lying from Reality

When I look up I see the colors of the sun melting in the distance.
A salty breeze embraces me with amity as I continue to watch the sunset.
The feeling was unimaginable, but I had no one to share it with.
It grew later and the sun was almost set when he came.
His glossy hair and full lips were positioned in just the right way.
And when I looked into his icy blue eyes I got lost in their moonlit gleam.

He sat down next to me and said nothing.
But his presence said it all.
His love was ten times greater than anything I had hoped for.
Back in my home I opened the door as the old fashioned tune rang.
There he was standing at my door step.
But he wasn't the same.

His hair a dirty brown with no life nor gloss.
His lips were plain and simple, not enough for me.
And when I looked into his eyes I could have cried.
Another night passed as my true love from before met me in the park.
But then I woke up and realized that the man of my dreams was only in my dreams.
And that one who falls in love with perfection,
will never have the heart to come face to face with reality.

I came to school the next day and kissed the imperfect boy.
And even though he was no prince charming, he'll just have to do.
Olivia Peterkin, Grade 7
Carson Middle School, VA

Only Me

Grief has filled me, such sorrow and anger.
Don't they understand? I want them to see me,
The real me, so I don't feel like a stranger.
I want to be open just like the sea.
They adore the other, who doesn't try
So why should I? When they do not try at all.
I'm telling you I don't feel high and mighty,
Feeling so down and low makes my heart fall.
They look at me and say that they love me,
No, they laugh to cover their guilt, from my pain
They never can tell that I am only me
And in this life I feel I have nothing to gain.
They don't understand how I feel today,
Agitated, a complete failure, every day.

Cindy Rushworth, Grade 9
Unami Middle School, PA

Life

Life is like a pool…
You never know what it's like until you dive in.
Life is like a waterfall…
You never know what's coming next.
Life is like candy…
They are both sweet and sometimes sour.
Life is like a soccer game…
You are always trying to reach your goal.
Life is like a roller coaster…
They both take you up and down.
Life is like a friend…
They both can put you down and build you back up.
Life is like a hurricane…
They both have calm in the middle of something rough.
Life is like a baseball game…
They both lead you back home.

Jordan Crills, Grade 8
Ephrata Middle School, PA

The Heart of Nature

Nature brings warmth
and joy to my soul.
Walking outside I smell fresh air,
hear chirping birds, hooting owls,
howling wolves in the night.

Nature should be cherished
forever because she is heartwarming,
enticing, and embracing everyone
to share in her beauty.

One day we should
all feel the same way about her,
think outside the box, be open-minded
because it's just the heart of nature
that brings this country together.

Mariah Rowell, Grade 7
Ocean City Intermediate School, NJ

All My Siblings Are Gone

All my siblings are gone
I hate it, I hate it, I hate it, so much
Not even having a hand to touch
A shoulder to lean on would be so nice
And when they come home it's like rolling dice
I never know how long they will stay
I wish they would move closer my way
When they both moved away from me
My eyes were so teary I couldn't even see
With nothing to do but sit around frozen
But then I realize this is the profession they have chosen
With my brother controlling investments
And my sister in commercials
Geez, I feel left out just learning how to use plurals
I take after my brother with his amazing math smarts
And of course I look like my sister with my striking body parts
One day they will both be famous
And me just sitting here
Maybe I'll be tackling running backs without one ounce of fear
One day I'll work for my brother; maybe manage my sister too
And all I can say is I wish I was there with you

Paul Emanuele, Grade 7
Franklin Regional Middle School, PA

Things Under My Bed

I lean down,
What's that thing, under my bed?
Is it a broken piece of lead?
Which has been there since last fall
Next to the pretty rainbow colored ball?
Or maybe it's my favorite teddy bear
Waiting to be rescued from the vicious dark air.
Could it be a lonely sock without its pair,
Right under that, dried up rotten pear?!
Let's see, what else we've got there, a book?
Oh no! It's long overdue; just look!
And pens, and papers, keys and chips
And even some old hair clips!
Oh cool! Look, there's an apple pie
I can eat it, but then I'll die…
The more I search below my bed,
The more I keep my mouth opened.
Well, I know one thing for sure
This is not a normal room.
So immature!

Aydan Rasulova, Grade 7
Carson Middle School, VA

field hockey

running, communication, participation,
strength, encouragement, turn and dribble past your opponent
one love, one team, one sport!

Mesa Alexander, Grade 8
Ephrata Middle School, PA

The Breeze

The gentle breeze rushes by.
Rushing things through the sky.
Slinking in between the trees.
Buzzing down beside the bees.

Swirling, twirling, whispering too!
High above the ground it flew.
Swaying trees of many faces,
Blowing through so many places.

The gentle breeze rushes by again.
Caroline Landrum, Grade 7
Ghent School, VA

The Crystal Clear Blue

The waves roll in,
The waves roll out,
As I sit,
In the cooling soft sand,
Watching the sunset,
On the beach,
In the presence,
Of the crystal clear blue.

As I approach the water,
For one last dive,
I get a tingling chill from my bare feet,
To my spine,
As the wind blows my hair,
I dive head first,
Into the crystal clear blue.

I am so at peace,
As I glide through,
The darkened soft,
Crystal clear blue.
Stephanie Jones, Grade 7
Lawrence School, MA

Love

Love is like a trap,
A trap you want to fall into,
And once you fall into one,
It's hard to get out of.

You'll know your love is true,
When your heart skips a beat,
Whenever he embraces you.

The sight of his beautiful eyes,
The scent of his skin,
The sound of his voice,
The feeling of his hand in mine,
Lets me know he's the one for me.
Julianna Pallone-Shehaiber, Grade 7
Intermediate School 381, NY

Frozen Dreaming

Silence can only be treated, with the hope of a cure,
Silence is this barren thing, that was just this occurrence to lure —
The ideas and minds of the patient ones, the ones we claim so much to adore.
But really, do we admire them, without a doubt to leave us obscure?
If our mind differs from their own, our most treasured dreams,
That defer from the realistic norm?
When we criticize them for their dreams, saying that they are not at all secure?
Silence can only be treated, with the hope of a cure,
It beacons at our feet — when the time comes to morn —
It slithers down our path — when we have not a thing to outpour,
Oh, how we wish to avoid the things we must endure.
We build ourselves with the hope at times, even though we are unsure,
What lies ahead, in front of our frozen solid doors.
Isn't it almost like velour,
Slipping away from the quandaries we make couture?
Silence can only be treated, with the hope of a cure,
Silence is this barren thing, that was just this occurrence to lure —
The ideas and minds of the patient ones, the ones we claim so much to adore.
But really, do we admire them, without a doubt to leave us obscure?
Is the silence that comes after frozen dreams,
A new kind of dreaming tambour?
Sahbrene Elmahalawy, Grade 8
Darul Arqam School, NJ

God's on the Right, Jesus Is on the Left of Me

God's on the right, Jesus is on the left of me.
The Bible works like a bulletproof vest for me.
When my feet get tired of walking in Christ, it works like a foot rest for me.
Life is the biggest test to me, with the reward of eternal life with Thee.
The Bible's the foundation; it gives you your salvation.
Jesus will be the key that'll set you free.
I'll be the 'modern-day Moses' and open your heart, like he did the Red Sea.
God's my best friend; He's always there around the bend.
He's the chief so give Him your belief.
He's the Boss; He'll find you even if you're lost.
He's so nice, He'll buy your soul no matter the price.
God's on the right, Jesus is on the left of me.
Proceed and concede to the One who's exceeded,
the One who succeeded, and
the decree will be acceded,
then your problems will be defeated.
God is superior, Satan is inferior.
That's why you always salute Him with a capital 'G'!
Devante Abraham, Grade 7
Life Academy, PA

Summer

Summer is a great season
This is due to many reasons
The weather is hot instead of cold
This makes us feel like gold
You can go to the beach and feel the sand on your feet
Or you can go to the pool and become cool
This is why I love the summer and the weather, could it be any better?
Julia Santoro, Grade 8
Floral Park Memorial High School, NY

Summer Rain

As the rain trickles from the sky,
I look outside to give a big sigh.
I want to go play out in the rain,
but I know it will give me pain.

As the rain keeps on coming down,
I hope that our house will not drown.
I sit there to be bored to death,
just hoping not to take my last breath.

I want the rain to go away,
then come again another day.
It seems not to listen to me,
but I'll just let it be.

I wish not to make it mad,
that would just make me much more bad.
I know we need some rain to survive,
it allow plants and animals to thrive.
It's good for the environment,
like a breath of new fresh air.

I just hope not too much comes,
then the rest of the day will just be a bum.

Daniel Li, Grade 7
Carson Middle School, VA

I Do Not Believe Them

Some see me as unlucky,
I don't believe them.
I have all I need to be successful.
Some see me as boring,
I don't believe them.
I interest myself.

Some believe I am unhappy,
I don't believe them.
I have my days of fun.
There are looks that are deceiving,
There are truths untold,
There are flowers yet to be bloomed,
And suns yet to rise.

I hold onto my four leaf clover,
I recite my life stories.
I laugh 'til earthquakes crack the earth below me.
I don't believe them.
Maybe someday you will see who the real me is.
I am not my looks, looks can deceive.

I do not believe them, you shouldn't either.

Audrey Baker, Grade 7
Ocean City Intermediate School, NJ

The Best Day of Fishing

The day dawned cool and cloudy
The wind was blowing strong
On the day that we went fishing
Nothing could go wrong
As soon as we got there
The wind she ceased to blow
On the day that we went fishing
Nothing could go wrong
We had caught naught
As time dragged ever on
On the day that we went fishing
Nothing could go wrong
The wind, she began to howl
And the waves grew tall
On the day that we went fishing
Nothing could go wrong
We began to enjoy the time as the sun came out
And we saw fish swimming 'bout
Then it all came crashing down
When my brother said "Dad, let me out!"

Dylan Grant, Grade 7
Depew Middle School, NY

9-11-01

The towers were standing strong;
The first plane hit
Craziness started in New York City and around the world
People thought it was an accident,
Then the next plane hit.
Now everyone knew it was an attack;
The towers start to burn.
People are jumping to their death;
It makes you wonder what it was like inside.
Suddenly, the towers crumble;
The country suddenly "sank" with depression.
New York City will never be the same again.

Max Dugan, Grade 7
Pine-Richland Middle School, PA

Cycle of Life

Is nature the ruler of the whole world?
The breath of nature rustles through the trees.
The leaves on the ground have swirled,
And the honey flows from the busy bees.
The cycle of life brings things to an end;
Mother Nature must bring and take things away sometime.
Though sometimes it must be our very dear friend,
Everything cannot be quite sublime.
But Mother Nature starts all things anew.
Through life it is fresh, grand and full of joy.
The cycle of life brings old, but new too.
The process of all life can be quite coy.
The whole kingdom of nature rules it all,
To spring, to summer, to winter and to fall.

Arden Ashford, Grade 7
Moravian Academy Middle School, PA

Drip Drip

Drip, drip
Drip, splash,

Dew drop from high in the clouds
Tangentially falls to the Earth

Drip, drip
Drip, splash,

Day and night
Hour by hour

Drip, drip
Drip, splash,

The sun rises as a rainbow appears
And the din resumes
Jasmine Edmond, Grade 8
Fairfax Collegiate School, VA

The Race

Down at the track, the intensity will grow
With people running to and fro
Some have wins, some have loss
The competition is thrown across
As I bend down to start the race
Sweat trickles down my face
On go, I start to sprint
Around the bend, I begin to squint
The finish line is in the distance
I ignore my body's resistance
I dash across the ending line
I'm in first — the prize is mine
Janice Tieperman, Grade 7
Unami Middle School, PA

Summer Feeling!

Take a deep breath
Do you smell it?
Taste it? Hear it? Feel it?
It's summer.
Smell the grass and the
New budding flowers.
Taste the flavor of
The rain and the juicy
Summer fruits.
Hear the summer birds that are
Going chirp-chirp
The motorcycles roaring.
Feel the warmth of the summer sun
And the electric charge of fun
Summer is here
Smell, taste, hear, and feel it.
Sabrina Kwiatkowski, Grade 7
Depew Middle School, NY

Summer

At long last school is out
Now it's time to scream and shout
Vacation days are on their way
All day long it's time to play
We'll hit the beach
And ride the waves
Soak up the sun
And enjoy its rays
We will look so cool
But before we know it
It's time to go back to school
Alyssa Martinez, Grade 7
Hammarskjold Middle School, NJ

From Me to You

Roses are red,
Violets are blue.
Why am I,
So addicted to you?
You say you're dumb,
As smart as a sack.
But it doesn't matter,
If you're bright as black.
No matter what you say,
Or what you do,
You say that you love me,
And I will always love you.
Nolan Birtwell, Grade 8
Memorial Middle School, CT

Summer

It's summer! It's June!
Let's all listen to a radio tune.
We can go to the pool,
To stay so cool.
Kiara Costarelos, Grade 7
St Agatha School, NY

Signs of Spring in the Forest

The creek is running merrily,
the forest is all aglow.
Buds turn to leaves or flowers,
So let the world know!

The snow is melting quickly,
the Earth is warming up.
Winds are blowing gently
through trees and last year's grass.

Bees are flying happily,
the fawns take their first steps.
Bears are making troubles,
birds are making nests!
Yulia Taylor, Grade 7
Alexander Middle/High School, NY

3 Seconds

It's not over yet,
own the moment,
time to be a king,
don't give up,
there's only 3 seconds.
Marty Blanchard, Grade 9
Unami Middle School, PA

What Is a Friendship?

What is a friendship?
Oh so many things.
It's a lasting relationship,
Flying on wings.

It's a ship
That is sailing
Through good
And through bad.

It's a bird
That is flying
Through happy
And sad.

A friendship's a dream
That already came true,
And was specially made
For a person like you.
Katerina Nozhenko, Grade 7
School Number 14, NJ

Rain

I wish I could be like the rain
So fearless to ruin any good day
Too modest once praised
When all the mammals graze
To stay forever watching the world
Wherever it may travel it still unfurls
To give life to dying
Without even trying
Continuing a traditional lifelong cycle
Falling so bravely
Even if ground is below
Peaceful to rest
Even when rain is venting its feelings
Rain picks itself up again
To nurture and let life flow
Doesn't care about mistakes
Doesn't get only a single chance
Has not a worry in the world
But whom to influence next
I wish I could be like the rain
That would be the best
Berin Simsek, Grade 9
Chartiers Valley High School, PA

Winter

Winter is cold, mad, unforgiving
Biting the noses
Of people who step outside,
Ripping the life out of trees and meadows.

As I looked out the window,
I noticed the snow was melted and gone.
The birds were singing a beautiful song
And the leaves on the trees were dancing in the wind.
Spring is warm, refreshing, new.

Summer is hot, fun, and full of life.
Kissing the ocean waters
With giant swirls of blue on the beach
People laughing, enjoying, loving
What will mother nature think of next?

Jenny Groblewski, Grade 7
Depew Middle School, NY

Our Revolution

What trouble this world is in
Almost everything is perverted with sin
The whole world is a scrambled mess
Every action results in Satan's test
One person can't change the word, it's said
But maybe we just need more than one head
A new generation is on the rise
Ready to go, eyes on the prize
How amazing would it be
If our generation set the world free?
An army of youth, ready to fight.
A unit of young people, shining our lights
Who says we're too young
To get the job done?
No one else is stepping up to the plate
If we don't act now it will be too late.
So come together, this generation of youth
Let's show the world that we have the truth!
Together we grasp hands and pray
Our revolutions starts today!

Hannah Moore, Grade 9
Ralph C Mahar Regional High School, MA

Bang!

Bang!
The sound of an old car muffler brings me back to that day
I remember it clearly
It was the day that fate cruelly took you from me
You stood there frozen in fear when death came
I tried to get to you in time but the bullet was faster than me
In a split second you were on the floor in a never-ending sleep
Guns are the reason my best friend is no longer at my side
Bang!
A gun-free world is but a dreamer's dream

Kelly Raso, Grade 9
Quaker Valley High School, PA

Friends

A friend is like a light
shines bright but has a low beam
A friend is like a roller coaster
that stays with you in your ups and downs
A friend is a fire
which has a flame exploding with excitement until it's put out
A friend is like a name
it stays with you forever until chosen to be changed
A friend is like a mountain
strong and bold
A friend is like a fairy tale
when you dream of what you want them to be like
but a friend can't be forever
not yours maybe
but my friends are wonderful
or what I dream of them to be.

Tytianna Williams, Grade 7
School of International Studies at Meadowbrook, VA

As One Day Ends

As one day ends
Another starts.
All mistakes
Have been forgotten.
We are all human.
We need to forgive,
And stay together,
Help each other,
Play with one another
Till we end.

Bridget Podgorski, Grade 8
Christ the Divine Teacher Catholic Academy, PA

Feeling Alone

I see myself in the darkness of rays.
No longer to be heard beyond my days.
All alone — not a sound to make,
Wondering what leads my faith.
Doubted and uncared for don't have anyone but me.
I just wanna go, I just wanna be free.
Always being judged and being compared
Always crying and being scared.
Just wanna know what my future contains —
(does it hold happiness or me in pouring rain?)
Not a single person gets me, not one at all —
By myself I'll either rise or fall.
Today and right now I write this as I cry —
The only thing I know, I'm left alone
Not to rise nor not to hit the ground,
But wondering who to trust, who at all.
And if found will they help me up or let me fall?

Alexandra Jean-Paul, Grade 8
Northern Lebanon Middle School, PA

Life

Sometimes life can be a little strange.
But we all get through the day.
Friends will always be there for you.
To help you find your way.

Stephany Ciprian, Grade 7
St Agatha School, NY

Earth

I see trees of green and clouds of white.
A wonderful world day and night.
The day is nice, the night is too.
Earth gives us gifts for me and you.

Eric Cabrera, Grade 7
St Agatha School, NY

The Eagle

Beak royal golden
Body frozen
Eyes watching
Always searching
For prey
Every day
Oh, so glorious
She swoops for the catch
Victorious
There's food for the eggs
That will hatch

Navid Chowdhury, Grade 7
Selden Middle School, NY

Musical Seasons

Winter; Music is everywhere
Open your door
Hear the flakes fall
Christmas abound
New Year is here

Spring; Music is everywhere
Animals awake
Children go out and play
Easter abound
My birthday is here

Summer; Music is everywhere
The wind blows
The wave's crash and the sun sings
No school abound
Halloween is here

Fall; Music is everywhere
Step outside
Hear the crunch of the leaves
Work abound
Start all over again

Jiana Babu, Grade 8
Floral Park Memorial High School, NY

Developing Your Life

Rushing to the hospital, baby is born.
Crying. Laughter. Joy. Relief.
Mother and staff up since early morn'.
As beautiful as an angel, protection underneath.

The boy begins to walk, preciousness to the ones that love him.
The father loves him even more than his own dear life.
First words spoken make it past his delicate lips.
The first words to his life story; one that someone shouldn't skim.

Starting school, the boy soon learns.
Making friends, learning right from wrong.
Loves the education, a thing he tends to yearn.
Here he spends half is time, soon feels he belongs.

Growing up so fast, after an eighth year, it flies.
First comes middle school, the school year dies.
High school begins, he enters the senior high.
With all the school work, another hard year goes by.

Parents attend son's graduation.
Crying. Laughter. Joy. Relief.
Fellow peers, teachers, guiders say their congrats and goodbyes.
He knows this is the start of a new life, a new ingredient to his life calculation.

Katherine Zell, Grade 8
Ephrata Middle School, PA

Truly

If someone told me I could change who I was,
Then I'd change everything about me
I'd change my arms, legs, face, everything would have to go

Everything about me would be perfect
And I would finally see how the other side lives
I'd look fabulous all day,
The media would center around me and I would finally live in luxury

But if someone said I truly wasn't happy
I would think back to the time
I had family and friends
Who would always comfort me in my time of need

Would life truly be perfect with money, clothes, and riches of all sorts?
Without family to care and love you
Without friends to make you laugh and cry
I think not

If anyone would tell me I was perfect the way I was
With all my flaws and mistakes
Then I would truly be happy.

Raisa Alexis Santos, Grade 8
St Sylvester School, NY

The Sun

The sun appears from east to west,
Brightens up the day to help you look your best,
Uses nuclear fusion to tan your chest.
Floating high in the sky,
Until it slowly creeps out and says goodbye.

Anthony Brady, Grade 7
Anthony Wayne Middle School, NJ

The Lost Teddy Bear

It is almost time for bed.
When I walked into my room, it was an absolute mess.
I should have listened to what my mom said.
I probably should have guessed
that she would be right in the end.
When I glance in the direction of my bed,
I see that something is missing…OH NO!
Where is my teddy bear?
I cannot sleep without my teddy bear!
"Mom!" I yell, "Have you seen my teddy bear?"
"Did you clean your room?" she responded.
Darn, she has caught me again.
I knew that she would be right in the end.
I know I can find it, I can, I can!
I begin cleaning my room like a bear cleans his den.
Throwing shirts and socks everywhere
Just to find my beloved teddy bear.
And moments later, I come upon the spot
That beholds the one I seek.
My furry teddy bear is safe and sound
And now I can peacefully fall asleep.

Alexis Drake, Grade 8
Unami Middle School, PA

Sleep

I am lying in my bed
Counting some sheep
All because I can't
Go to sleep

I will toss my sheets
Or play with my feet
Because I have
A lot in my head
As I try to go to bed
But my body wants to leap
Because I can't go to sleep

I tried warm milk
And sleeping in silk
Now I have the need
To catch some Z's.

Christopher Craighead, Grade 9
Bishop Ford Central Catholic High School, NY

The Final Exam

For ten long months, we've been in school
But now we're almost through,
The school year has come to a closing
Yet the hardest part is still coming too.

Everything we've been through,
Everything we've learned,
Is coming back to haunt us,
And take all the grades we've earned.

There is no way to escape it,
We've been studying for days.
The test is meant to confuse us,
In ever so many ways.

They barely gave us warning,
As if they had not thought
That we'd have trouble remembering
Everything they had taught.

What if I'm not ready?
What if I'm not right?
Well that test is not till tomorrow,
So I'll forget about it for tonight.

Nick O'Connell, Grade 7
Carson Middle School, VA

Mountains

Snowcapped mountains white
Standing there tall and lofty
An amazing sight

Dallas Zuk, Grade 7
Our Lady of Grace Elementary School, PA

Standing Tall

Here I am, standing tall
after all you put me through
you took me, and held me
you stroked me and said what I wanted to hear
but then you constricted me
and squeezed and crushed
until my heart was given up
until the pieces slid between your greedy fingers
and shattered on the ground
you took me, and you broke me
but somehow, here I am
I was found and held once more
but it wasn't a hateful hand
no, it was a loving hand
a healing hand
it took me and helped me
it put me back together
so here I am
standing tall

Rosemarie Lenz, Grade 9
Clarence High School, NY

Withering and Dying

Our world has provided us with all that we need.
We constantly tear away at our almost limitless supply of resources.
Nobody truly realizes the damage we do daily by simply tossing a piece of trash on the ground.
Nature is being desecrated and its inhabitants slaughtered just so we can live a glamorous life.
We've cut down millions of trees to make room for industrial buildings that suffocate our world.
Our rivers blackened and our air poisoned because of man's greed and stupidity.
People take and take, yet few give back what they take.
Our world is slowly withering and dying from within.
If we do not stop this destruction, our world will be destroyed.

Dylan Scott Lowery, Grade 7
Pine-Richland Middle School, PA

Hollywood Rose

I'm that chick called a Hollywood rose, I'm the girl with the loaded guns
I'm the girl that always knows, with climbing I ain't never done
I'm the girl with the barbed wire heart band, but the soul of a pure white dove
I know you think I live in dreamland, and honey you need more than love

Ya gotta have a steel ambition, ya gotta fight life tooth and nail
No one cares if you're not in fighting condition, ya gotta stick to the wheel and use your sails
Ya gotta know how to sprint before you crawl, ya gotta stand up and never back down
Ya gotta know before you achieve it all, ya gotta spin this world around

Ya gotta brush off blood, sweat and tears, ya gotta plant those heels in the dirt
Ya gotta face your darkest fears, no one cares if you're sad and hurt
Ya gotta have you pistol out of your holster, ya gotta fight like that Hollywood rose
You're gonna ride life's roller coaster, ya gonna fight for places for your dreams to go

Promise me you'll dance to your own tune, and always run safely on a reckless road
Keep that head up, a break is coming soon, remember; stand strong under that heavy load
I live in the City of Angels, it's where I grew my steel hard nerves
It's where I've fought all my battles, and through being a Hollywood rose
I got what I deserved

Emily Mihailescu, Grade 9
Falmouth High School, MA

Zoë Libby

Zoë
Who is funny, mischievous, spastic,
Usually very random.
Relative of Ellen, Nathan, Max, and I like to think, the world.
Lover of horses, food, the beach,
Who feels glad to be alive, sad there is war,
Ecstatic that I am who I am.
Who needs attention, but not too much, a lot of laughter, so much it could fill the world, but mostly,
I need to belong.
Who fears being hurt, physically and mentally, failing tests, others, and myself,
But mostly being outcast.
Who gives people a hard time, bad advice and
Strong friendships.
Who would like to see Paris, France and the whole of Europe, Assateague and the wild ponies,
But mostly a peace-filled world.
Resident of Norfolk, Virginia.
Libby

Zoë Libby, Grade 7
Blair Middle School, VA

A Day by the Lake

A day by the beauty of heaven
Looking at the playful ducks
The graceful swans
The beautiful water lilies
Listening to the chirp chirp of the birds
The zzzzz of the dragonfly
The plink of a stone dropped in the water
Smelling the fresh grass
The sweet fragrance of flowers
The clean new air
Touching the flawless water
The feathers of birds left behind
The fur of a little baby bunny
This is the best day of a life
Quiet peaceful and calm
A day by the lake

Sahaja Yerramsetti, Grade 7
Carson Middle School, VA

Journey

The road is long,
Winding,
Twisting,
And you're not sure which way it will go.

Challenges you face,
Friends and foe entwined,
Lead to heartbreak or
Victory.

One goal drives you through the night,
Long and weary you are at the end,
But if the goal is accomplished,
It was worth the struggle.

You met friends and some friends
Turn to be foe,
Death follows, shadowing behind,
What seems to be a never ending struggle.

Samantha Dorman, Grade 7
School of International Studies at Meadowbrook, VA

Friends Forever

Through the ups   and downs in
Our friendship we're   always looking out
For each other. You're always there for me and
I'm always there for you. When one of us is sad
We always try to put a smile on one of our faces. We
Laugh till we cry over our funniest moments.
You're my true best friend and I don't
Know what I would do without
You. I hope we can be
Best friends
Forever!

Stephanie Bobeck, Grade 7
Depew Middle School, NY

Clueless*

He was so young.
And the pain for him had already started.
But what could I do?
Nothing.

He was just a child,
Young, and playful.
I didn't see it coming,
Until I heard the news of course.

He was diagnosed with Marfan's Syndrome.
Only two years old and having to start on drugs.
I didn't want to sit here and watch this happen to him.
The only thing I could give him was love.

The doctor's aren't one hundred percent sure,
But it runs in the family so there's really no doubt.
People say that things happen for a reason.
The reason in this case, I'm clueless.

My cousin.
The only thing I could ask is why him?
I hope he stays for as long as he can,
Because I wouldn't be able to watch him go.
The only thing I could do was love him.

Taylor Losel, Grade 7
Depew Middle School, NY
*Dedicated to Parker Spruch.

Jet Flyover in NYC

An airliner and supersonic jet
zoomed past the lower skyline in a flash.
Within minutes a nightmarish replay;
September 11th, circled the site,
calls and witnesses, but nothing
but a series of flights,
little warning, infuriating
and putting on the defense.
To fly so near the site,
One approved the clear mission,
confusion and disruption.
"I apologize and take responsibility for any distress."
Provide few answers and wouldn't say why.
A wise decision.
Requested anonymity,
Combined with another,
To speak, one would be taken
Above Liberty.
"Had I known about it,
I would have called them right
away and told them not to."

Julia Wunderlich, Grade 9
Unami Middle School, PA

Frightening Fog

I am fog
   I envelop everything around.
Anyone who sees me
   wonders
     what lurks in my ghostly shadows.
I send a spooky shudder
   that trickles down the spine
   of all who see me.
I hide my victims
   in my ghastly chamber.
Soon they are trapped
   in a foggy fortress.
Feel my misty wetness,
Taste my groggy moistness,
Hear a haunting "ooooooh"
as people
   pass
     me by.
Kyle Moore, Grade 7
Christ the Teacher Catholic School, DE

Cancer

Anyone, every year
cancer hits its corner.
Anytime, anywhere
where you're standing it's nearer.
Anyone, anybody
beware, you can get struck.
Be alarmed, beware
that you are out of luck.
So clutch on your skin,
and take a big, deep, breath,
for you aren't the only one
whose life is quick to its end.
You might be the lucky one,
the one who survived.
Please still pray for others,
that really might die.
Katie Culver, Grade 7
Floyd T. Binns Middle School, VA

Fourteen

Fourteen is just a number
A number I have surpassed
I'm on a different level
because of what I have seen
and because of my powerful past.
My life is full of lies and pain
slow moving and
full of all those love games.
Now just saying I'm 14
would be an understatement
because I am more than your average
number 14.
Jasmine Johnson, Grade 8
Beacon Middle School, DE

June

June will come, after May.
I can hardly wait for the day.

Many happy songs will be sung.
when the final school bell has rung.

I have sat in the cafeteria all school year with my bunch.
we have all eaten our last lousy lunch.

It will be a great summer.
when all my friends get together and do things we will remember.

The summer will go fast
it can never last.

Next school year will start.
I will once again try for good marks.
Jim Daniels, Grade 7
Garnet Valley Middle School, PA

Ode to Green Crayons

I love to draw with crayons.
They're vibrant, smooth, and clean.
Of all the many crayons, my favorite one is green.
Green means eco-friendly, a tribute to the Earth.
Green means life and luck, and it's the color of money's worth.
Green crayons are special and produce a beautiful hue.
Can you tell me now dear person what green crayons mean to you?
Hayley Morgans, Grade 7
Bloomsburg Area Middle School, PA

A Chocolate Chip Cookie Coma

The mahogany drawer shuts with a snap of the magnet, I have what I need,
My socked feet glide over the newly placed tiles,
As I sink the glittering metal spoon into the bowl on top of the granite counter,
I stir three times and inhale deeply,
The aroma of raw eggs, sugar, flour, and vanilla extract
Crawl into my nose and fill my lungs,
My hand leaves the spoon and is joined by my left,
I greedily reach for some chocolate chips,
Although I am tempted to take more, they must be saved,
I slowly devour the cold cocoa flavored sweetness,
Sadly I must pour the rest of the chips into the batter,
However, I know what will be the result,
And quickly the chocolate no longer blankets the batter,
But are dots in a beige basin,
Even faster the dough is equally placed on our old,
Tattered tray and into the oven 350°F
Beep, Beep, Beep, for a total of 15 minutes

Over the long, agonizing 15 minutes the familiar smell
Makes my tummy grumble in response
After nearly burning my hand, I separate my masterpiece
There are no words to describe, except a chocolate chip cookie coma
Rachel Fischer, Grade 7
Westwood Jr/Sr High School, NJ

Losing Then Finding You!

You were gone
You said you would never return
So I climbed the mountain
And cried there all night
Thinking about you
Thinking about how stupid I was to believe you loved me
I continued to cry away my pain
Tear, tear…drop drop like the rain at night
Rain on me
Let it pour
I won't cry for you any more
But one day I will get over you
One day I will finish this adventure
Finish looking for another
But for now the view is great

Emily Adams, Grade 9
Professional Performing Arts School, NY

Families

We are family
We are brothers and sisters
We are moms and dads
We are grandmas and grandpas
We are loving and caring
We are compassionate and considerate
We are united and thoughtful
We are faithful and loyal
We are people who love each other
We are friends who have each other's backs
We are loved ones who sacrifice for each other
We are family

Katie Grace White, Grade 7
St Stephen's School, NY

Life

Love is pure
As gold is to thee.
Times grow into memories
As we grow old and wish
To go back to the
Happy moments and change
The mistakes.
Life does not let you
Go back, but it gives
You a chance to live
In this unbelievable world.
The mistakes are what
Makes you human and the happy
Moments are that people are grateful
That you are on the planet and they are not
Alone in this world.

Anna McElroy, Grade 7
Marblehead Veterans Middle School, MA

Anger

Anger,
is like a raging fire,
in the forest of hatred.
dried souls ready to be lit,
like raging forest fires
burning through innocent homes and villages,
people screaming and running in fear,
some will have to face the raging fire,
because they couldn't escape soon enough,
innocent souls suffering a horrible fate,
the only thing to do is run away, as fast as you can.

Mina Girgis, Grade 7
Hammarskjold Middle School, NJ

Starred Death

I miss the clear night sky,
The stars are burning out before our eyes.
Do you notice it happening? I do.
When the stars burn out I shall die, my spirit at least
Love shall conquer me and I may live again.

I'm not afraid to die, for I know
That I'll be happy where I end.
My spirit shall begin anew
And I, I shall die
As the stars burn away, I die.

As the stars fade
My breathing begins to cease.
I close my eyes and review my life, I'm happy.
As I lay dying my spirit begins to leave me
It slowly slips away, and I close my eyes
One final time.

Amber Lyn Paul, Grade 7
Trinity Middle School, PA

Pinto Times

Dad is as happy as a lark.
Mom is glowing with joy.
I'm just here to play baseball.
Baseball, baseball, baseball.

Sweat is streaming down the faces of players,
And bats sitting in the scorching fire have a little extra
POP!
Pinto State Tournament,
Delighted to be here,
Playing the game of enjoyment,
With cheek to cheek smiles on the faces of athletes.

Dad is as happy as a lark.
Mom is glowing with joy.
I'm just here to play baseball.
1…2…3…

Ryan Rohrbacher, Grade 7
Trinity Middle School, PA

Yearning…Wanting…Waiting

I stood astride the flower,
as the cold, icy wind
tore at my shoulders, mystified.

The lonely flower
like a quarantined puppy,
yearning for attention.

Drip,
    Drip,
        Drip,
The final drop…
descending from the sky,
as the calm, peaceful, serene
environment s-p-r-a-n-g to life.

Happiness crept through my body.
Slowly turning my back
inching farther and farther away.
Melissa Busch, Grade 7
William Penn Middle School, PA

The Forge in Silence

Bonds in silence
Forever holding
Brotherhoods form
No longer separate
But part of a whole
In bad or good
Bonds hold steadfast
Forever, forever
Bonds are forged
Brian Kelly, Grade 8
Charles F Patton Middle School, PA

Innocence

Waves crash down on shores
Making an unyielding blow
Downward towards the earth.
Over time the waves grind down
The helpless sea shore
And destroy the mighty Earth.
This is the cycle
Of erosion. It is like
The destruction of
Innocence. This thought occurs
Throughout daily life.
Even though we may not see
This, it's always there.
A good example is in
Harper Lee's novel,
Called *To Kill a Mockingbird*.
Even the title
Shows the harm of purity.
Matt Ricci, Grade 9
Shenendehowa High School, NY

Come Back to Me

Peeling bark, sitting in the park,
off the vibrant tree, come back to me

All the white lies walking down the street,
ruining all they meet, asking who are we?
come back to me

The two great pillars that support the living sky
that fall into the dying sea, come back to me

Shimmering sidewalks, holding all who talk,
where we can be free, come back to me

Peering lions that guard the sanction of knowledge
reading into all they see, come back to me.

Whispering wind, holding many a breeze,
soothing my oppressed senses, will you please
come back to me?

The link between the concrete jungle and the rest of the world, answer my pleas
and please, please, come back to me.

Ted D'Anna, Grade 8
Beacon Middle School, DE

Shattered

I let myself fall.
I broke into a million pieces and there all of me lays.
Broken and shattered.
All of my remains just lay there
As I attempt to pick the pieces up they cut me deeply
They slip through my veins and return to their destination — the ground
The hard demanding concrete asking for my pieces as I already handed them to it

Now I'm lost
I'm broken and alone
With no one to help and no one to hold

Because along with myself
I let them fall too
I distinct myself away in time with my mind

I let my mind empower me
Control and devour me
I let my mind make choices and gave my mind access
To me to them to it all

Here I lay from the floor I'm speaking
I'm broken shattered
into little pieces

Jeffrey Perez, Grade 8
Public School 528 Bea Fuller Rogers, NY

A Walk in the Woods

My walk in the woods is quiet
The wind brushes my cheek like a kiss
Far from the noise and riot
Life in the city, I will not miss
As the wind blows through the trees
On this starry night in June
Branches are stirred by the breeze
And the only light is the full moon
This evening will be forever mine
Though from my home, I am far
Away from where electric lights shine
My only companion is my guitar
Nothing made by man here is included
And I wish this walk in the woods to never be concluded

Georgia Miller, Grade 8
Ephrata Middle School, PA

Not Enough Time

Every day there is so much work
And there's always so little allowed time
Not even earning a tiny small dime
In this work there is not even one perk
Trying to make my personal work prime
When all I feel like is just dirt and grime
Always feeling tossed and bossed around and irked
Doing this kind of work should be a crime
Not sitting here and talking, like a mime
Or going there and acting like a jerk
Out of this nightmare I try to climb
But always seem to fall into the slime
Not wanting to cry and trying to smirk
There will always be not enough time

David Keeley, Grade 9
Unami Middle School, PA

Laugh

I close my eyes
And let out a laugh.
A joyous laugh,
Gurgling and giggling,
Rising up to the sky
Like a bubble,
Only to pop,
Scattering goodness across the nation.
A laugh
Not because of hate
But because of love.
A laugh that will soar,
Soar like an eagle
And bring everyone
A piece of hope,
A glimpse of a fairy tale,
A possibility of a happily-ever-after
That we all wish for.

Grace Chuang, Grade 8
Kilmer Middle School, VA

School

School is so boring
It makes me sleepy
In the class kids are snoring
And the girls are so annoying
In the halls it is very creepy

My first class is math
Where we learn many numbers
And kids dream about taking a bath
And others dream about great wrath
By the end they all fall into a deep slumber

Next is gym
This is kind of cool
My gym teacher's name is Tim
Who teaches us to get slim
So we don't look fat and like a fool

Finally, it's French
It's loud and crazy
The class has a bad stench
Since everyone looks drenched
Because they are too lazy

Brian Chu, Grade 7
Simon Baruch Jr High School 104, NY

The Never Ending Cycle

Every tree in the rainforest,
Has an endless horizon of green.
But on one certain tree, is an ordinary leaf,
On which a small, round white egg remains unseen.

An exhilarating journey is beginning,
As the egg shivers and splits into two.
A small, hungry caterpillar emerges from its shell,
And as weeks went by, the ravenous creature grew.

The caterpillar spins a home of silk,
People today call it a cocoon.
It takes a new form, one elegant and graceful,
The caterpillar shall unveil its beauty soon.

A glorious animal, wonderful to behold,
The creature takes wing to the sky.
No longer an egg, nor caterpillar, nor a shimmering cocoon,
But instead a magnificent butterfly.

Its journey was short but amazing,
With surprises around every bend.
And all that remains is a tiny little egg,
In a cycle that never shall end.

Meaghan Mahoney, Grade 8
Commack Middle School, NY

California Dreamin'

Hello summer!
Hot beach with sunshine,
And luminous sunny blue skies.
True blue waves,
Passion for my shades.
Shiny-licious style,
California dreamin'.

Alyssa Lynn, Grade 9
Unami Middle School, PA

Smiley Face

I make you
As
Happy
As
You could
Possibly be.

I refill
Your joyful meter
With only
One glance.
You see the world
Turn wrong
To right.
What a sight!

I make your day
Turn yellow
For joy
And happiness.
I have NEVER
Made someone
Frown.

Brandon Judy, Grade 7
Olson Middle School, NJ

A Secret

Blooming flower, hidden man
Orange petals, flowering fan
Feathers blowing in the wind
Cup around the hidden man
Five black marks in the
Petals deep
Meaning calm and peace serene
Petals deep
And meaning far
Painters flower, colors calm
Mysterious man
But hidden within
The flowers veil
A surprising secret
For you to guess…

Benjamin Brule, Grade 7
Whitin Middle School, MA

Clear Night Sky

There I stand alone,
Staring at the sky,
Stars spinning around me,
But I know I cannot fly,
Searching for answers,
But none of them are here,
I want to walk away,
I want to disappear,
But here I still stand alone,
Staring at the sun,
As morning breaks through the clouds,
I still see no one.

Lauren Devens, Grade 7
Garnet Valley Middle School, PA

What Is a Miracle?

What is a miracle?
Winning the lottery, or
Being a millionaire,
Not just that but many more,

Waking up each day, is a miracle itself,
Beating the odds,
Food to survive,
Living life to the fullest,
And appreciating the small things in life,

Everything is a miracle,
Miracles don't come to you,
You have to go out and find them,

Nature's beauty,
The earth to live on,
And parents that love you,
Making a change,

Are all miracles in life,
Miracles come in all shapes and sizes,
Both big and small,
So what is a miracle?
Everything in life.

Shivani Patel, Grade 7
Hammarskjold Middle School, NJ

Football Players

F ull of good players
O wning other players
O nomatopoeia on every play
T all people rule the game
B ig fat guys blocking
A ll the guys are fast
L ike a lion
L ook at them run

Brian Kramer, Grade 8
Ephrata Middle School, PA

Yankee Fan

Just because I'm a Yankee fan
   Doesn't mean I'm a snob
   Doesn't mean I'm rich

Just because I'm a Yankee fan
Doesn't mean I live in New York
   Doesn't mean I'm smart

Just because I'm a Yankee fan
Doesn't mean I'm a front-runner
   Doesn't mean I'm dumb

Just because I'm a Yankee fan
   Doesn't mean I'm a jerk
Doesn't mean I'm a sore loser.

Just because I'm a Yankee fan
Doesn't mean I'm a sore winner
   Doesn't mean I think I'm cool

Just because I'm a Yankee fan
   It doesn't make me great!

Harrison Bender, Grade 7
Anthony Wayne Middle School, NJ

The Fight for Freedom

The war was never ending
You were called upon to fight
You signed on the dotted line
And pledged to keep us free
They sent you off to a foreign land
To fight a senseless war
We had never seen one like this before
The guns they were a blazing
The bombs continuously falling
Every step was filled with danger
Land mines were buried there
A hidden enemy that was never seen
Lay in wait at every turn
You gave your life to save us
Thank you for keeping us free

Mike Oakes, Grade 9
Pine-Richland High School, PA

Shine

Shine perfectly
party in neon pink
hot glam
rich summer dreams
precious glitter
Big thrills
believe in extreme
sweet golden days.

Jessica Waskiewicz, Grade 9
Unami Middle School, PA

Have You Ever?

Have you ever frowned on your wedding day?
Have you ever smiled on a rainy day?
Have you ever laughed when no ones around?
Have you ever cried, when hope is found?
Did you ever find the meaning of day?
Have you ever wished those nights away?
Have you ever thought these thoughts before?
The days and nights go by quiet for sure.

These things have happened to me,
when the first time in my life I was carefree,
my mind was telling me something was missing,
then I saw the forsaken missed blessing.
The thoughts and words that were shared that night,
will haunt me forever in my life.

I asked and I wished to know the answer,
of where my father had been after all this banter.
Where he ended up I do not know,
where his life is now is still unknown.

I've never seen my father face to face,
but someday I will,
from his base to his face, face to face…

Haylie Wood, Grade 7
Altmar Parish Williamstown Middle School, NY

Who I Am Becoming

As days go by,
And time seems to fly,
I wonder who I am becoming.

So I will not be a fool,
Every day, I go to school.
I wonder who I am becoming.

What better to have then friends,
Who will be there for me days on ends.
I wonder who I am becoming.

My family will always be there,
Memories, we will always share.
I wonder who I am becoming.

Living each day,
As if in a play,
I wonder who I am becoming.

I am starting to see who I am becoming,
With the pen in my hand that I am a drumming,
I'm learning I'm becoming unique.

Laura Zakowski, Grade 8
Maple Point Middle School, PA

The Majestic Tree

When this tree sways in the breeze,
It looks like it's waving at me.
Then as I stare at the bark,
I see ants looking like they're screaming.
So I decide to observe the leaves,
And I see they're smooth and green.
But then I see a leaf fall off,
As though it's sky diving.
Then I look towards the soil,
And I noticed a root poking out of the ground.
It looks like it's gasping for air.
While I looked and stared at this tree,
I realize nature's as good as it can be.

Ashley Sheen, Grade 7
School of International Studies at Meadowbrook, VA

Change

Will you change?
Will you change like Barack Obama did?
Will you change like some of America did?
Will you change if I ask you to change?
Yes?
No?
Maybe so?
Will you work hard for a change?
Did Barack Obama stop you from changing?
Did I stop you from changing?
I ask you do you want a change?
If so be the change.

Hecmar Smart, Grade 7
Link Community School, NJ

Government

I can't stand you.
Always looking over my shoulder,
Why? Is my question?
Why do you shackle me?
For doing what you call wrong?
For breaking your unfair laws?
Where can I go to be free of your oppression?
Free of your views of so called "justice."
Free from your killing and death.
What do you want from me?
To fight with you, along with your armies?
To be a slave to your views of "peace" and "victory?"
When will you go away from me?
And go to some other country that needs what you think is help.
And unshackle my bleeding wrists from your bonds.
Who do you think you are?
The almighty God that so many pray to,
Or just the people above everyone else.
Why don't you just leave me alone?
Why won't you let me be myself?
Why do you shackle me?

Max Brungardt, Grade 7
Westwood Jr/Sr High School, NJ

Entranced

A stream of liquid silver,
A tendril of shining mist,
Flares across the horizon,
Swift.
A great black vulture,
A herd of dirty sheep,
Watch from far above,
Silent.
A crack of a whip,
A round of applause,
Leap through the air,
Alive.
A small pink girl,
Sitting at a foggy window,
Gazes at the storm,
Entranced.

Evelyn Wang, Grade 7
Carson Middle School, VA

Perhaps

Perhaps trees
    don't grow leaves
        but instead
            only catch them.

Maybe leaves
    fall from heaven in spring
        onto branches
            of waiting trees.

Perhaps trees
    wait to catch them
        and care for them
            until they grow old.

And in winter
    they must drop them
        and mourn
            until spring
                returns again.

Monique Medina, Grade 7
Bedford Middle School, CT

To a Random Friend

Some days you were cool;
other days you treated me like a fool.
I thought you were my friend,
but it turns out you were just a user.
We could've been good friends,
but I guess not.
All because of your foolishness,
we cannot be friends.
So it's time to move on.
See you later, when you act right.

Brittanie Diaz, Grade 8
Life Academy, PA

Survival

The hot summer sun sizzles, as the day moves on
I croak and croak for the dark god
Shade to us to finally come
No! No shade ever comes

As the sun gets hotter the day grows longer
We sit in the sun while my kind begins to bubble and disintegrate

We are frogs
Pipsqueak-sized frogs
Who grew up in the Amazon
One with a canopy to protect us
From the steaming ferocious devil we call the sun

Shipped to the U.S. when we were just two
Where the devil waits to burn us to bits
Like a piece of cheese crackling in the microwave

When the sun disappears out of the light, blue sky
And the moon settles in its place night comes
We roam around the yard listening to the hoots of owls
The singing of crickets searching for food while our bellies mumble at us

We watch our backs as a dog could come at any second and slurp us up
Swallow our guts and walk away with pride while we float down to his insides

Ryan Bradway, Grade 7
Olson Middle School, NJ

Very Silly Billy

There was once a mischievous boy named Billy.
Everyone in his family had magical powers, except Billy who was silly.
He lived with his three sisters and had a brother named Willy.
His sisters like to sing, but their voices are quite shrilly.
During the night, Billy likes to scare his sisters by making a din.
His sisters got mad and with a flick of a wand, turned Billy's head to a can of tin.
He felt silly, he did it again, he just won a pair of fins.
Silly again, he did it again, he has to walk around with feet as small as a pin.

Oh, Billy he will never learn, he tricked his sisters.
He put the cusp of a pencil on the seat of his sister. Boom! Found himself in a twister.
He survived amazingly, with 1000 blisters.
He was nursed by a boy named Kister.
They became friends, but they had to part.
He goes back home and hits his sister with a dart.
He made his other sister sit on a strawberry Pop Tart.
His sisters attacked him, Billy yelled, "You guys have no heart!"

Now Billy knows not to do it again. He might go insane.
But, Silly Billy did it again. Now he has to walk with a cane.
Because he got attacked by 30 Great Danes.
He just yelled in pain.

Oh, Silly Billy, will he ever learn?

Joshua Shin, Grade 7
Fairfax Collegiate School, VA

Hidden

Look away from those prying eyes,
Never hear those sweet, sweet lies
Shield yourself from those terrible truths,
That no one wants you around.
Hide yourself from all those
Who pretend who backstab who lie.
Don't keep yourself with them
Who look away and laugh
And say they care but don't not really.
If they did, would they look away, laugh,
And leave when you really need them?
Hide yourself behind a veil of hair:
Look down. Look away.
Pretend not to hear when they laugh
They whisper and stare and point
Pretend not to see
When they break off their conversations
Just as you walk into the room.
Because it's best
To stay hidden.

Wendy Zhang, Grade 9
Horace Mann Upper School, NY

Friends

They're all you ever need in the world
Especially when they have a heart of gold.

Friends always have your back,
Even when you hit the sack.

You can always rely on a friend,
Even if they can't comprehend.

And when we say goodbye,
We know we'll be friends forever, even until we die.

Carlos Solis, Grade 8
Floral Park Memorial High School, NY

Animal Cruelty

Animals have feelings, too.
What gives people the right to hurt them?
What if they were the people?
And they treated us
How we treat them?
What would happen to them?
Would you save them?
Put yourself in their position;
How would you feel?
Look out for the animals;
Help them stay safe.
How can people look at them
And treat them bad?
The people are the animals
Treat animals how you would treat yourself.

Andrew Kline, Grade 7
Pine-Richland Middle School, PA

Life…

Life is like a book
There are chapters
With many different pages
If the book is torn
It is incomplete
The same tear will pull the book apart
Bit by bit
'Til there is nothing left but memories

Life is like a die
It has different sides to everything
Many different results are possible
And you can never tell what the next will be

Life is like a test
Not knowing what's in store
You have to get a perfect to pass
Or else

Life is many things
But it's never the same again
No repetitions
So enjoy life while you can

Sunny Eltepu, Grade 7
Carson Middle School, VA

Change

Life is like a puzzle, each day
You hope another piece will fit into place.
Life is like a pattern, each day
You hope nothing will break the chain.

Life is like a boat, each day
You hope that the wind won't blow you far off course.
Life is like a lake, each day
You wonder if something will disturb the water.

Life is like a road, each day
There are going to be bumps along your journey.
Life is like a book, each day
Has a beginning and an end.

But what happens when something goes wrong?
The pattern breaks, you hit a bump,
Something disturbs the water,
And in the middle of the book, a new chapter.

You are blown off course,
Struggling to hold on.
All this over one thing:
Change.

Morgan Hennessy, Grade 8
Holy Family Elementary School, NJ

Our Past Is Unforgettable

You can't forget your past, no matter how hard you try.
It teaches us lessons we would never forget, and answers the question 'why?'
It tells you the reason you go to school, and tells you stories that might make you cry.
You have to remember the past, for it is where you came from.
Your ancestors are waiting for you to discover them.
Great-Grandmothers were queens, and Great-Grandfathers were kings. Your past is rich, and we have
Just begun.
They arrive from a land where they were free, and others arrive to this land in chains.
When they came to this land, they created a new world with a government for all.
They had children, grew crops, and acquired skills from the Indians.
They built towns and cities, and then expanded them.
They invented lights, phones, and automobiles.
They also made steel and learned how to build a railroad. They fought for their rights to live free,
So today you can go to school, dream big dreams, and grow up to be who you want to be.
Yes, our, your past is truly unforgettable.

Lydia Johnson, Grade 8
Wise and Pure Sr High School, PA

An Angel Looks Down on Me*

An angel looks down on me, smiling from the sky.
Helping me see what's right and what's wrong.
When I saw your smile my whole face would smile back at you.
You were the one guy I looked up too.
When you took your journey up the stairs, I never thought I would be able to ever deal without you.
But when I look back on those days I realize what you've taught me.
Though you were afraid of failure, you taught me to follow my dreams.
You got angry easily, teaching me to be patient.
You taught me that when the world gave you all of the reasons to cry, you smile up at the sky.
You were afraid to try, afraid to see the possibilities of the good, just saw the possibilities of the bad.
You told me to view all the possibilities, expect the best, prepare for the worst.
You were the one I came to with my problems, the one who would teach me about life.
You will always be in my heart. Big brother. When I look back on what there was, I look forward to how those lessons will help me in the future. I am who I am because of you.

Kelliann Dancy, Grade 8
Aberdeen Middle School, MD
*RIP Bradley Michael Bandy

The Birdman of the Cherry Knoll

There once was a place where the red cherries rolled, it was my most favorite place to have strolled
On the branches birds would sit, waiting for their daily visit
They would peep and they would turn, waiting for their bread they earned
Because they'd preen and then they'd dance, and put me in a soothing trance
But as my friends would peep and twirl, they told me fresh news of the world
They told me far off in the east, there were goose-footed marching beasts
And in the south it was warm, and they, my friends, would come to warn
"Crows beak there, crows beak there, if you go be fully aware"
But I would laugh and say to them: "I'm no rooster, I'm no hen"
But they didn't understand that I wasn't a bird, but a man
But at least they understood not in a tree, I grew up in a hood
There was one day though, I did not stroll by the birch tree in the knoll
Because I was indeed a man, I shook a cold and dour hand
That day they did not get their bread, but finally — and instead,
On that quiet and rainy day, I flew with them, merry and gay.

Hannah Mades-Alabiso, Grade 9
Melrose High School, MA

Where I'm From

I am from hair ties and hair clips,
From the laundry detergent I drank when I was five.
From the Cactus garden,
Coming out as red as a rose, whose pricks scarred me for life.
I'm from the "Don't you dare"
And the occasional "That's spelled wrong"
From the broken promises and the kept secrets.
I am from the smell of butter cookies
Being burnt on Christmas Eve,
And the worried look on my mother's face.
I am from the fog of cigarettes
And sweet hard candy we cleaned out
When he was gone,
And the tears he left for us.
I am from my father's nose,
And my mother's bright eyes,
From the tire swing still swaying in the wind.
I am from the love and laughter from all,
And the great times with them.

Michele Katora, Grade 7
Hammarskjold Middle School, NJ

My Neighbor's Cat

I always feed my neighbor's cat
Although I know I shouldn't do that.
He scratches the door with his little front feet;
He begs me to give him something to eat.
He eats a lot, he's getting big.
Although he's a cat, he eats like a pig.
He's an orange tabby with big green eyes,
And I think he deserves a beauty prize.
Now he's left, but he'll be back
As soon as he wants another snack!

Abigail Blumkin, Grade 7
Westwood Jr/Sr High School, NJ

I Come Home from School

I come home from school, work needs to be done.
Rather than sit down and do some homework,
I'd prefer to hang out with friends and have some fun.
Looking for a snack, through the kitchen I lurk,
I manage to find some Oreo cookies.
I sit at the table, still no homework complete.
Playing *COD4*, I whoop all the rookies.
After two hours, I rise to my feet,
Sliding downstairs, I call up a friend.
I ask to hang out and meet at the park.
I begin to realize, the day's at an end,
I tell by the sky as it grows pitch dark.
I return home, play *COD4*, just one more game,
Homework not done, with just myself to blame.

Evan Wyatt, Grade 9
Unami Middle School, PA

Is There a God?

Is there a god?
Or am I just seeing things
That man wearing white with the eyes of an eagle
reminds me of him

If God is out there
Then can He hear us?
Or are we just murmuring souls
Desperate for love and attention

Is He the Creator and we, the created?
Or are we just a side effect of evolution
One by one dying
And one by one beginning life anew

There is an internal debate within me
Deciding whether or not God is real
I'm not ready to choose yet
But one day I'll have the answer

Samantha Brennan, Grade 8
Charles S Pierce Middle School, MA

Bird's Song of Life

In my egg, I sit waiting, eating, resting.
Ready, one, two, three!
Out comes my beak!
I squirm and wiggle and chip away,
On my most important bird day,
The day of hatching!
As I chip away,
My parents sing and sway,
the joyous song of life.
"Come child come, break your shell,
Come chick come, do it well!"
Singing your song of encouragement, I break out!
Oh, how joyous is this feeling,
Breath of first air, taste of first feeding,
I thank thee!
I live through the bird's song of life!
I rejoice!

Ted Gervais, Grade 9
Bishop Ford Central Catholic High School, NY

The Tulip

It begins to bloom filled with pink,
Always seeming to make me think
How all the colors begin to mix,
They are perfect with little to fix
And now the sun is starting to make it shine,
Beginning to show all its wonderful lines,
Leaves of the color green,
With stems that must be seen
Extending high over the rest
This tulip twinkles its very best

Kristina Sefakis, Grade 7
Whitin Middle School, MA

When the Season Is Fall

As the breeze blows by,
when the season is fall,
some leaves may fly,
although, not them all.

As the years go by,
when the season is fall,
life stories may end.
Remember to mourn them all.

As the days go by,
when the season is fall,
mistakes may happen.
Even so, forgive them all.

As the breeze blows by,
when the season is fall,
moments become memories.
Forget none, remember all.

Keenan M. Witmer, Grade 7
Trinity Middle School, PA

July

July leaps in
POWERFUL and expected.
It scurries around
In the warmth and excitement,
Flashing joy.
But soon enough, it sinisterly
Begins to
F   a   d   e.

Tyler Kulcsar, Grade 7
Anthony Wayne Middle School, NJ

White Night

I am a snowflake
    I am white as whipped cream
and still as
    night.
I shimmer and sparkle
    as I drift softly to the
Left
    and softly to the
                right.
The wind carries me
    gently
like the feather of a bird.
I am like a butterfly
floating softly and
    Plunk!
    I hit
    the
    ground.

Emily Lare, Grade 7
Christ the Teacher Catholic School, DE

Johny May

Your honey kiss
Is what I miss,

O my Johny May!

Your bluebird song
Is for what I
Long,

O my Johny May!

For your elm tree hug
I cannot
Shrug,
My dear old Johny May!

Patricia May Smith, Grade 7
Ocean City Intermediate School, NJ

Lion

Lion! Lion! In the light
Feasts on his prey with great might,
Golden locks flow in the wind,
His mighty land he will rescind.

Kristen Haverstick, Grade 9
Unami Middle School, PA

The Liar

Liar, Liar. So unclear,
In my heart that's hurt severe;
What sinful smile so sly,
Could thee be hiding in tonight?

Patricia Le, Grade 9
Unami Middle School, PA

Watertrees

Waterfalls
Fall
All because of the call
They nourish
The trees
As you see
Waterfalls
Are the keys to succeed
In this flourishing
Watertree

The trees live for the waterfall
And their lives are taken by surprise
They fall to the ground
And lose their lives
Ending the beautiful
Flourishing
Waters of life

Jor-El Sanchez, Grade 9
Leonardtown High School, MD

It May Be too Late to Turn Back

The soft breeze
Whispers quietly in your ear
Of troubles up ahead,
But you do not hear

The hard ground
Under your feet
Tries to push you down,
But you keep them firmly down

The brilliant blue sky
Above you
Tries to warn you,
But you don't see

The gentle breeze turns to
A fierce wind
The stable ground
Gives way
The sapphire sky
Turns jet black,
But it is too late to
Turn back,
Too late to turn back.

Megan Davis, Grade 8
Matoaca Middle School, VA

Fall

Walking through the park on a fall day
hearing the children play
seeing people walking
hearing them talking

seeing the trees swaying
and the kids that are playing
seeing the kids playing football
and the others shooting a basketball

Michael Jounakos, Grade 8
Floral Park Memorial High School, NY

Obama

He is a magnificent man
Saving the world the best he can.
He is trying his best
To keep us at rest.
He works for the red, white, and blue
For everyone, like me and you.
He does it all
So we will never fall.
The people can't wait till when
The time we will vote for him again.
Obama, Obama, Obama
With him there is no drama.

Adrian Gilbert, Grade 7
Whitin Middle School, MA

Commitment

She offered so much devotion,
poured out all of her emotion.
She just wanted him to see
kept repeating why not me.
All she wanted was a little love
just a some guidance from above.

It had been an eternity —
after this her life would be recovery.
She had her kids so she kept on trying
but she knew she was done lying.
She finally told him it was done
all she had left to do was run.
She felt like she was playing a game
but she knew she was not to blame,
Finally, it was over and though she still felt cold
she knew soon enough she'd find someone's hand to hold.

Katy Van Ness, Grade 9
Hudson Falls High School, NY

Summer

It is hot today,
jump in the pool and come play.
Flowers are booming they may make you sneeze,
and the trees have a wonderful breeze.
Today is the perfect day!

Shannon Jones, Grade 7
Ellington Middle School, CT

Chopsticks

"Chopsticks or a fork?"
"Chopsticks,"
"Thank you."
Getting the full experience
With chopsticks.

First comes the rice
It's chopstick time
Read the instructions
One chopstick between fingers
The other anchored by my thumb

Going in for some rice
I drop a chopstick
"Excuse me, may I have another chopstick?"
"One second."
I wait, my hunger growing.

Try a second time,
Rice flies everywhere.
All over the ground,
"Excuse me,"
"Yes."
"May I just have a fork?"

Matt Mahoney, Grade 9
Summit Sr High School, NJ

Remember the Person

Remember the person
That sacrificed his life
To save yours
He fought for truth
He fought for pride
Remember the hero
Remember him well
He gave himself, he gave his best
His headstone will fade away
No one remembers the price he had to pay

Brooke Cote, Grade 7
Sanford Jr High School, ME

Owl

Sleeping in a tree during the day
Gliding at night just hooting away

Looks like a bird and a raccoon in a way
Hooting an prowling the whole day

Hunts like a blood thirsty wolf
Faster than a lightning bolt

When heard hooting at night
Gives such a great fright

Sound of the owl hooting on and on
Screeching like a ghost mourning forever on

Alexander Wang, Grade 7
Hammarskjold Middle School, NJ

A Paw Print on My Heart

I lay up in bed. Aware of the plight
My baby Kelly would not live for another night.
We made her day perfect. As she lay in the sun,
Kelly no longer walked. Her swimming days were done.

Her eyes were swollen. And red, droopy too.
She took insulin daily. Her tumor grew and grew.
Nothing could be done. Believe me, we tried.
Her case was hopeless. The end of her ride.

We loved her so dearly. I cried day and night.
The house seemed empty. Her doggy door locked tight.
She was my sister at heart. Her tail wagging fast,
Kelly didn't bite or bark. Oh her life flew past.

She loved us all. Always eager to please,
She's surely in heaven. Free from pain, disease,
My life's not the same. It's missing a part.
She's gone away. A paw print on my heart.

Sarah Ogren, Grade 9
Fox Chapel Area Sr High School, PA

The Paintbrush

I am like a paintbrush, sitting on the easel
Looking cowardly and small.
Just sitting there, my talent building inside me
While I wait.
Waiting for the moment when I burst and all
The creativity flows outward onto the canvas called my life.
A rainbow of colors, each one reflects my mood.
Red for the burning intensity of anger.
Yellow for the sunny moments that cover my canvas.
Green for that little green monster that seethes with
Rage, jealously.
Blue for the sorrows.
Then there's that mixture of colors that blend together
To make a new color, a whole new section of my life.
My canvas.

Paige Griffin, Grade 8
Rock L Butler Middle School, PA

The Trees

The Trees;
I am surrounded by the sweet smell of maple,
My family inside while I am out,
I sit under the big maple tree,
Doing my work slowly,
Quickly I grow tired of this,
I stretch up on my toes,
Grab a low branch and begin my climb,
I ascend myself higher as my hands stick to sap,
I taste it,
Its tasteless except for the faint resemblance of dirt,
Quietly I laugh to myself,
In amusement I climb even higher,
Towards the top,
And look out,
To see The Trees.

Elizabeth McClelland, Grade 7
Trinity Middle School, PA

A Day at the Beach

Listening to the waves crashing on the ground
Oh that's a wonderful sound
Watching the fish jumping in the air
While my friends stared and stared
Watching a fisherman casting his pole
While a little kid was digging his hole
Standing on the burning sand
As me and my boyfriend were holding hands
Watching the seagulls fly
Then I saw a little crab go by
As I stood up to go away
I wondered if I would have another good day

Audriana Miller, Grade 7
Thorne Middle School, NJ

Summer

I can't wait for you to come
And to soak up some sun
School is almost over
This year will be fun!

I can't wait for you waves
I'm your biggest fan
Just like the good old days
I can't wait to get tan

Too many good times
Fun for all
There are no crimes
I can't wait for your call.

Tyler Nowak, Grade 8
Township of Ocean Intermediate School, NJ

False Praise

The cold winter breeze was silenced by "Play Ball"
The Phils return to Citizen's Bank Park
Although no one truly watches 'til fall.
Yet they still fight for the Eastern Title.
Late summer, early fall, they won't give up.
Now the fans come around, hey, might as well.
Here comes the bandwagon, now showing up,
Though I'll never not savor the season;
I will always be a fan, through and through.
The bandwagon is an act of treason.
Still, nice to see they hate the Brew Crew.
They took out the Dodgers and then the Rays,
And out of nowhere, earned everyone's praise.

Garrett Pirollo, Grade 9
Unami Middle School, PA

The Ocean

Take a look at the ocean.
Oh, how I love it so.
Though I still must take some lotion,
I must say, it surely beats the snow.

Oh, how I love it so.
The ocean truly is a wonderful thing.
It surely beats the snow,
And I swear I even hear the ocean sing.

The ocean truly is a wonderful thing.
To my face, the smiles it may bring.
Sometimes, I swear I even hear the ocean sing.
And oh, how lovely its sounds do ring.

Take a look at the ocean.
To my face, the smiles it may bring.
And oh, how lovely its sounds do ring…
And note to self: I still must take some lotion.

Amber Winters, Grade 8
Ephrata Middle School, PA

Impossibility

Impossible, to run a mile in less than four minutes.
Impossible, to visit the moon.
Impossible, to pass the limit.
If everything seems impossible what should I do?

Impossible, said those who had no faith.
Impossible, said those who did not believe.
Impossible seems like a wraith,
or something that just frightens us.
And for that reason nothing we achieve.

Impossible has to do with our excuses
to not attempt what we desire.
Impossible sabotages what we admire,
and inspires us to brake through barriers.

Impossible is for the weak.
Impossible is for the lonely.
Impossible is for those who don't try.
Impossible is for those that quit!
Impossible is nothing…

Impossible does not exists in God's dictionary!
So why is it part of our everyday vocabulary?

Wendy Marroquin, Grade 9
Framingham High School, MA

Joy

Joy means spending time with family
being happy, and sharing love.
Having time to be with people.
Joy is what makes people get along.
Joy is what makes people strong inside.
Joy is spending time with family,
which means an awful lot to people
thinking of what good memories we have.
Joy is just like happiness
Love is all around
Even deep beneath someone
Joy is happy, joy is sad
Joy means sharing the love
with all the people around them.

Jacqulyn T. Elliott, Grade 7
Trinity Middle School, PA

Life Is Like

Life is like an hour glass;
There is no way to turn back time.
We can't press rewind;
Some friends will go; others will stay.
Where will you be twenty years from today?

Ashley Miskowski, Grade 9
Unami Middle School, PA

Wilt Chamberlain

Tall and bold
Wore yellow and gold
Set a record for scoring
Would never play boring
Nicknamed "Wilt the Stilt"
Off of how much talent he built
What a great inspiration
To the basket was his destination
Fourteen seasons never fouled out
Improving the league is what he was about
And now we are all pleased to say
That Wilt Chamberlain is remembered today

Richard Larcher, Grade 7
Floral Park Memorial High School, NY

The Advent of Autumn

A chilling Autumn wind
cuts through the summer's last, lingering days.
A shudder runs rampant down the spine,
rattling bones
and tickling nerves,
Autumn is near.

Summer's sunset is soon forgotten,
Distant memories of July
hover in a young child's mind,
appeasing his longing cries.
Trees begin to grow weary of the change,
slowly, shriveling away.
Autumn is here.

Julia Vance, Grade 8
Shady Hill School, MA

God Speaks Through the Rain

God speaks through the rain.
He speaks to you in soft angel whispers,
knowing your weaknesses, your insecurities.
His voice is firm but comforting.
Pitter, Patter, Pitter, Patter
You listen.
Pitter, Patter, Pitter, Patter
A voice calls you, calls your name.
All is well
for the moment.
You know He is with you.
You feel His presence, and you are at peace
Looking at the beautiful rain.
He calls your name again, again.
You are not afraid.
Pitter, Patter, Pitter, Patter
The clouds separate.
The sun shines.
All is well
for this moment.

Maria Sutton, Grade 7
Christ the Teacher Catholic School, DE

The Everlasting Life Cycle

People have gone on
Though the portals of time,
Showing the people,
The people that shine.

The one with the brains
The one with the mind,
Two people working together
Taking their time.

People wishing for more
Some wishing for none.
Waiting for things to end
And just want to have fun.

As time goes on
People will be lost
But we must cherish that
As there is an innumerable cost.

The everlasting life cycle.
Richard Chen, Grade 7
Simon Baruch Jr High School 104, NY

Harmony

Peace, solitude, and tranquility,
we all need these in small quantities,
for going full speed all of your life
can lead to anger, chaos, and strife.
The gentle silence cures distress.

Peace, solitude and tranquility,
the keys to live life healthily,
are found in forests, gardens, and ponds,
the carefree nature of small baby fawns,
found everywhere without misery.

Peace, solitude, and tranquility,
in large doses can no longer be
helpful to the mind and soul,
for isolation can take a toll.
Have caution with this medicine.
Rachel Scaman, Grade 9
Chapel Field Christian High School, NY

The Leader

A leader is what I'll be
No matter what the world thinks of me
I'll have a heart of compassion for all
And I will never ever fall
I have a dream for a nation
And my soul overflows with motivation
A leader is who I am
I am the leader with a plan
Kai Gilford, Grade 8
Talley Middle School, DE

Pool of Truths

Lies,
Cheats,
Harsh words that stab the heart, over and over.
And the truth spills out like blood against the crystal clear water.
"You're only hurting yourself" says you.
But really you have no idea of the pain searing against my chest
As an undying reminder of simple little fibs sewn together like a web.
And you are my little fly.
How does it feel to be in a sticky pool, of the undecided truth?
My fly, I apologize, I continue feeding you words
Plumper, more gullible you become to my every word.
You poor, poor fly the things I've spun! The tales I've told!
With you hanging on my every word unbeknownst to you
You become my victim

My victim of my bloody lies.
It was you, fly, who stabbed my heart,
Because of you I drown in my own truth.
You believed every word,
Can you believe,
That you are
The murderer?

Eileen Clevenger, Grade 8
Beacon Middle School, DE

Sarah

I look out to the horizon; a single tear falls from my eye,
Rolls off my cheek,
And drops to make a tiny splash in the water.

Invisible waves roar, and seagulls scavenge for buried food.
The sun lines the tips of the houses behind me.
Stars awake from their nocturnal sleep.
The moon comes out to welcome anyone
Who is brave enough to explore the dangers and darkness
When all things have shut down here in this majestic place.

Being me, the strong wave I am, have come to think about something.
Something so wretched. Something that was taken from me.
My sister lingers around me, and I know it.
I have come to think about her; her fragile body laying somewhere safe with God.
She comes to visit; I see her dance across a wave,
Then crash and disappear with the white water.
She washes up to me; I take her hand and wrap it around my finger.
I know this is the way it is supposed to be.

A second tear drips from my eye,
Rolls off my cheek,
And washes away to meet my first sister, Sarah,
Somewhere beyond my reach.

Caroline Bowman, Grade 7
Ocean City Intermediate School, NJ

Sonnet 1

In human's sick, dark, cruel world, so much hate,
Why must the innocent pay for their deeds?
More people lie dead, was this their true fate,
No peaceful meetings, talk about their needs.

Love ones of victims left alone to mourn,
So much destruction, all the lives are lost.
Mothers of children, some not yet born,
They express their hate, is it worth the cost?

Better security, lower the kill count,
Security guards watch, lower the threat.
Random security check, the right amount,
They defend their country well? You bet.

Security is great all the lives it saves,
Terrorism will end, peace in future days.

Austin Schuck, Grade 9
Unami Middle School, PA

All About School

True, smart, or, funny
School is always fun
Friends have secrets they love to share
This is a happy side
Dreaming, talking, or walking with buddies or pals

We all look handsome or pretty
And playing sports is something we're good at
Asking questions may be helpful
But…let's face it, we all enjoy a
Break every once and a while.

Ashley O'Brien, Grade 8
Charles S Pierce Middle School, MA

I Am From

I am the beat of the music,
the song and dance.
Practice made perfect,
after a much needed second chance.
The Outkast CD's, singing at the top of my lungs,
faded memories now covered with dust.
I am the tiger costume outgrown, matted, and torn,
now in a box, unused, unworn.
I am from the days of trying two wheels,
thinking, "Oh, I can't do this."
falling head over heels.
But now I am pedaling, as if a pro,
up and down the hills, boy, did I grow.
I am from the dreams of fitting into the prom dresses,
of shimmering gold,
once my sisters, soon my own.
I am from the laughs at home teaching me how to be,
nervous and excited for the day I am free.

Kayla King, Grade 8
Mars Area Middle School, PA

Why

Why?
Do we take for granted what we have?
When we live a life of luxury, with so much more than we need?
Are there millions who sleep on the streets?
Are we willing to receive, but give nothing in return?

Why?
Do miracles happen every day?
But other lives slip away?
Does the sun come out, even after dark skies?
Do people risk things, and end in a trap of lies?

Why?
Do we turn little things into big issues?
Do we yearn for drama, and items we don't need?
Is there so much fighting in the world?
Can't we have a world of peace and love?

Why?
Do I care?
Why doesn't anyone know how to answer these questions?
I have to wonder,
Why?

Megan Reid, Grade 9
Inter-Lakes High School, NH

The Lies We Believe

"Get super-thin quick!"
"Make your teeth white!"
"Make your tresses thick!"
"Increase your height!"

This world is full
Of lies, fibs, and tall tales.
We go with the tide's pull,
Without paddles or sails.

There are false things
We are led to believe.
With the pain this world brings,
We just need a reprieve!

The world wants you
To alter who you are.
This you're going to rue —
Your image it will mar.

Without a doubt
They'll try to pull you in.
Never worry about
Everyone's opinion!

Heather Van Voorhis, Grade 9
New Jersey United Christian Academy, NJ

My Friends

My friends are all I need
They're all I see and all I breathe

They're always by my side
and help me stand up high

They help me through bad times
and they always make time

My friends are people I will never forget
But if I do Jessica, Adilia, Jessie, Maria
and others too

Those friends and more will
be in my heart all the way through

Friends are the ones
who love you the most

Friends are the ones
who need you the most

A friend is a person who walks in
when everybody else walks out

A friend is a person
who you tell all your secrets to

A friend is like a charm
you love it and love it till the end of time.
Megan Pierre, Grade 7
Scofield Magnet Middle School, CT

Rainbow

I am like a rainbow,
Red, orange, yellow, and lime.
I am like a rainbow,
Brightening days one color at a time.

I am like a rainbow,
Big, medium, or small.
I am like a rainbow,
Helping everyone and all.

I am like a rainbow,
After a big gray storm,
I am like a rainbow,
Making everyone feel safe and warm.

I am like a rainbow,
As bright as the sun.
I am like a rainbow,
Made up of every color crayon.
Meghan Kelly, Grade 7
O.C.I.S.

I Remember

I remember
Dreams
Of being
The next great
Being
Flawless
Believing
I'm the best
Knowing
They can't stop me.
Chris Torgalski, Grade 9
Unami Middle School, PA

Animal Abuse

Full of love and care
Furry and sweet.
Always wanting to play,
And loving the attention.
Wet noses, long tails, floppy ears,
And big eyes that stare at you like beads.
All they want is your attention,
But some people are hard stones,
That refuse to care about them.
Those people have no heart,
So they don't feel anything that they do.
They neglect them.
How could they not feel anything?
What were they thinking,
When they beat those innocent animals?
All they wanted,
Was love.
Kelly Rodgers, Grade 7
Pine-Richland Middle School, PA

Our World

What would the world be like
if no one would ever fight
What would the world be like
If there wasn't violence every night

If everyone could go to bed
and not be sad about what lay ahead
if everyone could wake up
to a world not so corrupt

Earth would be a peaceful world
where violence would never occur
but to make these dreams come true
there is something we can do
we can love everybody
and go help somebody
that is what we must do
to make these dreams come true
Gabriel Murcia, Grade 8
Ephrata Middle School, PA

Summer Season

Summer is fun
Under the sun
Go to the beach
Party all the time
Meet with friends
Swim in the ocean
Have some good food
Go on vacation
Summer is fun
It always stinks when it's done
Dan Faulkner, Grade 9
Unami Middle School, PA

Long Island

New York
Much is overshadowed
By the city
And the farther you go
From the city
The more they forget
About you and your land
Though we are related
And not so far apart
I suppose it is better
To be a shadow of a king
Than a shadow of a nobody
Ryan Bannon, Grade 9
Kellenberg Memorial High School, NY

Blade on Blade

A single blade of grass
is a green dress dancing in the wind.
But more than just that,
blade on blade becomes
an entire meadow,
the mother and base of all life
creating
homes for insects,
runways for birds in long migration,
fashion shows for butterflies,
and miniature mountains for ants.
Chandler Russo, Grade 7
Ocean City Intermediate School, NJ

Never Forgotten

He may be gone,
he may never come back,
But he will never be forgotten.
He will be remembered,
Not only by me,
But everyone who knew him.
So now I wonder,
What's it like to never be forgotten?
Jordan Brasslett, Grade 8
Glenburn Elementary School, ME

Heaven

I picture heaven as being a wonderful paradise,
With light blue skies and fluttering butterflies.

I can picture everyone relaxing on the beach,
While listening to God's excellent speech.

I can picture everyone with a smile on their face,
Because they know everyone is accepted in this place.

I picture choirs of angels singing for joy,
To please every little girl and boy.

I picture a brilliant palace with a big, golden throne,
Which sits God where his glory can be shown.

Samantha Jarrett, Grade 7
St Hilary of Poitiers School, PA

New York City

Cars are…
Honking
Beeping
Revving
As they screech to a halt for a…
Man as he whistles
Woman as she screams
Ladies around are click-clacking
In their heels as they walk to work
Doors around the city slam
As the local McDonald's croaks at dawn
The city is awake and all are stirring
The buildings blink as people storm in the doors
A day in New York City has begun

Madison Walmer, Grade 8
Ephrata Middle School, PA

The Animal in Me

There is a cheetah in me
It lives inside my soul
It is fast as a race car,
Fast as lightning strikes,
Fast as fast can be
It unleashes itself when I run
On the track
It makes me fierce to my enemies
But gentle to my friends
It darts around my body through my veins
Like a cheetah prowling in the night
It bolts out like lightning and
Gives me a great wave of energy
A cheetah is in me
It is like the control center of my mind.

Caroline Keegan, Grade 7
Christ the Teacher Catholic School, DE

Poppies

Purple, peach, and white
These flowers are quite a sight
Although they make you sleepy
They are far from creepy
Their colors fly in the wind
And they are beautiful from the outside in
These poppies awake in the sun
And fall asleep when the day is done
You can see the children smile
Even from a mile
Seeing these poppies will make you glad
And at certain times they will make you sad
Purple, peach, and white
The poppies are truly quite a sight

Kelsey Wojnowski, Grade 7
Whitin Middle School, MA

Lost

As lightning strikes
Just as quick
Everything made sense
I DON'T BELONG HERE
Lost among these pretty faces
Gone without tying my laces
Let my hair flow in the wind
Tried before
But I couldn't fit in
Ran on an empty road
Found a bog and kissed a toad
And I think
I've found myself alone
While I streaked down that empty road
Hair in my eyes
Tripped on laces
Wanting to be lost in those beautiful faces
But as thunder booms
Loud and clear
I knew for sure
That I belong here

Richelle Kota, Grade 8
Julia R Masterman Secondary School, PA

Why?

Why did I have to meet you?
— knowin' that we were gonna come to an end
Why did I fall for you?
— knowin' that we were impossible.
Why did I trust you with everything?
— knowin' that you weren't truthful to me
Why did I put my heart on the line for you?
— knowin' it was gonna get hurt
Why did I believe when you said you'll be there for me?
— knowin' that you were always too busy for me
Why was I so stupid to fall for you?

Joel Ordonez, Grade 9
North Bergen High School, NJ

I Lost…

Wasted…time, discombobulated…thoughts, past…memories.
To spare, organize, and recollect…I could have done so.
I should have said it; there was no point not to…the words were there, dancing on my tongue.
Kicking, pushing, tearing, and fighting…
trying to pry my lips. Yet they did not budge!
Time after time I wasted…to get you to understand how I felt,
though I did not comprehend it myself.
It was all in my head…but I couldn't get it together.
Reaching, grasping, pulling, and collecting…
restraining my thoughts to prepare them to come out right.
Yet all they did was escape, and followed the words elsewhere.

I had to overcome and present superiority,

however, I let them run over me and do as they pleased.
Thoughts, confusion, hurt, words, and time…
reaching, grasping, pushing, tearing.
You're slipping. Your shadow's so faint.
"STOP!" My voice cracks and silence breaks.
It's too late. All that is left is memories…

P.S.: It's better to say too much, then to never say what you need to say again!

Keisha Lloyd, Grade 9
GAR Memorial Jr/Sr High School, PA

My Dedication to Hip-Hop

This is a dedication to hip hop.
Everyone on the streets want to be like them
But let's wake up young men and women of African Descent.
I mean the music is a culture we can relate to maybe the artists went through what we went through.
I know hip-hop is my name say it once, say it twice it's all the same.
When we feeling down we listen to our hip-hop it's like a band-aid someone puts on to heal our wound.
That's why I listen to it every day every morning and afternoon.
See the hip-hop is reality it blends into everyone's personality.
When we have our soul food dinner its like hip-hop is the main course.
But hip-hop will live today, tomorrow on until that day were gone.
To all the people who trying to make it
Look up to your favorite artists they won't fake it
So I won't put a fake smile on
Because I'm not going to unless I did it along
We got Philly, Cali, and New York to they putting something on the streets every day something new
So lets get it together if we going to be somebody
But when you guys make it please don't be snobby
We not going to get into that so lets stop
Because this is my dedication to hip-hop.

Arlana Brown, Grade 9
Science Leadership Academy, PA

Soul

What is a soul?
Is it really just an extension of the brain? Knowledge that comes from within? Or is it a God presence that can't be explained? Was Socrates right? Or maybe Plato? Did the Greeks know better than the scientists of today? Maybe it is a road map that leads us with knowledge attained over centuries and passed on? Or is it something that dates back before time began or the universe? Does it survive beyond death or does it die off with our last breath?

John Daniel Coburn, Grade 9
Sanford School, DE

Death

In the open field —
A symbol of mournful loss; a treasure for families,
An open casket, holding a former loved one.
A peaceful expression on the face —
Blank, but smooth, with no signs of distress.

Through the fire and ice
They hold on together.
A feeling of terror — but the calm, peaceful kind of terror,
Watching the coffin being lowered into the ground.

Not managing to dodge all the obstacles,
Trying to find a way through the impossible thick gloom.
Seeking a way through the twisting path,
Looking past the tangled web,
And finally finding a light at the end of the tunnel.

Walking toward the light, all troubles fade away.
Every stress is forgotten; each trouble unheard of —
Dilemmas evaporate.

Touching the light —
Reaching a trembling hand out towards it;
The glow is warm,
And the world fades away.

Younah Park, Grade 7
Carson Middle School, VA

Best Friends

Best friends are hard to find especially today
every time you think it's them you go your separate way.
Kids don't like to hear it but what your parents say is true
friends will come and go in a year or two.
Don't let it slow you down just keep pushing through
there will come a day when you find the one for you.

Vito Marcello, Grade 8

Techno

Exciting but not great,
Bringing a new revolution,
Adding on to both sound and movement,
Going on for a limited time,
Just waiting to be able to become a legend,
Not knowing when to stop,
In genre and task,
Having every element to bring,
Having its own
Sound?
Giving the world a beat every day,
Containing waves of crystal vision,
But owning the lives of some,
Bringing in a new revolution,
The sound
Techno?

Eric Lantz, Grade 7
Franklin Regional Middle School, PA

Unforgotten

We never thought this could happen
This terrible thing that will take you away from me
The doctors kept messing up
Giving us hope then crushing it
I know right now it is a bad time
But try to be strong and you'll be fine
I know you don't have much time to waste
So go and live your life
There will only be pain for a little while
Then it will be fine
I know you will be going to a better place
But still, I can't help from being scared
So I just wanted to let you know that…
I LOVE YOU

Marissa Martinez, Grade 7
Depew Middle School, NY

The Invitation

When I look into the sky
I see no clouds
only the sun inviting me
to put my toes in the ocean.
With calm, tickling waves
gently touching my feet
making my toes sink
deep into the sand,
I become still and washed
with peace and tranquility.

Connor Benjamin Louis Green, Grade 7
Ocean City Intermediate School, NJ

Little Person Big Dreams

I sit, gazing up at the stars
The sky, a blanket with sparkling dots everywhere
As I lay in the grass, staring up, I feel small

I am small compared to the big night sky
The cloudless, star-filled night
But somewhere in that, looking up into the moon
I find something

I find myself dreaming
Staring into the moon I see a teacher
I am looking up at my future
The stars are my students and I am the glowing moon
In the night sky, I lead them on their way
To follow their big dreams

Although I might be a little person, I have big dreams
Dreams bigger than this night sky
Dreams that will one day come true

Katie Perreault, Grade 7
Carson Middle School, VA

The Girl Ran

The girl ran as fast as a cheetah
Away from school she ran
She did not turn back
Hearing sirens made her panic
Away from school she ran
She jumped behind a bush
Hearing sirens made her panic
Her chest pumping hands sweating
She jumped behind a bush
Hoping not to be seen
Her chest pumping, hands sweating
She didn't know what to do
Hoping not to be seen
She did not turn back
She didn't know what to do
The girl ran as fast as a cheetah

Dana Davis, Grade 7
Garnet Valley Middle School, PA

Trust

Trust is a special gift
It doesn't come in a box with a bow

Some give it away
Many keep it locked away

When trusted is given away
Trust is accepted in return

Sometimes trust is mistaken
And betrayal is forsaken

Lauren Epstein, Grade 8
Floral Park Memorial High School, NY

Baseball

Jon is my name,
Baseball is my game.
I play baseball day and night,
When I'm at bat, I use all my might.

Crack, the ball goes flying in the air,
Try to catch it if you dare.
Running the bases one by one,
Hope our team gets it done.

We go to tourneys and win them all,
Everyone on my team has a ball.
We are really fantastic,
I'm sometimes too enthusiastic.

I hit the ball whack, whack, whack,
It's not that hard to take a hack.
Playing first base is what I do,
You should try it, too.

Jonathan Snyder, Grade 7
Dallastown Area Middle School, PA

Never Ever

Never have I ever met a guy like you, that is why
Forever
Forever
I will love you
Each hug you give me makes me feel secure and I know
Never
Ever
Would I want you to let me go
Each dream I have I think of you
And I will dream of your kiss through and through
I will
Never
Ever
Forget you because your personality has got me flying off walls
I will love you forever
Forget you…never
I will dream of your kiss forever
And I will hold you forever
But one thing that I will say that makes me feel forever gray
I will never tell you how I feel, even with my nerves of steel
You will never, ever know how I feel, so the dream of you being with me is
Never…ever…

Khadjiah Johnson, Grade 9
Abraham Lincoln High School, NY

Observing Nature

I sit observing nature
As the sun stalks me as if watching my every move
As I bask in the sun
I think about the stones that gleefully skip across the water
They skip as if ignoring the water that's angrily crashing against the shore
To me, that's what makes nature beautiful
That's why I sit and enjoy the trees that dance in the wind
Observing nature equals beautiful results

Tayla Boyd, Grade 7
Ghent Elementary School, VA

Roller Coaster

Anxiously waiting in line,
The feeling of excitement as you slowly make your way to the front,
You're almost there.
The fear finally begins to kick in,
It's your turn.
Step into the ride and wait,
Then finally you're off.
Flying through the air.
Butterflies in your stomach and the wind on your face.
Throw your hands up and scream,
As loud as you can.
The thrill of the ride is coming to an end.
Slowly you calm down,
And then it stops.
It's over.

Alexa Lenskold, Grade 9
Unami Middle School, PA

Goodbye

You were my mentor
my lifelong friend
time caught up
and brought the end

You tried to erase
my greatest fear
but it wasn't fair
to keep you here

You weren't really
mine to keep
I stayed with you
and watched you sleep

You sprouted wings
flew above the sky
I caught a feather
and said goodbye

Those were my words
but even so
I will never
let you go

Rachel Leah Schild, Grade 9
Monsey Beis Chaya Mushka High School, NY

The Sky

The sky started crying last night.
It was beautiful to watch but still didn't feel right.
I know that it helps the plants and the trees,
But I couldn't help feeling, it's crying because of me.
I know there is nothing to whine about,
But something inside makes me want to shout!

We pollute the word today,
Thinking we will never pay,
But the rain comes down, and I know things are not okay

Imagine the world a boat,
Thinking it will always stay afloat,
But the moment we stop caring and thinking
We slowly, but surely, start sinking.

As I turn my attention to the rain fall
I can't help but start to bawl
Because no one will look at the rain
And see that it is actually tears of pain
As I look at the sky, I sigh
Because all it can do is cry.

Janell Spigner, Grade 7
Westwood Jr/Sr High School, NJ

Someday

Someday…
I will not only reach for the stars, but touch them
I will look at the Earth in a different way
I will learn to overcome adversity
I will grow to be a mature adult
I will have kids to love and watch blossom
    Someday…
The world will be a safer place to live
The world will come together in peace
    Someday…

Allison Fournier, Grade 7
Anthony Wayne Middle School, NJ

Raindrops on My Heart

I stared out my rain splattered window,
Looking into the sky.
My heart was filled with sorrow,
My face stained with tears that dried.

Sometimes things can happen,
That can leave you feeling torn.
But when one door closes, another will open,
Another life is born.

In life there are always ups and downs,
An extra mile you have to run.
But experience different sights and sounds,
Remember the obstacles you won.

Now I look out my shiny window,
Looking into the bright sky.
Staring at the lovely rainbow,
Until the drops of rain will dry.

Tammy Gu, Grade 7
Green Brook Middle School, NJ

On the Inside

Here stands a girl, her face so plain and pale
She's strong on the outside, yet sick within
She lives a free life, yet she's trapped in jail
The same, yet different under her skin.

She seems normal, but she's out of control
Always afraid because there is no cure
Will not say what's wrong, but it haunts her soul
Like toxic waste, her body is far from pure.

This girl is before you, this girl is me
It is thanks to my mom that I'm alive
There is so much below that you can't see
If I do what I'm told I will survive.

Only I can save myself from the pain
I cannot ever let my life be drained.

Kaylee Carmichael, Grade 9
Unami Middle School, PA

I Never Saw

I never saw a monster,
Something that hides in the dark;
Yet I know its features,
Whether it talks or barks.

I never saws lightning high above,
That zaps around in the sky;
Yet I know it comes in color,
Whether it moves faster than my eye.

Jia Jun Li, Grade 7
Simon Baruch Jr High School 104, NY

Pineapples

The spiny outer shell
Hiding a juicy inner core
Like the lock on a chest
Guarding the treasures in a drawer
One tasty fruit like another
Teaching us not to
Judge a book by its cover

The green stiff leaves
Are like his battle spikes
Also daring its enemies
To come and chance its pikes
The rewards are great
If the battle is won
Your stomach will soon be its fate

So cut up a juicy pineapple today
You will agree with me on the first taste
That eating one will be a great idea
So hurry to your grocery store with haste
The yellow pulpy meat
Inside its hurtful skin
Will be too great to admit defeat

Ben Ekeroth, Grade 7
Franklin Regional Middle School, PA

If Only

If only she had more time to live
If only they could find a cure
If only cancer didn't strike just yet
If only she had less to endure

If only her life could be saved
If only the searing pain had gone away
If only the burn wasn't there anymore
If only we all could forget that day

If only the hospital had worked miracles
If only she hadn't fallen sick that fall
If only her optimism had prevailed
She would have been amongst us all

Neha Goswami, Grade 7
River Bend Middle School, VA

A Shade Darker Than Black

There's nothing more mysterious, than the deepest depths of the ocean,
Where the jellyfish float
And the giant squid swims,
But beyond all that
Is darkness.
Where no creature dares to go, for miles around all there is
Is black.

If silence is deafening, then darkness is blinding.

And there is nothing more mysterious, than the wilderness at night,
And the moon is hiding,
Where the wind whistles
And the coyote howls,
But beyond all that
Is darkness.
Where no creature dares to go
For miles around, all there is
Is black.

And there is nothing more mysterious, than a shade darker than black,
An unimaginably dark tone
Where no creature dares to go, and for miles around all there is
Is black.

Emma Annunziato, Grade 8
Floral Park Memorial High School, NY

Icarus

I was gathering all of my fishing equipment.
Then I headed outside.
I set all of the equipment up.
Then all of a sudden I saw something flying closely toward the water.
As it got closer I noticed that it was Icarus.
He was flying in the air with wings. Him and his father.
I was so fascinated.
So I decided to go and tell the others,
So I went to get the plough man and the shepherd.
They were already outside looking.
Then after a while we all got board.
So we went back to work.
All we could hear was Icarus yelling of excitement.
Icarus' dad warned him not to go to close to the sun,
But Icarus did not listen.
He kept going closer and closer.
Soon his wings began to melt.
Then all of a sudden we heard Icarus scream and fall into the water.
He was drowning.
There was nothing we could do.
We were too old and we could not swim.

Telly Coley, Grade 7
School of International Studies at Meadowbrook, VA

Wings to Fly

I got myself some wings and thought,
Now I can let go and fly.
It turned out that the world was spinning,
You were winning,
I was held down against my will.

I must let go and fly
This is my only chance.
I'll fly to somewhere near or far,
Somewhere I can freely dance.

Life isn't fair,
You loose control,
But sometimes,
You just have to
Let go,
Spread your wings,
And F
L
Y.

Ellen Sukharevsky, Grade 8
Milton Academy, MA

Violin Color

Bach is brown as antique furniture
Mozart is green as fresh leaf in May
Beethoven is black as tough wooden desk
Handel is salmon pink as spring flower
Kreisler is yellow with a purple dot
These are the colors my violin sings

Michael Lear, Grade 7
Carson Middle School, VA

The Wonders of the Nightmare Before Christmas

In the deep forest, just before night,
Jack came upon an amazing sight.
He saw 5 large trees
With pictures on them
The one that came to surprise was a Christmas tree
Jack opened the door sighting with awe
Then a flurry wind came and Jack left his dog

When Jack popped up in the place he was now
He discovered that he was in a place called Christmas Town

Jack loved this place so he took everything in sight
He even grabbed snow and took a big bite
When he got back to his group of peers
They all stared in amazement at Jack's wonderful souvenirs
No one saw this coming
Everyone thought it would always be Halloween
He ordered a town meeting about how Santa was king
Since Jack was always so bored with Halloween
He thought that he would try to be the Christmas king

Seleste Stahmer, Grade 7
Whitin Middle School, MA

Time

As time marches through the days,
to its side flock many men
of broken hopes and shattered dreams
looking for refuge.

And yet they will not find it there,
among the lost and broken
victims of a savage past
enslaved to their despair.

Lurking in life's corners dark,
they seek to claw a life
out of the grime
the deep dark black
and build one
for themselves.

And yet they can't — they wont, they don't
they remain forever bent.
Broken upon life's steepest cliffs.
In swift pursuit
of the shadow, of a life
that could be theirs.

Arnav Sood, Grade 8
Thomas R Grover Middle School, NJ

Rumors

People spreading gossip are flies,
Searching for juicy news to devour.
Swarming around spoiled things,
They might get swatted away,
But even more come back.

Spying silently like flies on walls,
They flit away to tell tall tales.
All the while, the stories are twisted and turned,
Into ones that are more exaggerated,
Exciting, and entertaining.

People spreading rumors,
Are like bees carting pollen.
Harvesting it and moving on,
From one flower to the next,
For mile after mile.

Gossip is their honey,
And they try to make the sweetest.
But one person alone cannot do it all,
Many people have to work together,
To ruin reputations.

Andrew Wang, Grade 7
Carson Middle School, VA

Eclipse

The sun shining as bright as possible,
Fighting off the clouds
Its light strong and powerful
the light warm, filling the people up
with joy and happiness.
As the clouds ran off
That brought pain and gloom
a new pain has come,
graying the sky
the sun rays dimming
as a large dark circle crosses the sky.
It gets colder, wind chilling the sky
The sun is hidden.
The clouds the sun can handle
But the sun can't fight with an eclipse.

Katie Pedernera, Grade 7
Hammarskjold Middle School, NJ

The Animal in Me

There is a dolphin inside me…
Peacefully swimming,
Always happy and joyful.
There is a dolphin inside me,
Not caring what goes on around me,
Enjoying life.
There is a dolphin inside me,
Easily swimming about my mind,
Freedom ringing within my heart.
There is a dolphin inside me,
Reigning forever.

Eva DelleDonne, Grade 7
Christ the Teacher Catholic School, DE

My Summer Was Like…

My summer was like a hyena,
with laughter all the time.
My summer was like broccoli,
because "going green" was my headline.

My summer was like a statue,
staying in one place.
My summer was like a beautiful rose,
blooming in a vase.

My summer was like a race car,
speeding by very fast.
My summer was like a firecracker,
with a big beautiful blast.

My summer was like a party,
with family, fun and friends.
My summer was like a good book,
at some point it had to end.

Angela Guido, Grade 7
Ocean City Intermediate School, NJ

Hockey Players

Skating, flying, shooting,
The hockey player,
Miraculously,
Scored,
Into the goal!

Anthony Poltronetti, Grade 7
Anthony Wayne Middle School, NJ

Murals Behind Closed Doors

The legacy
Of art behind locked doors
New York art scene
Urban street scenes
Photograph art
The legacy
Of art behind locked doors.

Arielle Peleg, Grade 9
Unami Middle School, PA

Skateboarding

I know skateboarding…
people chatting
boards braking
rails sliding
I know skateboarding…
the smell of the new wheels
the smell of the new wood
I know skateboarding…
people talking
landing tricks
having fun
I know skateboarding…
"land that trick"
"try again"
"do that again"
I DO KNOW SKATEBOARDING!

Zachery Dunn, Grade 8
Ephrata Middle School, PA

Graduation

The last day of school
The final drop-off
The final walk down the hallway
The final greetings
The final prayers
The final classes
The final ceremony
The final hugs
The final goodbyes
The final memories of a class
That took in the new students
And treated them as one of them

Jeremy Loss, Grade 8
St Stephen's School, NY

Depths of the Dark

In the depths of the dark,
a heart is breaking.
In the depths of the dark,
a body is shaking.
In the depths of the dark,
all hopes are fading.

The darkness is a scary place,
where nothing's what it seems.
Where every day's a nightmare,
and monsters steal your dreams.

In the depths of the dark,
a devil is lying.
In the depths of the dark,
a child is crying.
In the depths of the dark,
all innocence is dying.

Brianna Thomas, Grade 7
Ocean City Intermediate School, NJ

Time

The table turns
The hands move
The world is spinning
But I have paused
Taking in every thing life throws
And shoving my own back
Stopping and staring
Thinking and caring
The clock ticks
The book flips
The world is spinning
But I have paused

Rachel Felt, Grade 9
Pine-Richland High School, PA

World of Wonder

So many things so beautiful and cute
So many things one cannot compute

A moonlit night
That covers the Earth

A wolf howling at the moon
Like a sad song crying out

A beautiful waterfall
Falling down and making a sound

So many things so beautiful and cute
So many things one cannot compute.

Bethany Hintze, Grade 7
Thorne Middle School, NJ

Goodbye

Goodbye,
Not any goodbye,
But saying bye for good.
Not just giving someone a wave,
But showing there is a chance you won't see them.

Never take people for granted,
Whether they are annoying or nice.

As we go out
We remember,
All the times
We spent together.

When it's time to depart,
You look around,
You put a smile on your face,
Chuckle, cry,
And leave,
For good
…Goodbye.

Kamal Abdelrahman, Grade 7
Joseph B Cavallaro Intermediate School, NY

Not Good Enough

What ever happened to,
"Everyone is beautiful?"
Why does it have to be,
"She's too fat or he's too ugly?"

Who says you need a face lift?
Your face is given as a gift.
Who says you need some collagen?
God didn't give your lips as a sin.

In a world with Botox and plastic surgery,
Not following the trend is like perjury.
The clichés that rule out originality,
Totally obscure your personality.

Why tan yourself? Why paint your face?
Why not take pride in what you brace?
When you strip away your natural way,
Have you ever acknowledged the price you pay?

When we look at our reflection,
We only see the negatives the media portrays.
The mirror taunts you, not at all in praise.
This all won't matter some day,
Only on how you thought it through.

Ashley Puk, Grade 7
Westwood Jr/Sr High School, NJ

The True Game

Butterflies come, that weird feeling I can't shake.
I need to make the move.
I need to be there for the people I have dedicated my time to.
Bursts of adrenaline, a deep roar.
I think all of a sudden,
What if, what if, what if,
The last minute comes before the signal, and I think…
"I need to do this."
I bend with the sourness swelling inside.
Then the CLAP of leather against my skin.
The natural motion backward,
And I see the figure at the end of the plain.
Hands tight to the laces you show them how pigs can fly.
Thud!
I fall sprawling to the turf.
As I lay I hear the sound of lightning in my head.
I see as I stand, tears!
Great pain comes, as my stomach tightens.
I grow older and older remembering that play!
Oh to try it again, just one more time!

Anthony Buono, Grade 7
Depew Middle School, NY

Just Because

Just because I'm a girl,
Doesn't mean I like makeup,
Doesn't mean I wear dresses.

Just because I'm a girl,
Doesn't mean I love the color pink,
Doesn't mean I like to sing.

Just because I'm a girl,
Doesn't mean I spend hours on the phone,
Doesn't mean I like to dress up.

Just because I'm a girl,
Doesn't mean I liked ponies when I was young,
Doesn't mean I like to dance.

Just because I'm a girl —
Don't judge me.

Rihab Mahmood, Grade 7
Anthony Wayne Middle School, NJ

Unkind

Something is beating me down
It's big yellow and round
It's not a wave hitting the sand
While at the beach with sand hitting my hand
No not with legs, arms, nor feet
I am really getting beat
It's the sun being mean
Just like my school dean

Cameron Irby, Grade 7
Rosemont Middle School, VA

Tears of the Clouds

Clouds gather in,
Gray like their mood.
Starting small,
The sea is their food.

Flowing over,
Tears fall back down.
A continuous cycle,
Endless returns to the ground.

Droplets return,
Back to the clouds.
Other foggy tears
Act as their shrouds.

Lightning and thunder
Emitting power.
A strength so infinite
Accompanying a shower.

The cycle continues,
Carrying God's heart.
The lightning and thunder
His touch on this art.

Alycia Park, Grade 8
Huntingdon Area Middle School, PA

Life and Death

Life.
Difficult, choices.
Discovering, growing, overcoming.
Love, friendships, emotional, peaceful.
Falling, ending, departing.
Empty, lonely.
Death.

Kristina Jubinsky, Grade 7
Anthony Wayne Middle School, NJ

Heaven's Touch

Harmonious
Causing your worries to go with the wind
Whistle
Blowing nature towards you
As if the grass is waving at you
Heat and sweat blowing away
Sway
The smell of fresh trees and their bark
Don't look
Just feel
Do you taste the moistness of the air?
Thrust
You just felt me
Cleansing all of your troubles
I am the summer breeze

Bradley Meyer, Grade 7
Christ the Teacher Catholic School, DE

There Is No Mystery Here to Be Found

There is no mystery here to be found.
This poem is but a quick smite of expression.
There is no deep meaning to be renounced,
But random true thoughts during a clean typing session.

I feel the breeze of cool winter rain,
Bringing life to all around me.
While the muscles of my mind they strain
To make a work that any could so clearly see.

To recollect a cooked chicken's scent
And thunder crashing through my skull.
I feel as though I must repent,
To make a piece of art so simple, bland, and dull.

My humblest apologies for wasting your time, my consent is all I can give.
For expressing with you a work of mine whose only purpose is to rhyme and live.

Richard Kruse, Grade 8
Girard Academic Music Program, PA

I

I am glad for the life that lies before me
I am sad for all the lives that I may lose
I am happy for all the family and friends I have today

I am grateful for all the close people around me
I am worried for all the troubles I may face
I am happy for all I have and will have

I am excited for having a great life
I am beautiful for the good person I have become
I love who I am and hope everything stays the same

I am scared for the life that lies before me
I am nervous for what could happen to me
I know what happens, happens for a reason

I know I should take every step cautiously
I hope nothing ever happens to me
I am excited for what lies before me in this vast wonderland of life

Mitchell Logan Moore, Grade 7
Trinity Middle School, PA

The Best Christmas Ever

What my favorite thing that is wrapped, you say
Well it all happened at Christmas one day.
I woke up and ran downstairs.
Knowing I should wake up my parents but thinking, "Who cares"
When I saw all the gifts, the big one stood out.
Then I heard my father wake up, he must know I am wondering about.
Once I got up to the presents and sat on the floor.
Man, I was excited since I was just four.
The whole family was up and they saw the presents and didn't expect much more.

Justin Von Ahnen, Grade 7
Garnet Valley Middle School, PA

What You Must Pay

I come to those who wait,
To those that leap,
I am everyone's fate.

Some call me grim
And your chances of escaping
Are quite slim.

But I am also a new start,
Though no one knows what I bring
I stop the beats of the heart

But no one should hope
For me to skip over their pulse
How would you cope?

To see all your loved ones sucked under my wrath
Trust me, your life
Would be a blood bath.

Although I do confess
You shouldn't be happy
About meeting death.

Olya Rizzo, Grade 8
Jefferson Central School, NY

School's Over

After nine years, it has come to an end.
It feels kind of weird 'cause I won't be back.
At this time of year school is always over.
I'm not sure if I'm sad because I'm too excited.
High school will be here before I know it.
So good-bye St. Stephen School.
Thank you!

Alan Wopperer, Grade 8
St Stephen's School, NY

Summer

Summer is always so much fun.
You get to go outside and play in the sun.
There are so many people having fun.

All of the children are now out of school.
You now see the opening of pools.
It is all very cool.

The trees and grass are now very green.
It is all a wonderful sight to be seen.
Everything is now very clean.

There are many parties going on.
People are vacationing and gone.
There are so many things going on,
During the summer of fun.

Ashley Colan, Grade 8
St Stephen's School, NY

Popcorn and M&M's = Memories

I can hear the crunch as I bite into the puffed corn,
I can taste the sweet sensation of chocolate
And the tangy taste of butter.
My mind flashes back to summer.
Clara's backyard.
A big bonfire with everyone that I'd give my own life to save.
I am reminded of love and laughter.
The tradition of making a wish at 11:11.
My mind fills with joy and sorrow
As I remember the best months of my life.
I feel sorrow knowing
It will never be the same.
As the taste fades away,
So do the memories that I'd give anything to relive.

Jill Wyatt, Grade 7
Unami Middle School, PA

Soaring

The parents gather debris to make their nest
They find this works the best.

The mother takes a little rest
Before the babies enter the nest.

The parents go daily to gather worms
And feed the babies on their terms.

They grow and grow and get stronger each day.
So they can finally make their own way.

They soon are chirping with glee
That they can finally be free.

The parents soon say good-bye
When their baby hatchlings soar into the sky.

Brandon Janca, Grade 7
Depew Middle School, NY

My Loving Neighborhood

My family is a neighborhood:
Dad is a house, protective and strong
But has weak points.
Mom is a garden, filled with flowers
But has more love than buds.
Matt is a sidewalk, quiet and boring
But sometimes walked over.
Mikey is a bike, only out once and a while
But never stops ringing his bell.
I am a pool, calm sometimes
But anger me and I will splash.

Abbey Yonta, Grade 7
Jamesville-Dewitt Middle School, NY

Nature's Senses

Do you hear it the cold wind is going and the spring wind is coming? Do you smell it the spring flowers are growing? Splish splash kids are splashing in puddles after the spring rain. Do you hear the howling wind of the night? More and more kids are running in the fresh dewed grass. Do you see the beautiful sunset sinking to the ocean floor? Do you hear the waves crashing against the rocks at the beach? Do you smell the sweet smell after it rains?

Katelyn Dykens, Grade 7
Marblehead Veterans Middle School, MA

Darkness

Darkness runs under his cloak of shadows,
exciting our imagination, as we hear him rushing by. And he rushes through
the trees as we turn round and round in dread. And if we dare enter the darkness,
then he crawls on our skin, wrapping us in fear. He stabs us with his knife of terror,
right through our hearts. And he rides upon his nightmare,
she is as black as he. She gallops in your mind, her ghost hooves
disturb your deepest fears, and remind you in your sleep. Together they race around and around.
And although you cannot see them you feel them,
you feel his knife and her hooves, and panic rips through you.
But Darkness is a coward, and is afraid of the light. He hides in the shadows,
and away from the Moon, who turns him into nothing with her rays
She is why he is always running.
He is fighting, but will never win. But the battle still rages and will never be gone.
He steals your senses and takes them away.
And as you stand blind he whispers in your ear, that he will release it, but won't tell you what.
And he sits and laughs as your mind races faster than your heart,
and cold fear runs through you. So stay in the light, and be afraid of the dark.

Hannah Anderson, Grade 8
Pathfinder Academy, NH

Regrets

If only I had known the regret you had inside you if only I had seen the pain that was inside you if only I had realized that everything wasn't quite right, if only I had looked and seen the pain alone you couldn't fight, maybe if I had done these things you would be okay. But now there's nothing I can do but cry another tear. The one thing I've always wanted, you couldn't do. But I only wanted to help you. The one thing I always needed you couldn't fill that need. Now all I wonder is what I did wrong. No matter what with no regrets I love you forever but this is what I get?

Cassandra Connors, Grade 7
Depew Middle School, NY

Saving the Environment

Do you like the planet we live on?
Everybody does.
Do you know what people are doing to our environment?
Rainforests around the world are being cut down
Leaving innocent animals without a place to call home.
A local stream is being heated up by the sun,
A place where fish swim daily every day.
Fish are flopping out of water trying to get a breath of cool water.
Trees are being cut down to make way for a new mall.
Have you ever seen a tree fall?
A falling tree looks like a soldier in a war falling to his death.
Animals starve without food from the local trees or abundance of animals for hunting.
These ideas in my mind make me frustrated because we need to stop people from doing this.
I understand people need furniture from trees, but how much furniture do we need?
I hope we humans can do something about it and live on this Earth for a long time.

Charles Colton Croskey, Grade 7
Pine-Richland Middle School, PA

This Feeling

I put on a smile to hide the truth,
my real smile faded into tears.
I put on a smile to hide the truth,
maybe it'll calm my fears.

Can you tell me where your feelings went,
once so strong but now no more?
Your feelings were spilled like water,
and I don't know how to make things right, anymore.

You said I gave you that feeling,
but I guess it didn't mean a thing.
Now I'm here crying,
and you're with her smiling.
You said I gave you that feeling,
but I guess it didn't mean a thing.
Now I'm here dying,
and you're with her smiling.

And now I wish I could melt away into nothing,
so this pain wouldn't exist.
And now I wish I could melt away into nothing,
so I wouldn't feel like this.

Michaela Kascak, Grade 9
Frank Scott Bunnell High School, CT

Camera

Camera! Camera! Moments embraced
Capturing scenes in their place
Oh so thoughtful; remembrance of the past
Could even that show, thy inner face?

Becky Pohl, Grade 9
Unami Middle School, PA

Don't Mess with Me

I start out as plop…plop…plop,
but then, as I get ANGRIER,
I BOOM, BOUNCE, and RIP,
leaving an ear-shattering, heart-thumping sound!
Now I am rushing to the ground,
like giant ice balls,
shaped like golf balls or baseballs.
I feel POWERFUL!
But what am I?
I am a…
HAIL STORM!
Hear me roar!
As windows shatter and shake,
the screens underneath rip and shred.
Maybe that is why I don't have any friends.

Ashley Barnett, Grade 7
Christ the Teacher Catholic School, DE

Walls

If these walls could talk
They could tell us the stories of those before our time
If only these ultimate eavesdroppers would dare tell
Of the gossip, the betrayal, the laughter,
The lies, the truths.
If these walls had courage
Would they speak out
Would they laugh or call our ideas stupid
If only these walls had energy like the Energizer Bunny,
But they don't.
They are shy like lambs.
They are not brave like lions.
They can't burst forth.
They prefer the shadow instead of the spotlight.
They hide in the back and become invisible to all
They remain silent as they always will
Besides what could they say,
They are only walls.

Jasmina Chatani, Grade 8
Beacon Middle School, DE

A Fairy Tale

His crown stood so very high,
With diamonds on every corner.
But the problem was the man inside the crown
A prince in the shape of a frog.
He was sad, very depressed.
A princesses kiss would mend his pain
It was fate when she stumbled among this special frog
Under the frog she saw his charm,
The gift of her kiss is what he received.
Then he transformed into the man inside,
And it was a celebration of marriage with laughter and fun,
And they lived happily ever after!

Jordyn Lustig, Grade 7
Hammarskjold Middle School, NJ

I Am From…*

I am from 42" Samsung Plasma TV
from Springhouse Milk and Rockband.
I am from the biggest bedroom in the house.
And the smell of fall candles all year round.
I am from the lilacs that dad always talks about.
And the "Umbrella" tree
whose long gone limbs I remember as if they were my own.

I'm from Christmas Eve dinner and
Fireman's Fair every year.
From cousins whose names start with "J"
and lots of aunts.
I'm from making feet pancakes and
homemade whipped cream with the chef of the house, Dad.
And from the whole family all swimming at Gram's pool.

Julia Handra, Grade 7
Trinity Middle School, PA
*Patterned after "Where I'm From" by George Ella Lyons

My Sanctuary

The birds, the tree, the bumble bee
How peaceful is thee
The bear, the rabbit, the coon
And me, a mini Daniel Boone
How important is his machete
Covering the forest floor in confetti
For why is the eye of the forest so keen
May it be because of man and machine
The forest has become depleted
"Stop!!! Stop!!!" I pleaded
But how…how could a small voice
Spread such savior and rejoice
The birds, the tree, the bumble bee
How peaceful is thee
For what is to happen to my sanctuary?

Akil Stallworth, Grade 7
Trinity Middle School, PA

See Me

Can you see me
Can you tell if I'm sad
Do I want to be free
Or am I mad

Would you say I'm cool
Am I easy to please
You see me this way
You're the only one this way

I'm an angel in all minds
They always say I'm easy to find

Do you see right through me

Christina Dana, Grade 8
Western Heights Middle School, MD

In the Web

I've been caught,
And tied up.
My past,
Coming back,
To bite me.

The things I've said,
Anything I've done,
Has got me,
Twisted up,
Into the grip,
Of my wrongs.

So I sit.
Waiting for my:
Judgment.
The Fly in the Web.

Sara Downey, Grade 7
Unami Middle School, PA

Home Sweet Home

Waking up,
A new day has begun,
Breakfast is ready.
"Come eat, Freddy!"
My steaming hot breakfast of eggs and juicy bacon call,
Yum,
Without my breakfast I would be quite glum.
As juice dribbles down my chin,
I just have to grin.

Glistening windows,
To look through.
Steady floors,
To walk on.
A backyard,
To play in.
A room,
For me.

Home Sweet Home.

"Where we love is home, home that our feet may leave, but not our hearts."
— Oliver Wendell Holmes

Mary Powathil, Grade 8
Farnsworth Middle School, NY

Standing in the Rain

Feel the cold rain on your skin,
as it falls down from the stars.
Ignore the sounds of the world,
and let night take over your soul.

Don't think about the past or future,
but think about the moment.
Think about the reasons to live,
and know to feel rain is one of the best reasons of them all.

Open your mouth,
let the drops come down.
Shut your eyes,
and let the water drip along on your face.

Smell the freshness in the air,
the bad things all getting washed away.
Lift your face up to the sky,
And open your eyes just barely to keep the water from coming in.

Then smile.
Smile for the rain.

Hannah Corderman, Grade 9
Needham High School, MA

Summer

Summer is the best time of year.
The kids start to play and you can hear,
The birds come out and the sounds of the children.
The sun is out and it is warm.
Summer is my favorite time of the year.

James Gallagher, Grade 8
St Stephen's School, NY

Grandpa

One last kiss goodbye
I march out and he sighs
Little did I know
One week later he would go
A shoulder tap
My heart takes a lap
My mom's swollen eyes told the story
I knew that it was time to worry
I had to be strong for Kara and PJ
To my grandparents house we were on our way
Sad shocked depressed and alone
The next few days I was a stone
5 years later
I try to help my younger brother and sister remember
You never really know what you've got
Until it goes and you're distraught

Kathryn Neary, Grade 7
Westwood Jr/Sr High School, NJ

Wind

I go where the wind boasts.
Left, right, up, down.
Sometimes sending me spinning in circles.
It's my compass guiding me
through the forests of life never leaving my side.

Lilting gentle breezes on a spring day guide me
onward toward my beloved summer
having me hug my excitement
more and more with every step.

Sultry summer winds hum against my face,
flustering my hair, asking me to follow.
But, warm winds sting my blistered skin
making me clench in pain.

Harsh winter blusters pierce my icy skin
forcing me to twitch in grief.
But, that doesn't keep me from playing in the squall
surrounded by snowflakes erupting from the sky.

Fall storms bask in the air.
The breeze touches my face
sending thrilling chills down my spine,
making goose bumps tingle on my calves.

Paige Broadley, Grade 7
Ocean City Intermediate School, NJ

When You

When you open a book,
You open your mind.
When you open your mind,
You open your imagination.

When you read those tiny letters and words
A lot can happen
Your brain starts running
Like a mouse on a wheel.

When your imagination runs,
Anything can happen,
Like a knight in shining armor
Riding a horse to save a princess.

When you turn pages,
It is like changing a scene
In a good movie
Or a nice play.

When you open a book,
You open your mind.
When you open your mind,
You open your imagination.

Christopher Watenpool, Grade 9
Pine-Richland Middle School, PA

The Heart Has Its Own Calendar

The heart has its own calendar.
For when the death of a loved one befalls,
Your mind goes blank, your heart stops.
You can't feel anything except the blood,
The blood pounding in your ears.
You see in your mind the black waters, the waves,
And they drown you, pulling you under.

You wake up, blinking groggily, and for a moment,
Everything is fine.
Until you remember, with a sinking heart, the death.
Disbelief washes over you.
Surely — surely you would know if they were dead!
Wasn't it only yesterday they were alive,
And you both were talking and laughing under the stars?

A cloud of anger descends upon you.
Then the pain pierces like a thousand knives.
Eventually, life goes on, you become yourself again.
But not quite, for a part of you will always remember.
A part of you died with them that day, because
The heart has its own calendar.

Smrithi Srikanthan, Grade 7
Carson Middle School, VA

The King of Pop

The King of Pop's career
Started with the Jackson 5
Singing "Abc" and "Thriller"
He slowly started to climb

He created the moonwalk
An unforgettable dance
He could walk the talk
He took a chance

Though he has left us now
He remains firmly in our hearts
Michael truly has touched the world
He was off the charts

May he rest in peace!

Christianna Tottossy, Grade 7
Corporate Landing Middle School, VA

Break the Circle Around Her

Break the circle around her,
the one that holds her in,
break this circle around her,
she no longer must hide in,
in the walls that hold her tight,
hold her from the truth,
the truth of life,
has to be revealed,
to her hazel eyes,
so give her a kiss,
and tell her you love her,
'cuz once the walls fall,
there is no stopping her.

Breanna Englander, Grade 9
Commack High School, NY

I Cry

I cry when I am lonely,
I cry when I am sad,
I cry when I am misunderstood,
I cry when I am lost,
I cry when I am fearful,
I cry when I am hurt,
I cry when I am isolated,
I cry when I am pressured,
I cry when I am joyful,
I cry when I am delightful,
I cry when I am dignified,
I cry when I am ambitious,
I cry when I laugh too hard,
I cry whenever I want,
Because that's just the way I feel.

Anna Lee, Grade 7
Hammarskjold Middle School, NJ

Hurricane

I am a hurricane!
I destroy and demolish towns
that get in my way!
I bring friends:
Rain
Thunder
Lightning
Nothing can stop us
There are no warnings
I hunger for land and
anything that gets in my way
Then I leave a path of
destruction
behind me!

Anthony Reynolds, Grade 7
Christ the Teacher Catholic School, DE

Redwood Trees

The mighty Redwood,
towering,
aged,
sturdy,
living to be hundreds of years old
has lived past history and time
and seen most of early life
of this country being built and
battles and wars fought to the death.

Mighty homes are given
to smaller more exposed animals,
cover from
cold,
rain,
snow,
a birthing house for young birds.
Standing the test of time
always to be there.

Matt Popp, Grade 7
Ocean City Intermediate School, NJ

My Thunder

Today I went to class
I did nothing but stare and wonder
About all my lightning and my thunder

I thought about what you did to me
I thought about how it came to be
I felt so lonely at the time
I felt like I didn't have a dime

Now I'm wondering what to do
Knowing I will always be thinking of you.

Justin Danatos, Grade 7
Hammarskjold Middle School, NJ

Tree

Tall and lean
Short and stout
Weeping in solitude
Swaying in joy

Thriving in the summer
Sprayed with color in autumn
Dormant during the winter
Reborn in the spring

Home of many
Birds, and animals alike
Covered in wreaths of leaves
Pointy, round and needle like

Cherry, Teak, Maple, and Oak
Thick and skinny
Round and hard
I am a tree

Eli Guseman, Grade 7
Ocean City Intermediate School, NJ

Spring

I know spring
Birds chirping, flowers blooming
Summer on its way
I know spring
Go for a picnic, take a walk, ride a bike
I know spring
Smell of sweet flowers
Play in the warm sun
I know spring
Sports start soon
Friends hanging out
Play out side with your dogs
I know spring

Morghan Howard, Grade 8
Ephrata Middle School, PA

Every Story Has a Happy Ending

As the year comes to an end
There is no more room to bend
We have experienced so much
At every single finger touch
Our memories are so great
It keeps us on the narrow straight
We realize that everything and everyone
Has had our good and bad times
We were stupid but smart
But don't like to be apart
Together now we stay hand in hand
As the end of the year comes to a stand

Carlee Conway, Grade 7
St Stephen's School, NY

When I Am in Boston

When I am in Boston, I would cheer.
I would cheer for the Red Sox, even if it was 96 degrees.
I would take my water, and pour it down my shirt.
I would have ice cream, spending my dad's money.

When I am in Boston, I would go to Yawkey Way.
I would get a jersey, and go to Game On.
My dad and I would sit at the bar, waiting for game time.
He would get a beer, and I would get a Coke.
Then it would be 7:30, and we would head for the stadium.

When I am in Boston, I would go to Quincy Market.
I would go to Cheers, and get lunch.
I would get a spray tattoo, just for the game.
I would get a new hat, if I liked one.
I would wear it, when we got to the game.

When I am in Boston, everyone is my friend.
I was in Red Sox Nation, and nobody liked the Yankees.
I got to meet the mascot, and dance on the dugout.
I had a ball, and the crowd went wild.
I went up on the Green Monster, and I enjoyed it.
I didn't want to go back, I was in Boston.

James Beal, Grade 7
Markham Place Elementary School, NJ

Two Paths

Two paths, formed a fork in my life.
I, being the pawn, was forced to choose.
For one path, joy; the other, strife;
Long I decided and looked, a decision larger than life:
I was choosing; what could I lose?

Then was forced to the path less worn,
Forced into strife, misery, pain.
Little did I know; how I'd be torn!
I'd hardly have enough time to mourn
Over not picking quickly enough, not being vain.

I'd hoped to keep the other path for another day,
Yet I later found I couldn't go back.
Too late; I would always say,
"I'll come back later to play."
But the other path was out of my reach; turned black.

I'll always regret not being able to choose again,
But it must be destiny, rather than my choosing.
And my regret is all in vain;
But if the chance, I ever obtain,
I'd certainly choose joy, rather than my losing.

Kelsey Pontz, Grade 8
Martin Meylin Middle School, PA

A Soccer War

The stretch, then run
just to play
the crowd is there cheering in the hot sun
oh it is a beautiful day

Just to play
the goal is to score
oh it is a beautiful day
the winning team will soar

The goal is to score
they kick the ball to be adored
the winning team will soar
and dribble and shoot to end the war.

They stretch then run
they kick the ball to be adored
they dribble and shoot to end the war
the crowd is there cheering in the hot sun.

Sarah Haddon, Grade 8
Ephrata Middle School, PA

Asylum

The lights are on
But the house is hollow
And I'm stuck staring into the glass half empty
Trying to penetrate its surface
But all I can see is a tiny mirror
Quivering to the pulsing rhythm of my heartbeat
Seeming so solid in my mind
But in actuality, so breakable
However, in the stillness of the night there seems to be no threat
So I sit and try to clear my head
And hope to God I'm still sane
Because I'm staring at a glass half empty
Fearing the eminent break in my reflection.

Molly Cesare, Grade 9
Huntingdon Area High School, PA

Sonnet 1

My life today is so crazy busy,
I go from track meets, to soccer, to school.
I get myself in a frantic tizzy,
I keep thinking this is really not cool.
My priority is homework and tests,
But it's hard to give up the game in me.
I stay up too late and sacrifice rest,
I tell myself, I have to find the key.
To eliminate mindless distractions,
Give up texting, gaming, endless TV
Allowing more time for proper action,
Focus on homework to prevent a "D."
I realize now that it's myself I cheat,
I will change these habits in a heartbeat.

Stephen Pieri, Grade 9
Unami Middle School, PA

Kathryn

He was once an insecure, shy boy.
Although he wanted to feel warm,
His heart was ice cold.
Never did he think he'd feel such joy.

Then along she came,
And feelings began to form.
Her smile was worth more than gold,
To him she wasn't just another dame.

When his feelings started getting strong,
He wondered how she felt.
And this feeling felt so wrong,
Because she caused his icy heart to melt.

Neither of us knew what was going on,
My feelings had scared me.
The waiting had seemed so long,
And foolishly I just let it be.

Now I haven't a clue what to do,
Because I will always be in love with you.
Daniel Costello, Grade 9
Medford High School, MA

City Life

Day by day,
I never see hay.
There are lots of streets and cars,
So people can go far.
Andrew Genao, Grade 7
St Agatha School, NY

I belong here

the silence is a song
that laces through my mind
the sun is a laugh
that dances on my tongue
the wind is a warmth
that warms my very soul
my smile is a mystery
a story not yet told
the clouds are my scrapbook
when I take the time to look
nature seems to glitter
and it makes me sparkle too
I belong here with the silence
that screams the beautiful truth
I belong here with the hidden
that is in everyone's plain view
I belong here and I'll stay here
as long as reality allows
for now the world is left behind
and I'll float among the clouds
Kendall Moyer, Grade 8
Central Academy Middle School, VA

What Is Beauty?

In our society,
beauty is everyone's, key element, in their lives.
When most people first hear the word beauty,
many if not all, imagine a girl,
with blonde hair as wavy as spaghetti.
Also imagined are pools of blue eyes, someone's figure,
whether it is a supermodel figure or not, personality is never a factor.
You can have the looks, maybe not the intelligence,
either do matter, blonde and blue eyed are assumed to be nice.
With looks and a body, blonde waves and blue sparkling eyes,
our society portrays this, as the perfect woman.
Brunettes exist too, along with redheads,
in our society, we are never as pretty as a blonde.
Everyone is picked on,
blondes with blue eyes, can be called dumb blondes.
Many of us judge, maybe not realizing it,
looks don't matter, inside counts more.
Blonde and brunette, brown and blue,
don't forget redhead, and green eyed too.
Our society is a monster, destroying anything it crosses,
it is up to you, if you want to believe it.
Alycia Monaco, Grade 7
Westwood Jr/Sr High School, NJ

God

I sit at my window, as I try to think.
Who made man? Who made us blink?

Who is the person, responsible for these things?
Who made wind? Who made the birds sing?

Is that person, more powerful than the sun?
Does he know, when the Earth will be done?

Who knows, the future is endless
I care about my future, but some people could care less,

We have to take this seriously, we could research it right,
Maybe we can meet that one man; even if it takes all day and night.

I want to meet that man, and someday I'll have to die
And someday I'll go to Heaven, and I can finally meet THAT man.
Natasha Collova, Grade 7
Westwood Jr/Sr High School, NJ

Me as a Free Person

In this world and time, I am free
I can be what I want to be, and not be judged by my skin color
I can be me
I am not bought by slave owners and bought for few dollars
I flee from the seas of hate and follow the breeze of prosperity
I have the power to learn, make my own decisions, and speak my own mind
I am happy God has created me
Jessica Valmont, Grade 8
Our Lady of Lourdes School, NY

When We Were Kids

Everyone in my life is progressing,
leaving me behind
to find that I'm alone,
trying to find somewhere I belong,
somewhere to be accepted,
someplace to call home.
I've realized that this place does not exist,
that my hopes are worthless,
that I'm not missed.
I hope that someday they'll look back and find
that I'm not trapped, alone,
and behind on my life and my dreams.
That my wounds have healed
and I can feel again,
chasing after something I believe in
like I used to
when we were kids.

Selina Avelino, Grade 7
Joseph H Martin Middle School, MA

Our Special Bond

They both come from different backgrounds
His eyes squinted, hers are round
They share a special bond, like nothing known
Best friends they said until they were fully grown
Long walks along the road
The countless things she made him hold
He was the best friend she could ever ask for
But now he's getting old
Will their friendship still behold?
Only time can tell.

Zoë Reda, Grade 7
St Stephen's School, NY

Land of the Free

One day I looked at our grand old flag,
and I thought to myself, it looks like a rag.
It's beaten, it's old, it's not that attractive,
and thinking about it, my mind was real active.

I kept on thinking about the reason it was there,
the more I thought, the more I cared.
Maybe our leaders wanted a sign,
maybe our country thought our flag was fine.

Did they originally want it to represent us,
did they spend all their time making a fuss?
Our flag stands for our country, and people are proud,
that life and liberty will always be allowed.

Our flag is not beaten, and although it is old,
I can see now it stands bright and bold.
The U.S. is my home, and in my mind I will save,
I live in the land of the free, and the home of the brave.

Gianna Dafflisio, Grade 7
Calvary Academy, NJ

Unlimited

One world among the stars
Amidst the swirling galaxies
Lost in the nebulae
Hidden in the star clusters
Sandwiched by black holes
And strange pulsing quasars
Smaller than quarks, up and down
More elusive and unknown
Than the master of disguise
Higgs-Boson, shamed
Earth, one planet of many one from infinity
The big picture, box, universe
The grand scheme of things
Renders our Pale Blue Dot
Insignificant, nothing, nada interstellar dust
And yet so important is our Earth
The Mother of life keeper of thought
Father of imagination
From these confines
The brain, as mysterious as the universe itself
Conjures up a boundless world

Daway Chou-Ren, Grade 9
Holmdel High School, NJ

Finding Day Amidst the Darkest of Nights

We work and we labor
All day in the sun
Little or naught a victory won
Water is scarce
And rations are little
Striving onward as our bones become brittle

In the eyes of the enemy, now I stare
With fury, hatred, and a rebellious flare

"Eli, Eli, rema sabachtani!"
The cries emerge from the crowd
And those beasts, that beat us, care not for our lives
Oh, I pity them not, for they march and wallow
In the filth of a leader they so blindly follow
The lack of humanity
Lives stripped away by their cold hands

And yet a man sits there kneeling off in the corner
Hands folded, eyes to the sky
"Jeremiah, how can you pray? Hath God not forgotten us?"

"My good friend," he responds calmly.
"I pray in thanks to our Yahweh,
That He hath not made me like them."

Johnny Milligan, Grade 8
Monsignor Haddad Middle School, MA

Where I Am From

I am from the old scooter in my cold, yet furnished basement that lets me speed by,
    everything allowing me to feel the wind pound against me.
I am from the colorful assortment of sweet-smelling flowers and the brand new blue trampoline, doused in a downpour of rain.
I am from little birds chirping and the fallen leaves rustling in the wind.

I am from a dirty soccer ball, played with by me and my brother kicked around senseless until it was flat,
    and a Christmas tree, embellished with many glistening ornaments that shine in the light.
I am from the breathtaking gifts I receive on a perfect Christmas Day.

I am from my mom's carefully handled cookbooks and my brother's shining black clarinet always played at least once a day.
I am from my cousin's, Tony, bad-boy act and my dad's, Hyun, constant care for me.
I am from sticky, white rice and the confusing language of Koreans.

I am from my grandfather's deafening fire of his gun in the Korean War.
I am from his achievement of fleeing it to escape death.
I am from his achievement that helped me and my father exist.
I am from the other great adventures my incredible ancestors had.
I am from the plentiful supply of stories my relatives have to share joyously with me.

Gregory Song, Grade 7
Lakelands Park Middle School, MD

Shopping Spree

A shopping spree is when you go shopping and have no limits.
A shopping spree is when you go out with friends or family and try on clothes take them off, try on another outfit and so on.
A shopping spree is when you just want to go shopping that day and just have fun.
A shopping spree is when you're done shopping at that store and you ring up your items,
receipt says way more than you expected.
A shopping spree is every girls' dream.

Christa Brown, Grade 7
School of International Studies at Meadowbrook, VA

Confessions of a Computer Addict

I just got off the bus, I can't think straight, I need to get home, and go to my safe place.
Running through the doorway, I drop all my stuff, and get out my computer, without a huff.
I turn on the machine and impatiently wait, for the screen to change from it's dark slate.
Finally it comes on, I silently grin, while I get on the internet, the cursor spins.
Alas, it's logged on, right on cue, oh sweet computer, how I've missed you.
I open tabs for facebook, youtube, and more, oh the internet, it holds wonders galore.
Eight hours later, my eyes are still on the screen, chatting and reading, I need some caffeine.
It's 2 AM, and I'm not even tired, mainly because the screen has me wired.
As I listen to music, I loudly cough, I need to sleep, I need to turn it off.
But I can't! There's still so much to do! Sadly, sleep is quite important too.
As I turn it off, I know I'll regret it. I know, I know, I will admit, I'm a computer addict, and I just can't quit.

Carlie Procell, Grade 7
Carson Middle School, VA

Life Is Like…

Life is like following a country road…you don't know where you're going, or where you'll end up.
There are ups and downs, and you take them as they come because you have to move with the land.
Life is like a blank sheet of paper, waiting to be written upon…a lot is out there waiting for you; you just have to get started.
Life is like a ball of yarn…things can get tangled, but if you have the patience and take the effort, it can turn into something beautiful.
Life is like a musical…you have lines to follow, but sometimes you just have to improvise.
Life is like a marathon…you're with a lot of people, but you're running by yourself.

Emily Vogt, Grade 8
Ephrata Middle School, PA

Sidewalk Chalk

Exploring a new place can bring up questions.
What is their history?
Are they different?
What is their ways of life?

There are new places!
Many new faces!
But limited time to spare.

Time cannot stop.
Time cannot freeze.
Time goes as fast as a wonderful breeze.
You can only wish you had more time.
Exploring a new place can bring up questions.

Why do I have to leave?
Why must time go so fast?
Will I never come back?

A new place can seem like a vast ocean.
You wait your whole life for an adventure like this,
And before you know it your adventure is over.

Sometimes you wish it would all just slow down
So you could enjoy your experiences.
Catherine Veiders, Grade 7
Depew Middle School, NY

Roses

Walking around the old church moonlight lit my path
Abandoned wreath on the door
Half burnt candle in the window
Sitting on an old gray stone wondering why they all left
Looking at the cracked sidewalk
Leading up to the wooden door
Walking around the old church moonlight lit my path
Abandoned wreath on the door
Half burnt candle in the window
Suddenly turning around color caught my eye
Fresh red roses on the ground next to the old gray stone
Cautious now I turn step away from the stone
Lightly on the side small engraved words
"In loving memory of SG"
Somebody had been here somebody still cares
Thinks about a loved one buried here for years
Someone comes visits this stone
The stone I didn't notice was a part of someone's life
Walking around the old church moonlight lit my path
Abandoned wreath on the door
Half burnt candle in the window
Laura McCarter, Grade 7
H B Dupont Middle School, DE

The Sunset

I glanced outside at a sunset —
One moment, one memory all but lost.
I saw the sky a brilliant blood red
Staining the heavens,
Stretching over the atmosphere like a sea of color
To embrace the night and the silence it brings:
A last farewell to that instant for posterity;
A glorious sight for weary eyes;
A hypnotic end for a chaotic day;
A blissful blessing given by God.
One moment, one second, one instant,
Making a memory to hold to for years to come.
Carly Moorehead, Grade 9
Cornerstone Christian Preparatory Academy, PA

The Feeling

The feeling I get when I pick up a softball is indescribable
When I make an excellent play,
The feeling cannot be explained
As I'm up to bat and I see that pitch coming,
There are no words to fit the meaning,
It's indescribable
When I'm running around those bases as hard as I can,
The feeling cannot be explained
As I make a great play in the outfield
I feel an excellent rush all through my body
As my teammates make great plays and try their best,
The feeling is indescribable
There is no way to explain the way I feel on the diamond
The feeling is INDESCRIBABLE
Samantha Wayne, Grade 7
Depew Middle School, NY

My Walk

Sloooowwwwly, I walked through the desolate park.
Listening to the dark leaves
crunching below my feet
watching the young quaint animals
get a taste of their surroundings.
I sat down on the cold indigo bench.
Alone. Thinking.
Watching the goose bumps
trickle up my arm.
I sat staring at the bark peeling off the tree.
Quietly, I got up off the bench,
when a squirrel scurried up the side of a tree.
I continued my journey down the never ending path
feeling the gentle breeze
run through my hair.
I came to a halt
when I reached the colorful playground,
I could vaguely hear the playful laughter
of the children.
You couldn't dream of a more beautiful day.
Sarah McDonald, Grade 7
William Penn Middle School, PA

Music to Me

I can hear the music with my ears.
It makes me smile, shed some tears.
The voice is so powerful, so clear.
The vision of the song appears.

The rhythm and notes are my warm soul,
Beating to my heart, keeping me full.
It draws my joy with a huge pull.
I end up losing all control.

The lyrics are what I truly love,
For a song that feels like an angel above.
I tend to sing just like a dove,
That is full of song, heart, and love.

Music is what I truly enjoy,
It leaves me to absolute no annoy.
I love it way better than a toy.
Music is surely my decoy!

Caitlyn Chale, Grade 9
Hauppauge High School, NY

Untitled

I love
Feeling happy
Among my precious friends
When they are honestly caring
To me

Ja'Sadie Nicole Cartagena, Grade 8
Life Academy, PA

Take Care

Take care of yourself when I am gone
Every day is a
Turning point
Have the power to be confident
Show the world how glamorous you are
Let your inner beauty show.

Angelina Crawford, Grade 9
Unami Middle School, PA

A Spoonful of Sugar

You slowly walk
It's an exquisite morning
The puffy pink clouds
Show the beginning of a story
You graze your hand over
A field of tulips
Inhaling the softness of the Earth
Feeling the light pounding of your
Filled heart
Your breathless mind bare
You walk that morning
Happy

Devon Winsor, Grade 9
The Potomac School, VA

In a Moment

In a moment, she dances, cheeks rosy, hair bouncing to the beat
In a moment, he watches his son, his own pride and joy,
Spreading his wings making his mark
Changing the world for the better

In a moment,
They stand together
On the edge of their own separate worlds
Contemplating their fate
The emptiness rising in their souls
Waiting just waiting for someone to save them
But no one knew they were in danger

In a moment, a mother weeps
A father's knees buckle
A son slams his fists down on the black and white keys
Friends sit dazed awestruck confused
With tear streaked faces wondering why
The heavens open their majestic gates
For the ones we loved so much

In a moment, all that we had
Suddenly fades away to
Nothing.

Zoie Chen, Grade 9
Fairfield Warde High School, CT

Pace

The race before just ended, so you are about to run,
You line up at the start, to get ready for the gun.
You are nervous but excited; your body starts to shake,
You are now ready for what is at stake.
You look at the official, he raises his hand,
While you are ready, but still in a stand.
His second hand goes up, you are practically jumping,
Your adrenaline is now pumping.
He fires the gun and you start to run.
You start to know the race isn't just for fun.
You pass another person you're gaining speed,
To come in first place; is what you need.
Another person past, you're in 4th place,
You just want to go faster but you know you must pace.
You are now in 2nd place with three hundred meters to go,
You start to speed up to put on a show.
You are now neck and neck for first, with one hundred meters left,
This race is now yours to theft.
You start to sprint so does your opponent,
You are waiting for the glorious moment.
The race is won, you won the race, and you knew it because you paced.

D.J. Mlodozeniec, Grade 7
Depew Middle School, NY

Sad Circle

Lights glint off the pond's deep blue
And reflects a color's deepest hue

That lonely slab stands in a line
A saddened circle forsaken by time

The names of those whose lives were lost
Reminds us of a deadly cost

But think as you stand there in fear
Defend yourself from cynical tears

For although they are long dead and gone
They lost their lives so we could live on

Chris Ptak, Grade 8
Monsignor Haddad Middle School, MA

My School

Saint Agatha School is the best.
We're one above all the rest.
We learn a lot with all our friends.
We hope Saint Agatha School will never end!

Alisha Medina, Grade 7
St Agatha School, NY

Summer Day in the Park

Walking in the park on a summer day
Watching little children laugh and play
Couples walking hand in hand
Picnics on the grassy land
Trees swaying in the light air
Wind blowing in people's hair
Flowers blooming on the ground
Birds singing with great sound
Families happily together
Knowing they will be together forever
Walking out of the park on a summer day
Leaving the beautiful park portray

Megan Rostkowski, Grade 8
Floral Park Memorial High School, NY

Global Warming

The world
Global warming affects many people including you.
It destroys our Earth day by day.
It destroys our ecosystem and kills our environment.
It kills the food sources for our animals.
It destroys our animals' habitats and homes.
It eats away our ecosystem and destroys our planet.
So help recycle and save our planet
Reuse bottles and carpool
Save our world, and save your life
Clean our Earth, and buy clean cars
Help our planet stay clean.

Alex Mueser, Grade 7
Pine-Richland Middle School, PA

Euphoria

Beads of water
rest on my hair,
streams run down
the sides of my face.

My shirt soaks through,
hugging to the small of my back.
Tendrils of hair, flat, drenched,
cling to the sides of my neck.

Raindrops dance off the sidewalk. Splashing.
A chorus of tick, tick, ticking on the car tops.
The rotting stench of soggy worms
and decaying earth lingers in the air.

My rubber flip-flops
splash water up the backs
of my legs
as I trudge towards the grass.

I slip them off, my bare feet
sloshing into the mud, black,
letting it ooze between my toes.
Thick and delicious.
Euphoria sweeps over me.

Marisa Purdy, Grade 7
William Penn Middle School, PA

My Desk

Its like a forest of lead and ink,
boundless and full of energy.

Light shines as bright as the sun,
burning the papers around it.

Wrappers provide entertainment,
as lunch money become banks.

CDs stacked high like skyscrapers,
and books stacked low like stores.

Doodles are citizens,
while post-its are tourists.

A computer is its capital,
representing freedom and endless possibilities.

But all in all this city of mine
is no other, then my desk.

Sarah Viens, Grade 8
Mount St Charles Academy, RI

Winter Desert

Toasty warm inside
Dressed snug, boots tied
And then...WOW
Silent vastness
I feel lost in the great abyss
Burrrr...

It charges through
My lips turn blue
I feel deserted in the winter desert
Snow covers me in a frozen sheet
Oh how I wish it would deplete
I begin to make my journey through the frozen land

It crunches under my feet
A solemn, rhythmic beat
Fall leaves or snow?
The world is heavily furred
So I am assured
No school

The smell of hot cocoa tickles my nose
The wind blows
Time to go inside

Jenevieve Ball, Grade 7
New Egypt Middle School, NJ

I Know What Camping Is

I know what camping is...
The sun hitting you on the head,
Kids running and playing, feeling the wind in your face.

I know what camping is...
The smell of campfire smoke,
Stinky kids, hot dogs,
Hunter stew

I know what camping is...
Clouds going about,
Trees and branches in your way,
Leaves on the ground, freshly cut grass

I know what camping is...
"Light the fire."
"Time to roast hot dogs."
"Time to make s'mores."
"Time to go to bed."

I KNOW WHAT CAMPING IS!!

Dalton Angelo, Grade 8
Ephrata Middle School, PA

This Is My Life

i'm the girl that everyone thinks they know
but on the inside i'm alone
i express my thoughts and feelings when i'm blue
but i'm the only one that knows what i've been through
the ones i call friends don't even get me
i can't say it enough that i'm just not happy
sometimes i hide my feelings just to save others time
so they worry about their own life and not mine
"everything has a purpose" they used to say
but not in my life, 'cause things never go my way
i want to think that it'll all get better
but with the things i go through
i know it won't anytime soon
"you don't know anything about me" i tell them each day
"so just let go of me and let me find my own way"
but this is my life and i'll never forget
that i know i'm stronger than this
and i need to stop with the regrets
but this is my life
yeah, my life and i'll make it through.

McKenna Rae Lemley, Grade 7
Trinity Middle School, PA

Baseball

Crack, and I'm off
The crowd is roaring as I round first
I'm passing second and the outfielder gets the ball
I keep running at full speed as I touch third
The crowd is on their feet as I race for home
The ball gets to the shortstop who rifles it in
It's going to be a close play
The ball gets in as I slide
The catcher puts the tag
Am I safe or out?
Only time will tell.

Edward Kao, Grade 7
Carson Middle School, VA

The Last Day

The greatest day of the year,
The last day of school...
Or is it.
Sure you get ten weeks of no teachers,
No homework,
No quizzes,
No tests,
But what about your friends.
For some you'll keep in touch,
But for others, you won't see them until next year.
Some may not even remember your name.
That doesn't sound very "great" to me.
The last day of school,
For some it's the greatest.
For me...

Dominic Lauricella, Grade 7
Depew Middle School, NY

A Few Pieces of Wood

One window is all I need…
To express my true colors and just be free
To reveal myself to anyone and everyone
And show what it means to be me
To scream and shout and sometimes pout
To unmask my true identity
To see beyond what eyes can't see
To see what lies right in front of me
To make my own choices
To be more than just an ordinary person
To express my true colors and just be free
One window is all I need.

Kanchan Railkar, Grade 7
Anthony Wayne Middle School, NJ

I Will Miss You

When we got the call,
We were devastated.
I knew this was coming.
I ran through the hospital,
Straight to our family.
What's happening?
Everyone is sitting in the room,
Their eyes full of tears.
When I saw you in your bed,
I began to cry.
I saw you laying in your death bed,
My heart sunk to the ground.
I never once saw you like this,
So alone.
I gave you a hug and told you I love you,
You whispered in my ear everything's all right.
That moment was the last,
I ever got to see you smile.

Rachel Dannheim, Grade 7
Depew Middle School, NY

I Guess

Bolts of lightning caress the sky
Their partner's sonic boom attacks my waking dreams
I lie awake, tossing and turning
Thinking, feeling nothing
Except my own heartbeat
Wishing it was joined with another
My Juliet's Romeo
My love's duet
He pays me no mind, no sense
"Just friends," he says.
I say, "I guess."

Sharra Neely, Grade 7
Medford Township Memorial Middle School, NJ

Do You Know?

Do you know why the grass is green?
Why the sky is blue?
Why the snow is white?

Do you know why children laugh?
Why babies cry?
Why writers write?

Do you know why?

Do you know why people are happy?
Why people are sad?
Why people love others who are their 'other half'?

Do you know why people help others?
Why compassion is shown?
Why they want others to laugh?

Faith Kim, Grade 9
Unami Middle School, PA

Skateboarding

The smell of the air
The wind in my hair,
Landing tricks
Feeling like you're on top of the world,
Until you fall
Things take a twisted turn,
But you're all right, you get back up and try again
You find a good spot to skate with your buddies,
And have fun
But already the day is done,
You're sad yet happy for tomorrow still will come
That is why I will skateboard until my days are done.

Brandon Berghold, Grade 7
Depew Middle School, NY

Puppet

And if this heart of mine shall cease to be
The sun will set upon this lonely page
Your face will be the only thing I see
Entrapped inside this suffocating cage

Of a love once loss to the depth of sound
And an ear that has heard such brutal noise
To your voice and will I'm forever bound
Cursed to be played with like your childhood toys

We fly so high only to sink so low
With an arrow too fragile hearts we bleed
The rain has come to stay and never go
Along with my new incurable need

And if this heart of mine shall cease to be
Your face will be the only thing I see

Destiny Jones, Grade 8
Woodmere Middle School, NY

Putting the Clothes Away

I hate to put the clothes away
I'd rather be outside and play
Bare hangers on the hooks
Always giving dirty looks
A pile filling high with clothes
Watching cautiously as it grows

I do not like putting clothes away
But I have to if I want to stay
My mother does not like a messy room
She tells me to clean it with a broom
So now I put the clothes away
Wishing to run outside and play

Haley Stab, Grade 7
Hammarskjold Middle School, NJ

April

I am the month of April.
I will bring many showers.
The sun shines bright,
Welcomed by many flowers.

Miriam Salazar, Grade 7
St Agatha School, NY

Worlds

Water
Blue, wet
Slipping, swimming, sliding
Many different worlds around
Walking, talking, running
Dry, land
Brown

Yvonne Highfield, Grade 8
Martin Meylin Middle School, PA

A Poem with No Point

This is going to be a boring poem
For often I can see
That when I have not one idea
No poem comes to be.

What is the use?
It is really bad.
And even as I write this
I know it's really sad.

Sad I wrote this thing
That has no point at all.
But as you may see now
This poem's not that small.

But since I have not one idea
I might as well go on.
But who would want a boring poem?

Ameer Khan, Grade 7
Floral Park Memorial High School, NY

Behind a Dancer

A dancer is not what you think
Seems graceful, but takes blood, sweat, and tears to become one
You need to set your mind
Need to have goals and ambitions
You work yourself 'til nothing's left
You give it everything you got,
You leave everything on the dance floor.
It's time to show off everything you've worked for,
Time to show how great you can be.
No time for flaws, perfection is key.

Crystal Witmer, Grade 8
Ephrata Middle School, PA

Rehoboth Beach

That year, that summer, that day.
The sand is a diamond: precious, unique, and rare.
The water is a reflection of fun days with friends and family.
The luscious air is new, bold, and refreshing.

The sand is a diamond: precious, unique, and rare.
The bold lifeguard plopped a squat on his chair and sat there without motion.
The luscious air is new, bold, and refreshing.

The bold lifeguard plopped a squat on his chair and sat there without motion.
The swimmers flourishing in the sea, trying new stunts on the waves.
The luscious air is new, bold, and refreshing.
Laughter filled the air as kids play together in the sand.

The swimmers flourishing in the sea, trying new stunts on the waves.
Laughter is a reflection of fun days with friends and family.
Laughter filled the air as kids play together in the sand.
That year, that summer, that day.

Bryan Kozlowski, Grade 8
Valley Forge Middle School, PA

Summer Is Coming

Happiness is felt all throughout the hall that school is coming to an end.
No work will need to be done; we'll just have fun with friends.
As the final weeks of the year are strolling right by,
All we need to do is take some final tests and in relief we sigh.
There are two weeks left to go,
In astonishment we say, "Whoa."
We have been here at school since last fall,
But it doesn't seem that long at all.
There are conversations about vacations,
And talks about visiting different nations.
All I hear today is that the end of school is fourteen days away.
As the end comes near we are having some fun.
Field day and awards are given to students that earned it.
We had an amazing year,
Still we all gave out a cheer.
That the school year was finally done,
Work has turned into fun.

Ajay Mehta, Grade 7
Carson Middle School, VA

Summer Is A…

Summer is a splash,
at first it goes up then down at different times
Summer is a hot fudge sundae,
it's filled with goodness and fun
Summer is a twisty road,
with exciting adventures around every corner
Summer is a 3-month long picnic,
food and fun for everyone
Summer is a coupon,
after 3 months it expires.

Liz Bender, Grade 8
Ephrata Middle School, PA

The Sea

Ripples wrinkle the surface in the distance,
while crashing waves intrude and disrupt.
Shells are formed
where water-dwelling animals stay.
Wind and storms direct the current,
every which way.

Waves erupt again,
washing upon the shore,
to dampen the already-wet sand,
and greet the land with a splash,
and a loud crash.

Then, the wave rolls back in,
pulled by the force of the current.
I watch it join the rest of the sea,
in a frenzy to distort the sun's reflection.

Stefanie Simoni, Grade 7
Unami Middle School, PA

Love Me or Don't Love Me

Love me or don't love me, I don't care what you feel
Love me or don't love me, you just want to steal
My heart, my soul, everything that I have
Love me or don't love me, I don't care what you feel

I am me, the only person I want to be
I am an African descendant, with a beautiful gold pendant
As I walk down the street, I see people stare
I go about my business, as if I'm not aware

I like the colors of the flowers, which are red and blue
I like them even if they're not beautiful to you
I visit an art museum, where people can't really speak
I look around quietly and admire the pretty antiques

So love me or don't love me, I don't care what you feel
Love me or don't love me, you just want to steal
My heart, my soul, everything that I have
Love me or don't love me, I don't care what you feel

Muibat Ajomagberin, Grade 7
Bronx Preparatory Charter School, NY

War

As people join,
others question.
They think violence
is the answer

So, they pack their bags
to go to training.
Then they're off to
where the action is.

When they're gone,
it is all sorrow.
And when they end up dead by tomorrow,
people still join to do what's right.

But is violence right?
As they die
as they suffer
they wonder what they have done to get this

Then, they remember families left behind.
Joiners think they are doing what's good
for the country
then comes the biggest question:

Is This Right?

Frances Akwuole, Grade 7
Parkville Middle School and Center of Technology, MD

Life

I look outside in the rainy night,
Where the rain goes out far beyond my sight,
I think and wonder, who am I, why am I here?
I sit and ponder while the rain patters near,

Why am I here? For my family for my friends?
What makes me who I am today? It really depends,
I think to myself I will not go through this strife,
I won't sit and think of this for the rest of my life,

I look out into rain once more,
It was not very easy ignore,
But I was anxious as if I was a child in a land of lore,
But all I can do is watch the rain pour,

I remind myself people can ponder this for their whole life
But I will not
There is one simple answer,
This is who I am and this is why I am here

Tom Zhang, Grade 7
Carson Middle School, VA

When Dawn Arises

When dawn arises
So will the world.
Cast out hopes
To a new day.

When the sky awakens
So will God's children.
Opening their eyes
To a new masterpiece.

When the wind starts to sing
So will the birds.
As their hearts flutter lightly
In a renewed breeze.

When the grass starts to dance
So will our lives.
Elegantly swaying
To an invisible song.

And when the sun hides once again
So will the world.
So all of its blessings
May sleep 'til the next day.

Brynleah A. Wiedorn, Grade 8
Waldorf School of Princeton, NJ

Beauty

We are all stars,
Floating in the sky,
Some are wide and skinny,
And others are low and high.

Some may be as dull as a dog,
Or neon bright,
But we are all beacons of inspirations,
A hope or a light.

No one is perfect,
No one is the sun.
Don't try to change yourself,
You know it isn't fun.

The media attacks our self-esteem,
The pressure will devour you,
People unfortunately change themselves,
If only they knew.

We are all beautiful,
In our own unique way,
Like a flawless masterpiece,
Despite what others say.

Ankira Patel, Grade 7
Westwood Jr/Sr High School, NJ

Terra Firma

Winds that blow
Trees that grow
Leaves that fall
But that's not all
Birds that fly
Soaring through the sky
Volcanoes that erupted
Lava that flowed
Land that moves
Around the globe
Sound in the sky
Can't you hear?
Light in the clouds
Can't you see?
All the wonders deep in the sea
All the tiny things, such as a bee
We live here
With no fear
And for all it's worth
This is our Earth

Nikko Tonolete, Grade 8
St Camillus School, NY

Where I'm From

I am from Staten Island New York.
Where all people
talk with an accent.

I am from Abercrombie and Hollister,
The preppy clothing
and nothing else.

I am from Italy.
Where you have festivals
and pasta every night.

I am from Great Adventure and Seaside.
With the humongous water slides
And roller coasters.

I am from dance studios
to dance mix
Since three years old.

I am from soccer.
Scoring a lot of goals,
And having a ball of fun.

I am from a very loving family
That always sticks together
No matter what.

Christina Renzi, Grade 7
Hammarskjold Middle School, NJ

Love's a Field of Glass

Love's a field of glass
When light shines on its surface
It is beautiful.

Love's a path of glass
The trail is very fragile
One wrong move, it breaks.

Love's a hill of glass
As all, it has ups and downs
There's no doubt of that

Love's a coin of glass
It'll be gone if you waste it
And more is better

Love's a bond of glass
When good, it's strong, when bad, weak
It hurts when broken

Matt Bell, Grade 7
Ballston Spa Middle School, NY

Sadness

Sadness is weeping with
Sorrow filled eyes
A smile turned around
Red, swollen eyes
Tissues always at hand
Wanting to be left alone
Depressed at everything
Hoping for something to come around
And cheer you up again.

Stefanie Dias, Grade 7
Dorothy L Beckwith Middle School, MA

Forever and Ever

Remember the promise
We made to each other
Forever and ever
Was what I thought
Promises have been kept
Promises have been broken
But our faith has kept us stronger
Tears in our heart
Has left us scars
But forever and ever
Has been washed away
I love you now
I love you then
But I guess
Forever and ever
Wasn't meant to be

CeCilia Sarkodee, Grade 9
Bartlett Jr/Sr High School, MA

Family Fun

Now that summer is coming
I can relax
If you don't believe me
I'll state the facts
School is coming to an end
Soon I'll be fishing
On a river bend
We'll have family gatherings
For those who graduate
Let's just say
I'll probably be late
We have our family camping
And our afternoon napping
What could be better than that
Oh I almost forgot our campfire chat
My aunt will get us soaked
Because my uncle joked
I have to admit they are fun
Especially when they're not bathing in the sun
I've got them and they're all mine
I really wish I could have them for the rest of time

Grace Olszewski, Grade 8
St Stephen's School, NY

Bonfire

Kevin and Kyle start the fire,
Adding wood it gets higher and higher.
With all the wood it starts to smoke,
Kyle grabs the rake and gives it a poke.

Fire a blazing it becomes very hot,
Causing Emma and I to find a new spot.
They add a huge pine tree,
Letting many sparks fly free.

In goes a plastic bottle thrown into the pile,
Oh no don't do it Kyle!
This fire can never be stopped,
Emma and I jump when the bottle popped!

All of a sudden a raindrop hits my face,
Kyle goes to find a dry place.
In their living room we sit on the ground,
On TV nothing can be found.

Kyle and I watch TV for a while,
We look over at Emma and Kevin as they smile.
When it's time to leave we all put up a fight,
But we couldn't have asked for a better night!

Erin McConnaghy, Grade 8
St Stephen's School, NY

The Sea's Sweet Melody

Listen to the song of the surf,
And think back to the time it began.

What a world we have been blessed with,
That has heard the sea's melodious tune.

Oh, what wondrous stories it must hold,
That go back to a time we think old.

Listen to the crashing of the waves,
And think back to the time it began.

Its ancient quarrel with the land
Has now left it broken and brined.

The once tall stone towers
Have been shattered by the cruel showers.

Listen to the sea's sweet melody,
And think back to the time it began.

Brian Boehm, Grade 7
Carson Middle School, VA

The Wonderful World of Soccer

Don't you love soccer
Come and play with me
Can you kick
Or can you dribble

What about a trick
Like a bicycle kick
What about a rainbow
And a scissor kick

Can you play keeper
How about striker
I like midfield
You want center

Nate Tedrow, Grade 7
School of International Studies at Meadowbrook, VA

I Am

I am
Strength, desire, belief
I care about the dedication in everything
God is important to me
Life is important to me
Education is important to me
Dreaming is a good thing
Anger is bad, but you can use it against your opponents
Your life is getting shorter
The way you appear is your choice
Trust in only the ones you love
This is me

Anthony Leggio, Grade 8
Hauppauge Middle School, NY

Going Back

I'm
going back
to
spend
my day in
Green Pastures
I never knew
gave me
safety

Colin Crawford, Grade 9
Unami Middle School, PA

Life

It's a mystery
Filled with occasional misery
And sometimes fun
When you're old
And when you're young
It's a pain
To some it's a game
To some it is lame
But it's fun too
Loving friends and family
Meet new people
You make choices
You hear voices
But the life you choose is up to you

Anthony Belgrave, Grade 7
Hammarskjold Middle School, NJ

The Sights of Nature

Climbing
Climbing up the charcoal rocks
Realizing the tall
Shining lighthouse
Shining over the coral sunset
The smell of rich pine trees
And the reflection
On the sapphire ocean
The beautiful sound
Of the waves crashing
Hoping life would be
Like this every day
Climbing
Climbing up on
An amazing journey

Samantha Lesmeister, Grade 7
Selden Middle School, NY

Poetry

I have to write a poem,
and it needs to rhyme.
My thoughts continue to roam,
so I need more time.

Fernando Placencia, Grade 7
St Agatha School, NY

In Memory of Grandpa Carter

I never really knew you; I really wish I had
You cried when I was born not because you were sad

I know you played the flute and the saxophone, too.
You were like another Mozart; yes that was you.

You smiled as you held me when I was like a little doll.
Your brown eyes looked upon me not knowing that was all.

Your hands were my cradle; your smile was the sun.
At that very moment, your heart I had won.

The animals loved you because you cared
This is a trait we could have shared.

Your love for rhubarb pie; it never did die.
Thinking about you like this makes me cry.

I love you more than air wherever you are.
I hope you're near and not very far.

Someday, we will be together; I know that is true.
So for now just watch me grow; I'm not the baby you once knew.

Miranda Clement, Grade 7
Medford Township Memorial Middle School, NJ

Beauty Is

Beauty is a suavity a certain person has,
A sun flower in a field of daisies.

Beauty is at the beach watching the sun set, and the waves crash,
Or running at full force into a pool with all of your friends.

Beauty is a penalty kick scored,
Or a penalty kick saved.

Beauty is swish three pointer,
Or a stuffed lay-up.

Beauty is pouring rain,
Or one single snow flake.

Beauty is a family picture,
A single rose on Valentine's Day.

Beauty is one word,
One feeling,
One touch,
Beauty is…

Amanda Sonntag, Grade 7
Westwood Jr/Sr High School, NJ

The World

Aloha, Chow, Konichiwa, Hello.
There are so many different languages,
Many ways to communicate.
Different ways to express our hate,
But that's not what you wanna do.
We should express our grateful emotions,
Like happiness, love, and friendliness.
Separation and segregation tears this world apart,
It might also destroy your heart.
Bring this world back together,
We need to create a better atmosphere.
There's really nothin' to hear.
I hope I am clear with this,
As clear as the ocean waters.
Separation shouldn't hurt you and make you blue,
As sad and blue as the rain.
Separation hurts more than constipation.
But hate should have never been a creation.

Larry Pirone, Grade 7
Westwood Jr/Sr High School, NJ

Heart

frozen in place
sharp as razors if broken,
but not sharp enough to cut the limbs of thy body.
filled with love, peace, and grace;
it makes thy breath freeze.
needing aid, you suffocate in thou presence.
needing you, though you're not there;
she might die for his presence.

Kyri Saint Germain, Grade 8
Galloway Township Middle School, NJ

Mist

Slowly I creep
over the fair countryside,
emerging gradually in the dawn's fading moonlight.
I creep little by little over hamlets.
I engulf whole cities
into my sinister, murky stomach.
I shall hinder all with my
blinding, obstructing advance.
My grey body will only disperse
when illuminating rays of sunshine pierce it
in one lengthy volley.
I sing no songs,
only an eerie silence shall follow me
wherever I venture.
The silence I bring forth is as
mysterious as the ocean floor.
For I am Mist, son of the levitating Clouds
in the wild blue yonder.
Forever I shall be present, because
I am eternal.

Tyler Sastre, Grade 7
Christ the Teacher Catholic School, DE

Heart Race

Screech!!
We entered a dark and mysterious room.
Suddenly, the room lightened with flames.
I could feel my heart beating faster and faster.

We entered a dark and mysterious room.
The coaster beamed to the left.
I could feel my heart beating faster and faster.
Slowly, the cart went up a big hill.

The coaster beamed to the left.
The piercing screams killed my ears.
Slowly, the cart went up a big hill.
As we fell into what seemed to be a never ending drop.

The piercing killed my ears.
Suddenly, the room lightened with flames.
As we fell into what seemed to be a never ending drop.
Screech!!

Bilal Ali, Grade 7
Garnet Valley Middle School, PA

An Unusual Summer for All*

I am in a furnace.
Sitting in a courtyard, limp,
brown and bone-dry.
The city around me,
once prosperous and seemingly interminable,
was thrown into an oven, and burned to a crisp.

There are no gray ashes.
A sickly yellow, they float in the air,
destroying all that they touch.
I beg for water,
so I could once more
be flooded with life and flourish.

A puddle sits beside me, murky, dusty, dark.
I am surrounded by a sound;
buzzing, loud and eternal.
I envy the mosquitoes. Small, yet full of life.
Prospering in the summer heat
on the blood of mortals.

Nobody waters me. I sit, ignored.
What was I to expect?
I am but a tree.

Evan Hale, Grade 7
Markham Place Elementary School, NJ
*From the perspective of a tree during the
Yellow Fever epidemic in Philadelphia in 1793.

Deep Beauty

Serene and quiet sounds of the rippling water catch my senses.
The beauty of the water with the perfect blue-gray mountains behind.

The small beach of rocks and sand with the sun beating down.
The breeze off the lake. All of it simply summed up in one word:

Beautiful.

Reading swiftly as I hear the waves come in.
The smell of gas from the boats that go by.

Seeing a family, a mother, a father and a child all in a boat ready to fish together.
Thinking I might like to have a family someday.

The miniature waves that bounce off of the boats; they come in and pour upon the beach.
It leaves the smell of a pleasurable and relaxing day filled with fun, love, and small quarrels.

Clouds high, the sun out, and rays pouring down from above to below me.
God opens His arms to the people who no longer live, opening the gates to Heaven.

Morgan Keller, Grade 9
Lebanon High School, NH

Someday I'll Be Happy

Someday I'll play high school ball.
I'll be the best, be the worst or something in between, but I'll still have fun
Someday I'll have a job.
I'll either make a lot of money, make none, or something in between, but I'll be happy I have a job.
Someday I'll have kids.
They will either be the best or the worst or something in between.
But I'll still love them.
Oh Someday.

Nico Aronson, Grade 7
Anthony Wayne Middle School, NJ

True Genius

Respect your elders, for they know so much more than you
But who are they to say such things while we children can
Make conversations out of silence, yet not break the quiet
We can find meaning in absolutely nothing
They tell us we are to young to know what love is
No they are simply to old to recall for their fires have died to barely burning embers
If only their stubborn minds would permit the memories of youth's deep passions
And bright imaginations then never would they say
We are too young or don't understand if they remembered
How when youth had them caught when they rebelled their own elders,
Would still they try to break our young spirit or dull our fevered minds and to quench our burning fires
If they remembered all would change, for their passions
Would burst to life, their imaginations would run wild
And creations would begin anew for only with the patience
And intellect of age and the passion and imagination of youth is there true genius
They have simply forgotten and misunderstood
The beauty of childhood and all of its glorious wonders

Zachary Thomas, Grade 8
Wareham Middle School, MA

The Secret

Sometimes people act a way,
A certain type, maybe timid one day.
It might be because they regret,
The thought of having a secret.

It could be something "cool" or fake,
Or maybe about a huge mistake.
It might make you laugh, or cry, or think,
It may have a special link.

It might be something serious,
Or even just ridiculous.
It might be big, might be small,
It might make you want to fall.

It could be scary, even sad,
Maybe it will make you mad.
You might care, you might not,
Maybe you will scream, a lot!

But even if one of those things,
It doesn't matter what it brings.
As long as you will understand,
The secret, your secret, in your hands.

Benjamin Alfonso, Grade 8
Floral Park Memorial High School, NY

Things You Hear on a Soccer Field

The whistle blows and the game has begun.
"Get the ball," yells my coach.
"Quickly, run!"
I sprint towards the goal,
"Pass the ball," I said.
"Offside" calls the ref.
I think to myself,
"Not again!"
We get the ball back,
Hopefully we will score.
The ball comes to me and
I beat three defenders,
There's just one more.
My teammates and fans start to roar.
I have a clear shot of a goal,
And I shoot the ball.
The ref blows the whistle, right in my ear.
"Goal," everyone starts to cheer!
The game is over, and we have won.
Everyone congratulates us.
The celebration has begun.

Kelly Wieczerzak, Grade 7
Anthony Wayne Middle School, NJ

Pap Fred

His once-smiling and happy face,
now pale and emotionless.
He is dressed in church clothes,
even though it's not Sunday.
I say goodbye for the last time,
as his box is lowered into the Earth.
I still remember him smiling and laughing,
as Carleigh tickles his nose
with a pink boa feather.
The memories of walking in the woods,
hide-and-go-seek, and mini-golf with him
will stay in my heart,
forever.

David Yencsik, Grade 7
Trinity Middle School, PA

Just Because I'm Small

Just because I'm small
  Don't think I'm in 3rd grade.
  Don't think I can't play basketball.
  Don't think I have a fiery temper like those midgets on TV.
Just because I'm small
  It doesn't mean I can't get back up.
  It doesn't mean you're stronger than me.
  It doesn't mean you can call me short fry behind my back.
Just because I'm small
  Don't think I can't reach my goal.
  It doesn't mean I can't dream.
Just because I'm small — give me a chance.

Dennis Park, Grade 7
Anthony Wayne Middle School, NJ

Inside an Engagement Ring

Inside an engagement ring there are promises of
Love
and
Devotion
Love so strong must be shown on own left hand.
Devotion so strong is worn with pride.
A gold band that shimmers
Reminding all
Gems that sparkle screaming
"Look at me! Look at me!"
Displayed not in a glass case
But on one's knee.
Black satin box
A small treasure chest
Opened up, like one's heart
Say yes
Slip onto left hand
And journey of
Love
and
Devotion follow.

Kelly Brown, Grade 7
Christ the Teacher Catholic School, DE

An Afternoon of Fire

An afternoon of fire.
Plumes
Flames
Clouds
Smoke
Charred beams and rubble of a house.
Sweltering heat
Embers blown by a slight breeze.

Amanda Glidden, Grade 9
Unami Middle School, PA

Here to Stay

Afraid to fall,
Yet strong enough to stand,
I'll do it all,
In God's hands.
The fear of the dark,
With its damaging remarks,
Tells me to fear,
Of what's coming near.
But nothing is there,
No burden to bear,
My savior will teach me to not be afraid.
My load is lifted,
My shoulders free,
Of the ominous terror,
That once encumbered thee.
My fear is gone,
Blown away,
By the Mighty One,
Who is here to stay.

Mariah Ricasa, Grade 8
Covenant Life School, MD

The Cat

Slipping through the quiet darkness,
Midnight fur brushing the ground.
He is stealthy, lithe, and limber;
Slipping through the woods — a cat!

Amber eyes glowing in moonlight,
Shining, deadly claws unsheathed.
Watching, scenting, tracking down prey,
Stalking through the brush — a cat!

Paw steps silent like the forest,
Head and tail are held up high.
Independent, lonesome shadow,
Needing no one else — a cat!

Slipping through the quiet darkness,
All is peaceful, nothing stirs.
Holds himself up, proud and mighty,
Master of the woods — a cat!

Jocelyn Huang, Grade 7
Carson Middle School, VA

A Past Time Waking Up

As I trot down the stone steps
to the click-clack, click-clack of my metal cleats,
I see the Pony Field begin to come to life.

At the crest of the hill, the constant ping of batting practice
echoes in the valley.
Far out in the vast, bright green field, athletes warm up,
tossing the ball back and forth.

Soon, all that is heard is the soft hum of each team's pregame speech.
Then, a sudden commotion arises as the home team takes the field.
The ball park has come to life.

Zach Kenny, Grade 7
Trinity Middle School, PA

The Opossum

The opossum lays sprawled out dead on the road.
It got hit by an 18 wheeler truck, that's a heavy load.
All it tried to do was walk across the road to get some food
Although I can't say I blame the driver because the opossum was rude.
What would you do if an opossum walked across the road and mooned you?
If you were drivin' a car, I bet you would have ran that opossum over too.
That opossum always was sassy and never listened to his mother.
He always pulled his sister's fur and tackled all his brothers.
When informed that he wasn't nice he said, "I'm bad to be precise."
And since he hardly went to school, the opossum failed the third grade twice.
That opossum ran away from home a lot, but his parents didn't mind.
They tried being nice to him, but gave up since he was never kind.
Maybe that opossum would still be here if he hadn't mooned that driver.
Maybe if had been a little nicer, he might have been a survivor.
And maybe if he was kinder, he might have had more people befriended.
Maybe he would have passed the 4th grade, but all of that depended.
Now I'm not saying that if you moon someone you're going to get run over.
But you should consider how you treat others before your life is over.

Kassi Auker, Grade 8
Ephrata Middle School, PA

Peace

I love the world,
The peaceful sounds.
I love the world,
For leaps and bounds.
Could there possibly be any greater cause than our lovely green earth.
I don't think so, not even before mankind's birth.
I love the world
The swaying trees
I love the world
Come bend your knees.
Come out and join in cleaning the planet
Everything must be shiny, even the granite.
Let's clean the globe
Down to every last cove
I love the world.

Daniel Hinterlang, Grade 7
Christ the Divine Teacher Catholic Academy, PA

A Summer Day

The sun was a shining star
Shining throughout the day
My father was a racing horse
Who needed a bale of hay
It was a hot summer day
There was a butterfly
The butterfly was a fighter jet
Shooting for the sky
I wish this day would never end
I could not get the time to bend
I love summer and all its glory
No school no sports and a late bedtime story
Summer is like a burning fire
It will sometime soon expire

Ryan Price, Grade 8
Ephrata Middle School, PA

Golden Bridge

Over a golden bridge
where the sun shines all year round
magical and mysterious
joyful and troubleless
as if all my problems run away
Embracing the sun's rays, shining upon me
where everything comes true
Back over a golden bridge
Saying good bye to the magical world
That is so dear to me
I wonder what new things would happen
To a believer like me

Chelsea Glover, Grade 7
Trinity Middle School, PA

Training Camp

All of the Bills starting to train,
Speed, strength, intelligence is what they gain.
The team gets ready by practicing plays.
They can practice on all the nice summer days.
Terrell Owens gets welcomed into town.
Looked like he had already had these plays down.
They have not put on pads yet,
But when they do someone will get hurt I bet.
The rookies get to meet with everyone,
But it does not mean they are done.
They have to work just as much.
They practice special plays to gain confidence and clutch.
They are taught how to play Buffalo Bills style.
Leaving the veterans to teach them awhile.
Everybody just getting to know each other.
Season's coming up quick, oh brother.
Still a lot of things to choose,
And lots of weight to gain and lose.
Lots of things still to get done,
As the team gets ready to give their fans a lot of fun.

Matthew Gagola, Grade 8
St Stephen's School, NY

What Do I Do

There's something wrong with me
I don't know what
I don't know what else to say but
Please don't hate me
Or make me leave
I'll change my ways
I'm begging
I promise
Please

They say to wait for the postman to bring you a letter
Or wait for the good Lord to make you feel better
But that won't work this time
We're separating. Yours and Mine.

I'm not going anywhere
I've told you times before
You're sick of me, I know it
You tell me more and more

You say I'm just like him
He says I'm just like you
But at this point, being myself…
Is the hardest thing to do.

Jordan Smith, Grade 8
Rondout Valley Middle School, NY

Summer!!!

This the season that school is over
We also have many sleepovers
The sun is up high in the sky
Where the birds fly high
We play outside
Or stay inside
But yet this month is very fun
When school is over you get excited
You get to swim in your pool
Summer is a time to hang out with family if that is cool
Or hang with friends
And wish summer would never end
Fourth of July is near and we cheer
For the independence of the USA
Then at the end of August kids become sad
They are becoming sad since school is coming around
We know no one likes summer to be over
But it's going to happen sooner or later
So have fun while you can
So make sure to make plans
For over the summer

Chris Gasiewicz, Grade 7
Depew Middle School, NY

Staying Here

I was just 3 years old when you left
You didn't even say good bye
They said you were in a better place
How can I find a way from my sorrow

Why did you leave me staying here
You could have taken me there
You're far from my soul
I've got nowhere to go
I'm staying here

They said I'll see you again sometime soon
But you're just 3 million miles away
They said you would feel no more pain
How can I find a way from my sorrow

Why did you leave me staying here
You could have taken me there
You're far from my soul
I've got nowhere to go
I'm staying here.

Olukorede Esan, Grade 7
Trinity Middle School, PA

Threats

Even the smallest threat can arouse us all

We talk and we rumble
Thinking till we stumble
Upon an idea of war
We hit them back like a boar
Or an idea to thwart
Yet we still spill more than a quart

Responsibility is on no one
A lot of trouble but no fun
Not all that is spilt may be necessary
Just a few hints and we will start to quarry
Causing more trouble than worth
Yet barely anything was put forth

Then when we don't do anything and there is an actual threat
Then we will have something to fret
And bring harm to a gigantic crowd
Then when we thwart them early we will be proud
But if we thwart them for nothing then we won't stop a brawl
Just cause extra trouble for all

Yet if the threat is true then we shall fall

Ceyer Wakilpoor, Grade 7
Carson Middle School, VA

The Words Will Echo On

As I walk towards them, they stare
As I walk past them, they whisper
Towel head, radical, terrorist

I shake my head in disgust
But the words echo on
Towel head, radical, terrorist

Why do the reckless attacks of the few, hurt so many?
Why is the whole community judged, because of they few?
Towel head, radical, terrorist

Do you know me? Do I know you?
Why are you whispering? Why are you judging?
I feel your pain, your loss
But do you see mine?

The words continue to echo
Towel head, radical, terrorist

I have learned to move on
Pushing the past behind
The words will echo on
But through this, I have grown strong.

Fareya Zubair, Grade 9
Fayetteville-Manlius High School, NY

'Tis Be Thine

'Tis be Thine morning
I arose to.
Whose morning I find
Uncontrollable sole.
For His gift to me
Is mine own.
The day is new and
Brightening.
Thy days are not
Numbered.
Such the morn is
Not mine.
Then this is His
Morning and this
Is His day.

Geoffrey Miller, Grade 7
Christ the Divine Teacher Catholic Academy, PA

Summer Sun

The bright sun sets over the sea,
It's as beautiful as nature can be.
The colors of orange and yellow,
Make me feel so calm and mellow.
The brightness burns my eyes.
A pretty bird stretches its wings and flies.
I love the summer sun.

Rosie Amrhein, Grade 7
Our Lady of Grace Elementary School, PA

Clouds

There I lie in the grass
Watching the clouds roll pass
My mind wanders, not a worry
There was no rush, no hurry

As I watch I notice a cloud
Big, wide and round
It covered the sun, and then I watch it pass
And I lied in the grass

The clouds are all over
Some round and some wide
Some small and stout
They are nature's blanket
They drift all about

They can be whatever you want
A bird, bee, whatever you see
They gallop like a horse over the sun
There I lie in the grass
Watching the clouds roll pass

Elias Bermudez, Grade 7
Westwood Jr/Sr High School, NJ

Flying Free

Feeling the wind, such a gentle breeze,
Flowing through my hair, I feel at peace,
Knowing that the world is full of opportunities,
I want my wings to be free, flying free.

Flying free with nothing pulling me down,
Is what I want unless I want to settle down,
No one telling me how to live my life,
Is a dream that I wish would come true,

Flying free is something that I want,
To explore the world on my own, in which no one can stop,
With love, courage, and wonder,
I will be able to succeed flying free,
Would the world like to help me?

Knowing that my loved ones will be there to support me,
Will help me believe that I can fly free,
Flying free, flying free, would be such a joy to me.

If I feel pain on my path to flying free,
I will overcome it so I can succeed,
Flying free is what I want and need,
Doesn't everyone want to be flying free?

Hannah Suarez, Grade 8
Floral Park Memorial High School, NY

I Am

I am
Crazy, happy, blonde.
I enjoy soccer and gymnastics.
Friendship is important to me.
Family is important to me.
Education is important to me.
Having fun is a great thing.
Bullies can be hurtful, but make you a stronger person.
World peace is needed.
Summer is the best season.
Take chances, you never know where they will lead.
This is me.

Whitney Post, Grade 7
Anthony Wayne Middle School, NJ

Sweet Pain

I do not know you well, but what I know
Enchants me, like a song far away
In the midst of a summer evening
Your voice makes me soar
Your touch warms my heart
I cannot hear the words, but what they
Say moves me I wish I knew your thoughts
Shared your cries
This love brings me sweet pain but I
Want more
I want to hold you in my arms
Protect you from misery
I love you enough to fight for you
And sacrifice myself for you
I'll always be there for you
To the very end
When our paths separate
Later to be reunited as one

Elizabeth Duckworth, Grade 8
Springton Lake Middle School, PA

What Is the Color of Love?

What is the color of love?
Is it red like a rose?
Or blue as the sea?
Is it yellow with happiness?
Or green with serenity?
Is it white: innocent and pure?
Or black: unyielding and strong?
Is it clear? Straightforward? Simple?
Or is it rainbowed? Confusing? Complex?
Is it mixed with all different colors?
Or is it a color we have not yet found?
Is the color of love hot pink and bold?
Or is it gray and soft?
What color represents love?
Or maybe, perhaps, the color of love,
Is different to everyone.

TingAnn Hsiao, Grade 7
Medford Township Memorial Middle School, NJ

Dad

My dad is like a hero in the sky
Though he hates to say goodbye
His eternal sleep must start

My dad was a genius man
He did everything he can
To try to fight forever

I know I hate to see him go
But I have to let go
I will see him once again

My friends and family help me grieve
But the one thing they don't see
He's standing right beside me

I will see him once again
I will see him once again

Alexandra Morris, Grade 7
Summit School, MD

The Passion Flower

Blossoming, blooming, blowing.
His face blows in the wind.
Whoosh, whoosh, whoosh.
Blowing his colorful petals.
Showing his face in the morning,
Hiding it at night.
Smiling up at the sun,
And sleeping under the moon.
Pinks, purples and greens
Always blowing in the wind.
Whoosh, whoosh, whoosh.

Kori Alston, Grade 8
Monument Valley Middle School, MA

Max

I know a boy named Max
Who knows how to use an ax
He puts it in his dishes
'Cause iron is nutritious!

Alexandra Beyder, Grade 7
Hammarskjold Middle School, NJ

Myself

I was looking in the mirror.
Thinking to myself
Is this the real me?
Looking at my hair, eyes, and mouth.
Is this the real me?
Not knowing if this were the real
Person that's inside of me.
Is this the real me?
The one that I used to be.

Joseph Gorsky III, Grade 7
Thorne Middle School, NJ

Love Always

There was something about the way she smiled.
When she walked into the room everyone lit up with joy.
She knew want she wanted out of life.
She had a strong head on her shoulders.
The night I got news, I felt like the whole world was crashing down.
The tears were falling.
My head was spinning.
The world was ending.
It will be all right grandma, the tumor will go away.
There will be no more coughing blood.
You'll see Matthew and I graduate.
It will all disappear.
Reality?
When I look up at the sky, I know you'll be there soon.
I don't know when, but I sure do know why.
I'll try to make the best of what I have left with you.
But before you go let me tell you something,
I'll always love you.
You're my true hero.

Anna Schiavi, Grade 7
Depew Middle School, NY

The Predator, the Lion

The lion is a predator, waiting to pounce.
Running through the grass chasing an animal.
Any animal that's in its view, is on pins and needles.
Hunting through the Savanna, living on meat, supporting his family.
The lion is fierce.

Ryan Goydos, Grade 7
Hammarskjold Middle School, NJ

Love, Hate and Confusion

Love is beautiful.
It's that feeling in your stomach when you hear his voice.
It's the way your heart jumps when she calls you.
It's a drop of water in a room of African children.
Love is beautiful.

Hate is evil.
It's the feeling of rage that comes over you when you see your ex-boyfriend.
It's the way you burn a picture of an ex-girlfriend.
It's a ring of fire in a circus of dreams.
Hate is evil.

Confusion is scary.
It's that feeling in your stomach when you don't know what to do.
It's the way you look around like a lost puppy.
It's a goldfish playing in shark-infested waters.
Confusion is scary.

DeJanae Griffis, Grade 7
School of International Studies at Meadowbrook, VA

Surf, Sea and Me

I yearn for the waves and the sea,
I feel they are a part of me.

When they crash upon the reef,
They rip my heart, oh what grief.

As I hit the surf in the early morn,
I feel like a babe newly born.

As the mermaids dance and the fish swim,
I can't stop and watch, for the light grows dim.

As I leave the beach that late afternoon,
I feel as though I could fly to the moon.

But, the beach will be apart from me,
Because there are many things I have yet to see.

Monica Merante, Grade 7
Franklin Regional Middle School, PA

Choices

On a dubious night
The breeze brushing my face
I look up at the stormy night
Wondering what's the case

Two paths to choose, two paths to go
The dark clouds arrive
The whispering winds blow
At the end of the road, the fork divides

Rain pours down, blocking my way
But soon the sun comes out from its hiding place
The path emerges as the shining day
I look up at the rising dawn,
Wondering what will be the case.

Rozana Rahman, Grade 9
Noor-ul-Iman School, NJ

Johnson June Please Clean Your Room

Johnson June
Please clean your room
Or meet your doom

Toys and clothes piled high
So far up
They almost reach the sky

Bulging doors
Filled with apple cores
And some wild boars

Oh why oh why
Do I have to clean this pigsty

Ahed Syed, Grade 7
Hammarskjold Middle School, NJ

An Ode to a Dreamer

John Lennon, John Lennon
You gave peace a chance
And wasn't afraid
To get up and dance

Your childhood was bumpy,
Your father left,
Your mother died
But all through that you did not cry

But as a Beatle
You were the Walrus
A Paperback Writer
Unlike anyone among us

But before you met
Your untimely death
There was a lot to show us
You still had left

You wowed us with "Imagine"
"Instant Karma" too
But as a person
Everyone still likes you

Sean Brautigan, Grade 8
Township of Ocean Intermediate School, NJ

My Family Garden

My family is found in the garden:
Mom is the bumble bee, hardworking and always busy.
Dad is the gate, strong and steady, keeping everyone in.
Grandma is the caterpillar, eating all the leaves,
But then transforms into a big, wise butterfly.
Nathan is the weed, sprouting up in unexpected places,
And very annoying.
Ethan is the soil, firm but sometimes gives away.
Sara is the vine, very pretty,
But sometimes gets confused and loses her way.
Madelyn is the ladybug, small and innocent,
But sometimes flies away.
Abby is the baby bird, small and helpless,
Always needing someone at her side.
Pepper is the dandelion, popping up like crazy everywhere.
Stinky is the sunflower, growing fast, but mostly boring.
I am the morning glory, bright and pretty in daylight,
But small and quiet when darkness strikes.
Families are unique in their own way,
My family is a garden where there is joy and happiness,
But sometimes it is a danger zone.

Kaylee Horn, Grade 7
Jamesville-Dewitt Middle School, NY

Urban Wasteland

Welcome the Issue:
Urban Wasteland:
The generation's Culture club!
The brightest splendor
is sunshine,
It nourishes my
Radar like broken English.
Gold delights Lemonzest,
Off the wall awaits the land of
un peu d'air sur terre.
Go your own way,
Live at least 55 seconds per day.

Mattea Kozari, Grade 9
Unami Middle School, PA

The Light

Bridge
And
Tunnel
Fall from
Grace
Fear before the
Twilight
If all goes wrong
Speak out
It's called
A constant state
Of motion.

Aslin Tressler, Grade 9
Unami Middle School, PA

Once Before

The river that you see
Once before I walked in free

That tree that just now fell
Once before stood up I'll tell

That leaf that is now dead
Once before was alive and red

That place you love to be
Once before you couldn't see

That paper you write on today
Once before was a tree I say

That bread that you now eat
Once before was a piece of wheat

Those history pictures you see
Once before were lived, by me

LeighAnn D'Andrea, Grade 9
Sacred Heart High School, MA

Inspired

In the dark still night,
ominous storm clouds engulf the sky
whipping over the mountains
colliding into the valley below.
The victim stands strong —
roots deeply planted in the earth
as the destructive team rages closer.
Using her branches to shield
against the raging tempest
plummeting droplets,
and wind slithering snakes,
she thrives —
survives
prevails
stands strong
and bold
and firm.

Amanda Leonetti, Grade 7
Ocean City Intermediate School, NJ

The Unknown

I live every day
with the fear of the unknown
I don't know what's coming my way
or what will happen when I'm grown
I worry about my future
I worry about the past
I pray they will find a cure
and I pray it happens fast
there are good days and there are bad
I am happy and I am sad
I know that I am strong
and with that I can't go wrong.

Daniel Foley, Grade 7
Depew Middle School, NY

Cabin

Going to the cabin
Hour and a half to get there
Can't wait to get there
I have to sleep in the car
We have to stop at Tops
We get to ride four wheelers
Cutting the grass all day
Weed whacking
Feeding the fish
Cleaning the barn and cabin
Help cooking
Going to Wal-Mart
Bonfires every night
Then leaving to go home
So sad to go home

Richard Shanor, Grade 7
St Stephen's School, NY

Summer

Sitting in the grass,
Soaking up the sun.
I can tell,
That summer's just begun.

Swimming in the pool,
The cold water feeling nice.
After being in the sun,
The water feels like ice.

Barbecues and picnics,
Food cooking on the grill.
Like hamburgers and hot dogs,
Which bring the taste buds a thrill.

Vacations on the beach,
Playing in the sand.
Building tall sandcastles,
Which are looking quite grand.

It is now September,
And school is about to start.
Our summer vacation has ended,
And it's breaking all of our hearts.

Allison Macri, Grade 8
Pine Grove Jr High School, NY

Life as an Army Brat

I watched him go.
I watched him leave
Then the first tear fell,
And time seemed to freeze.

He was going to Afghanistan,
In the midst of a war.
When I thought of it again,
I began to sob more.

Another year without Daddy,
Brought me sorrow and pain.
The notion of him gone,
Drove me insane.

Another Christmas missed,
My birthday missed too,
His niece's graduation,
And the Thanksgiving food.

Scared for Daddy,
Sad again and again.
Maybe the anguish will end,
In the year 2010.

Tierah West, Grade 8
N.B. Clements Jr. High School, VA

Wish

As I approach the well,
So many things run through my head.
What should I wish for?
There are so many things.

I wish for the end of fighting and hatred
For the end of war and weapons.
I wish for the beginning of a green planet
For recycling and eco-friendly lifestyles.

I wish for people to stop the bullying
Stop the teasing, the whispers, the hurting.
I wish for the discovery of a cure
For cancer, malaria, AIDs, heart disease.

I wish for love and peace worldwide
For every child to be loved and cared for.
I do not know which wish to choose,
I want each one and more to come true.

So many could make the world a better place.
So many could make people's lives easier.
So many could help all of Earth.
So many.

I am going to need some more pennies.

Melissa Chen, Grade 7
Portsmouth Middle School, RI

Stranded

Hang in there,
For soon you will be free,
For life is like a speck of dirt
Stranded out at sea.

And that little speck of dirt,
As hopeless as it seems,
Is waiting to be free
While stranded out at sea.

"Soon I will be free,"
Says the dirt with a plea,
"But for now I'll have to wait
For I'm stranded out at sea."

Just remember
That you're not alone,
There are other specks that you can't see,
For they too, are stranded out at sea.

Rachel Rosa, Grade 7
Sanford School, DE

Beach

I hear the waves crashing.
I hear the kids splashing.
Also, the gulls calling,
And see beach balls falling.
I look out far and see sail boats sailing.
I turned around and saw kids flailing.

I ran into the water and turned around.
I ran into the water like it was a playground.
When I got out, I waved to my dad.
When he saw me he said, "Hey, what's up, lad?"

These are all the things I like to do when I'm on the beach.
How about you?
I jumped into the air to catch the ball,
But the way it ended was with a big fall.

The beach is a wonderful place to play.
Why don't you come and stay?
We can go surfing or swimming; whatever pleases you.
I'm telling you, it's up to you.
It's the beach just come and play.

Cooper Gallagher, Grade 7
Ocean City Intermediate School, NJ

One Last Goodbye

I didn't want to believe the truth
It's just a lie in my fading youth
Then it hit my dying heart
Remember the one you tore apart
I couldn't believe you had what it took
It's my ending to a lucky book
Lies were apart of my everyday life
Fairy-tale ending said I'd be your wife
Then you added your little twist
You shook your head and grabbed my wrist
Told me you were never going to be mine
Let go of me and didn't look behind
As you told me one last lie
You left me with your last goodbye

Kayla Glossner, Grade 8
Central Mountain Middle School, PA

Beards

Beards come in all sorts of colors.
Almost everywhere except on your mother.
Beards make you so rugged and cool.
They give you mad skills in billiards and pool.
You can use them as ladles and/or razors.
They are the ultimate defense against clowns and blue lasers.
Use them to cut cheese or melt silver bricks.
Or you can use them to remove giant ticks.
Everyone will think you're so very weird.
But they're all just jealous of your super awesome beard.

Patrick Dinh, Grade 7
Galloway Township Middle School, NJ

Paths Touch

Paths touch. Arms crossed, they say hello! Hi! What's your name? Hoping to hear an answer, a person to play with, someone to call. Under the table, she crawls out. Wanna be my friend? I say.

On the playground, in the box, the backyard. Finding frogs and turtles. They dress up, the time flies. Closer and closer they become, then we cry, I leave.

New school, house, lakes, neighborhood. Sounds of cars, horns, sirens and a searchlight on the very first day! Hoping for the same, she stays protected, and without a bubble, I never had. Who is she? Loud, we meet. Different arms, open to others. She and her orange, skirt, shirt, smile, on picture day in the hallway, walkway, bridge over the glass. They connect together in the morning, on the way to school, over ice cream, bee stings, saxophone case. Their friendship gives her hope to find a clear pathway. But school is almost done, we cry, I leave.

Paths touch, cross, and stay…together, forever.
Footprints in the sand, never washed away
Even if she moves, I stay, close to all who have touched, helped, loved, my life in a day.

Alexandra Porrazzo, Grade 8
Garrison Forest School, MD

The Living Earth

The breeze sings through the trees and grass making them sigh in contentment.
Slowly, through the brick, saplings grow. Do you hear them cry though?
Crack crack crack (sigh) "ahhhhh" you hear them say as they hum oxygen.
Look at the wonderful land, it shines like no other! Yet we tarnish it, look closer.
Do you see as it moans in pain for help? Do you hear? Listen as it tells you its many secrets in a mere whisper.
"Shhhh" It pleads for help from the trash we so casually throw at it.
Do you feel its pain? Listen as it cries out. "HELP!!" The living earth speaks, all you have to do is listen.

Asia Anderson, Grade 7
Ruffner Middle School, VA

Life's Problems

"I have to let you go." My boss had said
We were doing great and the best of friends
How he let me go? He knew I needed the job
My wife is concerned, I'm running out of resources

Kids are getting hungry, wife is never home working two to three jobs a week doing the best she can
Loretta 5, Max 13 both unable to work, Max trying to help, being my little man
Loretta stunned, confused, and shocked I am out looking, desperate for work
Family growing distant, Margret exhausted
With no break, withering her down slowly arguing and fighting
Pulling the children out of school, missing their friends
Loretta trying to learn, Max on the street with no end.

"We are in debt, we have to go." My wife says.
Go? Go! We have no where to go but the streets and sidewalks.
There? There! We lost our apartment, can't afford rent
Margret and I roam the streets, Max carrying little Loretta on his back
We roam the city for hours on end finding a place as our last resort

Having to use Loretta to bribe for money as our last hope.
We are gone. No home, food, water, or shelter.
We are hungry, tired, thirsty, and weak.
"Think positive," I encourage as we keep slugging along.
All ends, life in our hands, love is what is left of us!

Molly McIntosh, Grade 8
Columbia Secondary School, NY

A Beautiful World

The trees,
The breeze,
The buzzing bees.
I lay,
I ponder,
I let my mind wonder:
What if factories were no more?
Air pollution would be old folklore.
And what if litter didn't exist?
One less thing on my "to do" list.
Just think — what if our world was like this?
The peace, the harmony, and all the bliss.
If you think about it, deep within,
It could work if we all pitch in.
Because this is our world, we must protect it,
We can't let litter and pollution affect it.

Morris Pulver, Grade 8
Tuxedo Park School, NY

A Silhouette of Bare…

As I sit on my back porch,
In the darkness of the almost setting sun,
The sheen of orange and blue cover the horizon.
The brutal winds bombard the never-ending woods
Pointed out a slender tree bent to a contortionist's limit.
The smell of brisk air drives a quiver through my body.
My dark hair is swept across my face,
But not enough to hide the now beautiful starry sky,
Casting a silhouette of bare trees for me to admire.

Annemarie Perilli, Grade 9
Unami Middle School, PA

Power of Death

Tears trickle down the face
The blurry vision of death
The face masked in fear and sorrow
A flower aged to the stem
Lying against the stone
Cold and Dead
A skeleton beneath it all
In a never ending slumber
A never ending
Inescapable dream
And surrounding it all are pretty flowers
But to the face
The mind
They are as ugly and brown
As the one on the grave
They are dead
To the eyes and mind
Evil tricks at play
Ones that have trapped this face in a mask
Of sorrow, fear
And of bitterness

Ian Sherman, Grade 8
Rippowam Cisqua School, NY

Gracie

Her zig-zag tail
Whacks, smacks, leaves me black and blue
When she sees me
Only after leaving her for 5 minutes

Her golden hair a pool of sunshine
Bronze and copper children mixed in
Depressed eyes lock in place
Cutting a hole in my heart
If I want a glass of milk
Departing from her for only a minute

Snoozing by the door, on the bed, on my floor
Any place that is roomy
A squirrel!
No, a rabbit!
Doesn't matter, will attack anyway
Attack! Attack!
My soldier of WW2
Always whining to go outside

Sydney Dydiw, Grade 7
Trinity Middle School, PA

Fright

Sitting in the darkness feeling my fear
Hearing the footsteps I hear you come near.
Sitting down in the silence locking my door
All I hear is the creakiness of the old floor.

Crying on the inside
Screaming on the out.
Warm tears slide from my eyes
Knowing all of your secret alibis.

Looking to the opposing wall
All I hear is my name being called.
A flash of light
A sickening sight.

You sit in front of me
You disgusting lying fiend.
Glaring at you through my hair
Feeling your cold dark stare.
Knowing the presence of your cold stiff form
Your breathing makes my storm.

Waking up scared half to death
Your warm body there
Knowing my dream was a lie.

Hallie Kicak, Grade 7
Depew Middle School, NY

Escape from Reality

I have one getaway
which connects me
to nature and brings
me tranquility.
Unleashed,
my thoughts and worries
melt with brilliant sunsets
above placid water.
The fleeting rays
dancing in the distance
reveal a glimpse of joy
before the night swallows
my contentment.
The rareness of this place
in time makes my escape
from reality so fulfilling.

Rachael Young, Grade 7
Ocean City Intermediate School, NJ

The Perfect Day

A child's laughter
Young helping old
A happy song
A hand to hold

A sky pure blue
The shining sun
Serene waterfalls
A world of fun

Sadness gone
Tears go away
Left to reveal
The perfect day

Lindsay Hazen, Grade 9
Mount Pleasant High School, DE

Love Is Like a Rose

Love is like a rose
Both beautiful but deadly
Love is like music
It can sound like a melody
Love is like a blind man
Both can be blind
Love is like a searcher
Looking for something valuable to find
Love is like shopping
Finding which item is right
Love is like fire
Not knowing when it'll light
Love is like cooking
Knowing which ingredients to add
Love is like life
It can be good or bad

Josiah Asso, Grade 8
Ephrata Middle School, PA

Great Depression

Dust billows up into a plume.
As it spirals higher my hopes sink into the ground.
The world I once knew is bleak.
What will happen now?

The small shanty town is in ruins.
I look up into the sky for a desperate answer.
It is vast and unchanged and speaks no reply.
Is the end coming?

The field, once full of life, is withered and gray.
The horizon is endless and wavers underneath the sky.
Rabbits eat clover and bound to safety when they notice me.
Why do they look happy and well at my expense?

Dust singes my face.
The revolving cyclone storm moves over the rabbits and consumes me.
I blink away the dust in my eyes.
The tears that roll down my cheek are not only from the sand.

Adam Kershner, Grade 7
Markham Place Elementary School, NJ

Timing

Don't forget to wake,
The day might leave without you.
Night into day is a hard thing to miss.

Stop and observe nature's beauty,
Art is all around you.
If you can't,
Then do the best you can.

Remember the notes that you make is the only thing that can be remembered!

Jacob Mitchell, Grade 7
School of International Studies at Meadowbrook, VA

School Morning

You wake up you're tired but in a good mood
But then, you remember, there's just one thing you forgot to include
Today is Monday, and you're late for school
You think to yourself, wow I'm such a fool
To make things worse you're extremely late
And your hair looks messy instead of straight

You run out the door yelling and screaming
You hope and wish that you are only dreaming
You're finally on the bus, and full of relief
Even though your morning was full of grief

But you walk into the door of your classroom
And your friends jump to you, like a big loud boom
Then it seems like the entire morning just goes away
Because you know that with all your friends, it's going to be a great day

Amanda Bruno, Grade 8
St Stephen's School, NY

Without You

When I'm without you,
I dread every second.
I need to hold you,
Smell your hair,
Taste your lips.

When I'm without you,
I think of all the past memories we've shared.
Holding you for hours,
Laying with you,
Gazing into your beautiful eyes.

When I'm without you,
I can't get you out of my head.
Your a fire burning strong in my heart.

When I'm without you,
I long to be with you.

And when I'm with you,
I know where I belong.

Kevin Carvalho, Grade 8
Dighton Middle School, MA

Ten Little Puppies

Ten little puppies climbing up a vine
One lost its grip and now there are nine
Nine little puppies walking through a gate
One got stuck and now there are eight

Eight little puppies searching for heaven
One found it and now there are seven
Seven little puppies looking for sticks
One got in a fight and now there are six

Six little puppies getting ready to drive
One got in a crash and now there are five
Five little puppies running out a door
The screen slammed shut and now there are four

Four little puppies climbing up a tree
An eagle flew by and now there are three
Three little puppies looking for something blue
One found the ocean and now there are two

Two little puppies sat under the sun
One sat out too long and now there is one
One little puppy said "there is no more fun"
He ran away and now there is none

Paige Hublein, Grade 7
Sanford School, DE

Just Because I'm a Kid

Just because I'm a kid…
Doesn't mean I should be treated differently
Doesn't mean I'm stupid
Doesn't mean I'm irresponsible

Just because I'm a kid…
It doesn't mean I have bad taste in games
It doesn't mean I have bad taste in music
It doesn't mean you can hit me

Just because I'm a kid…
You can't push me around
You can't make fun of me
You can't laugh at me
Just because I'm a kid doesn't mean you can break my spirit

Kyle Croll, Grade 7
Garnet Valley Middle School, PA

Clean My Room

My mom told me to clean my room
She told me to use a broom
I said no way mom
She said my room smells like a stink bomb
She was in a bad mood
I said I want food
She said I'm not a waiter
I said fine, I'll clean my room later
There was clothes everywhere
My room looked like it got attacked by a bear
I finished and was tired
My room was so clean, my mom admired

Zach Schrier, Grade 7
Hammarskjold Middle School, NJ

Hope in the Tide

Drifting along the waterside,
As all life long dreams wash in with the tide,
All cries, all tears, all bad wishes disappear,
And all bad moments are soon washed in a tear.

I give thank to my world around me,
I give thanks to the people I see,
I give thanks to peace on Earth,
And I give thanks to the ones that are worth.

The water is slowly making its way,
And all I can see is a soothing day,
Every second I feel a sudden gust,
And every moment I pray of piece through us.

I give thanks to my community around me,
I give thanks to the people I see,
I give thanks to the clouds above,
And thanks to the ones we all love.

April Stein, Grade 7
Ocean City Intermediate School, NJ

Number 1

Number 1 is a lonely tree in a forest,
all alone, about to die.
Number 1 is a snake that does not move,
by himself on the ground.
Number 1 is an umbrella that is closed,
because the sun is not shining.
Number 1 is a first place ribbon,
you won the competition.
Number 1 is a pencil on a desk,
untouched by the student.
Number 1 is the pencil,
it is the beginning to a great poem.

Allison Lane, Grade 7
Charles F Patton Middle School, PA

Epiphany

I hear it in each word you say,
Wishing you'd never go away,
Not knowing 'til now,
I have feelings on behalf of you.

My heart is beating faster,
Trying to avoid disaster,
Not present 'til now;
My epiphany concerning you.

Hoping to see you soon again,
Not knowing if it's for certain,
Not caring 'til now,
How much I tend to mean to you today.

Wondering why these things ensue,
Not knowing what I ought to do,
Not thinking 'til now,
That I desperately want you to care.

Kaitlyn Vollmer, Grade 9
Unami Middle School, PA

Dreams

Onto the pillow,
Through the door,
Down the street,
Into the sky,
Through the clouds,
Down through the valley,
Between the mountains,
Back up to the clouds,
Between the stars,
Back down to the street,
Through the front door,
Back on the pillow,
Dreams flew.

Tanner James Craig, Grade 7
Trinity Middle School, PA

Basketball

I love to play my favorite sport,
at home or on a court.
Although my favorite position
is to play on offense,
it's fun to play defense, too.
I love it when I make a basket;
I'm elated when we win.
Basketball is fun.
With me it's number ONE!

Chance Roberts, Grade 8
Holy Trinity School, PA

Washing the Floor

yelling and screaming
for me to wash the floor
it's oh so annoying
for it's such a bore
i took out the mop
and the bucket too
i filled it to the top
so i could start washing
from tile to tile
from inch to inch
i washed that floor
boy did i want to give my mother a pinch
i finally finished and let out a nice sigh
until my mother told me
you missed a spot nice try
so i went back to my mop
i really do despise this a lot

Emily Hutchinson, Grade 7
Hammarskjold Middle School, NJ

The Zone

There's a place I can wander
Whenever I wish,
Or when I feel as if I'm alone.
I'll crawl into the world
Of foes, best friends,
And heroes.
They'll beg for me,
Asking me to never depart
When the last page has been
envisioned.
I'll dive into the hardcover,
Whose soft pages cuddle
Against my fingertips.
I'll play
With the new world's
Characters
And plot to never
Come out.

Megan Sheehan, Grade 8
Whitinsville Christian School, MA

One Blurry Mirror

Thought the heart was about to show
Thought the guy knew the thing
But now it's true
He didn't know

Thought I was part of the group
Thought I was one of them
But now I know
I'm alone

Thought my mom had liked me
Thought she will spoil me
But now she has shown
It's only my thought

Life is life
Never true
Just think deep
And you will know

Not everything's out there
But it's just deep
Way way deep
In its soul

Jenny Lee, Grade 7
Simon Baruch Jr High School 104, NY

The End That Leads
to the New Beginning

Tears touch the cheeks of
hearts that are too weak.
Sorrow fills the eyes of
hearts that are too deep.
If you care you would
never bare letting the
souls know that
you are the one that
made them weep.

Peri Zarrella, Grade 9
Red Hook Sr High School, NY

Thumb Sucker

His cute chubby baby face,
pale warm skin,
fuzzy little head,
red rain coat.
Crying and whining.
Not sucking on his own thumb,
but mine.
The whining ceases,
the crying becomes a whimper,
and the picture becomes a memory.

Maria Grande, Grade 7
Trinity Middle School, PA

Life

Life is like a flowing river
Always going, never stopping
It may hit a bump, just as the water would
But you continue as if it never happened
Signs of caution or stop may pause you
But it will never get in your way
People may put you down
So you pick yourself up again
Never let your dreams fade away
Hold them forever and ever

Krista Mau, Grade 7
Depew Middle School, NY

Our Two Hearts Became One

With your hand in mine, our two hearts became one,
with your eyes locked on mine, our two hearts became one,
with our small inside jokes, and understanding of the other,
our two hearts became one.
When our eyes locked on each other the first time,
the Earth's rotation stopped,
when our hands touched the first time,
the oceans grew clam,
when our thoughts were formed into the words "I love you"
our legs grew weary,
and with our stomachs in knots, our vision grew impaired,
our two hearts became one,
when we are near, the skies grow deep blue,
and when no one else loves you, you know that I do,
your generosity and love, brings my heart in the light,
and when we see each other, everyone disappears from sight,
your loyalty is true, and your love is pure.
And when you first kissed me good night,
our two hearts became one.

Marisa Lynn Tomsic, Grade 7
Trinity Middle School, PA

Nature

Nature is like a happy memory,
It embraces me in a cloak of leaves.
All of the forest smells of hickory.
All concepts come true — my beliefs, my dreams.

I love the rush of the wind in my hair,
The shine of the sun on my eager face.
Many things rush past, carried by the air.
All seems to be, with a calm, fluid grace.

Beauty of the moon leaves me in wonder.
The glimmer of the stars catches my eye.
The heavens break in fragments by thunder.
Everything is alight in the night sky.

The sweet smell of the woods runs through my vein.
All is tranquil in my peaceful domain.

Diana Correia, Grade 8
North Arlington Middle School, NJ

I Remember

I remember when I was saying goodbye
To the mom
Who was taking care of me?
For 4 years and they were crying
I didn't know what was going on
I remember them putting me in a car
I remember going across the Brooklyn Bridge
I remember when I got out of the car
I remember going up the stairs
I remember meeting this man who I don't know.
I remember sitting on a couch
The same one I sit on today
I remember when she asked me,
"Do you know this man?"
I said, "No."
She said, "This is your new dad."
I didn't know what she meant
By new dad
At the time
I remember
When she left.

Arthur Cook, Grade 7
Simon Baruch Jr High School 104, NY

Deadened Emotions

Tears. Gushing down my face
seeking so hard
a crack in my pain

Lost. There is no way back
I'm eluding the control of the past
shattering the pain

Fear. Seen in my eyes
only one means out
my pain growing stealthily

Blindness. It never halts
can't hold it back
Blowing pain

Clear. Achieved coup détat
finally ended it all
my pain perishes completely

Return. Back to my first initiate
going through memories
Living over it again
agony creeping through

Raashika Goyal, Grade 9
Advanced Math and Science Academy Charter School, MA

Baseball Champs

In every game
only the brave have
a big
shot at
a baseball
championship.

Colin Rowbottom, Grade 9
Unami Middle School, PA

My Flower

This is my flower;
all mine with its innocence
and hidden beauty
planted in soil.
With roots deeply embedded,
the warm rays of sunshine
invite a bud to appear,
a bud which holds
the most furtive of all secrets;
a tall and proud explosion,
of a vibrant orange fireworks display
creating the most exquisite blossom!

Justin Goucher, Grade 7
Ocean City Intermediate School, NJ

Vacation

School's out!
Let's all give a shout!
We're going to have fun,
Tanning in the sun.

Gabriella Torres, Grade 7
St Agatha School, NY

The Magic of a Pen

I scribble all day long,
From thoughtful poems
For friends and family,
To secret notes,
For few to see.
I can draw pictures,
Or write an essay,
All while I am
Bitten on,
Stepped on,
And chewed on.
But every day I see paper.
I am magical.
I make magic.
But not by making objects,
But by making words,
Words that appeal to the imagination;
Words that can make anything happen.
I am as magical as a magic wand.
I am a pen.

Margareta Ianosi-Irimie, Grade 7
Hammarskjold Middle School, NJ

I Love You Kassi

Kassi, you're the greatest sister I could ask for
You're my mentor, my best friend, and, oh, so much more
Your art is as good as Picasso's masterpieces
No matter what, your excellence never decreases
At playing Sweeper, Kass, we all say you were a Beast
You were definitely the best, not even close to the least
Kassi, I hope you had fun in Italy being an artist
You'll be the best brain doctor; you're already the smartest
Taking me to the Big Apple was certainly the best,
After the art, the park, and Nathan's, I needed some rest!
Every time mom sees us, she says we look completely alike
We've always looked the same, ever since I was a tike
Our personalities differ so very much, this I know
It doesn't matter to me, I still love you so
I know that to you, I always seem like I'm a disaster
Yes, and I know all that advice is to make me become a master
Kassi, hopefully you now clearly see
That I love you, and I know you love me!

Allison O'Brien, Grade 8
Medford Township Memorial Middle School, NJ

Like the Sun

My brother's like the sun,
Used for such good,
But can do such devious things.

When you look straight to the sun, your eyes may go blind
When you follow its path though, only good you will find
With too much power it will overtake your soul
But with though the sun, were just a mere hole

The sun can damage our earth out of existence
But can also save us from a spiraling disaster
Sometimes it seems the earth "revolves around the sun"
But that's just because it's #1

The sun is responsible for some unhappiness
But you can't go on without it, and no one will ever forget or undermine the sun
The Peacemaker.

Jessica Silverman, Grade 7
Commack Middle School, NY

There Once Was

There once was a bird
A bird that struggled to fly, yet it had wings of an eagle
There once was a bear
A bear that struggled to fight, yet had the strength of a giant
There once was a man
A man that had found love so many times before
Though still can't confine it for its true meaning
There once was a superman
To whom love was his kryptonite, yet desired it to overtake him.

There once was…

Daniel McCauley, Grade 8
Middle School /High School 141 Riverdale/Kingsbridge Academy, NY

Spirits

We walk in the grass, we whisper in the wind
Spirits come and go in this place of ours
When you grew, I grew with you
We were one person, for some time
But now, we have changed; still one but not the same

I remember when it was just us
Me and you, you and I
Rolling in the grass, whispering in the wind
Then the world came and invited us in
It took us from our world; it molded us
It shaped us, even if we didn't want it to
It taught us how to act, how to lie, how to win
But I know you're in there somewhere

You are different, but you will always be the same
I am different, but I will always be the same, too
I will be there for you when you need me
I will let you go when you need to be let go
I will be angry with you, but not for long, never for long

Because I will always remember when there was no grass
And screams turned to whispers in the wind
Spirits come and go in this place of ours

Taryn Pochon, Grade 8
Branchburg Central Middle School, NJ

Gone for Good

You left without a kiss
Not wondering if you were going to be missed
I tried to hold back the tears
But I have been holding them for years
But know I don't have to cry
All you are to me is just a fry
You are a fog
You make me want to blog
You are no where to be found
So you don't know if I am safe and sound
I don't need your love
I have people who love me and are as peaceful as a dove
Loving and kindness was all I need
But that was too BIG of a deed
You couldn't do a little task
So what can you be ask
You shot me in the heart with a dart
But my heart mended quickly
Now I am happier that I have ever been
But knowing that he will never see
Of what I will ever be

Yasmene Kimble, Grade 8
Page Middle School, VA

Where I'm From

I am from endless baseball games,
An always shinning television,
And nonstop video gaming.
I am from my cape cod styled home,
Surrounded by a mountain of rocks with beautiful colors.
I am from my dogwood tree,
To the high school's tennis courts.
I am from a town,
That believes my well being.
In traditional family gatherings,
That includes succulent apple pie and turkey,
I am from my mom, dad, and brother,
And a family that loves a variety of foods.
I am from memories,
Captured and stored,
Under my bed in my room,
Left to be revisited.
I am from the love,
My family shares with me,
Awaiting to share it,
With the rest of the world.

Kevin Baliga, Grade 7
Hammarskjold Middle School, NJ

You Know

Why did you
ask me to go
with you to Famous Dave's?

You know
I'm a
vegetarian.

But I wouldn't have
gone with you
anyway.

Catherine Turner, Grade 9
Appomattox Governor's School for Arts and Technical, VA

Lazy Days

On a day that the sun shines bright,
When the air is warm and the breeze is slight,
Sleeping in and staying comfy
Is all that matters to me.

Waking up and going outside,
Reading a book at the pool side,
Being lazy and staying comfy
Is all that matters to me.

No alarm clocks, no schoolwork,
No rushing, no rude jerks,
Just relaxing all day and staying comfy
Is all that matters to me.

Samantha Murray, Grade 9
Unami Middle School, PA

Goodbyes Are the Worst
I see a tear fall from your eye
I wipe it away with my thumb; I can't stand to see you cry
I'm leaving, turning to walk away
You catch my arm and tell me not to go
Yet you know I must, you know I can't stay
Goodbyes are the worst, with our never ending tears
Goodbyes are the worst, as I walk away, you cry for me
I head to my car and open the door
I turn to see you running, running for me; I get in the car and close the door
Tears soak our cheeks, as you pound on my window
I put my hand to the window, then put the car into drive
Goodbyes are the worst, with our never ending tears
Goodbyes are the worst, as I walk away, you cry for me
Tears soak my cheek the road starts to blur
I see you behind my eyes as I close them
Goodbyes are the worst, with our never ending tears
Goodbyes are the worst, as I walk away, you cry for me
The car hits something but I don't care
All I see is your tear soaked face
And your arms wrapping around me at the hospital
Goodbyes are the worst, with our never ending tears

Samantha Satterfield, Grade 7
Depew Middle School, NY

The Northern Knights
In the oppressed South there lay in this kingdom no queen, no king, and no gentry.
There on the sweat filled crops of injustice lay the tarnished ones, beaten and belittled.
For the peasants of the "Cotton Kingdom" must labor until the blessed dusk.
But engraved by hope there lay a path through the warm hearts of kind souls
That will lead them to their birth right, a reincarnation of freedom
The Northern Knights take mount at night
They fear no fright for in their sight
It is God's mission unearthed, from Sir Douglas, Sir Brown, and Lady Tubman
The monarch of freedom will prevail
The Northern Knights take their flight
Shh, can you hear the gallop of freedom?

Malik White, Grade 8
St Francis of Assisi School, PA

My Night Sky Adventure
The sky so bright, showered with stars gleaming so nicely like a quiet lake. The moon round, enormous and beautiful so near feels like you can reach it with your hands, sitting beside my window feeling the reflection of the night sky on my eyes wishing on every star that I can fly, fly oh so very high and swim through the stars including the moon. As I go to bed I dream. Finally touching the moon with my hands and the stars spiraling around me like a tornado, after my adventure had finished the stars drove me to my bed and I slept. 'Til morning the sun was up shining as bright as a flashlight and the clouds as big as a frog's bulgy eyes. It's another day for me to wait until the night sky shall come again.

Michelle Belen, Grade 7
Borough Elementary School, NJ

Forever and Always
I'll always be there my angel through good and bad times.
If you ever need me, all you have to do is stare by the moonlight and I'll be there in a blink of an eye.
I know you need me now to be there by your side, to tell you everything will be all right.
As long as your heart is beating with mine, I will be there for you my dear friend, forever and always.

Alexa DiBlasi, Grade 8
Oakdale-Bohemia Middle School, NY

Mistake

This was such a huge mistake;
I don't know yet, where my life is going to go.
Say hello to the crossroads,
That's where I stand.
My life is passing oh life grains of sand.

I'm falling, I'm breaking down;
There's too much weight on me.
My life is heading towards disaster,
And that's not where I want it to be.

I'm stuck in this moment, observing my life;
If I stay in this corner, it won't turn out right.

I can't decide where to go;
Everything's spiraling out of control.
It's getting dark,
And I can't figure out what to let go.

Emily Hart, Grade 9
New Jersey United Christian Academy, NJ

Big Sis

When I think of you leaving, graduating, and moving on,
I can't help but cry.
You're my big sis, my best friend.
I don't know how I will live without you.
You taught me everything on how to be the best.
From sports to school.
You pushed me to the top.
If I didn't have you there by my side,
I would have nobody to keep me going each day.
So here's to you sis.
Good Luck.
I'll miss you with all my heart.

Jen Wasielewski, Grade 7
Depew Middle School, NY

Technology

Lights are bright,
Like stars in the night.
Wires, lines, and underground pipes,
Modern weapons like guns and bombs,
Some think it's right, and some think it's wrong.
TVs, computers, handhelds, and more,
Lawnmowers and weed whackers to help with my chores.
Cars, trucks, vans, and trains,
Printers and copiers,
Like food to my brains,
Keeping me warm during the cold winter season.
Movies and shows all have a reason.
I won't worry a bit,
And I won't throw a fit,
I'll sit back, relax and enjoy it.

Cole Hawbaker, Grade 7
Pine-Richland Middle School, PA

A Place to Go

A quiet, little place to go,
Where I can think and be alone.
No one there to bother me,
It's just myself and my fantasy.

That place would be my dreams,
There I can be whatever I please.
A skydiver, a shark, super hero, or even a bat,
No place I know can ever top that.

It's my little world I create on my own,
It's like a home away from home.
My dreams are a fairy tale,
Where all my wishes set sail.

Everything is going great,
Until something happens that makes me shake.
Something takes over my dreams giving me a scare,
But these aren't dreams anymore they're known as nightmares.

Then not too soon the wonders and scares come to an end,
I wake up, but don't feel sad because tonight I'll do it again.

Debbie Stanley, Grade 7
Garnet Valley Middle School, PA

The White Thief

When my family went to the beach,
It seemed like nothing could go wrong,
As we raced in and out of the ocean,
Listening to the harsh seagull song,

Little did we know
That a little white thief,
Innocently standing there,
Could give us so much grief,

We left our belongings on the ground,
Before running to play in the water,
And as we were mesmerized by the ocean's sound,
The thief made its move,

The seagull found our unattended food,
Munched on our sandwiches made on rye,
Before making his escape,
Into the clear blue sky,

In the end my family left,
And we all went hungry,
Because of that nasty seagull's theft.

Emma Brown, Grade 7
St Hilary of Poitiers School, PA

I Want the Real You Back

When we were little I would always look up to you.
You taught me so many things that were new.
People said we were alike,
You even helped me learn how to ride a bike.
You shared your music,
You showed me your magic trick.
But ever since we learned the truth that day,
Never again were you the same way.
I asked you to stop and think,
But when you left it made my heart sink.
Why did you chose that over us?
Why not pick the house instead of a bus?
I'm afraid that the cops will come here,
And have the word death ring in my ear.
Where did you go, the you that's real?
Is he hidden by an invisible seal?
I would do anything to get you back.
So please pick the right track.
I want you back here with me.
Before the real you gets lost out at sea.

Holly Borz, Grade 9
Bethel Park High School, PA

Endeavor

Broad leaves taunt a porcelain-like face.
Sharp green blades jut out between rosemary toes.
Thin stubs spread vast like a black hole.
Droplets roll downward, inching toward the bone.
A melody flowing from the stumps, booming and smooth.
Spine sprawled out, almost shattered at the joints.
The rosemary toes crack.
A squeal breaks the barrier of silence.
Walnut brown portiers droop over round pale blue seas.

A deep exhale.
Nothing.

Broad leaves shrivel then dance to get sliced by the blades.
The blades shrink, transforming into a dreary tan.
Thin stubs curl inward, digging into skin.
The droplets turn into a current and wash the leaves away.
Spine and rosemary toes loosen.
Squeal fades to a hushed breath.

A fall into the vermilion matted green blades.

Sara Stoneroad, Grade 9
Hershey High School, PA

Scoliosis

Squeezes you tight like a vine
It seems as if you're running out of time
It is crawling up your spine
You claim to be fine

But they know you're not

You've battled and fought
Until you're at the spot
Where you're caught

Where it comes to an end
You can't pretend
Or bend

The truth be told
You begin to fold
You're cold and not so bold
Since you've been told

In the end it's only the beginning

Tia DeCesare, Grade 8
Unami Middle School, PA

I Know a Fire Call

I know a fire call…
pagers beeping, fire whistles blowing,
air horns, sirens blaring.
I know a fire call…
the smell of diesel fuel, fire engine exhaust,
the smell of thick black smoke.
I know a fire call…
"Chief 1-5 to county, we have a working fire."
"Truck 1-5 to county, we are on location."
"Engine 1-5-1 and Engine 1-5-2 are on scene."
I DO KNOW A FIRE CALL!

Matthew Shirker, Grade 8
Ephrata Middle School, PA

Index

Author Autograph Page

Author Autograph Page

Author Autograph Page

Author Autograph Page

Author Autograph Page

Author Autograph Page

Author Autograph Page

Author Autograph Page

Author Autograph Page

Author Autograph Page